The Florida Folklife Reader

The Florida Folklife Reader

Edited by Tina Bucuvalas

UNIVERSITY PRESS OF MISSISSIPPI / JACKSON

www.upress.state.ms.us

The University Press of Mississippi is a member of the Association of American University Presses.

"Key Largo to Marathon: A Report on the Folklife of the Upper and Middle Keys" by Brent Cantrell appeared in *South Florida Magazine*. Guest editor, Tina Bucuvalas. Vol. 3 (Summer 1990): 19–22.

"African American and West Indian Folklife in South Florida" by Joyce M. Jackson appeared in *South Florida Magazine*. Guest editor, Tina Bucuvalas. Vol. 3 (Summer 1990): 11–18.

"The Patronal Festival of Vueltas in Cuban Miami: 'No One Loses, They Always Win!'" by Tina Bucuvalas was presented at the American Folklore Society Meeting, Jacksonville, Florida, October 1992.

Michael Kernahan: A Life in Pan by Stephen Stuempfle was published as a booklet by the Florida Folklife Program, Florida Department of State, Tallahassee, 1999.

"Folklife of Miami's Nicaraguan Communities" by Katherine Borland appeared in *Nicaraguan Folklife in Miami/La Vida Tradicional Nicaraguense en Miami*, edited by Brent Cantrell. Occasional Papers, No. 2. Miami: Historical Museum of Southern Florida/Folklife Program, 1993. Pp. 1–9.

"Exploring Peruvian Music in Miami" by Martha Ellen Davis was presented at the Latin American Studies Association Meeting, Gainesville, Florida, March 2003.

"The Seminole Family Camp" by Ormond H. Loomis appeared in *A Guide to the 33rd Annual Florida Folk Festival, May 24–26, 1985*. White Springs: Florida Folklife Program, 1985.

"Sacred Steel" by Robert L. Stone appeared in *FHC Forum* (Winter 2004): 28–31.

"'The Rest Is Up to You and Me': Sunday Morning Band and Ritual Identity in the Florida Panhandle" by Jerrilyn McGregory was presented at the Florida Folklore Society Meeting, Ybor City, 1998.

"Maritime Folklife" appeared in *A Guide to the 35th Annual Florida Folk Festival, May 27–29, 1987*. White Springs: Florida Folklife Program, 1987.

Manufactured in the United States of America

First printing 2012
∞
Library of Congress Cataloging-in-Publication Data

The Florida folklife reader / edited by Tina Bucuvalas.
p. cm.
Includes bibliographical references and index.
ISBN 978-1-61703-140-3 (cloth : alk. paper) — ISBN 978-1-61703-141-0 (pbk. : alk. paper) — ISBN 978-1-61703-142-7 (ebook) 1. Folklore—Florida. 2. Florida—Social life and customs.
I. Bucuvalas, Tina.
GR110.F5F564 2011
398.209759—dc22 2011013551

British Library Cataloging-in-Publication Data available

For Alexandra & Chloe Curran

Contents

Acknowledgments ix

Introduction xi

Key Largo to Marathon
A Report on the Folklife of the Upper and Middle Keys 3
BRENT CANTRELL

African American and West Indian Folklife in South Florida 10
JOYCE M. JACKSON

The Patronal Festival of Vueltas in Cuban Miami
"No One Loses, They Always Win!" 23
TINA BUCUVALAS

Michael Kernahan
A Life in Pan 35
STEPHEN STUEMPFLE

Folklife of Miami's Nicaraguan Communities 50
KATHERINE BORLAND

Exploring Peruvian Music in Miami 67
MARTHA ELLEN DAVIS

The Seminole Family Camp 84
ORMOND H. LOOMIS

Sacred Steel 90
ROBERT L. STONE

Musical Practice and Memory on the Edge of Two Worlds
Kalymnian Tsambóuna *and Song Repertoire in the Family of Nikitas Tsimouris* 96
ANNA LOMAX WOOD

Eternal Be Their Memory! 154
STAVROS K. FRANGOS

Richard Seaman's Presence within Florida's Soundscape 161
GREGORY HANSEN

Legacy and Meaning in the Changing Sacred Harp Tradition of the Okefenokee Region 178
LAURIE K. SOMMERS

Nativism and Cracker Revival at the Florida Folk Festival 207
MARTHA NELSON

"The Rest Is Up to You and Me"
Sunday Morning Band and Ritual Identity in the Florida Panhandle 225
JERRILYN McGREGORY

Maritime Folklife 237
FLORIDA FOLKLIFE PROGRAM / FLORIDA DEPARTMENT OF STATE. INTRODUCTION BY NANCY MICHAEL, ORAL TRADITIONS BY NANCY NUSZ, BOATS BY DAVID TAYLOR, FISHING GEAR BY ORMOND H. LOOMIS, MUSIC BY PETER ROLLER, FOODWAYS BY MERRI BELLAND

Selected Florida Folklife Bibliography 275

Appendix I
Early Folklife Research in Florida 282

Appendix II
Public Folklife Programs in Florida 287

Contributors 291

Index 296

Acknowledgments

THERE ARE MANY PEOPLE TO THANK FOR THEIR GENEROUS CONTRIBUTIONS of time and information. No one could have a better colleague than Kathleen Monahan, director of Cultural and Civic Services for the City of Tarpon Springs, who provided the time and enthusiastic support necessary for this book. Mike Knoll, of HistoryMiami, gave generously of his insights and assisted in collecting images for a number of the essays. I am truly grateful to Jody Norman, State Archives of Florida, who always saw to it that images and other materials were delivered with the speed of light. Susanne Hunt, Florida Department of State, graciously provided needed permissions and materials. Marisella Veiga provided wise counsel in Spanish translation issues. Craig Gill, editor-in-chief of the University Press of Mississippi, provided strong support and encouragement from beginning to end. Anne Stascavage, managing editor at the University Press of Mississippi, and copy editor Debbie Upton were instrumental in bringing this work to fruition.

My cherished colleagues, who have brought to public attention the richness in talent and skills of Florida's incredible tradition bearers, have been the inspiration for and foundation of this volume. And as generations of Florida ethnographers have known, there is no separation between us and the people about whom we write—in the process of learning and teaching, appreciating and being appreciated, we have shared and immeasurably enriched one anothers' lives.

My continuing gratitude goes to my children, Alexandra and Chloe Curran, for tolerating a mother often missing in the field.

Introduction

AS A CALIFORNIA EX-PATRIATE, I APPROACHED MY FIRST ETHNOGRAPHIC contract position in Florida with low expectations. In the 1980s, few Californians considered that they could exist elsewhere—and especially not in Florida, with its slow-driving retirees and right-wing refugees. I was to conduct an ethnographic survey of Miami-Dade County, with a special emphasis on Latin American culture, for the Florida Folklife Program. Peggy Bulger, who supervised the project, drove with me to Miami through a blinding tropical storm. She stayed long enough to introduce me to several neighborhoods and to the staff at the Historical Museum of Southern Florida, where I would have an office. I found an apartment in the Miami Beach compound of the Scull sisters, eccentric twin Cuban painters who always appeared in clothing styles evocative of 1950s Havana, then I embarked on a quest to document south Florida's people and culture.

It was love at first sight.

I marveled at the jumble of urban and rural (chickens roaming the streets of Hialeah or the hallucinatory sight of tugboats hauling huge commercial ships past quiet suburban houses on the Miami River), the shady coolness of enormous ficus trees and the fantastic colors of tropical flowers contrasting with the hot gritty streets of industrial neighborhoods, the glitz of abundance next to the hopelessness of absolute poverty, cultures colliding and merging—and looming over all the towering clouds of the tropical Atlantic in a brilliant sky. It was the most complex place I had ever been, it was a mess, and I have never been able to get enough of it.

As I have subsequently journeyed throughout Florida, I have found countless other fascinating niches offering their own distinctive blends of cultural traits and natural beauty. To my way of thinking, Florida is the most remarkable state in the nation. Not only is it blessed with a semitropical climate, beautiful natural inland areas, and over a thousand miles of warm seas and sandy beaches, but Floridians themselves are every bit as colorful and vibrant as the tropical foliage they nurture.

THE ESSAYS

Although several publications detail the traditions of specific Florida regions or folk groups, to date no single work provides an overview of Florida folklife. This book brings together essays written by folklorists, anthropologists, and ethnomusicologists on an array of topics. Some of the essays are new, while others appeared in ephemeral publications that never reached a wide audience. In particular, the Florida Folklife Program and the Historical Museum of Southern Florida[1] produced dozens of essays, booklets, exhibition catalogs, recordings, and musical liner notes by folklorists who have achieved national respect—and many of those essays address topics that have not otherwise been examined. Since the writers often address multiple genres, topics, or groups, I have organized the book in geographical sequence from south to north, with the final essay covering maritime folklife statewide.

Many of Florida's diverse folk groups have been documented by ethnographers. In northern Florida and southern Georgia, Laurie K. Sommers spent several years exploring "Legacy and Meaning in the Changing Sacred Harp Tradition of the Okefenokee Region." Several essays are the result of field surveys organized by the Historical Museum of Southern Florida. Joyce M. Jackson wrote about "African American and West Indian Folklife in South Florida" for a survey of the traditional arts of the African Diaspora. Katherine Borland's "Folklife of Miami's Nicaraguan Communities" reflects her documentation of Nicaraguan culture in Miami for a field project. Likewise, Brent Cantrell's "Key Largo to Marathon: A Report on the Folklife of the Upper and Middle Keys" grew out of the only comprehensive folklife survey of the Keys by a public organization.

Many of the best examinations of Florida's occupational folklife have resulted from group research projects initiated by the Florida Folklife Program. Thus I have included their collective essay on Maritime Folklife: "Introduction" by Nancy Michael, "Oral Traditions" by Nancy Nusz, "Boats" by David Taylor, "Fishing Gear" by Ormond H. Loomis, "Music" by Peter Roller, and "Foodways" by Merri Belland.

Two essays deal with the unique built environments created by Florida folk groups. Ormond H. Loomis contributed a detailed study of *chickee* architecture and its use in "The Seminole Family Camp." The study was precipitated by an invitation by the Florida Folklife Program to have Seminoles build a camp at the site of the Florida Folk Festival. Stavros K. Frangos's "Eternal Be Their Memory" looks at the unusual gravesites in Tarpon Springs's Cycadia Cemetery.

Florida's traditional music is among the most diverse and exciting in the nation, and we are lucky to have many fine music specialists. In "'The Rest Is Up to You and Me': Sunday Morning Band and Ritual Identity in the Florida Panhandle," Jerrilyn McGregory documents the little-known Sunday Morning Band tradition in Florida's Panhandle. Robert L. Stone achieved national recognition for his groundbreaking discovery of an exhilarating musical genre in the House of God churches, which he explores in "Sacred Steel." In "Exploring Peruvian Music in Miami," Martha Ellen Davis recounts the process of investigating Peruvian music and discusses its function in the community.

By definition folklife is the product of communities, but the soul of our traditions is the people who maintain and enhance them. There are several fascinating profiles of individuals who have achieved excellence within their cultural traditions. "Michael Kernahan: A Life in Pan" by Stephen Stuempfle examines the art of the steel drum maker and musician. In "Musical Practice and Memory on the Edge of Two Worlds: Kalymnian *Tsambóuna* and Song Repertoire in the Family of Nikitas Tsimouris," Anna Lomax Wood provides a detailed ethnomusicological and contextual analysis of a Tarpon Springs family and the unusual musical traditions they preserved. "Richard Seaman's Presence within Florida's Soundscape" by Gregory Hansen explores the life and art of an old-time fiddler.

Not a week goes by in the Sunshine State without the possibility of attending dozens of fascinating community celebrations. Tina Bucuvalas discusses the changes in a Cuban patronal festival tradition in response to new conditions in Miami. Martha Nelson worked several years for the Stephen Foster State Folk Culture Center in White Springs, the home of the Florida Folk Festival. Her "Nativism and Cracker Revival at the Florida Folk Festival" is a probing examination of the development and implementation of the festival.

FLORIDA'S FOLK

Florida has so many different facets that it represents many things to many people. Outsiders often regard it as a destination where fantasy is reality or sometimes reality seems like fantasy. For north Floridians it is a slow-moving, rural part of the old South, while south Florida moves at a frenetic, *café cubano*-fueled Latin pace. Its high-tech industries lead the exploration of both space and the ocean, yet it is the home of the oldest city in the United States and a national leader in historic preservation efforts. Florida encompasses those identities and more, then combines them with its subtropical environment to produce many unique cultural syntheses. But in order to understand Florida it is essential to know more about its people.

The Seminole and Miccosukee are among the few native peoples who organized after Europeans colonized the Americas. As a result of conflicts with Europeans, Americans, and their allies, fragments of many Native American groups from Georgia, the Carolinas, and Alabama fled south. After settling in Florida, they were joined by survivors from local indigenous groups and in time they developed their own distinctive culture—though the core were Creeks from Georgia and Alabama. The early Seminole were hunters, traders, and warriors, and they gradually established agricultural villages with cattle and took advantage of the rich maritime resources. By the end of the eighteenth century, there were many Seminole towns in northern and central Florida. The Seminole wars of the early nineteenth century drove the Seminole deeper into the wilds of south and central Florida to avoid conflict and removal to Oklahoma. By the late nineteenth century, fewer than five hundred remained, but in the twentieth century they fared better. By the end of the century the Seminole and Miccosukee had made great strides in political autonomy and economic viability, while maintaining much of their traditional culture. In addition to these groups, the Panhandle is home to bands of Poarch Creek, Perdido Bay Creek, and Choctaw Indians.

Florida's Crackers are descended from the rural white settlers of Celtic heritage who migrated from Alabama, Georgia, and the Carolinas. Their culture reflected many traits derived from rural Scotland and Ireland: they maintained an economy based on open-range herding; a leisurely lifestyle with an emphasis on hospitality, food, drink, and outdoor sports; a strong sense of honor, self-reliance, and tenacity; and a tendency to take the law into their own hands. In Florida, they adapted to different regional environments. Some developed ranching traditions that combined British and Spanish techniques, while others survived by fishing, growing sugar cane, or collecting bird plumes. In the central north they raised hogs, gardened, and hunted wild game, while those near inland waters hunted gators and caught catfish. Many Floridians still take pride in their Cracker heritage, though today they are a small percentage of the population and reside primarily in northern and central rural areas.

African Americans first came to Florida as participants in Spanish explorations and settlements. In the seventeenth and eighteenth centuries, many

African-born blacks fled south to Florida, where military service and conversion to Catholicism offered a release from slavery. By the mid-seventeenth century, communities of free blacks lived in St. Augustine and Fort Mose, a fortified town built by the Spanish for runaway slaves and the first legally sanctioned black town in North America. Others preferred to associate with the Seminole in a benign form of servitude. These black Seminoles maintained separate villages, where they raised crops and cattle and worked as translators and advisors to the Seminole.

African Americans continued to flow into Florida throughout the nineteenth and twentieth centuries. In 1887, Eatonville became the first black incorporated municipality in Florida. Known as the home of the famed African American folklorist, anthropologist, and novelist Zora Neale Hurston, it continues its legacy of proud self-government to this day. While most black Floridians trace their roots to Georgia, Alabama, or the Carolinas, a significant portion have family ties to the Caribbean islands. Especially in south Florida, there are also many black Hispanics who hail from Cuba, the Dominican Republic, Puerto Rico, Costa Rica, Nicaragua, or Peru.

Florida has had strong continuous connections with Latin America and the Caribbean since colonial times. From early European contact to the present, but especially since the early 1960s, there has been substantial immigration from Latin America. The U.S. Census Bureau estimated Florida's 2009 population at 21.5 percent (or over 3,985,600) Latin/Hispanic—making them our largest minority group. Florida's Latin communities are dominated by peoples from the Caribbean, whose culture emphasizes a synthesis of European and African-based cultural elements.

The peoples of Florida and Cuba have long crossed the narrow passage between them on the tides of history—often profoundly changing and influencing each other. Throughout the Spanish colonial period, Florida came under Cuba's governmental and religious jurisdiction. Cuba provided most settlers and supplies to the Florida frontier, resulting in a constant interchange of people and trade. Later, the first unsuccessful struggle for Cuban independence (1868–1878) led to the emigration of many Cubans to Key West and New York. At the same time, several cigar manufacturers relocated to Key West to avoid paying American tariffs. By the mid-1870s, forty-five factories employed fourteen hundred workers who rolled about 15 million cigars each year. The cigar workers' custom of listening to *lectores* read from newspapers, essays, and political tracts while they worked created an educated and politically sophisticated society. In the mid-1880s, some manufacturers relocated to Ybor City, near Tampa, or returned to Havana in order to avoid strikes by Key West workers. The transplanted industry flourished in

Tampa/Ybor City, and by 1900 a Cuban population of over thirty-five hundred worked there in the cigar factories or related industries.

It is estimated that over one million Cubans emigrated as a result of the profound social and political changes instituted by Fidel Castro's government in the mid-twentieth century—and the majority settled in Miami. In establishing new homes and businesses, they created a dynamic world financial center with powerful links to Latin America and the Caribbean.

Cubans are not the only Latin American immigrants to make a significant impact. In the last thirty years, there has been an unprecedented influx from Puerto Rico, Mexico, Nicaragua, Colombia, Peru, Honduras, and other countries—bringing with them varying blends of Spanish, African, and Native American cultures. Puerto Ricans are the second-largest group statewide and are the dominant Latin group in Orlando and Tampa. Florida's Mexican population has been increasing rapidly since the 1990s, especially throughout central Florida.

Many West Indians have settled in Florida, where they are often referred to as "the Islanders." English speakers from Jamaica, Trinidad/Tobago, and other islands share many cultural elements and often live in contiguous neighborhoods. The largest West Indian population is from the Bahamas. Bahamians were fishing and scavenging wrecks on nearby Florida's southeast coast and the Keys by the early nineteenth century. By the mid-nineteenth century, many had found good jobs fishing, turtling, or sponging and settled permanently in the Keys. They constituted a third of Key West's population by 1892. From the late 1890s, Bahamians flocked to south Florida for jobs in agriculture, construction, railroad and maritime services, and tourism. They created their own buildings, churches, fraternal organizations, and artistic societies, and have maintained their heritage through a continued flow between Florida and the Bahamas. A smaller number settled in maritime Gulf Coast communities such as Cortez, Tarpon Springs, and Cedar Key.

Since its early independence, Haiti has suffered a succession of oppressive dictatorships which have impelled many to seek better conditions elsewhere. During the 1970s and 1980s, tens of thousands fled the harsh political and economic circumstances to Florida. While Haitians live throughout the state, Miami's Little Haiti and North Miami particularly bustle with shops, restaurants, nightclubs, and community events.

Florida supports a wide variety of ethnic European and Middle Eastern communities. It has one of the largest Jewish populations in the country, especially in the southeast from Palm Beach County to Miami-Dade County. Jewish settlement commenced early in Florida's history, but most families settled here from the 1920s through the late twentieth century. In 1905, hundreds of experienced divers, captains, and crew members from the Greek Islands began immigrating to Tarpon Springs to support the burgeoning commercial sponge business. Although the sponge business has diminished, Tarpon Springs remains a commercial maritime community with a strong Greek character. In Jacksonville, there is a substantial community from Palestine, Lebanon, and Syria that dates from the early twentieth century, and there are Iranian and Turkish enclaves in most major cities. Throughout Florida, there has been substantial settlement by a variety of other European-based ethnic groups from the northern and midwestern regions of the United States. In south Florida, there is a concentration of Finnish residents in Palm Beach County, and a large community of French Canadians in Hollywood. Near Tampa, Masaryktown was settled by Slovaks and Czechs; Dunedin has a strong Scottish ethnic identity; and St. Petersburg is home to many East Europeans.

A diverse array of Asian and Pacific Island peoples call Florida home. Florida's first Asian settlers were in Delray Beach, where the Yamato colony founded in the first decade of the twentieth century brought young Japanese to grow pineapples for shipment to northern markets. The U.S. Census Bureau revealed that over 463,000 Asians and Pacific Islanders had sought greater economic stability, abundant farmland, better educational opportunities, escape from political unrest, or closer proximity to family members. They maintain a strong desire to express their native cultures, adapt them to their current circumstances, and pass them on to future generations. Southeast Asians are among the fastest-growing groups. In particular, the Vietnamese community is gaining momentum in numbers and economic importance throughout central Florida.

In addition to communities based on a single folk group, pockets of unique cultural syntheses exist in several regions. Many residents of St. Augustine still trace their ancestry to the Spanish colonists as well as the New Smyrna colonists of the British era (1763–1783). In 1768 the Scottish physician Andrew Turnbull received over 100,000 acres south of St. Augustine to grow agricultural products for export. Having served as the British Consul in Smyrna in Asia Minor, Turnbull believed that Mediterranean peoples would be well suited to Florida and recruited Minorcan, Greek, Corsican, and Italian colonists from Europe. Because they were not awarded their promised freedom or land after completion of their contracts, some seven hundred colonists fled to St. Augustine in 1777. There they created an enduring economic niche for themselves by employing maritime and agricultural skills from their Mediterranean homelands. Although time has obscured much of their heritage, some traditions persist—especially those involving occupations, domestic arts such as foodways, and religious life. It is interesting to note that by 1786, St. Augustine's population was 50 percent Minorcan, Italian, or Greek; 31 percent free African; 9 percent British; 5 percent Spanish or Spanish colonial; and 4 percent Native American—in many ways, providing the precedent for today's multicultural Florida.

As part of a larger culture area stretching along the Gulf of Mexico from east Texas, Florida's Gulf Coast shares with the Caribbean islands a semitropical physical environment and a history of colonial development by the Spanish and French. Moreover, Caribbean settlers entered the region through Savannah, Mobile, Pensacola, and New Orleans, bringing with them a blend of African and Latin cultures. In the Panhandle there are reminders of this heritage in the distinctive Gulf Coastal vernacular houses, with low-pitched roofs, central dogtrot hallways, tall foundation pillars, and detached kitchens, that survive in old Pensacola. A few boatbuilders still make *bateaux* that derive their name and shape from their French heritage. And in Pensacola, long-surviving Catholic communities maintain Mardi Gras traditions.

Similarly, Ybor City owed much to Latin and Caribbean influences. From the mid-1880s, the transplanted cigar industry flourished, with thousands of white and black Cubans working in the cigar factories or related businesses by the turn of the century. They were joined by large numbers of Spanish and Italian immigrants. These three communities existed in harmony for decades, even publishing a trilingual newspaper, *La Gaceta*. They established a wide range of clubs, mutual aid societies, dance halls, and cantinas—some of which, such as Centro Asturiano, Circulo Cubano, and La Union Martí-Maceo, survive today.

According to the 2000 census, Latins/Hispanics were about 62.5 percent of Miami-Dade County's population and blacks accounted for 19.5 percent. Thus Florida's largest city contains a majority Latin American population, a large black minority with a significant Caribbean element, and a significant Jewish population. The result is the gradual development of a unique local culture that synthesizes aspects of all cultures.

The Florida Keys curve more than one hundred miles south and west from Miami to Key West, the southernmost city in the continental United States. In the eighteenth century, the Spanish used the Keys as a base for fishing, pirates hid in the coves and channels, and Bahamian wreckers salvaged cargoes from ships destroyed on the coral reefs. Claimed at times by Spain, England, private American citizens, and the United States, by the mid-nineteenth century the Keys were inhabited by a mixture of Americans, Cubans, Bahamians, and Spaniards. The wrecking, sponge, and cigar industries employed most of the Key West population, while fishing and agricultural activities dominated the Upper Keys. Long periods of isolation had a formative effect on the people of the Keys, or "Conchs"—many of whom never left the islands until the railroad was completed in 1912. These elements produced a traditional life unique to the Keys.

Florida's abundant natural resources have also generated a variety of folk groups who practice traditional skills and occupations distinctive to various regions. Water, in particular, is an important element of life in Florida. Traditional culture associated with both marine and inland waters is extensive and several aspects of Florida's fishing industry are unique in the United States. For example, in the Everglades Anglo "gladesmen," Seminoles and Miccosukees, and African Americans formerly traveled the interior glades and mangrove fringes to hunt alligators, deer, turtles, and frogs or to fish. The people who settled the Everglades developed unique modes of transportation to navigate the wilderness in search of fish and game. Seminoles and Miccosukees built dugout canoes and Anglo gladesmen created the glade skiff. These modes of transportation and the skills necessary to make them have all but vanished, now largely replaced by the airboat—a south Florida invention used in wetlands worldwide.

Florida preserves extensive rural areas where people raise crops and animals. For years Florida was the leading beef-producing state east of the Mississippi River, and today it remains in the top five. Florida ranching has evolved from many different cultural traditions, though the most important sources were the marshy coastal areas of Andalusia, Spain, and the hill regions of Britain and Ireland. The Spanish and British took these traditions to the West Indies, where they were adapted to the tropical climate and combined to create ranching systems used throughout the Americas. For example, Florida cow hunters or cowmen still crack their whips near the cow's ear, nose, or leg in order to move the cow in the required direction. They also use cow dogs to flush strays from hammocks, scrub, and swamps that riders cannot penetrate; control cattle from the sides and front as cowmen drive the cattle from the rear; and gather cattle into tight groups by circling them while barking and nipping. Many objects used by cowmen are imbued with a high level of aesthetic excellence, for craftsmen still create beautiful and functional saddles, cow whips, branding irons, and spurs.

With its mild climate, ample rainfall, and long growing season, Florida is one of the nation's leading agricultural states. It leads the nation in citrus and provides 80 percent of the nation's winter vegetables, but the production of tropical crops—primarily by Latin American and southeast Asian farmers—distinguishes it from other agricultural regions.

CONCLUSION

Florida's environment and peoples have created distinctive complexes of traditional life unlike those of any other American region. Its location and history bind it as tightly to the Caribbean as to mainland America.

While some of Florida's cultural syntheses developed from the sixteenth through nineteenth centuries in locations such as Key West, Tampa, St. Augustine, and Pensacola, they have intensified today with large-scale immigration from Cuba, South and Central America, the Caribbean, Africa, and Asia. Although south Florida leads other regions in the development of a contemporary cultural synthesis, all parts of Florida are affected. Orlando and Tampa are rapidly evolving, but even sleepy north Florida is experiencing a significant change as Floridians of all backgrounds drift north in search of greater economic opportunities and less-crowded conditions.

Note

1. The Historical Museum of Southern Florida changed its name to HistoryMiami in 2010.

The Florida Folklife Reader

Key Largo to Marathon

A Report on the Folklife of the Upper and Middle Keys

BRENT CANTRELL

THE HISTORICAL MUSEUM OF SOUTHERN FLORIDA'S FOLKLIFE PROGRAM completed a project to survey the folklife of the Florida Keys in 1989. The last general survey of Keys culture was conducted in the 1930s when the WPA Writers' Project documented folk arts throughout Florida, including the Keys. Since then, there have been only limited and sporadic efforts to research Keys folk arts.

Long periods of isolation had a formative effect on the people of the Keys, often called "Conchs." Many never left the islands until the completion of the railroad in 1912. The Conchs made their livelihood through the harvest of the land and sea, sometimes supplemented by smuggling and tourism. The isolated nature of the Keys, combined with the mixture of Anglo, Bahamian, and Cuban settlers, produced a traditional life unique to the area. Rapid development of the Keys in recent decades and the influx of outsiders have added new forms to Keys folklife.

Many of the oldest and most developed of the traditional arts found in the Keys are associated with maritime industries and occupations. Maritime commerce, fishing, sponging, and trapping have always been central elements of life in the Keys, and the arts, skills, and craftsmanship of the maritime occupations are held in high esteem by both longtime residents and newer arrivals. Even those residents who have little to do with the sea recognize the preeminence of the fishing captains and the people who supply them.

At the center of activity are the fishermen and trappers. There are two distinct types of professional fishermen in the Keys: commercial fishermen

Crew of *Take It Or Leave It* fishing off Islamorada. Photo by Brent Cantrell. Courtesy of Historical Museum of Southern Florida.

and fishing guides. The former make their living by catching fish or crustaceans in large quantity and selling them to local fish houses; they work with a crew and often go out with several other boats. Guides, on the other hand, work alone, taking sport fishermen to likely spots and instructing them in technique.

Fishermen carry tremendous traditional knowledge. Boat captains who catch fish must have knowledge of their equipment, weather, the typography of the seabed, and the behavior of their quarry. This knowledge is gained over years, or even decades, of apprenticeship. In the case of commercial fishermen, most work first as a deckhand and then as a mate on a successful captain's boat. Some of the most capable fishermen are from families who have been fishing in the Keys for several generations. Techniques and knowledge are passed from one generation to another, and at any given time there may be several family members earning a living by fishing.

Fish are notoriously capricious, and successful fishermen rely on friends and family for tips, pointers, and help at sea. While nominally in competition with each other, captains will share information about location, tackle, and techniques. There is often a great sense of comradeship and friendly competition among commercial fishermen, though it is governed by a complex etiquette system. Successful fishermen seem to feel an obligation to pass on information to others; in return, they receive respect and recognition from their peers.

Commercial fishing as practiced for generations in the Keys may be ending. The recent influx of new residents has brought pressures on the environment that have in turn resulted in an ensemble of new laws governing fishing and boating. These new regulations are forcing men whose families have fished the Keys for a century to give up the profession. Sport fishing, conversely, is doing well. Sport-fishing guides rely on the thriving tourist industry, which seems in no danger of collapse.

Besides the fishermen themselves, there is a host of related occupations dependent on the sea. Foremost is boatbuilding. Boatbuilding technology has changed considerably since World War II. Before the war, boats built in the Keys were of wood. Their construction required an intimate knowledge of woods and the properties of timber. After the war, plywood became widely available and builders switched from planks to that strong, relatively lightweight material. Finally in the sixties, craftsmen began shifting to fiberglass and resins, which are not only lightweight and strong, but also resist decay. Some of the older boatbuilders in the Keys have worked with all three methods.

William Roberts of Tavernier, a third-generation boatbuilder, began working in his father's shop in the thirties and, over the years, has built scores of wood, plywood, and fiberglass boats. Though he has built boats for many different purposes, he is well known for his backcountry skiff, a small, shallow draft boat designed for use in Florida Bay. Roberts and most other commercial boatbuilders have worked primarily with fiberglass for the last several years, but the art of wood and plywood boatbuilding is not dead, and wooden boats may be glimpsed under construction in back yards throughout the Keys.

Sail making, an allied craft, supports four or five businesses in the Keys. Today most sail makers use a synthetic sailcloth and a computer-generated pattern to make new sails, but older tools and techniques are used in the repair and alteration of sails. Setting grommets and rope work are still done by hand, and sails may also be sewn using techniques acquired through apprenticeship.

Utilitarian and decorative rope work is one of the traditional arts associated with sailing practiced today as much for pleasure as for practicality. George King of Windward Sails in Marathon has mastered scores of knots,

Willie Roberts working in his father's boatyard in 1932. Courtesy of Historical Museum of Southern Florida.

bends, and splices, including the decorative "Turk's head" and "crown knot," as well as the more practical but complex long splice and rope to wire splice.

Although at least one net maker works in Key West, hand net tying seems to be largely a thing of the past in the Upper and Middle Keys. Several people who tied nets in the past are still alive but inexpensive, commercially available nets of monofilament line have put most net makers out of business. Some still repair nets, retying ripped and torn sections. One such veteran of net fishing is R. R. Brawner. Now in retirement, Brawner has spent his life seining and netting fish and still occasionally repairs nets for friends in Marathon.

Making traps, particularly those for the Florida lobster, or crawfish, is also a thriving commercial concern in the Keys. Traps are made by both large lumberyards and individuals. Crawfish traps are of a standard design: a rectangular box made of wooden slats about two feet square and a foot high with an entrance hole on top. Two of the more accessible trap makers are Jose and Eugene Garcia; they make traps for their own use and to sell to the public at a roadside stand in Tavernier.

The Garcia brothers participate in two other traditional Conch occupations, sponging and scavenging. At their roadside stand one may buy sponges hooked by the brothers, as well as driftwood, bamboo, buoys, rope, and

Richard Blaes installing mandibles on his giant crawfish. Courtesy of Historical Museum of Southern Florida.

other items that have washed ashore or that they find while trapping and sponging.

The Garcia brothers' roadside stand brings us to a second important Keys industry—tourism. Although many of the objects sold at tourist shops are mass-produced or imported items, some are the work of talented local artists working within a community tradition. Most notably, shell sculpture and the decorative use of shells must be recognized as an indigenous south Florida art form. Surprisingly, the number of locally produced shell sculptures for sale in shops is rather small; most are now imported from the Philippines.

There is at least one exceptional quilter, Ida Wellborn, who sells to the tourist trade in Key Largo. Wellborn sells her own quilts, which she sews in the Keys, as well as quilts made by members of her family in other parts of the country.

The wealth of monumental sculpture associated primarily with roadside attractions is particularly striking in the Keys. Whaler's Plaza in Marathon displays examples of this genre of folk sculpture, including a reinforced

José and Eugene Garcia making lobster traps in Tavernier Key. Courtesy of Historical Museum of Southern Florida.

concrete conch shell and a whale tail. Massive sculpture of this sort also marks public buildings, especially public schools.

One of the most remarkable examples of monumental sculpture is in Marathon on Coco Plum Road. Over the past four and one-half years, Richard Blaes constructed a scale model of a crawfish twenty-four times the size of the original. Blaes used his knowledge of materials acquired as a fisherman, boatbuilder, and boat repairman to sculpt this thirty-eight-foot-long resin and fiberglass model, which is an extraordinary example of occupational folk art. Other types of monumental sculpture may also be seen marking schools, souvenir shops, and malls.

Foodways, in the Keys as elsewhere, is a conservative genre. Because of the limited resources and the physical isolation of the Florida Keys, a unique cuisine developed.

Seafood, of course, plays an important role in Keys foodways, and the conch is especially associated with old-time cooking. Conch chowder and conch fritters are two mainstays of island cuisine. A second peculiarity of Keys foodways is its reliance on sweetened condensed milk. Sweetening and canning milk was one of the first methods devised for the preservation of milk. Its use became popular in the Keys, where limited pasture and fresh water made fresh milk unavailable. Key lime pie is one of the most famous condensed milk recipes; others include Queen of All Puddings, a bread pudding with guava paste, and custards. Tropical fruits also feature high in Keys cooking: calamondin, guava, and sea grape jellies are common, and key limes are used for desserts and "old sour," a piquant sauce to which salt and sometimes hot peppers are added.

Music in the Upper and Middle Keys is not as well developed as in Key West. Several accomplished musicians of modern popular forms like rock and country and western perform in clubs in Marathon and Key Largo, and at least one group of musicians plays popular songs from the big band era at the retirement home in Tavernier. One notable musician, Elgie Brown, learned to play bones and saw about sixty years ago in Illinois. He still maintains those genres in Tavernier, but older forms of secular music are rare north of Key West.

Several people, particularly retirees who have made their home in the Upper and Middle Keys, have turned to wood carving, especially the carving of birds. Some of their efforts are spectacular. Nancy Quinn operates a private bird sanctuary in the Upper Keys and carves native birds from live models. Sales of the carved birds support the operation of her sanctuary. Other carvers produce statuary for sale and to decorate their homes.

In the Keys, as elsewhere, forms of folklore are constantly evolving. While we may bemoan the loss of many of the old ways, we may be confident that new ways are developing which will become the old ways of the future. Documenting this process of change is one of the most exciting aspects of folklife research, and the speed of change in recent years in the Florida Keys gives us an excellent opportunity to record the rapid evolution of folklife forms.

African American and West Indian Folklife in South Florida

JOYCE M. JACKSON

PRESENT-DAY METROPOLITAN MIAMI, WHICH ENCOMPASSES MOST OF Dade County, is an evolving environment that illustrates the historical flow of cultural ideas between diverse populations. The black population provides an excellent example of this diversity. Although the *1980 Census Summary of the General Population Characteristics* reported that there were 280,434 blacks in the county, it did not mention that they came not only from the United States, but also from the Caribbean, Latin America, and Africa. In this essay, I will examine some aspects of the folk culture of two African Diaspora groups in Miami—African Americans and West Indians.

THE AFRICAN AMERICAN PRESENCE

Since they first came to the Miami area in the early nineteenth century, African Americans have responded to a broad range of experiences—slavery, urban migration, disenfranchisement during the Jim Crow era, the struggle for civil rights and economic freedom, and today, a new political activism. Throughout the episodes of their history, African Americans have found ways to educate, strengthen, comfort, inspire, motivate, and entertain their minds and spirits, thereby making it possible to survive and grow beyond the external circumstances of their lives.

A rich and immense body of tradition has emerged from this struggle for survival. African American folk culture includes the songs, verbal lore, crafts, and occupational skills that African Americans brought from both rural agricultural areas and other urban centers. These traditions are composed of more than skills that can be learned by example, such as improvising the lead in a gospel song, piecing a quilt, or break dancing. They also include the concepts, cultural values, aesthetics, and worldviews that make African American folk expression unique. Many of these emerged directly from the values shared by various African societies.

When Africans were transported to the sugar plantations of the Caribbean, then to the cotton plantations and farms in the southern United States, they brought their traditional ways of thinking and living with them. Since many Africans had lived in close and prolonged proximity with European-derived culture, they were able to exercise a cultural selectivity by tenaciously retaining those elements of their African heritage that were most valuable to them. This selective process and subsequent synthesis of African and European elements defines the evolution of a distinct African American culture. In African American folk traditions, however, the African elements are usually more prevalent.

Religion

The culture of urban African Americans reveals much about the boom, bust, and subsequent redevelopment of their communities. Throughout the process of community change, African Americans have selectively chosen to hold on to long-cherished ways of doing things. The rhythm and flavor of African American urban community life takes one in many directions. The church is a good place to begin, for it serves as the most important community institution for newly arrived families. It is also one of the strongest and most-enduring transplants to urban life. For many African Americans, the church family replaces to a substantial degree parts of the extended family that were left behind.

African American migration patterns follow well-traveled corridors. People from rural areas leave some relatives and move to urban areas with other branches of their families; over time, others may follow. In this manner, entire communities can be gradually transplanted. Many of the African American churches in Miami were organized with memberships based on rural congregations. Some of the smaller churches are still shaped by members arriving from rural areas in Florida or other southern states. In the early 1920s, some residents of Calvin, Georgia, moved into the West Perrine community and founded the church that became Mt. Moriah Baptist Church. Families from Perry, Georgia, moved into the Goulds community in the mid-1920s, and some still have their church membership at Mt. Carmel Unity Baptist Church.

The church is the place where the raw edges of migrational change are softened, where old flavors and sounds from home are not discarded, but blend in comforting ways in a new urban gospel pot. There you can find the elders who perform black sacred songs and prayers holding on to a tradition that surely represents continuity not just from the rural South, but from older African roots as well.

One can go to the Church of Christ in the Goulds community and still find a strong traditional unaccompanied song service led by elders who maintain the old, rich pattern of singing a song phrase followed by the congregation repeating that same phrase, a practice which is known as lining-out. One also hears the old patterns with "amen comers" (i.e., a group within the congregation that responds verbally to the sermons and songs) and general congregational singing in unison and heterophony. The call-and-response structure, which is a common performance practice in West African music, is prevalent not only in this folk church setting, but in most African American traditional music. Call-and-response is an alternation between a leader and a chorus, purposefully done so all can join in. Many West African, and thus African American, musical events are of a participatory nature. Their songs—spirituals, hymns, and jubilees—are accompanied by handclapping, foot stamping, and interjection of a shout, cry, or holler from someone who "feels the spirit."

In many churches, especially the larger ones, old gospel songs led by the elders in the traditional way have been supplanted by the newer sounds of songs accompanied by electric organs and/or instrumental combos. New songs that serve new needs evolved from traditional ones. Many of them combined the musical structure and poetic forms of old secular and religious songs with new musical and textual ideas. These gospel songs can be heard in Mt. Carmel Missionary Baptist Church and New Macedonia Baptist Church in Liberty City or Glendale Missionary Baptist Church in Richmond Heights.

The highly emotional and spirit-filled music called gospel evolved from the Holiness and Pentecostal churches, and first penetrated more established denominations through the "storefront" Baptist and Methodist churches that permeate areas where African Americans have lived in Miami. Today, denomination is not a determining factor, and one finds gospel music in Baptist, Methodist, Catholic, and Episcopal congregations throughout the communities.

Going out to a "singing" is another urban-based Christian sociocultural event that takes place in churches, schools, community centers, and auditoriums. Singings, "gospel extravaganzas," and "gospelfests" are programs of gospel music, with between two and ten vocal groups performing a few songs each. A minister usually opens the program, and many times it is closed as the "doors of the church" are opened in an invitation to accept Christ as one's personal savior.

Smaller community-based vocal groups often perform along with choirs at singings. These groups are organized in churches and schools, and among occupational, community, and family groups. The Calvary Travelers (mixed group) is an example of a family group that continues to perform in the unaccompanied, or a cappella, style. The emphasis is on blended ensemble singing, with group harmonies serving as the only needed arrangements for the solo singing of the lead. Their arrangements include the whole group singing choruses in harmony, with the lead performing words and melody over repeated, harmonized, rhythmic phrases sung by the group. Performances by the Heavenly Jewels and the Disciple Travelers have remained a cappella. However, some quartets and other smaller groups who performed unaccompanied for many years, such as the Stars of Harmony, have added instruments. Although it is not the norm, Miami also has its share of female a cappella quartets, including the Gospel Lyrics, the Goldenaires, and the Wimberly Sisters.

Secular Music

Music, sacred and secular, is a powerful force in all communities, but is perhaps even more so in the African American tradition, since it was something that could be held on to under the most adverse circumstances. When the blues, which is traditionally African American, rural, and southern, came to the urban areas, it immediately took root and became the main song form used for entertainment. The blues of the country fields and small "juke joints" became urban when musicians employed amplified instruments in the 1940s. During that era many such bands could be heard while strolling down N.W. Second Avenue in Overtown—then Miami's "Little Broadway." Today you still hear the familiar sounds of the blues bands in clubs such as Tobacco Road (Miami's oldest extant nightclub), Sensations, and Studio 183. Singers like Charles Wright and Alice Daye have also carried on the tradition. Blues and many other African American folk traditions have survived largely by oral transmission from senior members of the community to the younger generation.

The blues performer provided music for dancing in clubs, at barbecues, house parties, and other social gatherings. The music also served as a means for passing time and making social statements. The solitary, transient lifestyle of many blues singers did not deter them from making use of the call-and-response performance tradition. In the twelve-bar blues, a singer makes a statement or asks a question related to some circumstances of life. The comment or response at the end of the phrase comes not from a chorus of other singers, but from his guitar.

Miami bluesman W. C. Baker was born in the rural outskirts of Live Oak, Florida, between Jacksonville and Tallahassee. At age six, he began to sing the blues while plucking chicken wire strung across an old box made from scrap lumber—his first guitar. Like many country bluesmen who made their first instruments, this was his rite of passage into the blues world.

Baker's first professional engagement as an adult came forty-six years ago at the Big House club in Brownsville. His early life was very transient, and he had to deal with many adverse circumstances caused by discrimination, financial strain, and lost love. Nevertheless, through discipline and cooperation, Baker gradually moved from the lonely life of a transient bluesman to the leader of a well-known Miami blues band called W. C. Baker and the Cooperatives.

Domestic Arts

Neighborhood community centers are another significant place in Miami's African American communities where many aspects of traditional culture can be seen. For many generations African American women in the South have made patchwork quilts for utilitarian purposes. Although quilt making is not a specifically African tradition, it is possible that both the tradition and styles of African American quilts are related to the African tradition of decorative textiles. The quilts made by members of other cultures are more formal and unyielding in design and color than African American quilts.

At the Goulds Senior Citizen Center and the Perrine Neighborhood Community Center, elderly women gather to work on quilts. Not only do they make new quilts, but they also frequently repair or restore older quilts for others. For them quilting remains a social event, during which they talk about things that interest them. Because of this social function, it is likely that quilting will survive in African American neighborhoods for a long time.

Pattern names are a part of quilt folklore. The ladies at the West Perrine Neighborhood Center have quilted the "Flower Garden," "Star," "Little and Big Bow Tie," "Square" or "Nine Patches," "Around the World," and "Stove Eye." The ties to West African textile art can be seen in the quilts they refer to as "String" quilts, which strongly resemble the woven fabric and designs of West African cloth.

Virginia Barrel came to the community of West Perrine from Atlanta, Georgia, thirty-nine years ago. She has quilted since the age of twelve, when she learned the craft from her grandmother and mother. Mrs. Barrel comments:

> I held the lamp at night, so they could see how to quilt. . . . They used a frame that hung from the ceiling by a cord or string. . . . I made my first quilt at age fourteen with strings left over from other quilts.

Some of the women hate to discard anything, and these leftover items provide materials for other crafts. For instance, some use the fabric left from the quilts to fashion rag dolls, as well as dresses for dolls they have made from plastic bleach and detergent bottles. They create yo-yo pillows, pincushions, fabric flowers, and rugs out of old stockings. In addition, they make items from plastic soft drink can holders, aluminum can pop tops, and egg cartons. The impetus to make these things comes from the strategy of survival that arose when people had to "make do" by making use of everything.

Doretha Carter, who moved to Miami in 1924 from White Springs, Florida, utilizes many old things. She continues to make her own lye soap because she does not like to throw away her leftover cooking fat and she prefers doing things the old-fashioned way. Carter also preserves fruits such as guavas, mangoes, and oranges when they are in season.

Many women in the community still employ home remedies to cure various illnesses. They gave several examples of remedies for fever, such as drinking fever grass tea or an alcohol, mustard, and turpentine mixture. For the common cold, they recommended a mixture of castor oil, cod liver oil, and honey. If children have worms, they might chew a piece of asafetida. Sores or burns may be treated by rubbing them with aloe vera or tobacco juice.

THE WEST INDIAN PRESENCE

In the 1890s, Coconut Grove became the first major settlement by people of African descent, most of whom were Bahamian. Since that time, thousands of Caribbeans have made Miami–Dade County their home. They continue to add a new and vital dimension to this city by the sea. No official count for each island nation represented has been taken recently, but there are several visible communities.

Even though many Caribbean groups have assimilated to the mainstream Miami culture to a certain extent, they maintain a very strong sense of shared identity through several strategies. First, a large number of Caribbean organizations or voluntary associations plan cultural activities and address social, political, and cultural issues. One example of this is the Miami Caribbean Carnival Association. In addition, there are newspapers, tabloids, journals, and magazines that keep the Caribbean community informed about issues and activities concerning them and their respective island nations. Furthermore, just as African Americans continued selected cultural practices when they moved from the country to the city, Afro-Caribbeans have bridged the gap from the island to the mainland by preserving some forms of their homeland's cultural practices that have become symbolic of their ethnic identity.

The West Indian sense of ethnic identity is also reflected in home interiors, which make important statements about the identity of their residents and the way they want others to perceive them. Home interiors often encompass vital aspects of family and homeland history, and reflect aesthetic patterns and values that are reiterated in other spheres of life. Far from remaining fixed and unchanging, arts and crafts displayed in the home always incorporate both continuity and change by reflecting their owner's travels to the home country. For example, in a Trinidadian home I observed beautiful embroidery done by the mother and the headdress of an old Carnival costume juxtaposed with a commercial wooden replica of the island of Trinidad, obviously made for tourists. The value of these objects, then, is not found in their function and aesthetic form alone. Clearly, the process of creating the items and the act of possessing them carry significance for community members and make important statements about how they perceive their identity.

Another strategy for reinforcing the traditional culture is the frequent journey home to the mother country. Since a large number of people frequently fly to the islands, a number of West Indian–owned travel agencies have been established in the north Miami-Dade vicinity. Many travel to their home island several times a year, depending on factors such as family, business, or vacation.

Music and Song

One of the most noticeable aspects of West Indian culture in Miami is the music. The remarkable richness of West Indian musical life is partly the product of its multilayered complexity and diversity, which reflects the encounter between European and African musical traditions. European folk music practices, whether of Spanish, French, British, or Dutch origin, have for centuries come into contact and fused with the musical traditions carried by slaves from West and Central Africa to the Americas. The various practices and the way they have combined differ from place to place. However, the fundamental cultural elements in the different colonies paved the way for a creative process of blending and fusion (sometimes referred to as "Creolization") that had similar results throughout the Caribbean.

In Miami, parties and other social events are held in peoples' homes or in rented halls, and generally involve a deejay who spins reggae, calypso, and soca (an invigorating musical synthesis of calypso with soul and funk elements) records. Occasionally, live reggae bands such as Zero Crew or Spice Roots, and live steelbands, including the Burt Reyes Steel Orchestra or the Rising Star Steelband, perform at the events. Staged dance performances, such as calypso and limbo, may also be featured along with informal social dancing.

In addition to local entertainers, major calypsonians, soca, and reggae stars, including David Rudder, Baron, Mighty Sparrow, Calypso Rose, Steel Pulse, and others, usually appear in concert several times during the year. These social events are often sponsored by a West Indian organization to raise funds for a cause or by a promoter for pure entertainment and monetary profit. West Indians flock to these events. The concerts are a medium wherein they can experience their common bonds, as well as express and solidify their West Indian heritage.

In all the previously mentioned West Indian musical styles—calypso, reggae, and soca—one can hear the synthesis of European and African elements along with indigenous island characteristics. For example, each style is performed on instruments of European origin and uses the European harmonic system based on the diatonic scale, but the African elements are very strong. They include the presence of the call-and-response structure, syncopated rhythms, improvisation, strong percussion, the relationship of music and dance, and the music's political as well as collective social nature. While all three styles are dance and party music, reggae and calypso also function as media for social and political commentary.

Musical and extra-musical affinities link the various styles with the individual characteristics of their island nations. Although calypso is performed today on European instruments, it is traditionally performed on steeldrums, or "pans" as they are referred to by Trinidadians. The rhythm of the Trinidadian and Jamaican dialects tends to exert a powerful influence on the music and the manner in which it is performed. It does not matter how urban or international these styles have become, they still retain a strong indigenous character.

Although currently a popular style, reggae has its roots in traditional styles of Jamaican music. Elements from the Kumina tradition (religious ceremonies of drumming and dancing, held for the purpose of communion with the spirits of ancestors) are evident in the rhythmic layering of the guitar and keyboards in many reggae songs. Reggae also has an "off-beat" phrasing of the rhythm guitar that strongly resembles that of mento songs. Jamaican mento music is similar to the calypso of Trinidad and Tobago in that it is sometimes comical while still making historical, political, and social comments. However, mento consists of a different combination of instruments than calypso. In addition to guitar and banjo, a rumba box is the percussive instrument instead of a drum. Mento phrasing can also be heard in the accents of reggae trap drummers, although their individual styles vary. Even the dance movements of reggae are similar to that used in mento dancing. This similarity is noted by Louise Bennett-Coverly, a Jamaican folklorist, poet, storyteller, and newspaper columnist. She refers to the dance movements as an "old African step," the "weak knee" or "dipping motion."

Carol Pratt has resided in Miami since 1980, but she still plays mento and other more traditional songs on her guitar, and sings the lyrics she learned during her childhood in Jamaica. Pratt has returned to some of the rural areas where people still practice the old folk songs of Jamaica in order to collect and learn more. She performs them at her church and other cultural events in the West Indian community.

Lucille Ranger-Brown, who has lived in Miami since 1971, is a celebrated Jamaican performer. She performs many traditional Jamaican songs and dances, including work songs that portray typical marketplace scenes, women washing their clothes at the riverside, men working on the railroad, and other aspects of "the old culture like it used to be." Ranger-Brown also recites stories in Jamaican dialect or patois, and intersperses songs and dances in the midst of them. She comments: "We tell stories through folk songs. You see everyday living and we'd make a song or dance out of it. We don't go to school for this."

Narrative

Narrative tradition is another vital aspect of the influence of African traditions on West Indian culture. Storytelling—expressing a concept, moral lesson, or day-to-day experience in dramatic imagery—is one of the strongest retentions of African narrative forms in the Diaspora. As in African communities, it is an important means of recordkeeping and transmitting information. Telling stories about animals that exhibit human behavior in familiar situations was a common method of instruction in West African society. A prevalent theme was the confrontation between a small animal, such as a spider or a rabbit, and a large animal, like a lion or a fox. The weaker animal prevailed by using its wit or cunning. Within the context of the oppressed lives of the slaves, the tales took on another connotation—that of the slaves outwitting their masters.

Lucille Fuller, also from Jamaica, has a large repertoire of animal folktales, particularly those about the Anansi (spider) character. She is a very animated and dramatic storyteller who tells tales in Jamaican dialect and uses voice changes to represent each animal. Fuller learned her stories from her grandmother, mother, and father. Now, she recites the stories in schools and in church and community programs.

Foodways

One can see the expression of West Indian identity in Miami through foodways. There are presently many authentic West Indian restaurants, such as the Pantry Restaurant, the Pepper Pot, and Pauline's. Taken as a group, they offer a considerable variety of foods, with the repetition of some dishes that are universally popular in the Caribbean, such as rice and peas. Other popular dishes include curried goat, oxtail stew, "jerk" chicken or pork, Escovich fish, fried plantains, codfish and oiled bananas, conch fritters or salads, callalou, and ackee with saltfish.

Shirley Sutherland of Tobago is proud of her heritage and traditional cooking. She still prepares the traditional foods of her island home for her family, friends, and West Indian community functions. For example, she cooks bigi, which has spinach as its main ingredient, and coo-coo, which is made from cornmeal, okra, and coconut milk. For special occasions, she prepares a main dish like callalou, made from dashing leaves, okra, green peppers, pig tails, and crabs.

Sutherland and other West Indians need certain basic ingredients to maintain the authenticity of traditional dishes. Therefore, Miami has many grocery stores that specialize in the essentials for West Indian dishes. Some businesses serve a triple purpose, such as Jamaica Products, Inc., which is a wholesale warehouse, grocery, and retail restaurant. Don Linton and his wife sell cases of canned goods, fresh produce, medicinal herbs, spices, pharmaceuticals, and other Jamaican products to clients in Miami and other parts of the United States.

Smaller West Indian grocery stores and bakeries may provide more than one service. Tai's Bakery, run by a Chinese Jamaican family, also serves hot lunches. The bakery abounds with West Indian breads and sweet treats, like sourdough and coconut breads, fry bake, plantain and coconut pastries, currant rolls, and fruit cakes. Two of the more popular items are the spicy lobster patties and meat pies.

Celebrations

Many Trinidadians from Miami make the annual journey home for Carnival. It is recognized that no single event in the English-speaking Caribbean engenders as much ethnic unity and comradery among West Indians abroad as the Carnival celebration. Not only do they make the annual pilgrimage back for Carnival, but also wherever they happen to be domiciled in large numbers, bands of masqueraders parade in imitation of the event.

Masquerading (mas for short in Trinidad) is an almost universal feature of the widely distributed pre-Lenten festivals, which culminate on Mardi Gras (Fat Tuesday), the day before Ash Wednesday, and the beginning of the Lenten fast. Trinidad is no exception. Early descriptions of the restrained European Carnival celebrations in Trinidad prior to emancipation mention maskers, and the custom was carried and elaborated by freed slaves. In recent years, many of the older traditional Carnival characters have disappeared, and the hundreds of mas bands that participate in Carnival usually construct costumes on a new and original theme each year.

Llewellyn Roberts, who remembers following old sailor bands around as a child in Trinidad, and who, like most Trinidadians, has participated in Carnival all his life, is committed to continuing similar celebrations through Miami's West Indian Carnival. Roberts, who is a master craftsman, has been designing and building costume headdresses for many years. His specialty is wire bending—the painstaking task of constructing frames of wire that can be shaped with foam rubber, cloth, paper foil, sequins, and paint into a finished costume. Jesse Lampkin, also a wire bender from Trinidad, designs and builds full costumes. He lived in New York for many years and always participated in the West Indian Carnival on Labor Day.

On Columbus Day, Miami's West Indian community turns out to "Jump Up" and "Play Mas," dancing through the streets of downtown Miami to calypso and soca music. The Carnival combines African rhythms, colors, and sensuous movement, with the West Indians' unique flair for hospitality, entertainment, and bacchanal.

Just as Llewellyn Roberts and Jesse Lampkin persistently endeavor to preserve and celebrate their Trinidadian culture, Billy Rolle and Bruce Beneby have played similar roles in the Bahamian community. Billy Rolle is the

Bruce Beneby performing with the Sunshine Junkanoo Band at the 1990 Pan-African Bookfest. Photo by Tina Bucuvalas. Courtesy of Historical Museum of Southern Florida.

executive director of the Miami/Bahamas Goombay Festival Celebration, which takes place in early June. His grandfather was one of the first settlers to come from the Bahamas in the 1890s, and his father emigrated around the turn of the century from the family island of Exuma.

Since it began in 1978, the festival has evolved into a large and celebrated event during which Coconut Grove's Grand Avenue turns into Nassau's Bay Street. The internationally acclaimed Royal Bahamas Police Band performs at Goombay events and marches in the parade. In 1989 close to 800,000 residents and visitors packed the Grove for the festival, feasting on traditional Bahamian treats, viewing the arts and crafts, and enjoying the music of Miami's Sunshine Junkanoo Band.

Bruce Beneby was the leader of the Sunshine Junkanoo Band, which consists primarily of his family and friends. He was born in Nassau, but lived in Miami since 1956. There are various theories on the origin of the term Junkanoo. Beneby believed that the term and the celebration of Junkanoo "all began in Africa with a gentleman named 'Johnny Enew,' leader of a band that

Bahamian American Junkanoo headdress by Sunshine Junkanoo Band with Martin Luther King image. Photo by George Chillag. Courtesy of Historical Museum of Southern Florida.

traveled from house to house, from street to street during certain holidays like Christmas and New Year's, which is when Junkanoo is celebrated in the Bahamas." Every year during the holidays, Beneby returned to Nassau, to participate in his country's traditional celebration, marching in the parade and beating drums.

The Sunshine Junkanoo Band members play horns, drums, whistles, and cowbells. Each year they create a new array of vividly colored costumes with headdresses based on a specific theme. The band has performed at the Goombay festival in the Grove since its inception, and also performs at other festivals and events throughout the state. Bruce Beneby was tragically killed in a hit-and-run accident, but his family and friends are continuing the tradition of celebration.

CONCLUSION

Traditional culture continues to pervade the lives of African Americans and West Indians in Miami. Many traditions, such as those mentioned here, not only provide an enduring basis for family and community life, but also serve as a source of aesthetic satisfaction for generations of participants.

The Patronal Festival of Vueltas in Cuban Miami

"No One Loses, They Always Win!"

TINA BUCUVALAS

A veces me pregunto dónde termina la verdad y dónde comienza el folclor en esas Habanas imaginarias que nos inventamos en las esquinas de Miami. [Sometimes I ask myself where truth ends and folklore begins in these imaginary Havanas that we invent on the streets of Miami.]

—NÉSTOR DÍAZ DE VILLEGAS

INTRODUCTION

Like many other immigrant groups, Cubans in Miami have reconstructed parts of their social and political structure in order to negotiate the difficult transition between their past and their present. For decades, most Cubans regarded themselves as exiles with a limited tenure in this country rather than as immigrants. Thus, they held on tightly to previous forms of social organization. Moreover, the community's large size (approximately 900,000 Cubans and Cuban Americans in south Florida) in combination with its concentration within a relatively small area (primarily Miami-Dade County and secondarily south Florida) also have contributed to the retention of many cultural patterns. This chapter will examine the patronal festival celebrated by former residents of Vueltas, Cuba, its significance within the social context, and its adaptation to new conditions in Miami.

Festivals are complex, periodic phenomena that celebrate significant times and events through patterned actions. Among their most important functions are the generation of positive emotions and social cohesion through the suspension of normal routine combined with activities that induce a sense of physical well-being. In the case of immigrant communities, festivals also serve as a buffer to a strange environment and a symbol of cultural identity. Continuities and changes within festivals often mirror similar phenomena in the general community.

Patronal festivals arose in Catholic religious practice as the devotions paid to local martyrs gradually evolved into the cult of the saints in the second century AD. This was related to the distribution of saints' relics to churches and the processions and popular festivals that grew up around them. Festivals dedicated to the Virgin Mary developed a few hundred years later.

Within Latin American folk religion, patronal festivals assume great importance as one of the few occasions on which a community comes together. Although the saint's day and its association with a particular town is the motivation for patronal festivals, religion is not always the dominant element. Patronal festivals vary considerably in the attention devoted to religious observations as opposed to activities that promote *alegría*, or joy. Moreover, many popular devotions or arts associated with patronal festivals reflect a strong Native American or African cultural heritage rather than a Catholic doctrine.

LOS MUNICIPIOS DE CUBA EN EL EXILIO

One way in which Miami Cubans have preserved their social organization is through *Los Municipios de Cuba en el Exilio* (Cuban Municipalities in Exile), the largest network of voluntary sociopolitical associations in the Cuban American community. Mutual aid organizations have a long history both in Cuba and among Cubans in Florida. In Cuba, people of Spanish and African background established separate fraternal orders or clubs that maintained their cultural heritage and provided them with economic assistance. Clubs organized by Cuban immigrants in Key West and Tampa in the late nineteenth and early twentieth centuries assisted the communities by coordinating social events and providing educational opportunities, financial assistance, and sometimes health care to those who needed them.

Los Municipios de Cuba en el Exilio was created in 1962 by former residents of several different municipios who thought such organizations would provide a good vehicle for get-togethers with others from the same vicinity. By 1963 about twenty municipios were participating, and they created a formal umbrella organization to unite them. By the end of the twentieth century, Los Municipios boasted about 60,000 active families. Although participation and membership levels vary considerably among the separate municipios, most meet at least two or three times a year to celebrate national holidays and saints' days or to hold community picnics. More than twenty possess permanent meeting places.

While it is not unusual for immigrant groups to form voluntary mutual support societies, the breadth of such organizations among the Cubans is remarkable. Of the 126 municipios in prerevolutionary Cuba, 117 organized in Miami. Each elects a president, secretary, and treasurer. In addition, they attempt to duplicate the structure of Cuba's prerevolutionary government by electing representatives to token provincial and national assemblies. The municipios also contrast with support organizations created by other immigrant groups in that membership is open to all and the separate municipios operate independently but maintain the umbrella organization.

While the municipios assert some political intent, their primary activities are social in nature. For the most part, each arranges events that bring together former neighbors and assists recent immigrants from the municipio. Many also publish newsletters to communicate information about members or to document their history. In addition, the umbrella organization sponsors an annual fair. The event features performances by local Cuban celebrities, rides, and a competition for queen. However, the core consists of stands built and decorated by the municipios, offering their traditional local cuisine. Each municipio provides tables and chairs for festival goers to eat, enjoy a beer or coffee, and chat with old friends.

THE PATRONAL FESTIVAL OF VUELTAS

A few municipios have revived their annual patronal festivals. The Spanish established this tradition early in Cuba's history. For instance, soon after they founded the central Cuban town of San Juan de los Remedios in 1540, the Spanish instituted patronal festivals in all towns within its jurisdiction. By the eighteenth century, *parrandas*, or secular festivities that include dancing and music, accompanied the patronal festivals.

The town of San Antonio de las Vueltas, in the province of Las Villas, was originally within the jurisdiction of Remedios. Its patron saint is La Virgen de la Candelaria, whose feast day is February 2. This day celebrates the Purification of the Virgin (called Candlemas Day in English), during which the principal Mass is preceded by the blessing and distribution of candles. Candles are essential elements in many rites and ceremonies of the Catholic church, signifying honor for holy things or people.

In the region surrounding Vueltas, every town was long ago divided into eastern and western sections, or *barrios*, to compete against each other in the parrandas. The residents of Vueltas's eastern barrio are called *hutios*, and those in the western barrio *ñañacos*. Hutias are rat-like rodents that measure eight to twenty-four inches and weigh up to twenty pounds, and many live in the rocky hills behind the eastern section. Since the western barrio included the majority of black inhabitants, they were called ñañacos after the *ñañambós* or *ñañigos* who were members of an Afro-Cuban religious society. Each barrio was also represented by a color and another creature. The hutios are identified with the color red and the *gavilán*, or Florida eagle. The ñañacos are associated with blue and the rooster. Both the gavilán and the rooster are associated with macho qualities. Vuelteños claim that there is no deep meaning to the symbols, but that they are simply results of happenstance.

Allegiance to the hutios or ñañacos was originally determined by residence, but over time there has been significant movement and intermarriage between the two barrios. Today loyalties are determined by a household's dominant personality, the family member with the greatest interest in the tradition, or merely personal preference. In a typical instance I encountered, the children of a ñañaco father and a hutia mother were a mixture of hutios and ñañacos. However, the issue of allegiance runs very deep in the consciousness of many Vuelteños. For example, the elderly grandmother of a friend of mine was hospitalized just before the 1992 parranda. The woman was semi-conscious and did not recognize any family member except for a daughter. Yet, when a grandson mentioned the upcoming festival and asked her if she was hutia, she exclaimed with fervor, "No!! I'm a ñañaco!!!"

THE FESTIVAL IN CUBA

In order to understand the changes undergone by the patronal festival in Miami, it is necessary to describe how the event was celebrated in Vueltas. Although a small town, Vueltas was famous throughout Cuba for its parranda and the associated fireworks. Each barrio raised money by sponsoring dances or collecting door to door several months in advance. Beginning two or three months before the festival, each side would start preparing their floats and costumes in a large warehouse. Artists designed the artifacts, craftspeople directed the process, and everyone helped. The themes and designs were kept secret from the rival barrio, and there was a great deal of excitement and tension between them. Within the same family, members belonging to different sides sometimes would not eat or talk together for months before the festival.

As February 2 approached, farmers from the surrounding countryside streamed into town, as did many friends, relatives, and total strangers from throughout Cuba. Early in the afternoon of February 2, the priest and the townspeople took the statue of the Virgin from the church, carried it in procession around the town, and then replaced it. Afterward, the two barrios flipped a coin to determine which side would be second in the parade. Each side preferred to start second because they believed they would be remembered more clearly and thus more favorably.

The parranda was held outdoors. The focal point was a parade of elaborate *carrozas*, or floats, that were built over cars or truck beds. The Vuelteños created the carrozas with strips of material soaked in plaster—something like papier-mâché. Themes usually concerned historic events or figures, such as St. George and the Dragon, Cleopatra, or Solomon. In 1964—the last year the festival was celebrated in Cuba—the ñañacos created a float featuring Nero enthroned with Pompeia, a grotto with running water, and people dressed as Roman statues.

In addition to the carrozas, the festival featured several other types of festival arts. There was a competition for the best *farolas*, large lantern-like ornaments hanging from the top of long poles, which were usually paraded down the street in groups. Festival artists also made *muñecones* or *cabezones*, tall figures topped with large papier-mâché heads, which were intended to entertain the children with their fantastic appearance. These are drawn from the Spanish tradition of *gigantes* that accompanied religious processions such as that of Santiago de Campostela in Galicia. In Vueltas, they created the muñecones in a male and female couple. Fireworks were another important festival art. Some artists constructed *tableros*: structures made from wood, wire, and paper, onto which hundreds or thousands of fireworks were attached. Over time, each barrio also created traditional songs with which they taunted the other side during the parranda. One such song complains that the hutios came out of their caves to fight, but found the rooster too sick for a confrontation.

The parade usually started between eleven and two at night, and lasted until dawn. Each side prepared two or three carrozas, which they brought out in alternation with the other side—both saving the most spectacular for last. The floats rolled down the main streets and through the central plaza, where they passed the table set aside for the judges. If a float could not hold together until it passed the table, it automatically lost. Roman candles illuminated their path.

Vuelteños evaluated the floats in a unique manner. Although they set up a judges' table, there were rarely judges because no one dared incur the wrath of the other side. As a result, both sides always claimed victory. As Vueltas's lay historian Esther Torres attested, "No one loses. . . . It doesn't matter what they do, they always win!"[1]

Spectators watched the parade from the sides of the street. After each float, members of the barrio joined those holding the various insignias (flags, rooster, gavilán) in dancing through the streets accompanied by musicians playing conga drums, tambores, a plowshare, and other percussive instruments. This aspect of the parade was called a *changüí.* During the night Vuelteños also held two racially segregated dances sponsored by separate white and black *sociedades* (societies). Most townspeople stayed up all night drinking, eating, dancing, and watching the parades.

The next day, members of each barrio again danced through the streets during the *entierro,* or burial. Each barrio carried aloft a small casket containing some item they had stolen from the other side. This action symbolically demonstrated that they had buried or vanquished the other side. The entierro provided another occasion for general merriment during the day.

Nearby towns developed slightly different traditions. Although Vueltas and Camajuaní built floats, in Remedios they created *trabajos de plaza,* or large tableaux. In both Remedios and Caibarién, *comparsa* groups danced through the streets but they did not build floats. Comparsas are groups of *conga* musicians accompanied by lines of paired male and female dancers performing choreographed dances.

THE FESTIVAL IN MIAMI

In Miami, Vuelteños organized as a municipio in the early years of exile. As membership gradually grew and the annual reunion became an established event, they revived the patronal festival. As in Cuba, the process of organizing the festival lasts three or four months. Vuelteños hold picnics and other fund-raising events during the preceding months, and also sell advance tickets in order to raise money and plan for the crowd.

Vuelteños have adapted their parranda to fit many new social and physical constraints in Miami. In accord with the American custom of scheduling holiday events on weekends so as not to disrupt the work schedule, the festival now takes place on the Saturday night closest to February 2. Since they cannot close the streets, they hold the event in a large hall, such as that of St. Sophia Greek Orthodox Cathedral. Floats will not fit through the doorways, so they have replaced them with comparsas and trabajos de plaza—which were known from the parrandas of nearby towns. In 1992 the ñañacos built two trabajos from painted styrofoam. One depicted a view of Havana and the other several enormous tropical fruits.

The hutia and ñañaco comparsa groups both organize and begin rehearsals in mid-January. A woman from each side designs and sews the ruffled, brightly colored costumes. The dance routines usually result from group efforts. In the case of the hutios, Esther Flores and the dancers themselves contributed ideas to create the 1992 routines. The dance steps are based on such Cuban forms as the rumba and conga. The dancers are all young people in their teens and twenties who are highly enthusiastic about participating in the event. Evita, a young Cuban American, explains, "It's fun. You get to wear the costumes, you get to rehearse. This is really good for the youth, because they get to learn about . . . how it was in Cuba. And then maybe when Fidel goes down, maybe they can go back to Cuba and make it there and start this tradition again."[2]

Among the Vuelteños in Miami are two acknowledged masters at creating the festival arts necessary to the parranda. Ñañaco Isaac Dueñas creates farolas and muñecones. Dueñas participated in the Vueltas festival from the age of nineteen, and learned the arts by assisting master artisans. Although he emigrated to the United States in the 1950s, he continued to return annually to participate in the festival through 1964. Dueñas began to work on the Miami festival in the mid-1980s. For the 1991 parranda he created a set of farolas and a muñecon of a ñañigo or *diablito*—a traditional Cuban figure depicting a member of an Afro-Cuban religious society that has become one of the standard national symbols for Cuban festive occasions. In 1992, Dueñas created a muñecon depicting a large older black man as well as a new set of farolas.

Among the hutios, Manolín Vega is responsible for creating such festival arts as the farolas. Vega, an older man who participated in Vueltas's festival for decades, was especially famous for his fireworks. During one well-remembered year, he created a tablero purported to have contained 35,000 fireworks.

As the Miami celebration has become more elaborate with each passing year, some Vuelteños have become newly involved in creating festival arts. For example, for the 1992 parranda, Ramón and Dennis Palomino (the president of the municipio and his son) created an impressively lifelike representation of a giant hutia. With eyes fashioned from red lights and a rubber chicken dangling from its mouth, the hutia resembled a hellish vision from Hieronymous Bosch. During the presentation, a friend of Dennis's held the hutia over his head as he danced wildly behind the comparsa group. Everyone at the gala was impressed, and the ñañacos were taken totally by surprise. The giant hutia now resides in the workroom of the Palominos's optical shop.

In 1992, over 700 Vuelteños and their friends attended the patronal festival. During the day, the active organizers from each side gathered at the cathedral to decorate the hall and prepare the tableaux. Many wore red or blue clothing to signify allegiance to their barrio. Inside, they covered the tables with alternating red and blue tablecloths. The most fanatic partisans sit only at a table bearing the color of their barrio. During the preparation there was constant ritual teasing culminating in heated but good-natured confrontations between members of the two sides.

The evening commenced with the hutio presentation at approximately ten o'clock. Esther Flores presented a skit she had written consisting of the reminiscences of an exile couple about the festival. She commandeered her parents to play the parts, prerecorded the dialogue, then directed her parents in lip-synching it on the stage. The conversation encompassed the different festival activities, notable events during past festivals, part of a traditional song mocking the ñañacos, and disparaging comments about the appearance of their rooster.

The main spectacle began with the entrance of a young woman dressed as the Virgin Mary. Next, six young women clothed in brightly colored costumes danced to a recorded song praising Cuba's six prerevolutionary provinces. The comparsa group entered shortly thereafter, accompanied by farolas, flag, gavilán, a man with a golden violin, and the giant hutia. The comparsa performed several choreographed routines. The golden violin was a personal joke directed at Abilio Amargos, a ñañaco who always complained that they did not have nearly the numbers or money as the hutios.

During the hutio presentation, a man emerged in blackface and smoking a cigar. His well-padded figure was clothed in a long gingham skirt and ruffled blouse, and his head was covered with a bandanna. This traditional figure is well known among Cubans as Mama Dolores, the epitome of the nineteenth-century Cuban slave woman. In many Cuban American celebrations, she appears as a sort of clown or trickster figure who often makes bawdy gestures or jokes with the crowd.

The climax of the formal hutio presentation was the 1991 hit, "*Nuestro día ya viene llegando*," written and recorded by Miami's Cuban American salsa star Willy Chirino. This powerful song had become an anthem for the Cuban community. In addition to fine lyrics that succinctly sketch the immigration process and its travails, the song announces that Cuba's time is near, and ends with a cry for the liberation of all communist states. During the Chirino song, a young woman dressed in the typical nineteenth-century

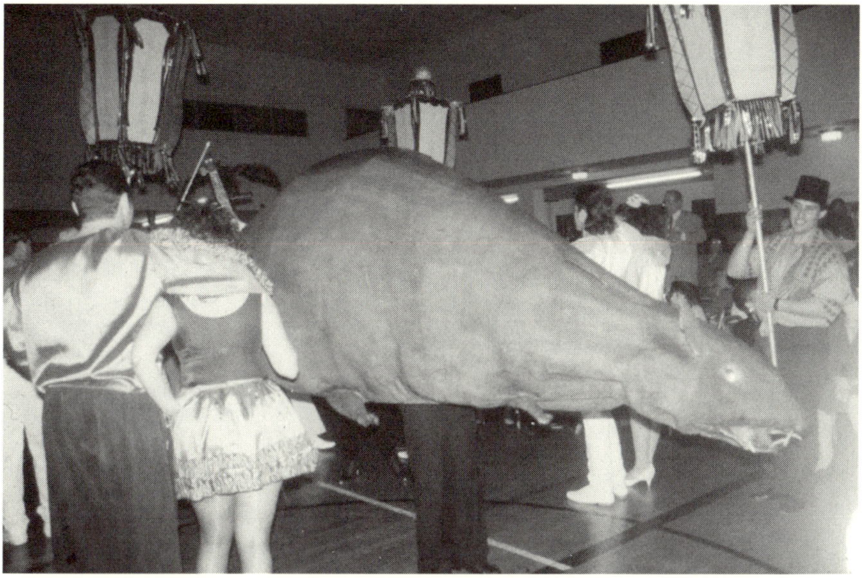

Vuelteños in hutio group parade with hutia at San Antonio de las Vueltas patronal festival. Photo by Tina Bucuvalas.

Cuban salon costume appeared with chains around her wrists. As Chirino shouted, "Cuba—Libre!!" the woman lifted her arms, broke the chains, and the crowd went wild.

Afterward, hutios in the audience joined with the comparsa group to dance joyously around the hall in the changüí. The song to which they danced was a remake of Los Matamoros 1930s' hit about going to a festival. The new version by Ricardo Montanel alludes to Miami's enormous Cuban-based Calle Ocho festival.

Immediately following the hutios, the ñañacos presented their comparsa routines, farolas, the rooster and flag insignias, as well as Isaac Dueñas's giant muñecon. Their primary routine revolved around a Brazilian theme, with the comparsa group dressed in Brazilian carnival garb and dancing to the song "Brazil." The finale consisted of the Chirino song, the release of hundreds of balloons, and then a changüí.

About half an hour after the formal presentations, a procession of hutios danced into the hall for the entierro. It was preceded by a man dressed as a priest, and the many mourners covered their faces with black veils or handkerchiefs as they danced around the hall. They carried a small coffin containing a farola they had stolen from the ñañacos. Although the ñañacos also had made a coffin, it broke before their planned entierro.

Comparsa of *ñañaco* group with *muñecon* and *farolas* San Antonio de Vueltas patronal festival. Photo by Tina Bucuvalas.

Finally, the Vuelteños settled down to an evening of dining, drinking, and dancing to a local salsa *orquesta* that played a variety of Cuban contemporary songs and old favorites. Despite the teasing and the joking confrontations of the day, they put all hostilities aside as they reveled late into the night.

CONCLUSION

Due to the grand scale of the Diaspora precipitated by the Cuban Revolution—with about one million or one-tenth of the population eventually leaving the island and a vast majority of that group finally settling in south Florida—Cuba is an entity that must be studied in at least two locations. In Miami's Little Havana and other Cuban residential areas, Cuban exiles have created what Benedict Anderson has termed an "imagined community"; that is, a community named for and/or in some ways parallel and comparable to the original home of the residents.[3] Yet this offspring of the original proceeds on a somewhat different trajectory.

The municipios represent perhaps the most overt and extensive form of social organization within the formal sphere that has been reestablished by Cubans in Miami. However, in Miami the content of their activities has ceased to be primarily political (the realm of political activity now being adapted to American political forms—albeit at times unsuccessfully) and has become increasingly oriented toward maintaining social ties. This is certainly the case with the municipio and the patronal festival of Vueltas.

In Miami, Vueltas's patronal festival has acquired a level of momentum that portends a long future. One reason for its success is that it fulfills a variety of important functions for Vuelteños. For those born in Cuba, it serves as a reunion with former neighbors, a way to maintain the old social order, a source of entertainment, and a vehicle for preserving traditional arts. Moreover, since the event features terrific music, dancing, and fantastic costumes, it provides an enjoyable and effective medium through which Cuban American youth learn more about their traditional culture.

It is apparent that the patronal festival itself has undergone a number of transformations in Miami. There has been some simplification or streamlining of the festival—part of which is directly related to the reduced number of Vuelteños available to work on the festival. One example of this is the blending of the dance with other events since all must now be held indoors on a single night. Another example is the creation of one rather than two muñecones.

Some changes, such as shifting the festival to Saturday, seem to be a consequence of the gradual Americanization of the Cuban population during the last three decades. Yet other changes may be a result of Americanization combined with additional factors. For example, whites and blacks now attend the same dance and the whole issue of racially separate formal societies has been dropped. This is probably attributable to several forces: American emphasis on at least token integration, a united Cuban approach to maintaining the tradition within the unfamiliar realm of American culture, the small percentage of Cuban blacks who emigrated, and the practical effect of blending the dance and parranda.

Other changes in the festival are more substantial—pushing it farther along a different trajectory than its Cuban parent. One such change is that the festival has become almost entirely secular. Although this trend was already evident in Cuba, in Miami it has escalated to the extent that religious elements have all but disappeared. In fact, when I questioned several Vuelteños as to the significance of la Candelaria, no one knew. In this instance, not only is secularization consistent with American tendencies, but the need to maintain regional unity and identity supersedes the need for religious observance. Another important change, the replacement of the floats by the comparsa tradition known from neighboring communities, reflects a practical move to recreate an aesthetic and social totality for the event by activating a passively held tradition.

Despite many changes, some things remain constant. Cuba has a long history of emigration and immigration, of ties with north and south. In Miami, Cubans are merely continuing to create and recreate Cuba outside the geographical boundaries of the island. And Vueltas, like other reestablished municipios, continues to hold its festival—each year adding more traditional arts from the Cuba Vuelteños remember and adapting other forms to reflect the Cuba they have reinvented.

Notes

Néstor Díaz de Villegas, "Un portal fuera del tiempo," *El Nuevo Herald*, June 4, 1993, 23D.

1. Esther Torres, interview with Tina Bucuvalas, Miami, January 29, 1992.
2. Evita, interview with Tina Bucuvalas, Miami, February 1, 1992.
3. Benedict Anderson, *Imagined Communities: Reflections on the Origins and Spread of Nationalism*, rev. ed. (1983; rpt. London and New York: Verso, 1991), 192.

Michael Kernahan

A Life in Pan

STEPHEN STUEMPFLE

IN A FIELD OF SAWGRASS BEHIND A WAREHOUSE COMPLEX ON THE EDGE of Miami's suburban Tamiami Airport, Michael Kernahan creates high-precision musical instruments, known as *pans*, from discarded oil and chemical barrels. He works in a small clearing under a tree that provides some limited shade. Assorted barrels are stacked around the space; some are full size, while others have been cut. A briefcase filled with metalworking tools rests on one barrel. From the edge of the clearing, a narrow path extends to another space, where pans are heated over a wood fire. In the distance is a third clearing, in which Kernahan's apprentice, Michael Phillip, sometimes works. This outdoor workshop is a peaceful place. Breezes blow across the acres of sawgrass, while occasional helicopters and small planes take off from the airport. The surrounding neighborhood consists of import/export, aviation, and other businesses. It is a good location for metal artisans. No one complains about the constant banging of hammers against metal barrels. Moreover, discarded barrels can sometimes be found at shops in the district.

One of the warehouse units next to the field where Kernahan works is the *panyard* or headquarters of the 21st Century Steel Orchestra. In addition to *tuning* (fabricating) pans, Kernahan serves as the leader and musical arranger for this band. He also plays an instrument known as the *double second* pan. While most individuals associated with the pan world today specialize in tuning, arranging, playing, or administration, Kernahan follows in the tradition of the old-time pan leaders of Trinidad who combined all of these activities. His versatility and accomplishments have earned him great respect from other pan musicians. At a recent party in 21st Century's panyard,

Michael Kernahan with tenor pan. Photo by George Chillag. Courtesy of Historical Museum of Southern Florida.

numerous members and supporters of the band took turns testifying about the multifaceted impact that Kernahan has had on the pan world. "We all can consider it a real privilege to have known him," suggested one panman. Indeed, Kernahan has inspired audiences throughout North America with his music, has taught countless students to play pans, has tuned instruments for numerous steelbands in Florida and other states, and is now patiently passing on his vast knowledge of tuning to his apprentice. In short, he has been one of the guiding forces in Miami's still-emerging pan scene.[1]

Steelbands, a creation of the twin-island nation of Trinidad and Tobago, are a relatively recent phenomenon in south Florida. Though a few *pannists*, such as the internationally known jazz virtuoso Othello Molineaux, were active in Miami by the early 1970s, most have arrived since the 1980s, as part of a growing migration of Trinidadians and other Anglophone Caribbean peoples to the region. Pannists have performed as part of small ensembles in the tourist industry and private party market, as well as playing with steelbands for the local Caribbean Carnival and other community events. Among the steelbands in Miami at present are 21st Century, Miami Pan Symphony, and Rising Star. There are also some school bands, most notably an ensemble at Florida Memorial College under the direction of Dawn Batson, a pan educator and arranger with many accomplishments in both Trinidad and the United States. Along with these bands, there are a number of individual pannists who play in restaurants, on cruise ships, and at other venues.

The characteristics of the Miami pan scene and of Michael Kernahan's remarkable career are best understood in the context of the development of pan music in Trinidad. What was once a disreputable type of street music eventually became a cherished national art and a new form of musical expression for the world.

THE HISTORICAL DEVELOPMENT OF PAN

The musical form that is now known as "pan" emerged during the late 1930s in Trinidad. Its immediate precursor was African-Trinidadian *tamboo bamboo* music, which was played by striking different sized pieces of bamboo together or stamping them on the ground during pre-Lenten Carnival street processions. During the 1930s tamboo bamboo men began beating on metal containers (such as paint and trash cans), automobile parts, and other metal objects. This metallic percussion proved to be louder and more durable than bamboo; around 1940 Carnival bands began to discard their bamboo altogether. During this period it was discovered that the bottoms of metal containers could be pounded into various shapes to produce musical tones when struck with sticks. Performance on different types of early pans was modeled on the roles of the diverse instruments of the tamboo bamboo band, though there was also influence from military marching bands, African-derived skin drums and, perhaps, East Indian-derived *tassa* drum ensembles. The earliest steelbands essentially provided a polyrhythmic background for the singing of Carnival revelers.

The creators of pan were primarily young and from the "grass-roots" (low-income) sector of the society. Steelbands were based in various urban neighborhoods and villages, and intense rivalries ensued as panmen developed their new instruments. Following World War II, panmen often named their bands after movies, such as *Casablanca, Destination Tokyo, Cross of Lorraine*, and *Desperadoes*. During Carnival the bands paraded the streets, often masquerading as sailors, and sometimes engaged in violent clashes. Panmen and their music were widely condemned by the middle and upper classes and even by many members of the working class. By the late 1940s, however, there were some prominent civic leaders, artists, and politicians who began promoting the steelband as an indigenous art form and arranged for bands to play in concert settings. Meanwhile, a steelband association was organized and middle-class youths began forming bands of their own.

By the 1950s steelbands had become an integral part of the cultural life of the colony and were performing in a wide range of settings, such as elite social clubs, nightclubs for sailors and tourists, and weddings and christenings in grass-roots communities. When Trinidad and Tobago achieved its independence from Britain in 1962, the steelband was already an important national symbol. During the 1960s businesses began to sponsor steelbands and state support for the movement grew. By the 1970s pan instruction was being offered in a number of schools, a development that encouraged women to join bands.

The institutionalization of the steelband movement was paralleled by a transformation of the music. In the course of the 1940s more notes were added to pans by grooving additional sections on the bottoms of containers and, by the end of the decade, the full-size oil barrel had become the most popular source of instruments. Meanwhile, the tonal quality of pans improved and the wrapping of the ends of playing sticks with strips of rubber helped to create a mellower sound. By the early 1950s the different types of pans (each with its own register) contained sufficient notes to make conventional Western harmony possible. While steelbands played only simple melodies during the World War II period, by the early 1950s they were performing a variety of local calypsos, Latin American musical genres (such as mambos, boleros, and sambas), North American popular songs, and European classical selections. Steelbands have continued to maintain eclectic repertoires up to the present.

In Trinidad today there are more than one hundred steelbands, ranging from massive orchestras with over one hundred members to small ensembles. The premier performance occasion for bands is the multi-round Panorama competition that is held during the Carnival season. Bands also perform in street processions during the Carnival, at other competitions, and in a variety of community events.

Though the steelband movement has its most vibrant manifestation in Trinidad, pans are also played in many other countries. The use of pans first spread to other parts of the Anglophone Caribbean during the 1940s, through migration to and from Trinidad. By the 1950s there were steelbands in immigrant communities in New York and London. Gradually, steelbands were established in other cities of the Caribbean diaspora. Meanwhile, the presence of many Caribbean pannists abroad and the distribution of steelband recordings inspired people from other backgrounds to form steelbands. In the United States, for example, there are numerous bands associated with colleges, high schools, and elementary schools. Steelbands can also be found in such countries as Venezuela, Switzerland, Nigeria, and Japan.

A CAREER IN PAN

Michael Kernahan is one of the many pannists who have left Trinidad in search of musical opportunities, adventure and, ideally, some income. At first he toured North America with a steelband; later he settled in the United States on a permanent basis. However, he continues to maintain close ties with Trinidad and returns for visits on a regular basis. His many contributions to pan in the United States are based on his firm foundation and extensive education in the Trinidadian pan tradition.

Kernahan was born in 1947 in Palo Seco, a small village in southern Trinidad. While a child, he moved to Manzanilla on the island's eastern coast and, around 1960, ended up in the St. James neighborhood of Port of Spain (the capital of Trinidad and Tobago). Though he missed country life, his encounters with pan kept him tied to the city. During this period St. James was the home of many fine steelbands, including the famous Tripoli Steel Orchestra. Kernahan was fortunate to have cousins who were members of Tripoli, and he soon started playing with the band, in spite of his parents' opposition. Even though pan was a widely appreciated form of music by this time, many Trinidadians still viewed panmen as disreputable and prone to violence and crime. Kernahan recalls:

> I started to play in Tripoli in 1964. My parents didn't know anything about that. I remember it was Carnival 1964. We were coming up the Tragarete Road, right by the Lapyrouse Cemetery [in the Woodbrook neighborhood of Port of Spain]. My mother was on the sidewalk. She saw me playing and she started to cry. She came in the band. Well, I had a cousin, he was an older guy. Luckily, my mother always believed in him. So he told her: "Well look, now, it's all right. I'm going to take care of him." Because she started crying and saying: "Oh lord, my son is a vagabond. You know, just now you start to walk with knife in your pocket." And she was really crying. I felt bad. But, when he talked to her and kind of calmed her down a little, it was all right. I continued playing until now. I never got in no trouble, and I never walked with a knife.

During the mid-1960s Tripoli was in its heyday: it played on the streets for Carnival with legions of followers and at so many Carnival *fetes* (parties) that it often had to split into more than one section in order to fulfill all of its engagements. The band was also a regular competitor at the steelband festival that was held in the elite Queen's Hall at the time. Through their sponsor, the Esso oil company, over twenty members of the band, including Kernahan, were able to participate in an overseas tour and play at Expo '67. Before arriving in Montreal, they played in several Caribbean locales and in New York, with appearances in Lincoln Center and on the *Ed Sullivan Show.* Throughout the summer they performed at Expo '67's Trinidad and Tobago pavilion and were a phenomenal success. During this engagement they also recorded an album—*The Esso Trinidad Steelband On Tour*—which included such tunes as "The Blue Danube," "Eine Kleine Nachtmusik," "Michelle," and "No Money, No Love," a calypso by the Mighty Sparrow.

Sales for this album were so strong that the following summer Tripoli was able to leave Trinidad on another tour, following the same path as before. This time the members appeared in the Expo '67 reprise, called "Man and His World." While performing they were visited by a fan from the previous year: Liberace. This encounter led to one of the more unusual chapters in steelband history. Liberace was so captivated with the pan sound that he contracted Tripoli to accompany him on tour. The band became a regular feature in his extravagant shows in top concert halls from Los Angeles to New York. Kernahan recollects:

> We came out at a certain point in the show. He would introduce the band. We did two songs by ourselves and then we did [two] with him: "Alley Cat" and "Twelfth Street Rag." It was a great thing. Every night it was something else: we got a standing ovation. We did songs like "Poet and Peasant Overture," "Die Fledermaus." Now and then we'd do the "Hallelujah Chorus." . . .
>
> That went on for two years [until 1970]. And luckily, again, we were the only act that he kept for that long. He had people like Barbra Streisand—he'd put them out in just like one year. But he kept us. It was a really good thing that was going. . . . He had always had something strange on his show. Something different. He liked the pan, but his manager didn't want it at all. And he [Liberace] said: "No, this is what I want."

When the engagement with Liberace ended, Tripoli continued to tour the country on their own. In 1971 they recorded an album for Warner Brothers, *The Esso Trinidad Steel Band,* which was nominated for a Grammy Award in 1972. That same year the band returned to Trinidad.

Back home Tripoli was able to further capitalize on its reputation by obtaining a gig as the resident band at Port of Spain's Holiday Inn and by playing on the docks for visiting cruise ships. The members were actually able to make a living from playing pan, which was fairly unusual in Trinidad, even during this period when steelbands were regularly hired for fetes and other functions.

Meanwhile, Kernahan found himself with some spare time and decided to experiment with tuning pans:

> There was no water coming up the hill [where his father lived]. Bob [Thomas], a tuner in town—he gave me six [oil] drums to take to my father, so you could put water in. But my father only ended up getting one. He gave me the six drums, and I went out and buy a hammer, a sledge. I going to try my hand at doing something. Well, I burst about four of them. I didn't know what I was doing. One came out—to me it was looking all right. But I tried to tune it, and it didn't come out right.
>
> So what I did, I decided I would bring it in town. When Alan [Gervais, Tripoli's expert tuner] comes, I'm going to show it to him. I took it to town and he came. I tell him I was trying to make a pan. He said: "Well, let me see what you did." I showed him it, and he started to laugh. He said: "All right, I'm going to show you." He started teaching me. Before long, I started doing like cello and guitar pans [types of pans]. I didn't take long because I think he was a good teacher. Because he always said: "I'll make you a tuner real fast." He always said that. Maybe because I did [automobile] body work, I already knew how to really hammer. So it didn't take me long to catch up.

Though he was progressing quickly, Kernahan felt that he was still not ready to provide any steelbands with pans. But in 1975 he had the responsibilities of pan tuning and "blending" (re- tuning) thrust upon him and, at the same time, had an inauspicious introduction to Miami:

> This guy approached us to come to Miami for ten days. Alan [Gervais] was supposed to come out as the tuner, but he was already committed to go to Switzerland with Solo Harmonites [another top steelband]. That's when he said: "Well, you'll have to take charge as a tuner." So we left Trinidad. We packed up all the pans and got here. I was the tuner. There were ten of us [all Tripoli members]. I'll tell you something: that was one of the strangest experiences we ever had. This guy brought us to Miami. We got to Miami. We were put up in a hotel on the beach. And we never saw the guy again. We were just here in Miami doing nothing. We were here for two weeks doing nothing. We tried to get in touch with people and we organized a few little places to play.

Fortunately, the brother of one of the band members called from Michigan and said that they could obtain work up there. As a result of this call, Kernahan and several members of Tripoli ended up settling in Michigan, where they re-grouped as the "21st Century Steel Band." This ensemble obtained steady work into the 1980s, playing at colleges, fairs, and other venues throughout the country. But Michigan's harsh winters were increasingly a burden and it was difficult to find work during that time of the year. By the mid-1980s they decided to give south Florida a second chance and started visiting every year. Among their gigs was one at the Miami–Dade County Youth Fair, booked by an agent in Michigan. Eventually, Kernahan, his wife, and four members of the band settled permanently in Miami.

Over the years Kernahan has devoted more and more time to tuning. In addition to making pans for bands and individuals in Florida, he has tuned for school bands in Michigan, Illinois, Mississippi, and South Dakota. The phone is always ringing in the Kernahan residence, with inquiries from as far away as Belize and Guyana. He even found himself tuning pans on a recent "vacation" back to Trinidad for Carnival.

THE TUNING OF PANS

Tuning a pan or set of pans is a complex process that takes many hours of work, generally spread over a period of at least two days. The first step is to obtain 55-gallon barrels. Pan instruments vary in terms of the number of barrels required, the number of notes on the playing surface, the depth of this surface when hammered into a concave shape, and the length of the "skirt" (the sides of the pan). The pans that Kernahan generally tunes include tenors, double seconds, double guitars, triple guitars, tenor basses, and six basses.

Though each pan instrument has its unique features, the basic tuning principles are the same. The procedures that Kernahan uses for tuning a tenor pan provide an illustration. This instrument requires a barrel with 18-gauge metal on the top and bottom and thinner 20-gauge metal on the sides. Once obtained, the barrel is turned upside down, with the top resting on the ground. (Since the barrel's top has a bunghole for removing its contents, the bottom is used for pan tuning.) The bottom of the pan is sunk inward, using both a bowling ball and a sawed-off twelve-pound sledgehammer. Once the surface has begun to assume a concave shape, a pencil and ruler are used to make some preliminary markings of individual sections, each of which will become a note. Sinking then continues with a forty-ounce hammer (with a shortened handle). Eventually, the surface of the pan is cleaned and the section markings redrawn to form three concentric circles of notes, totaling thirty. The sinking process concludes when the pan has reached a depth of 7.25 inches and the metal is "tight."

The next step of the tuning process is to "groove" the individual note sections with a twenty-four-ounce hammer and a nail punch with a blunted point. By carefully hammering the punch, a shallow indentation is made around the perimeter of each section. After finishing the inner sections, the surface is again hammered to remove any looseness from the metal and to pull it back toward the sides of the barrel. Without this additional hammering, one might puncture the metal when grooving the outer sections.

When all of the sections have been grooved, the pan is ready to be cut. This can be done either with an electric jigsaw or a hammer and chisel. A cleaner cut is then made with a pair of scissors until the skirt of the pan is 5.5 inches long. Next the pan is heated in a wood fire to release stress in the metal. One half of a discarded barrel serves as a furnace. Once the fire is blazing, the pan is rested in the flames. In the course of the usual three to seven minutes of heating, the pan is shifted from time to time to ensure that all parts of the surface are affected.

After the pan has cooled, the actual tuning of notes can begin. Like most tuners, Kernahan uses an electronic tuning device: a Korg Chromatic Tuner with a range of three octaves. Before tuning the notes, however, the individual sections have to be "ponged up" from underneath the pan. First, the sections on the outside perimeter of the pan are prized up with a 2 x 4 piece of wood, wedged against the pan skirt. This process helps to separate the note sections from the rest of the pan's surface, thus allowing them to vibrate and sound. When the outside sections have been ponged up, the pan is rested on an automobile tire, with the playing surface facing up. The notes are then tuned with a twenty-four-ounce hammer and a pan playing stick, which, in the case of a tenor pan, is approximately seven inches in length and has a tip wrapped with a piece of rubber. As Kernahan strikes an individual section, one can hear the note moving up and down in pitch. Strikes to the center of the section lower the note, while those to the edge have the opposite effect. At times, the pan is turned upside down and hammered from below or even ponged up again. Kernahan periodically compares the pitch from each pan section with the corresponding pitch selected on the electronic tuner. At this point, he simply tries to place all of the outside notes at their approximate pitches.

An even more complicated part of the tuning process involves amplifying the harmonics or overtones of each note. Over the years tuners have perfected techniques of hammering certain parts of a note section to bring out fifths and octaves above the fundamental. This must be done uniformly for all notes, if the pan is to have a consistent tonal quality.

After working on the outside notes, Kernahan pongs up the inner sections with a hammer and proceeds to tune them. This invariably affects the outside notes. Thus, he must keep working with the inside and outside notes until all of them correspond to the required pitches and have consistent harmonics. When the pan is fully tuned, it is cleaned with acid and taken to a metal shop where it is chromed. Chroming hardens the metal and helps the pan to retain its tones. While tenors and double seconds are routinely chromed, other pan instruments are usually painted, due to the expense of chroming large amounts of metal.

In addition to tuning the variety of pans used by a steelband, Kernahan also builds metal stands for suspending all of the instruments except the basses. Basses are rested on wooden blocks when played. It is also necessary to make playing sticks, which vary in length, diameter, and the amount of rubber on their ends. For example, portions of rubber balls are generally attached to bass sticks. If pans are kept indoors and periodically cleaned, they will last many years. But, with regular use, their notes eventually fall out of tune. Thus, from time to time, one must re-tune all of the notes on all of the pans in a steelband.

For Kernahan there is always more work to be done. When not tuning pans for 21st Century, he is busy tuning for other bands and pannists throughout south Florida and beyond. His tuning is an almost meditative process. While working he is highly focused, carefully engaging the metal with his tools and listening to nuances of sound. This deep feeling and appreciation for metal connects him to the long tradition of great tuners from Trinidad. From time to time, he puts down his hammer and talks about these masters—their many discoveries over the years and their ceaseless efforts to perfect their instruments. Pan tuning is something very tricky, he concludes, and something that one must keep doing all the time. With each pan, one learns something new.

THE 21ST CENTURY STEEL ORCHESTRA

Since relocating to south Florida, Kernahan's 21st Century Steel Orchestra has grown in size. During the 1990s, a number of local pannists joined the band, several of whom had previous experience with pan in Trinidad. The 21st Century has its largest contingent of performers during the Miami

Carnival, which is held on Columbus Day weekend. During the 1998 Carnival, for example, the band included thirty-five players: six tenors, six double seconds, one quadraphonic (an instrument consisting of four pans), five double guitars, three triple guitars, four 6-basses, and an "engine room" section of drum set, congas, bongos, cowbell, and six "irons" (automobile brake drums). For other engagements, far fewer players are used. The band's 1996 Christmas concert at the Joseph Caleb Auditorium in Miami, for example, featured fourteen musicians. Between five and ten players are used for most events, such as civic festivals, museum concerts, private parties, and the Trinidad and Tobago Independence Day Mass at Miami's Trinity Episcopal Cathedral.

Like steelbands in Trinidad, 21st Century has a diverse repertoire of music. Among their many tunes are calypsos, such as Sparrow's "Birthday Party," Kitchener's "Iron Man," and Robert Greenidge's "Fire Coming Down." American popular tunes include such selections as "Moonlight in Vermont," "You Go To My Head," and "Have Yourself a Merry Little Christmas." European classical pieces that they frequently play are Handel's "Hallelujah Chorus," Strauss's "Voices of Spring," and von Suppé's "Poet and Peasant Overture." Original compositions include Kernahan's funk-influenced "Mess Around" and a calypso titled "What Is a Pan?" Given this range of musical selections, the band is able to perform for a variety of occasions and audiences.

In addition to playing double seconds in 21st Century, Kernahan arranges all of the band's music. He started to perfect his arranging skills during the 1970s and notes that he has been influenced by four of the finest arrangers in Trinidadian pan history: Junior Pouchet, Beverly Griffith, Ray Holman, and Earl Rodney. Pouchet led and arranged for Silver Stars in Trinidad during the 1950s and 1960s and also arranged for Tripoli for a brief period. From the 1970s to the 1990s, he led a small pan ensemble at Disney World in Orlando. Since the 1960s Griffith has periodically served as an arranger for Desperadoes, one of Trinidad's premier steelbands. He currently resides in south Florida, where he plays in small combos. Holman lives in Trinidad and has arranged for numerous top steelbands, such as Starlift, Invaders, and Tokyo. Rodney also lives in Trinidad and is renowned for his arrangements for Harmonites and for the Mighty Sparrow, the calypsonian. For his own arrangements, Kernahan draws on the smooth, lyrical styles of all four of these masters. He also continues to play some old Tripoli arrangements, such as Pouchet's interpretation of Gershwin's "The Man I Love."

Though 21st Century performs around the year, the Miami Carnival season is the period during which the band is most active. Miami's Carnival draws tens of thousands of participants from Florida, northern cities, and

21st Century Steel Orchestra in concert at the University of Miami. 1995. Photo by Stephen Stuempfle. Courtesy of Historical Museum of Southern Florida.

the Caribbean. It is, in fact, the grand finale of an annual cycle of Carnivals that are held throughout the Caribbean diaspora, all of which are modeled on the pre-Lenten Carnival in Trinidad. The climax of the Miami festival is the street parade on the Sunday before Columbus Day. During the weeks leading up to this event, there is much activity in south Florida's Anglophone Caribbean community: *mas* (masquerade) bands prepare their costumes in their *camps*, calypsonians and "brass bands" perform at fetes, and steelbands rehearse the calypsos that they will perform in the local Panorama competition (often held on the Saturday night before the parade). Steelbands also play in the parade itself, though the music for most of the mas bands is provided by deejays or brass bands, ensembles that include guitars, keyboards, and percussion, as well as horns.

Like other steelbands, 21st Century spends several weeks preparing for the Panorama and Carnival parade. In addition to cleaning and painting pans, it is sometimes necessary to build new mobile "racks" for moving the pans onto the Panorama stage and through the streets. Racks are made by welding pieces of metallic electrical tubing together to form a frame for suspending the pans, covering this structure with a sheet metal canopy and attaching wheels. Friends of the band often drop by to assist with the preparations and to listen to the late-night rehearsals.

Kernahan follows traditional practices in developing a Panorama musical arrangement. After selecting a calypso that was sung in the most recent Trinidad Carnival, he works out musical parts for each section of pans. These parts are taught by ear to the section members phrase by phrase. Typically, the tenors play the melody, the double seconds play a harmonization of the melody or "strum" chords, the guitars strum chords and play short runs, and the basses provide the bass line. The other percussion instruments in the band maintain a basic beat and generate dense polyrhythms. Musical phrases are drilled by the individual sections of pans and then by the whole band for hours until they are committed to memory. Over the course of a few weeks, new material is gradually added. The finished arrangement is usually ten minutes long and comprises an introduction, the calypso verse and chorus, variations on the verse and chorus, and an ending. Often the arrangement includes counterpoint (the interweaving of different melodic lines), the shifting of the primary melody to different sections of pans, and key modulations.

The Panorama and Carnival have been held in different locations around Miami, such as Bicentennial Park, the Hialeah Racetrack, and the Opa-locka Airport. For the Panorama, 21st Century and the other competing bands perform on a stage in front of a panel of judges and an audience of steelband enthusiasts and general revelers. Often, the evening's entertainment also includes a competition for the finely crafted costumes of the "Kings," "Queens," and "Individuals" from the various mas bands. The following day the steelbands join the mas bands for hours of festivity on the surrounding streets. Steelband supporters help push the racks of pans through the streets and dance to the invigorating rhythms of the calypsos. Some join the bands by beating rhythms on pieces of metal. The Miami Carnival, like all Trinidadian-style Carnivals, represents a dazzling blend of tradition and innovation in masquerade and music. Each year creativity and revelry are pushed to the limits as people celebrate the human capacity for expression and communion. After the sun sets, the participants' energy begins to subside and they eventually wander home. The 21st Century loads its pans and racks into a semitruck and heads back to its panyard. Though the Miami Carnival is over, there are other engagements to play and the Carnival season in Trinidad is only a few months away.

On most days Michael Kernahan can be found at 21st Century's panyard. Usually he carries out the fine tuning of new pans in the warehouse, surrounded by the band's pans, racks, and equipment. In a loft above the rehearsal space is his office. On a desk is the paperwork generated by a career of making pans and managing a band. An answering machine records messages for a phone that rarely can be heard above the sounds of rehearsals and pan tuning. In one corner of the room is a stack of vintage calypso and steelband albums, including some of Tripoli's masterpieces. Though always overburdened with work, Kernahan is never too busy to welcome a visitor and to reminisce about some of the adventures of his life in pan. He looks over a few old Tripoli photographs and recalls the many personalities he has met through the years. Across from his desk are a tenor pan and a pair of double seconds, tuned by his deceased mentor, the great Alan Gervais. He walks over and plays a few runs; though the pans are over twenty years old, their tone is as rich and pure as ever. Kernahan says that he loves these pans and that he continued to use them at gigs until a few years ago. Now they serve both as a model and inspiration for his own work as a tuner:

> I try to stick with it [the Gervais method]. Why I could relate close to it is because I still have some of his instruments. So I could go back and try to keep it like that. . . . I've met people, Trinidadians, they come around and say: "Boy, Alan really taught you." It looks like his work.

Though Kernahan perpetuates his mentor's techniques, he has also developed his own style. He ceaselessly explores ways of improving the sounds of pans so that they will continue to captivate audiences in south Florida and around the world. For him, each pan, like each musical arrangement, is a new experiment.

Note

1. This article is based on field research carried out during 1996–1998 and describes Miami's steelband scene at that time. Funding for the research was provided in part by a grant from the National Endowment for the Arts to the Historical Museum of Southern Florida. Many thanks to Michael Kernahan for his participation in this and other museum projects.

Suggested Reading

Allen, Ray, and Les Slater. "Steel Pan Grows in Brooklyn: Trinidadian Music and Cultural Identity." In *Island Sounds in the Global City: Caribbean Popular Music and Identity in New York*, ed. Ray Allen and Lois Wilcken, 114–37. New York: New York Folklore Society and Institute for Studies in American Music, Brooklyn College, 1998.

App, Lawrence J. "The Professionalization and Commodification of Steel Drum Music in Florida: Musical Continuity and Change in the Caribbean Diaspora." M.A. thesis, Florida State University, 1997.

Averill, Gage. "'Pan Is We Ting': West Indian Steelbands in Brooklyn." In *Musics of Multicultural America: A Study of Twelve Musical Communities*, ed. Kip Lornell and Anne K. Rasmussen, 101–29. New York: Schirmer Books, 1997.

Dudley, Shannon. *Carnival Music in Trinidad: Experiencing Music, Expressing Culture.* New York: Oxford University Press, 2004.
Goddard, George "Sonny." *Forty Years in the Steelbands: 1939–1979*, ed. Roy D. Thomas. London: Karia Press, 1991.
Hill, Errol. *The Trinidad Carnival: Mandate for a National Theatre.* London: New Beacon Books, 1997 [1972].
Johnson, Kim. *If Yuh Iron Good You Is King: Pan Pioneers of Trinidad and Tobago.* Port of Spain, Trinidad: Pan Trinbago, 2006.
Stuempfle, Stephen. *The Steelband Movement: The Forging of a National Art in Trinidad and Tobago.* Philadelphia: University of Pennsylvania Press, 1995.

Folklife of Miami's Nicaraguan Communities

KATHERINE BORLAND

THE NICARAGUAN COMMUNITY IN MIAMI IS COMPRISED OF THREE distinct culture groups: the Creole peoples of the southern Atlantic coast, the Miskito population of the Rio Coco and Puerto Cabezas area, and the Mestizos of the Pacific coast. These communities do not have much contact across cultural lines. No overall Nicaraguan cultural organization unites them, and, though they share some foodways, their cultural heritages are quite distinct.

The Creole population is perhaps the oldest Nicaraguan population in Miami. Most are professionals—nurses, teachers, accountants—and many came to study in the United States as early as the 1950s. Others have worked on ships that have taken them around the world. Like other Caribbean rim populations, they are a mixed-race people. Their sense of independence and separateness from the Pacific coast Nicaraguans is well described in A. Sambola (1984).

English-speaking Creoles find it relatively easy to adjust to North American culture, as historically, American influence through trade and missionary work has been long standing. Institutions like baseball, Boy Scouts, and Girl Guides[1] constituted an established part of Atlantic coast town life by the 1930s.

In Miami, the population is concentrated around the Moravian Prince of Peace Church in Carol City, and scattered through the Jamaican and Spanish Nicaraguan neighborhoods of the west and southwest. For churchgoers, the Moravian church provides a strong unifying influence. Non-churchgoers gather to drink and socialize at the ball fields around the Carol City neighborhood on Sundays. Yet, Bluefieldians, regardless of their religion, know one another and keep in touch in Miami.

The Miskito population is estimated to be from 3,000 to 5,000. Some are professionals, but most have found work as janitors, cleaning women, and guards in Miami hotels. Miskito families are concentrated in particular apartment complexes throughout Miami Beach and Miami Shores. Although an indigenous people of Nicaragua, they are typically of mixed blood and quite westernized in their living habits. Many of their traditional cultural practices were supplanted decades ago by Moravian and other missionary church traditions. As Mary Helms points out (1971), ever since their first contact with Europeans, Miskitos have engaged with cultural outsiders, trading their labor for foreign goods or wages in a variety of commercial ventures. Their most binding cultural traits are a common language and the Moravian religion.

While Miskito people expressed no strong political views, they are generally bitter about the Sandinista and Somoza "Spanish" exploitation and destruction of their Atlantic coast communities. The Contra War severely affected the Miskito community and forms an important reference for many of the young men who fought in it. Jorge Jenkins Molieri (1986) gives an excellent history from the Sandinista point of view of the "Spanish" and other foreign incursions in the life of Miskito communities.

Enerio Danny tells an unfortunately typical story. In the late 1970s he worked with the Sandinista indigenous movement, Misurasata, and served in the Literacy Crusade in Miskito. Increasingly suspicious of Sandinista policies, he eventually joined a Contra military band. He now expresses disillusionment with the Miskito leaders, who drew a peace-loving people into armed conflict but subsequently failed to honor promises to promote community improvements.

The Pacific coast population, the largest in Miami, has been reported as high as 400,000 (*Estrella de Nicaragua*, November 30, 1991). It is concentrated in the middle- and upper-class neighborhood of Sweetwater and in the more working-class areas of Little Havana and Hialeah. Most cultural organizations are run by professionals and business owners, as working-class people generally complain that the demanding American work schedule prevents them from participating in cultural activities. Married women voice particular frustration at being isolated in their homes by husbands who resist their attempts to establish new contacts or join outside activities. Most Pacific coast Nicaraguans arrived in the years after the revolution of 1979. Nevertheless, they have already made a definite mark on the city.

Primary genres of Nicaraguan folklife in Miami include music, patronal festivals, Moravian church celebrations, and foodways. Material culture traditions outside the festival context have generally become latent as craftspeople enter new lines of work.

PATRONAL FESTIVALS

Nicaragua is a predominantly Catholic country. Patronal festivals for each town constitute the major folk expression of this religiousness and provide a context for artistic practices of all kinds, as well as for the expression of local identity. In Nicaragua, these festivals are organized by traditional *mayordomías* and *cofradías,* which are charged with shouldering the expense of festival celebrations. Members have usually made a promise to the saint to join a mayordomía after having been granted a favor (a family member's or farm animal's miraculous recovery from a serious illness, for instance).

Patronal festivals are processional in nature. After a mass, the saint is paraded through the streets of his town accompanied by brass bands called *chicheros,* dancers, fireworks, and devoted followers. After the processions *mayordomos* host public feasts or give away food and drink to festival participants. Individual families who own their own image of the saint may host a private procession and feast as well. Often the festivities will include carnivals, big social dances, crafts fairs, and traditional games such as a *corrido de toros* or the *palo lucio.* Moreover, in recent years, elite groups have introduced horse shows at these festivals. Thus, the patronal festival involves a series of activities that span from eight days to, in the case of Masaya's San Jerónimo, over three months. (For more information see Enrique Pérez Estrada, 1986.)

Although the *baile de la marimba* has become the national folk dance and is performed at most patrons' festivals throughout Nicaragua, each town typically has its own set of traditional festival dances as well. Dancing is an important expressive form for Nicaraguans, as dancing for a saint is a primary form of devotion. The original significance of costume, dramatic miming, and dance step, however, has been lost over time.

The degree to which dancers are organized into formal groups varies in the different towns. Normally, though, a patron will organize the dance and sponsor a series of rehearsals in order to prepare for a street performance. Traditional festival dance groups should not be confused, however, with the more recent folk ballet groups that arose in the 1950s. These folk ballets combine traditional and modern classical dance forms to provide interpretations of the folk tradition for large stage or televised environments.

The Miami Nicaraguans continue to celebrate many of their patronal festivals, but with some differences. Small businesses and professional organizations have taken an important role in fostering and organizing the festivals in the absence of mayordomías. Given the more rigid North American work schedule, festivals are held on the Sunday closest to the actual saint's day, and all festival activities occur in a single day.

As recently arrived immigrants, Nicaraguans are intimidated by Miami laws requiring parade permits for street activities. Additionally, the former residents of any one town tend not to be concentrated in a single area. Therefore, celebrations are located in rented park areas or halls, and their processional character has been modified to fit these new spaces.

Finally, the prohibition against fireworks in Miami has fostered some creative adaptations. At the *Fiesta de San Sebastían* and at many home *Purísimas* multitudes of balloons are strung overhead. At a certain moment in the festival when firecrackers would be set off, a signal is given, and adults and children furiously pop the balloons, simulating this important festival sound.

Cultural activities are also reduced in the Miami celebrations. While a mass and modified procession are usually performed, the varieties of dancing and masking traditions that adorn any Nicaraguan town festival are represented by just one or two symbolic enactments. Some festivals have included horse shows, but the palo lucio and corridos de toros games appear impracticable in Miami.

SAN SEBASTÍAN

Diriamba's festival of San Sebastían is known throughout Nicaragua, especially for its street dance-theater performances: *El Gueguense, El Toro Huaco, El Viejo y La Vieja,* and *El Gigante* (David and Goliath). In 1990 Pedro Facundo Pomar and Horacio González, both former mayordomos, got together to organize a patronal celebration in Miami, complete with the traditional *tope* that marks the formal beginning of the festival. In Nicaragua San Sebastían is taken to the village of Dolores, where he is met by the patron saints of the nearby towns of San Marcos and Jinotepe. This tope constitutes a ritual invitation to Diriamba's neighbors. When Santiago's (Jinotepe) and San Marcos's festivals approach, their mayordomías also stage a tope, inviting San Sebastían (and Diriambans) to attend. (See the work of Leopoldo Serrano Gutiérrez, 1960, for a fuller description.)

In Miami each of these patron's festivals is celebrated with a symbolic tope staged at the festival site. San Sebastían occurs on the closest Sunday to

January 21; Santiago is in July; and San Marcos, only recently organized, is in April. Each group of townsmen parades with its saint's image from a given corner of the grounds. When they all meet in the center, the saints are made to bob a greeting to one another.

At the San Sebastían festival, the Silva family presents the Toro Huaco, the dance that traditionally "breaks" or leads the procession. Dance director José Silva says that this dance constitutes a family as well as a town tradition. His wife makes the colorful costumes, while the wooden masks of Spanish colonial soldiers and the *chichiles* (tin rattles) are imported from Nicaragua. The dancers, mostly children, form two lines facing one another. Between them twirls a man sporting a cow's mask attached to a kite-like structure he holds over his back. The dancers alternately charge and retreat from this cow, employing a methodical stamping step.

The Toro Huaco is the only large-group traditional Nicaraguan dance performed in Miami. It employs the ancient indigenous music of flute and drum. While the slow, repetitive, ritualized steps of the dance make it somewhat monotonous, the elaborate masks, peacock plumed hats, and costumes provide a feast for the eyes.

SANTA ANA

Santa Ana of Nandaime has been celebrated occasionally in Miami on the Sunday closest to July 26. The festivities were organized by a family, María Teresa Chavarría and her son, Ismael López, who own a painting of the saint. Some years many Nandaimeños prefer to return to Nicaragua for their hometown festivities, so there are only occasional celebrations in Miami.

Unlike the Diriambans, Nandaimeños have no organized dance performance groups. Their traditional festival dance, *Los Diablitos,* is a simple hopping step that anyone who has made a promise to the saint must learn. On July 24, hundreds of these *promesantes,* dressed in brightly colored silk capes and wearing wire mesh masks, go to the valley where Santa Ana is said to have first appeared. On procession day the dancers escort their patroness the several kilometers back to town, accompanied by the music of chicheros. Auxiliadora Acevedo explains that in Miami, participants reenact this form of devotion and express their local identity by dancing Los Diablitos in their street clothes on the festival grounds.

El Viejo y La Vieja, Fiesta de San Sebastían (Old Man and Old Woman dance, San Sebastían festival). Photo by Laurie K. Sommers. Courtesy of Historical Museum of Southern Florida.

SANTO DOMINGO DE GUZMAN

Reportedly the first Nicaraguan patronal festival organized in Miami, Santo Domingo of Managua draws on participation from all Spanish-speaking Nicaraguans. The festival is held in August and was originally hosted in 1987 by a group of professionals who were looking for a way to unite the community. Unfortunately, as in Managua, the Miami festival has fractured into two celebrations, one among the elites and one among more working-class Nicaraguans.

The elite celebration generally constitutes a party with a horse show and represents an opportunity for socializing. The other festival, which takes place in the Nicaraguan part of Little Havana, is a rowdy affair. Young men paint themselves with black and red grease and then dash through the crowds smearing this noxious substance on unwitting members of the public.

Managua has its traditional dances as well. Chony Gutiérrez has organized a performance of *Las Vacas* for the Santo Domingo festival since 1988. In this dance women wearing hoops around their waists designed to represent cows mimic a bullfight with companions holding colored scarves.

SAN JERÓNIMO

Masaya's festival of San Jerónimo is known as the longest of Nicaragua's patronal festivals. Beginning September 30, festival activities continue every Sunday to the beginning of December. Two major traditional events are the *Torovenados*, carnival-like processions in which masked participants mock local and national personalities, and the Bailes de la Marimba. The most elaborate of the Masaya marimba dances is *Las Negras*, an all-male masked dance in which half the men masquerade as women. In Miami, natives of Masaya have recently begun honoring San Jerónimo with a one-day celebration at the end of September. After an outdoor mass and short procession at the festival site, *marimbero* Alonso Montalván provides the music for participants, who are invited to dance on a raised stage, either in costume or in their street clothes. Additionally, a group of friends, organized by Alma Vega and Chester Carrión, have formed a dance troupe that performs Las Negras, *La Mama Ramona* (a humorous marimba dance), as well as the more standard Baile de la Marimba. The other great Masaya festival tradition, the Torovenado, has not taken root in Miami, perhaps because emigrees are embarrassed by this boisterous, somewhat bawdy display.

LA PURÍSIMA AND LA GRITERÍA

Of all the patronal festivals, that of the *Virgen de la Asunción*, patroness of Nicaragua, is the most widely and most traditionally celebrated in Miami. Purísimas are private parties, to which guests are invited to recite the rosary and sing *villancicos* to the Virgin. They are then thanked for their participation by being given traditional foods and presents: *el paquete*. Most are held in the early evening on the host's lawn during purísima season, which lasts from November 26, the first day of the novenario of the Virgin, through January. The public *Gritería* is held on the final day of the novenario. In Miami the Purísimas are usually hosted weekend nights, and the Gritería falls on the Sunday closest to December 7.

On this night, altars are set up outside homes, churches, and stores throughout Little Havana and Sweetwater. People, especially children, roam from one to the other singing snatches of villancicos, "shouting" the traditional phrase: "*Quién causa tanta alegría? La concepción de María!*" and receiving their "paquete" in return. (For a description of these festival events in Nicaragua, see Edgardo Buitrago, 1959.)

Doña Elvia Vega, an ardent celebrator of the Gritería, claims she hosted the first family-sponsored Gritería in Miami in 1982. After being disappointed that friends, busy with work, didn't attend her Purísima, she decided to move her altar onto the street and reward passersby who would sing. From that time on, more and more of her neighbors on 103rd Avenue began setting up altars, until this street became a major focus of Gritería activity.

Another cluster of Griterías are held in the residential neighborhood around Ninety-fifth Place. One hostess, Gloria Ortíz, emphasized that she held a party every year *por promesa* after the Virgin Mary helped cure her son of a serious illness. Doña Socorro Castro de Sevilla, who hosts a yearly Gritería in Little Havana, said she does so because she enjoys the custom. Centro Comercial Managua and the Holiday and Laguna Plazas in Sweetwater provide a concentration of Griterías, as shop and restaurant owners host their own festivities. Moreover, San Juan Bosco Church and the Church of the Divina Providencia erect large platforms on their grounds with altars for an outside mass and group singing. At some of these locations the crowds of carolers number in the hundreds. Listings of at least some of the addresses for Gritería altars are published in both *La Estrella de Nicaragua* and *La Prensa Centroamericana* newspapers.

Gritería altars in Miami are relatively simple compared to those erected in Nicaragua. For instance, Chony Gutiérrez remembers designing a model of an active volcano for one particularly elaborate altar in Managua. Churches in Nicaragua often contract professional altar decorators to paint *telones* or backdrops with scenes of Jerusalem or Nicaragua. In Miami, private home altars often display the Virgin surrounded by potted plants and flowers or cleverly nestled in an existing tree or shrub on the host family's lawn. Christmas lights and balloons provide additional decorative elements.

Storefront and church altars are somewhat more elaborate. For instance, in 1991 Fritanga Monimbó on North Twelfth Avenue displayed the Virgin in a skyscape of blue and white tissue paper. Rincon Nica and Nicaraguan Grocery in Little Havana contracted Douglas Barrios, a specialist in altars and religious floats, to construct altars in which the Virgin stood on a tin foil-wrapped crescent moon among painted styrofoam clouds.

Fine artists have also been inspired by the purísima theme. In 1991, Doñald Estrada, a noted primitivist painter, depicted the Virgin against the Miami skyline with a logo thanking the United States for its hospitality to Nicaraguans. Like much of his other work, this painting reflects a unique blending of the traditional and the new that strikes a chord with the Nicaraguan community in Miami. (For an illustration of this work, see *La Prensa*

Centroamericana, November 29, 1991, 7.) Petronio Caldera, a painter and world-renowned caricaturist, painted the Virgin surrounded by angels, each of whom wears the face of one of Caldera's nine grandchildren. This very personal work was intended for his daughter's purísima party.

ATLANTIC COAST FESTIVALS

Unlike the Mestizo Pacific coast Catholics, Creole Moravians celebrate most of their religious holidays within the church. Standard festive practices include a special mass and beautiful Moravian hymn singing. At Christmas, for instance, a candlelit mass is held. At Advent, many Moravians still make or purchase a many-pointed paper Moravian star to hang over their porch lights. The old Watch Night custom, in which church members gather and sing hymns together all night to herald in the new year, is also still observed. Yet other social events related to New Year's—a dory race and games of kitlaly, or outdoor bowling—are impracticable in Miami. As will be described later, Harvest, the Moravian version of Thanksgiving, is perhaps the most distinctive and beautiful of all Moravian church celebrations.

One non-Moravian festival of the larger Atlantic coast towns, May Pole, represents a local Creole version of the English May Day rites. Discouraged by Moravian missionaries because of the erotic dancing and heavy drinking associated with them, May Pole parties were avoided by Moravian Creoles. Nevertheless, Maggie Harrison fondly remembers slipping out secretly to watch the dancers as a child. She describes makeshift bands of banjo, guitar, and homemade drums accompanying dancers who executed a subtle dipping step similar to a limbo.

Miss Maggie complains that with the popularization of May Pole music and dancing throughout Nicaragua in the late 1970s the dance has become exaggeratedly eroticized and has strayed from its original local form. In Miami, Creoles still tend to have parties during May, and they may even play records and dance May Pole, but the event as festival is not enacted.

Moravian Miskitos celebrate the same traditional church festivals as the Moravian Creoles, but they hold their services in Miskito, and sing the old Moravian hymns in translation. Their church band includes some traditional Miskito instruments like the grater, shake shake, and a homemade bass, constructed of a piece of string, a broom handle, and an overturned wash pan. George Dixon and Mary Bushy, who organize both the choir and the band, also sponsor a youth fellowship, which presents a nativity play for Christmas.

Ironically, while the Moravian church provides an important outlet for artistic expression, it has worked to obliterate other forms of native artistry.

Mary Bushy speaks of the *sukias*, old women who acted as midwives, shamans, and storytellers in the more remote villages. Their *kisi*, or animal tales, are no longer a part of living Miskito folklife, and Mary cannot tell these stories herself. Yet she collected and wrote down some of these stories while she was working for the Ministry of Culture in the early 1980s. Thus, adult Miskitos, while devoutly religious, remain interested in exploring and preserving lore from a more remote past.

FOODWAYS

One need not look far to find the influence of Nicaraguan foodways on Miami. Along the streets of Little Havana and in the Sweetwater shopping malls Nicaraguan food establishments abound. Most characteristic, the *fritanga* is a good place to start sampling this satisfying fare. The word refers to street side, open-air grills that serve inexpensive meals to hungry passersby. In Miami, fritangas have moved indoors, and refer to both take-out and sit-down cafeterias. Fritanga Monimbo, with three locations, is popular among working people and families. The Cuban-owned Yambo Restaurant is a fritanga that doubles as a nightclub. But perhaps the most interesting place to visit is La Fritanga in the Centro Comercial Managua shopping center.

Owner Emelina Tellez opened this Nica version of a fast-food stand because of her own nostalgic longing for things Nica. The walls of her shop are lined with old photos of Managua before the earthquake. Two carved coconuts, humorously labeled Daniel Ortega and Rosario Murillo, dangle from the ceiling. While there are no tables, her shop forms a natural gathering place for the local community. Doña Emelina's *quesillo*, soft white cheese wrapped in a corn tortilla and topped with Nicaraguan sour cream and pickled onions, is an excellent alternative to a sandwich.

While staple items like fried plantains and green bananas, broiled chicken, beef, and pork, and fried cheese are prepared on location at fritangas, the specialty meat dishes—*chorizo*, *moronga*, and *nacatamales*—and cheeses, tortillas, and baked goods are prepared by cooks working in their homes or in cottage food industries. The nacatamale, a combination of cornmeal, pork, rice, potato, onion, tomato, and green pepper packed in a banana leaf and boiled or steamed, is considered Nicaragua's national folk food. While cottage industries have sprung up throughout Miami specializing in this product, Nicaraguan housewives also run smaller nacatamale businesses out of their homes, just as they did in their native towns.

Other kinds of Nicaraguan *tamales* (the word refers to any cornmeal-based food wrapped and steamed in banana leaves) include *tamal pisque*

Making tortillas at Fritanga Yambo. Photo by Laurie K. Sommers. Courtesy of Historical Museum of Southern Florida.

(made with lime), *tamal relleno* (filled with brown sugar and aged white cheese), and *yoltamal* (made with fresh instead of dried corn and packed in the original corn husk). One adaptation that Miami Nicaraguans have made in cooking these tamales is to substitute aluminum foil for expensive banana leaves. Most cooks also use packaged cornmeal, rather than grinding the dried corn themselves.

One interesting foodways development in Miami is the ubiquity of *vigorón* at any activity identified as Nicaraguan. This snack food consists of fried pork rinds arranged on a bed of boiled cassava and topped with cabbage and tomato salad. In Nicaragua vigorón is often eaten for breakfast on weekends, but the meal is not considered culturally emblematic. Nicaraguans in Miami explain that the ease and rapidity of preparing vigorón, especially since the fried pork rinds are available in packaged form, makes it more compatible with their faster-paced Miami lifestyle. Thus, this snack has been declared "a little taste from home."

Traditional sweets like homemade *cahetas de coco*, coconut bars; *cosas del horno*, cornmeal-based pastries and sweet breads; *sopa borracha*, a sponge cake soaked in a rum syrup; and *tres leches*, a custard cake made with three kinds of milk, are also frequently displayed in groceries and fritangas. Some sweets are especially related to particular holidays. During Easter season *buñuelos*, fried dough made of cassava, white cheese, and egg, topped with hot sugar syrup are traditional. *Almívar*, grated candied fruit, is a Christmas delicacy. Purísima specialties include the *gofio* or *alfajor* (a crumbly bar made of ground corn, ginger, and sugar), *ayote en miel* (autumn squash cooked in honey), and *espumillas* (meringues).

Pacific coast Nicaraguans also have a strong tradition of consuming grain-based drinks. Cereales y Café El Vencedor, a small cottage industry owned and operated by Ramiro and Helen Álvarez, specializes in beverage mixes. One room houses several small electrically powered mills, sacks of corn, cocoa beans, barley, oats, *jícaro* (gourd) seed, and the cartons that Don Ramiro and Doña Helen hand pack themselves. The popularity of *Pinol*, a hearty beverage made from toasted corn, as an early morning pick-me-up has earned Nicaraguans the nickname "Pinoleros."

Nicaraguan tortillas, larger and thicker than their machine-made Mexican cousins, are also available in Miami. Ninosca, a family operation run by Perla Marina Castro in Little Havana, occupies what looks like a converted garage. Walk by any day and you can see young women standing around a large table, hand-palming tortillas that are baked on a huge griddle.

Small, inexpensive, homestyle restaurants serving Nicaraguan food also abound. Two excellent examples are El Masayita in Little Havana and El Taquito in Sweetwater. Try the *baho* at Masayita, a weekend specialty dish of seasoned pork steamed with vegetables, cassava, plantain, green bananas, and Nicaraguan potatoes, and topped with fresh cabbage and tomato salad.

Nicaraguan high cuisine is also plentiful in Miami. Perhaps the most famous elegant dining spot, Los Ranchos, is one of the most successful Nicaraguan businesses in the United States. Other restaurants include The Galloping Lobster and La Parilla, both in Sweetwater. All these restaurants offer a mixture of Nicaraguan and continental cuisine. Nicaraguan specialties include *churrasco*, a perfectly grilled steak or pork cut served on a wooden block with a special dipping paste made of ground herbs. *Puntitas a la jalapeña* (strips of sirloin topped with a creamy sauce laced with hot peppers) is another spicier selection.

While sharing many Pacific coast foodways, Creole and Miskito Nicaraguans also preserve many distinctively Atlantic coast dishes. Perhaps the most emblematic of these are run down (pronounced "ron don") and rice and beans. Similar to baho, run down is a one-pot meal in which seasoned fish or meat is boiled atop a bed of local vegetables and tubers. As it slowly cooks, the flavor of the meat is said to "run down" into the vegetables, thus giving this dish its name. What makes run down distinctively rich is that coconut milk is added to the water halfway through the cooking. Similarly, rice and beans are boiled together in coconut milk to make a delicious variation of Pacific coast *gallopinto*.

Coconut milk constitutes the secret ingredient in many Atlantic coast breads, tarts, and biscuits as well. The milk is extracted by grating and squeezing ripe coconut meat, either by hand or with an electric food processor. Atlantic coast cooks are emphatic about the medicinal qualities of this favorite ingredient, claiming that coconut milk acts as a purgative for parasites and generally eases digestion.

Among the Creole population traditional drinks include sorrel wine and ginger beer, a peppery beverage made of mashed ginger root boiled in water, then cooled and sweetened with sugar. Perhaps the most distinctly indigenous Miskito specialty, wabul, is a drink made of pounded breadfruit or other tubers, mixed with coconut or cow's milk.

In contrast to the Atlantic coast communities, Pacific coast peoples have not established their own food businesses in Miami. However, informal food sharing and selling does take place within the communities. Rosa Lau, a Miskito Indian living in Miami Beach, explained that when someone in her apartment complex had time to make a traditional dish, they often made enough to sell or give to their enthusiastic neighbors.

One place where the outsider can sample native Atlantic coast cuisine is at the November Harvest festivals of the Prince of Peace and New Hope Moravian Churches. At these thanksgiving services, church members place home-grown and store bought fruits and produce, home-canned pickled vegetables, baked goods, plants, and flowers around the altar in an elaborate display of ethnic food traditions. Palm fronds and sugar cane decorate the church walls, and after a service embellished with beautiful Moravian Harvest hymns, the offerings are sold off, and churchwomen dish out Nicaraguan, Creole, Jamaican, and American hot foods.

The culinary contribution of Nicaraguans to Miami is rich indeed. Representing the most pervasive and forceful retention of native country traditions within the community, Nicaraguan foodways are also slowly becoming popular among outsiders. In fact, a recent *Washington Post* article announced that Nicaraguan delicacies appear to be Miami's next dining craze (February 6, 1991, "The Latest in Latin-Miami's Explosion of Nicaraguan Cuisine").

MATERIAL CULTURE

Although Nicaragua, and especially Masaya, boasts a rich tradition of crafts and festival arts, and though many emigrees formerly practiced one or more of these arts, the handcrafts industry remains undeveloped in Miami. Most craftsmen arrived with few financial resources, often without their tools or work companions. As a result, most seem to have found factory or service jobs and are making the difficult adjustment to a more demanding schedule that allows little time for leisure.

Many Nica groceries and fritangas, however, import artisanry directly from Nicaragua through informal trade networks. The best quality items can be found at the Mercadita Nicaraguense and La Fritanga in the Centro Comercial Managua at 104th and Flagler, and at El Pinolero at Sixteenth and Flagler. Here one finds children's machine-embroidered clothing, embroidered cotton shirts and "maxi" dresses, wooden bowls, spoons and decorative dishes, small baskets, carved jícaros (gourds), leather and reptile skin belts and wallets, and small oil paintings. Moreover, two Nicaraguan-owned furniture shops imported *sillas abuelitas*, a fancier version of the Cuban rocking chair with a decoratively carved backboard and lathed dowels. Merchants remark that it is cheaper to buy in Nicaragua than to produce in Miami.

Nicaraguan goldsmithing is another trade that has suffered from the transition to a new setting. Several goldsmiths reside in Miami, but the old, hand-crafted colonial jewelry famous on the Pacific coast and the delicate gold filigree work from the Atlantic coast are not being produced. Independent goldsmith Enrique Robleto and jeweler José Miguel Chow explain that these arts demand a high degree of hand-crafting and are thus more expensive and less marketable than the machine-caste gold jewelry available in most Miami shops.

Likewise, among Creole and Miskito populations, traditional fishing crafts, and mahogany and rosewood carving and furniture making have proved impracticable. For instance, on the Atlantic coast the dory or dugout canoe remains the major means of transportation. Thus, any adult male who grew up there knows how to build a dory. He simply goes to the forest, chooses a suitable tree, and starts chopping. As retired Miskito-Creole carpenter Sydney Willis queried, "Where would you get the tree trunk around Miami without getting arrested?" Nevertheless, a fine example of this native boat making is on permanent display at The Galloping Lobster Restaurant in Sweetwater.

One set of crafts that has continued to thrive in the new environment, however, is Moravian Creole women's textile arts. *Hardangar*, a form of embroidery originally from Norway, is perhaps the most distinctive of these arts, and many Miami Nica Creoles still make elaborate hardanger altar cloths, table runners, and doilies. Lillith Robinson, an accomplished embroiderer, learned the technique as a schoolgirl from her home economics teacher, but said that her mother and grandmother also embroidered in hardangar.

The embroidery involves delicacy and precision, but Miss Lillith insists that the actual technique involved is very simple. Initially, one makes the border of a design, counting fabric threads carefully to ensure geometric accuracy. Once the solid work is finished, one cuts and removes some of the threads inside the pattern. Finally the remaining threads are woven together in new open patterns with a finer strand of embroidery thread.

Tatting is another textile art practiced by many Moravian Creole women. Using a crochet hook and a shuttle, one knots fine threads into lacy patterns at lightning speed. Joyce Bradford, an adept tatter, says Bluefieldians used to make tatted collars for dresses when these were popular, as well as doilies and decorative pieces. In Miami, Joyce has creatively experimented with the form, tatting snowflakes to use as Christmas tree ornaments. She has even decorated stationary with delicate tatted flowers made of regular sewing thread.

Fine, lacy crochet and cross-stitch embroidery are other textile arts brought to a high degree of refinement by Creole Moravian women. Perhaps one reason for the survival of these textile arts is that, unlike other Nicaraguan crafts, none seems to have been practiced as a means of earning money. While they represent European and North American traditions brought to the Atlantic coast by missionaries' wives, they have, over the years, become intimately associated with Bluefields women, forming a major part of their education and allowing for artistic expression and social interchange.

One versatile Nicaraguan folk artist, Chony Gutiérrez, preserves a number of festival-related arts in Miami. Years of investigation and practice of her country's material culture have earned her an envious reputation within the Pacific coast community. She began her career in *manualidades* as a small girl, when an extended illness forced her to find ways to amuse herself. Her mother, who was a seamstress, later taught her to sew. As an adult, Doña Chony studied regional folk dance costumes of Nicaragua, and she even directed one of the first *ballèts folklóricos* while working for the Ministry of Tourism. Doña Chony continues to make dance costumes, decorations for weddings, baptisms, and communions, and paper purísima decorations on consignment. *Congolomas*, hanging paper chains, *banderillas*, little tissue paper or origami flags with cut-out patterns that are stuck into sweet lemons, apples, or oranges for "paquetes," and tiny paper baskets and animal figures used to hold purísima sweets are just a few examples of her delicate work.

Doña Chony is also an accomplished piñata maker. She explains that Nicaraguan piñatas differ from the Mexican variety because their skeleton is of cardboard or pottery rather than wire. Her tiny home on the edge of Little Havana is always crowded with projects and visitors who stop by for a cup of coffee and a chat or just to see what new creations Doña Chony is fashioning.

FOLKLIFE IN THE MIAMI COMMUNITY

Despite dramatic changes in their work practices and general way of life, Nicaraguans in Miami have sought to retain those aspects of their cultural uniqueness that are most symbolically resonant. For Pacific coast peoples patronal festivals offer an opportunity to gather together and celebrate not only their religious devotion but also their sense of identity in their new, more ethnically diverse environment. For Atlantic coast peoples the Moravian church provides a center for religious, social, and artistic expression.

Fritangas, restaurants, and groceries offer the much-needed antidote to nostalgia for those who find it increasingly difficult to consider a permanent return to their native land. They also represent a burgeoning field of business opportunity both for the proprietors and for the home cooks who supply specialty items.

While taste in clothing, jewelry, and furniture has shifted to American-style, factory-made items, imported folk crafts have taken on symbolic significance as they become reminders of the home country rather than everyday items. A visitor to almost any Nicaraguan home will discover at least one silla abuelita, a decorative ceramic bowl, or a painted scene of the Nicaraguan countryside gracing the living room. With characteristic friendliness, Mestizo, Creole, and Miskito Nicaraguans are eager to share their culture with those who show interest in things Nicaraguan. The contributions that this new community has made and will continue to make to the city are rich indeed.

Note

1. Girl Guides were the British antecedent of the American Girl Scouts. The name has been retained in the Caribbean and Caribbean Rim.

References

Buitrago, Edgardo. 1959. *Las Purísimas: su forma y sus origins*. Leon: Editions de Cauldrons Universitarios.

Cortázar, Julio. 1989. *Nicaraguan Sketches*. Trans. Kathleen Weaver. New York: W. W. Norton and Co.

Cuadra, Pablo Antonio. 1976. *El Nicaraguense*. 7th ed. San Jose: Editorial Universitaria Centroamericana.

Cuadra, Pablo Antonio y Francisco Pérez Estrada. 1978. *Muestrario del Folklore Nicaraguense*. Managua: Fondo de Promocion Cultural Banco de America.

Helms, Mary. 1971. *Asang: Adaptations to Culture Contact in a Miskito Community*. Gainesville: University of Florida Press.

Jenkins Molieri, Jorge. 1986. *El desafio indigena en Nicaragua: el caso de los Miskitos.* Managua: Vanguardia.

Mejía Sanchez, Ernesto. 1946. *Romances y Corridos Nicaraguenses.* Mexico: Imprenta Universitario.

Peña Hernández, Enrique. 1986. *Folklore de Nicaragua.* 2nd ed. Guatemala City: Editorial San Piedra Santa.

Pérez Estrada, Francisco. 1971. *Estudios del Folklore Nicaraguense.* Nicaragua: n.p.

Sambola, A. 1984. *Trabil Nani: Antecedentes historicos y situacion actual en la Costa Atlantica.* Managua: CIDCA.

Serrano Gutiérrez, Leopoldo. 1960. *Folklore Nicaraguense: Cronica folklorica de las festividades de San Sebastian de Diriamba.* Diriamba: Paco Aleman e hijos.

Sommers, Laurie Kay. 1991. *Nicaraguan Traditions.* Final report submitted to the Historical Museum of Southern Florida, Folklife Archives.

Exploring Peruvian Music in Miami

MARTHA ELLEN DAVIS

> They say that the wealth of Peru is not in its mines, nor its soil, nor its mountains, nor its jungle, nor its sea. Rather, the wealth of Peru is in each Peruvian, wherever he or she may be.
>
> —JULIO REY, PERUVIAN JOURNALIST, INTRODUCING THE MUSICIANS AT A FAREWELL PICNIC FOR RESIDENT AYACUCHO HARPIST, ARTURO GÁLVEZ, BARNES PARK, MIAMI, AUGUST 12, 2001

THE AMERICAS, NORTH AND SOUTH, ARE COMING TOGETHER. THEIR point of encounter is Miami, crossroads of the Americas. Five decades ago, Cubans laid the cornerstone for a Latin American presence in Miami. Today, every Spanish-speaking country in the Americas is represented in Florida and most, if not all, are in Miami.

In the summer of 2001, all other Latin Americans taken together surpassed the number of Cubans in Miami. Among these other Latin Americans, the South Americans constitute a growing presence in the city. Colombians are the largest group (104,058 estimated in 2000 for Miami-Dade County alone).[1] Peruvians in Miami-Dade number 18,579 (2000 estimate) with another estimated 15,119 in adjacent Broward County, and others undocumented. Many left Peru due to tremendous insecurity during the height of the Shining Path guerrilla movement of the 1980s. Peruvians in Miami include upper- and middle-class as well as lower-class and rural-derived people. They hail from all of the three major regions comprised of north-south geographic and ecological zones: the Coast (*la Costa*), the Andean Highlands (*la Sierra*), and the eastern Peruvian lowlands, part of the Upper Amazon jungle (*la Selva*). For all sectors, music is a fundamental symbol of identity, an antidote and a response to crisis, and sometimes a business.

FIELD RESEARCH

In recognition of the South American presence in Miami, the Historical Museum of Southern Florida, in the summer of 2001, launched the South American Traditions Project to document the traditions of selected South American communities—Colombian, Peruvian, and Venezuelan—"making history" in present-day Miami-Dade. The project was supported by the National Endowment for the Arts' Folk and Traditional Arts Program. The goal was to develop an archive of data and audiovisual materials for public access, a bilingual online exhibit,[2] and future public programming. Three researchers participated: the writer and another researcher on Colombians, the writer alone on Peru, and a third researcher on Venezuela, later assumed and completed by the writer in 2002.

The first phase of the project entailed field research to identify and document key traditions of symbolic identity—music, festival, and foodways (culinary arts)—among members of these three communities. With regard to music, the interest, as specified by Stephen Stuempfle, chief curator at the museum and supervisor of the project, was not in artists imported from home countries for specific functions. Rather, it was in music, musicians, and musical events of South American origin residing or based in Miami—thus forming part of the artistic fabric of the city. Special interest was to be given to how South American traditions are adapted to the limitations, inspirations, opportunities, cultural contacts and fusions, and other circumstances of Miami, and to musical composition and recordings made in the United States and specifically in Miami.

The initial and major phase of the writer's work in 2001 on Peru and Colombia had to be carried out in only some twenty-eight paid days for research, cataloguing, and reporting, although the writer had never before lived in Miami. She had few contacts in Miami as well as only limited personal experience in the three countries themselves, namely less than two months' residence in Peru, specifically in the Andean area of Huancavelica twenty-one years previously, four very short visits to Venezuela, and no experience in Colombia. However, the research period was timed to coincide with both Colombian and Peruvian independence, July 20 and 28 respectively, high season for music, festival, and food symbolizing homeland identity. This intensive summer period was followed up by a few days in October 2001, and a couple of weeks in May 2002, focused on Venezuela and Peruvian coastal traditions.

The writer launched the project by collecting musical-event announcements from free newspapers, flyers, and publications from Peruvian restaurants and other businesses.[3] In the free papers, the most-promising Peruvian independence activity was a multipart festival organized by the nonprofit MADELMA Foundation, founded by Martha del Villar. The call to *Señora* Martha, *tocaya* of the writer (i.e., person of the same name), was the initial contact that gave entry into the Andean world in Miami. In addition to the independence event, several subsequent ones were attended, including an enactment of "Inti Raymi" in October 2001 by the Centro Qosqo de Arte Nativo of Cuzco. It was directed by the Peruvian anthropologist and public servant Luis Huayhuanca Villasante, who played the part of the Inca. Since visas were denied to many in the troupe who applied on the heels of the 9/11 attack, they were replaced for the U.S. tour by members of a Miami-based dance troupe, Inti Perú. Thus the spectacle was rendered a Miami-based event, suitable for museum documentation.

In addition to special events, the free papers provided advertisements for restaurants with fixed musical engagements. A notable group thus encountered was the guitar trio Los Bardos de América.

Follow-up on the writer's prior contacts and referrals also bore fruit. The former president of the Peruvian student organization at the University of Florida was from a family of Peruvian professionals who fled the Shining Path movement. In Florida, they own a bakery in Sweetwater (west Miami area, just east of Florida International University). They were interviewed and their bakery documented not only as part of culinary traditions, but also because of the role bakery products play in rites of passage events for the upwardly mobile society of Latin American Miami. The bakers recommended that the writer contact Juan Reyes, a former folk dancer and folk troupe director, significant community leader, and publisher of *Perú Hoy*, which is circulated nationally in the United States. He and his wife, Rosalva, have directed various troupes and a folk dance academy, attended by the bakers' daughter.

A referral provided by the Historical Museum was the Afro-Peruvian guitarist and singer Víctor Manuel "Chocolatín" Casanova, a versatile artist of many international styles and genres, one of which is Afro-Peruvian. Through him, the writer also met *cajón* player Luis "Cotito" Balarezo and thus entered the coastal world of *música criolla* and *música negra*. Cotito's recommendations were further pursued during the second brief research phase in May 2002, by attending a multipart *noche de gala* to launch the CD of the música criolla guitarist Luis Enrique "Quique" Negrini.

Initial contacts thus produced leads that formed networks of musicians, venues, and events. These were pursued as time permitted. As in any urban research, the telephone was very important, both for initial contacts as well

Víctor Manuel "Chocolatín" Casanova performs Afro-Peruvian music with *cajón* player Luis "Cotito" Balarezo. Photo by Martha Ellen Davis. Courtesy of Historical Museum of Southern Florida.

as follow-ups. In fact, some entire interviews were conducted by telephone, especially when they included musicians who formed part of the Miami-Dade Colombian, Peruvian, and Venezuelan communities but who lived in the greater geographical region beyond Miami-Dade, as discussed below.

NATIONAL AND CULTURAL IDENTITIES

Political and Cultural Boundaries

Political boundaries are artificial cultural boundaries, both in South America and in the United States. Many South American countries have the *costa*, *sierra*, and *selva*, geographical and ecological, hence cultural, divisions, that cut across national borders. The commonalities within a geographical region transcend these political boundaries. As Chocolatín states about Afro-Peruvian music in the international context of coastal South America and the Caribbean: "It's all one music."

Likewise in the United States, although the writer was instructed to restrict research to Miami-Dade in order to limit the scale of the study, the cultural community of Peruvians and other South Americans actually embraces

Broward and even Palm Beach Counties to the north. That is, it stretches from at least Pompano Beach over to Coral Springs and down to Homestead. Musicians from a broad area may be tapped to form an ensemble, and likewise audience members, including restaurant patrons, are drawn from this wide area.

A third dimension of political and cultural boundaries is the relationship, in the minds and lives of Peruvians in Miami, between the United States and Peru. Immigrants of an earlier era, whether from Europe, Africa, or Asia, came to the New World to stay. Nowadays, immigrants from areas contiguous with the United States do not entirely break contacts and allegiances to the homeland, but expand their identities. In fact the same is now applicable to South American communities farther afield, such as Peru, thanks to better mail service, telephone, Internet and satellite communications, and accessibly priced air travel.

These ties are enhanced by the dual nationality status recognized by Peru that facilitates dual loyalties and even political participation. Peruvian American journalist Dr. Julio Rey, who enjoys double nationality (proudly boasting of his U.S. citizenship and Michigan State degree in journalism), recently ran for congress in Peru.

With regard to intracity media that bind the Miami Peruvian community, during the period of research, Peruvians dominated local community-access TV (Channel 36 TAP) with three Saturday programs totaling 2½ hours: "Perú y su Gente" ("Peru and its People"), "Contigo Perú" ("With You, Peru") produced by Julio Rey, and "El Panamericano." Julio Rey announced on the air (2001) that "Contigo Perú" soon would be retitled "Contigo USA"—again indicating a dual and evolving identity. Peruvians in Miami also receive Cadena Sur (Channel 75) on cable service that connects them to South America.

Musical Dialectics

The result of a dialectical musical relationship with Peru is the development of a sort of dual cultural nationality. Martha del Villar, founder and director of the MADELMA Foundation (www.madelmafoundation.com) travels to Ayacucho annually to participate in its carnival in the prize-winning *comparsa* of 160 people called "*Huamanga Tunante*" ("Rascal Huamanga"—Huamanga being the region where Ayacucho is located). She asks rhetorically, "How is it that a person from here wins a prize there?" The fact is that for some forty years, she has been from both the United States and Ayacucho, and she views her mission as one of cultural ambassador for highland Peruvian culture in the United States and promoter of folk arts, particularly crafts, in Peru. In 2001 she was so acknowledged by the Peruvian Consulate in Miami.

This exchange relationship of Peruvian artists and arts promoters in Miami is one of dynamic feedback, in which energies are directed both toward the conscious conservation of tradition and toward innovation. With regard to cultural conservation, it is well known that expatriate communities often preserve tradition more faithfully than in the homeland, because of isolation from the homeland and/or because of the symbolism of traditional music and dance with regard to national identity. The Peruvian Andean music singer Victoria de Ayacucho, in residence in Miami during July–August 2001 through the MADELMA Foundation, performed at a Barnes Park picnic with the simple accompaniment of resident harpist Arturo Gálvez ("*Quri Soncco*"—"Heart of Gold"), also from Ayacucho. The performance contrasted with the complexly orchestrated arrangements on her CDs, produced in Ayacucho. She remarked after her first piece (translated from the Spanish):

> It is immensely moving to be here in Miami and sing with just the traditional harp—as if we were in the country back home. The magic hands of Quri Soncco have impressed me; his style is truly authentic. This is how people celebrate in their villages. With just a harp or a fiddle, they party for days. For days and nights they dance and sing.

It appears that different musical arrangements and instrumentation symbolize different identities. For sentimental expatriates, a traditional arrangement recalls the homeland; but for Peruvian highlanders in Peru, a modern accompaniment represents upward mobility within a national hierarchy.

PERUVIANS IN MIAMI

The Reconstruction of Peru in Miami

As is the case with other Latin American communities who have gone north to seek safety or economic progress, Peruvian society has been reconstructed in Miami, socially and symbolically. Social reconstruction of Peruvian society is of course intended through the regional clubs, a phenomenon that started in Lima and has been replicated in Miami and elsewhere in the United States. Professional clubs serve the same purpose. Other venues of social liaison are replicated as well, such as the *peñas* (music clubs), an institution in turn of southern Spain replicated in Latin America. During a multifaceted performance event produced by the couple Quique Negrini and Nedda Huambachano, discussed below, *Don* Quique was serenaded by friends from the peñas of Lima and his hometown, Callao (Lima's port city and the epicenter of Afro-Peruvian music), reconstituting that social-musical network in Miami.

Examples of symbolic reconstruction are the names of Peruvian restaurants, venues of the identity symbols of music, food, and dance, which refer to Peruvian national icons; for example, El Rincón de Chabuca (named for the most famous *vals criollo* composer, Chabuca Granda, 1920–1983), La Flor de la Canela (named for Chabuca Granda's most famous song), and El Chalán (the first touristic restaurant in Peru).

However, it must be noted that for no country are all symbols of identity accurate. Don Quique Negrini, who is extremely knowledgeable of Peruvian popular music history, of which he is part, considers the "true voice of Peru" not to be Chabuca Granda but Felipe Pinglo Alva (1899–1936), "The Immortal Bard." Likewise, he thinks that the true second national anthem should not be "*La flor de la canela*," rather Pinglo Alva's "*El plebeyo*." But he died young and never had the opportunity to travel in order to gain visibility.

Regional Identities

In Miami today, Peruvians represent the three major regions of the country, and a wide range of social sectors, as discussed above. However, the coastal identity, site of the capital, Lima, dominates in music and dance, as well as food, since it is more prestigious than the highland identity—in Peru as well as Miami. Journalist Juan Reyes commented that 80 percent of the Peruvians in Miami are from the Sierra but they all want to be *criollos*—"Creoles," that is, from the coast. Thus, both for Peruvians themselves and for cultural outsiders, the Peruvian cuisine as well as the music in Miami restaurants represents the Creole culture of the coast. To savor the culinary and melodic flavors of Sierra and Selva, one must visit homes or specially organized regional events, such as those of the MADELMA Foundation. In promoting Andean culture in the United States, then, Martha del Villar is fighting on two fronts: for inclusion of Peruvians within a multiethnic United States and enhanced prestige of Andean Peruvians in the Peruvian social hierarchy.

Social Organization

Peruvians are superb organizers—perhaps more so than any other South American community—both in Peru and in the United States.[4] In Miami and throughout the country, Peruvians are known for their regional clubs, which seem to transcend differences of class within the regions. Regional clubs in Miami connect people from Ancash, Ayacucho, Arequipa, Huancayo, Cajamarca, the Selva region, and perhaps other regions. There are also professional societies, the most active of which is said to be that of physicians (the Peruvian American Medical Society). In addition, ad hoc associations are activated in response to natural disasters, usually earthquakes, and are often allied with or part of the regional clubs. Miami also has an association of Peruvian associations, and at a national level in the United States, the Convention of Peruvian Associations has been meeting annually since circa 1986.

The most important organization is a recreation of Lima's religious brotherhood of *El Señor de los Milagros* (Our Lord of Miracles). In Miami, and probably elsewhere in the United States, the brotherhood of El Señor de los Milagros draws in Peruvians of all origins, since Lima is a way station in migration abroad. Accordingly, the phenomenon of regional clubs starts in Lima, which nowadays is home to people from all areas of the country, as the country's major metropolis.

In Lima, there is a single brotherhood with parish chapters. In Miami, there are four different brotherhoods, with yet another in West Palm Beach. Based on oral history, the first brotherhood in the region was founded in Broward County, followed by one in Miami based at Corpus Christi Church, followed by one in North Miami Beach, recently followed (ca. 1999) by a break-off from the Miami brotherhood in Kendall (southern area of Miami), due to alleged corruption. Regional identities within this greater metropolitan area are central to the debate about division or unification and the purpose itself of the brotherhoods. The debate raged during the summer of 2001 on the Peruvian community-access television program *El Panamericano.* The question posed was: Should there be but a single brotherhood in greater Miami? The spokesperson for one of the brotherhoods who was interviewed on the program aspired toward a single brotherhood among Peruvians not only in the greater Miami area, but in fact throughout the entire United States.

MUSICAL VENUES

Apart from special events, restaurants are the usual venues for music performance. For immigrants, the restaurant is a cultural embassy where three symbols of identity intersect: food, music, and often dance. However, Peruvian restaurant fare is entirely the coastal—that is, Creole—seafood-based cuisine. Interestingly, in the well-known restaurant El Chalán, the symbol represented by the name refers to the horse-and-cattle culture of the foothill region, the visual symbol on the menu—Machu Picchu—refers to the Andean region, and the cuisine is coastal. Similarly, the music in such restaurants includes música criolla, música negra, and international Afro-Latin dance music.

Restaurants where musicians have, or have had, fixed or occasional engagements in Miami-Dade and Broward Counties during and recently prior to the 2001–2002 research period included but probably were not limited to:

- Restaurante Mi Perú (North Miami Beach), where Los Bardos de América plays on Fridays
- La Flor de la Canela Peruvian Restaurant (just west of the Turnpike on Coral Way)
- Restaurante El Pulpito (on Calle Ocho in Little Havana), where César Ríos plays on Fridays, and Sonido Elegante plays on Saturdays
- Perú Place Restaurant (Miami Springs, just north of the Miami International Airport)
- Giralda Café (behind Plaza de las Américas)
- El Rincón de Chabuca (northern Miami Beach)
- Restaurante La Terraza de Cojimar (Doral area)
- Restaurante Perú Riko (Hollywood)
- Peruvian Grill Restaurant (Kendall area, southern Miami)
- Crazy Pollo Restaurante Peruano (2175 SW First Street)
- Restaurante (El Nuevo) Perú Deli (Snapper Creek Plaza, Kendall area)
- El Inka Restaurant (SW Eighth Street), the first Peruvian restaurant in Miami where Juan Reyes's ensemble, Perú Canta y Baila, performed some ten or fifteen years ago

Restaurants are unstable musical venues because they are unreliable sources of income. Musical engagements are low paying or tip-based. Hence, there are frequent changes of performers that restaurants offer and, likewise, musicians frequently change their engagements.

Special-events venues are rented by promoters, arts organizers, or clubs. MADELMA uses the Benevolent Police Association on SW Fourteenth Street. Quique Negrini and Nedda Huambachano, who organize musical events as semiannual business ventures, use the St. Brendan Parish center in western Miami. The free newspapers indicate that other places rented for musical events in 2001 included the Greek Community Center on Coral Way and El Teatro Tower on Calle Ocho.

A PANORAMA OF PERUVIAN MUSIC IN MIAMI

The Peruvian Miami music scene is dominated by música criolla, which entails the vals criollo plus the Hispanic *marinera* dance, whose focus is the northern coastal city of Trujillo. In addition, there is a growing presence of música negra or *negroide*, characterized by the wooden box drum (cajón), often encompassed by música criolla as a generic term. This includes such music/dance genres as the *festejo* and others such as the *landó*, whose best interpreter in the greater Miami area appears to be Giomar Antonio. The vals criollo itself is indeed a creole, that is, hybrid genre. Although the rhythm is of Central European origin from the mid-nineteenth century, in the versions of Afro-Peruvian communities, it is accompanied by a very punctuated, percussive *requinto* (guitar that plucks the melody in a guitar ensemble) and the cajón. This illustrates the fact that the Hispanic and Afro-Peruvian cultures really comprise a single creole (criollo) coastal culture, exemplified by the musical culture, in contrast with highland music.

The most notable vals criollo singer in greater Miami is Nedda Huambachano, who was to launch her first CD produced in the United States in June 2003, although she already has recordings in Peru. She is accompanied by her husband, Luis Enrique "Quique" Negrini, former guitarist for the renowned Perú Negro music-dance ensemble in Peru, the basis for the Miami ensemble Perú Expresión directed by Jhonny More [*sic*]. Other música criolla singers in greater Miami heard or identified during the study—although not all documented due to limited funded time, and some not commercial artists—include Lucy Watanabe and Tina Bianchi, Isabel Banses (who has a CD), and Martha Deza; Adolfo Barrantes and César Palomino (singing friends of Quique Negrini from the peñas in el Callao); and others. It is this music that is heard in restaurant venues, with live or recorded accompaniment.

Afro-Peruvian dance music such as the festejo is increasingly popular in restaurant performances. Live accompaniment of Afro-Peruvian music implies the cajón. *Cajoneros* include Luis "Cotito" Balarezo, mentioned above, who played Saturdays in Coral Gables with Chocolatín, Carlos Avalos (main cajero on the CD of Quique Negrini), Alberto Esquén, Lucho Armas, and others.

Afro-Latin dance music, which may include Afro-Peruvian, is also performed at restaurants. Ensembles documented during the project include a Friday engagement (2002) with the César Ríos ensemble at El Pulpito in Little Havana. Sonido Elegante, another Peruvian dance band, plays at the same place Saturdays. A modernized Peruvian adaptation of the Colombian *cumbia*, an Afro-Colombian dance genre from the Caribbean coastal region,

Los Bardos de América. Photo by Carl Juste. Courtesy of Historical Museum of Southern Florida.

is the so-called *tecknocumbia*, which is very popular among Andean people in Miami. Recorded tecknocumbia is played between live music or dance performances at the MADELMA Foundation musical events.

The Latin American guitar duo and trio are standard fare at Latin American restaurants in the region and the United States. Peruvian ensembles of international experience and fame include the trio Los Bardos de América directed by Ernesto Chávez ("El Zurdo Chávez"—Lefty Chávez), *segundo* (lower voice); Marco Antonio García (*primo* or tenor); and Armando Echeverría (requinto), who is actually from Quito, Ecuador. Los Bardos plays every Friday in Mi Perú Restaurant in North Miami Beach. A broad range of customers is welcomed by such Peruvian restaurants' designation as offering "Peruvian and international cuisine" (meaning Peruvian coastal cuisine but everyone is welcome). Don Ernesto says, "Sometimes we don't have a single Peruvian in the place." Rather they have a diverse Latin American clientele enjoying music of their homelands while savoring seafood from coastal Peru.

Los Bardos excels in the vals criollo, but also plays a wide range of hits of yesteryear symbolizing the national identity of other Latin American countries, such as "*En mi viejo San Juan*" and "*Preciosa*" played for Puerto Ricans. The customized repertoire pleases the pan-Latin American clientele, which is the objective since the band plays for tips. The audience is also delighted by the constant humor of Don Ernesto and Don Marco Antonio, who introduced one oldie saying, "This is from when the rainbow was in black and white."

Other duos and trios play largely Peruvian music, though representing both highland and lowland musical styles in which their renditions of the vals criollo characteristically show the pentatonic influence of the Andean region. Such ensembles include the guitar duo Los Acordes de América directed by Pedro Ferrer, who once had a trio with two brothers (Los Hermanos Ferrer) until the two left Miami for other U.S. locations due to economic reasons. He now plays sometimes in duo with Orlando Robles and in other ensembles, including with Ernesto Chávez of Los Bardos, while working full-time on the night shift at Walmart to make ends meet.

Coastal dance of northern Peru is represented by the *marinera norteña* of Trujillo, danced in Miami to recorded brass band music typical of the genre. The most notable representatives, who have won awards in Miami and elsewhere in the United States, are Natazha and Luis Armas.

Highland music is comparatively underrepresented with regard to the population of such origin. Music of the Selva or eastern Peruvian Amazonian jungle area is not represented at all, except through recorded genres from elsewhere (such as the Colombian cumbia) enjoyed but not produced in this area.

Music of the Sierra seems to have little market in Miami with cultural outsiders, unlike the Andean music enthusiasts in New York or Boston, for example. The leading highland music or dance groups in Miami included the following at the time of research: (1) the large musical ensemble Alma Andina of Miguel Sulca, only seasonally active around Peruvian independence, with fluctuating membership; (2) the revivalist folk dance troupe Inti Perú (formerly Ballet Folklórico Inti) directed by Walter Delgado—the ensemble also offers the coastal marinera norteña—in which Natazha and Luis Armas perform with two other couples from the group; (3) Kuyayky, comprised of five siblings and their father, from Jauja, north of Huancayo (see www.kuyayky.com); (4) there is also Andean regional affinity with the Bolivian music/dance ensemble Grupo Masis directed by Nilda Heredia.

Miguel Sulca, perhaps the most professional of Andean musicians in Miami, studied music at the School of Music in Ayucucho, a very musical city, and plays traditional string, wind, and percussion instruments. He is also a sound technician who worked in radio, recording, and television production in Ayacucho. He founded Alma Andina with his brother Abel, former president of the Ayacucho Club of Miami. They are from a renowned family ensemble of Ayacucho that included his father on harp; himself on fiddle; Abel on mandolin, as well as *charango* (mandolin-like instrument made of an armadillo shell), guitar, *quena* (the ubiquitous Andean notched flute), and other instruments. He affirms that they recorded for U.S. circulation

Miguel Sulca. Photo by Martha Ellen Davis. Courtesy of Historical Museum of Southern Florida.

without ever visiting the states and toured Europe for three months, recording there as well.

His ensemble, Alma Andina, has about ten musicians, all men, including a couple of Bolivians. The ensemble includes Amerindian traditional instruments of the flute family which abound in the Andes: the quena and the *zampoña* (panpipes—also known by other terms); European-derived stringed instruments such as the fiddle, folk harp, guitar, mandolin, and others—all long adapted to Andean music; band instruments including the saxophone and the bass drum; as well as a popular European and now Latin American dance band instrument, the accordion. The vogue of coastal music has also drawn the Afro-Peruvian cajón into the ensemble.

The membership is rather fluid, depending on availability, and the ensemble is constituted as needed. *Señor* Miguel has an "open-door policy" with regard to participants. Musicians may also play in other, different ensembles. For example, in addition to playing guitar in Alma Andina, Ankash native Orlando Robles performs in the guitar/vocal duo Los Acordes de America with guitarist Pedro Ferrer of Lima, who in turn performs with other ensembles.

BI-NATIONAL ARTS PROMOTION AND PERFORMANCE

Some key community figures are not artists themselves, rather arts promoters. Such is the case of Martha del Villar, and her nonprofit MADELMA Foundation, established in 1971 to promote Andean Peruvian folk arts. Others are both artists and promoters, inspired by both philanthropic and business motives, as is the case of coastal music event producers Luis Enrique "Quique" Negrini and Nedda Huambachano. Some musicians view their musical promotion and/or performance as simply a business, such as appears to be the case for the somewhat jaded Ernesto Chávez, founder and director of the trio Los Bardos de América.

And there are many musicians who perform for love and harbor dreams for their hometown and promotion of its arts in the United States, but are absorbed in their own survival in Miami. Such is the case of Miguel Sulca, a lost talent in Miami. He does house and car painting, yet dreams of touring the states with a highly professional ensemble which modifies traditional Andean music for an international palate and records it with the best sound technology. He is also interested in anthropology and served as Quechua-Spanish interpreter for an American documentary film crew. He would like to direct a video documentary of the Quechua marriage ceremonies in villages near Ayacucho. These objectives seem remote, and during the research period he appeared increasingly frustrated with the disparity between his high objectives and the banality of his life in Miami.

Another case of musical underachievers in Miami is Pedro Ferrer, mentioned above, because the trio with his brothers dissolved when they left for greener pastures—not an uncommon scenario. Yet another is Marco Antonio García, a native of Chiclayo on the Peruvian north coast and primo (lead singer) for years with the trio Los Bardos de América. In Peru he had a much higher profile as a popular music singer, not replicated in Miami. He began his career by singing for Sonoradio, the eminent Peruvian record company, where he recorded over thirty LPs with different ensembles. He has traveled in Latin America and North America as a soloist with dance bands under well-known conductors, performing a variety of music. He relishes his role as soloist because "in a trio, one goes unnoticed." He also is a song composer; Los Bardos performs several of his works. But he sadly confessed over the telephone that, during the research period, he had to take a job as night cleaner in a hotel, a role that embarrasses and depresses him.

Singer Nedda Huambachano and guitarist husband Luis Enrique "Quique" Negrini, are the major organizers of coastal creole and Afro-Peruvian music events. She is a renowned singer of vals criollo as well as a clinical psychologist. She says, "Singing comes easily to me. My real vocation is medicine; I love hospitals, love to talk to and encourage the sick. Since I couldn't afford to study medicine, I studied psychology." She also is a superb craftsperson in knitting, crocheting, and sewing; she designs and makes all the evening dresses for her shows. She says that when she returns to Peru she loves to give free concerts for "her people" and fills an amphitheater of 5,000. Don Quique, musician and guitar teacher, was the guitarist for the internationally known Afro-Peruvian troupe Perú Negro. He is the only direct link with that ensemble, hence is advisor to its Miami incarnation, Perú Expresión.

Twice a year Doña Nedda and Don Quique, as an enterprise, rent a hall, charge admission, and sell food for multifaceted galas mainly of coastal Peruvian music and dance. One such event was a "Noche de Gala" in May 2002 to launch Don Quique's first CD, entitled "*Criollo No . . . ¡Criollazo*!" (Not Creole . . . Super-Creole!). In February 2003 they organized a similar event to celebrate thirty-two years as artists. And in June 2003 they planned a launching event for Doña Nedda's first recording in the United States. At the May 2002 CD-launching extravaganza, Doña Nedda was master of ceremonies. She and others present in Miami from Don Quique's past in the peñas of Callao and Lima came to serenade him. Singers featured were Giomar Antonio, noted for his landó, vals criollo singers Adolfo Barrantes, César Palomino, and others including Doña Nedda herself. Perú Expresión offered dance performances, including an impressive cajón drum ensemble that accompanied a virtuosic dance duel, the *contrapunto de zapateo*. Quique Negrini's aspiration is to diffuse Peruvian música negra throughout the United States.

For the Andean region, Martha del Villar is their counterpart, and she has been at it a long time. However, in 2003 the Andean performance group Kuyayky established a philanthropic nonprofit to benefit their town of origin, Jauja, north of Huancayo. As young people who are fully bilingual and bicultural, they offer great promise in this area as well as serving as bi-national cultural ambassadors of Andean Peruvian culture through their music and dance.

During the research period, however, Martha del Villar, who lives for folk arts, was the central figure in Andean Peruvian arts promotion in Miami. She is the "godmother" of Inti Perú and says she facilitated their costumes. During the research period of 2001, she organized a marinera competition as well as a staged performance of "Inti Raymi" mentioned above, and her Web page is full of her many activities and accomplishments before and after. Although a lover of the most conservative of Andean traditions, her multipart, day-long programs as business enterprises also include local música criolla and even Latin rock and tecknocumbia. She also includes the Peruvian Amazon, where her mother is from, in the food sales at her events.

Del Villar's MADELMA Foundation brings traditional artists from Peru. In 2001 these included *huayno* singer Victoria de Ayacucho and harpist and saxophonist Arturo Gálvez, mentioned above. He gave a shot in the arm to young men from the region in Miami by founding an ensemble performing a special Peruvian style: the "Santiago music" associated with the animal-marking ceremonies of Huancayo during the St. James (*Santiago*) season (July 25). This music is characterized by an ensemble of tenor saxophones (presumably replicating the traditional use of the cow horn associated with animal-marking ceremonies), with harp and fiddle. The musical style is characterized by large intervals, like the overtones blown on a cow horn. Gálvez taught young men to play the saxophone and one, Edgar Chambi, the harp, adequately to perform the Santiago music. However, the group may have become inactive since Gálvez, who was going to leave the United States, was considering entry in the butchery business in Miami. Prior to coming to Miami, Edgar Chambi traveled throughout Peru performing the scissors dance of his native Huancavelica.[5] He is willing to perform it in Miami and train others to join him, but says that their work schedules may not allow such a commitment.

Señora Martha is also an avid craft and costume collector. In fact, it is through craft sales at various folk festivals that she earns a bit of a living, as well as providing a living for the craftspeople in Peru. However, she is distressed about how miserably they live, and wishes to develop a market for them, so that gallery prices for the *retablos* with figurines depicting life in the Andes trickle down to the artisans. This is why in 2002 she founded a folk arts organization in Lima called Jori Marquicuna ("Golden Hands" in Quechua). As a tireless champion of Andean folk arts and their culture bearers, Martha del Villar has t-shirts imprinted with this statement:

> *Recuerda . . . Una patria sin Folklore es una patria sin Alma.*
> *Hay que amar primero lo nuestro y después el resto.*
>
> [Remember . . . A country without folklore is a country without a soul.
> We must first love our own traditions, and afterward the others.]

Notes

1. See the author's article on Colombian music in Miami, "An Antidote to Crisis," in *Hemisphere* 11 (Fall 2002): 4–7, published by the Latin American and Caribbean Center of Florida International University, which conducted an extensive research project (2000–2001) on Colombians in Miami.

2. www.hmsf.org: Exhibitions—Online Exhibitions—*South American Music in Miami.*
3. At the suggestion of Laura Quinlan, director of the Rhythm Foundation, a Miami Beach-based nonprofit organization which presents "world music" international artists in south Florida, www.rhythmfoundation.org.
4. University of Florida anthropologist Paul Doughty, personal communication.
5. Also performed in Ayacucho, and filmed at the Ayacucho regional club in Lima by John Cohen for the film *Mountain Music of Peru* (1984).

The Seminole Family Camp

ORMOND H. LOOMIS

THERE IS NO BETTER EXAMPLE OF A TRADITIONAL FLORIDA BUILDING type than the *chickee,* the traditional Seminole Indian building which has long been a part of Seminole life. Most Floridians recognize these structures and associate them with the Seminoles whether the name of the building and its background are familiar or not. Chickees provide an environment for the Seminole Folklife Area at the Florida Folk Festival.

The Seminole Tribe of Florida has generously installed a temporary family camp on the festival grounds to serve as a base for interpretive demonstrations of several Seminole traditions. The crafts and foodways found among the chickees complement the building tradition itself. The domestic activities suggest the customary daily routines that might be encountered in a camp on a Seminole reservation. In one of the chickees at the folk festival, men are on hand to demonstrate and discuss chickee building. The symbolic as well as practical significance of this kind of structure makes the chickee a central element in Seminole folklife and an ideal setting for the appreciation of Seminole heritage.

The chickee is undergoing a major transition. It is tempting to say that, like many reflections of folklife, this form is vanishing and that surviving examples will be gone within a generation or two along with the intimate knowledge of its construction and use. Signs of its decline are easy to find. The current status of the chickee, however, shows cultural tenacity, mirroring in a sense the evolution of the Florida Seminoles themselves.

The chickee grew out of the Seminole experience in nineteenth-century Florida when the Seminole Wars and tribal migration into south Florida made building an older type of permanent Indian dwelling impractical. History does not supply an account of the development of the chickee. From

Seminole chickee, Big Cypress Seminole Indian Reservation. Photo by Blanton Owen, Florida Folklife Program. Courtesy of State Archives of Florida.

period photographs it is evident that the basic chickee structure was thoroughly established among the Seminoles by the end of the nineteenth century. The form, found today with little change since the late nineteenth century, is well adapted to local climate, relies on the use of materials available in the immediate, natural environment, and is unique to the Seminoles.

FORM AND CONSTRUCTION

Chickees were traditionally built in clusters. A single chickee served as a room rather than as a complete home by itself. The total number of these rooms changed to accommodate the number of individuals in the extended family who lived in a given encampment. According to James Billie, tribal chairman and former chickee building contractor, the elementary camp consisted of at least four chickees, each of a different design and use, usually arranged in a circle such as the one in the Seminole Folklife Area. A cooking chickee stood at the center. Around it were a dining area, utility area, and one or more sleeping chickees.

The basic structure of the chickee resembles that of any pole shed. Posts set into the ground support a rafter system, which, in turn, is covered with roofing. The arrangement of the corner posts is usually rectangular, but rounded ends are built occasionally as are square and circular floor plans. Most chickees have open sides, but enclosed chickees, sided with materials such as palm leaves, boards, or paneling, are not uncommon. Doors and windows in sided examples are installed at points adjoining the posts. The floor of the chickee is dirt, and permanent furnishings such as platforms and counters are built on small posts sunk into the ground.

All the structural members of the chickee are of cypress. On the Big Cypress Reservation, these trees grow plentifully. Builders cut the poles shortly before construction begins and peel off bark. The wood is highly resistant to insects. A layer of bark on the poles will harbor bugs and promote decay. Poles vary in size according to their use in the structure: main posts being the largest, about eight inches in diameter for a standard-sized chickee, and rafters the smallest, two inches at the small end. The Seminole terms for many of the members refer to parts of the body. For example, posts are called "legs," and rafters are "ribs."

Traditionally the roof of the building is thatched with the leaves of the cabbage palm, which grow in abundance on the Brighton Reservation. The broad fronds, or "fans" as the Seminoles call them, make an excellent natural shingle. They are attached by their stems in rows to the rafters. The leading edge of the fans on the bottom row is rolled under to channel water. The top row is capped with a line of fans laid lengthwise along the ridge and secured with short lengths of crossed or broken limbs.

A characteristic, three-sided overhang on the end of the roof extends beyond the corner posts, increasing the area covered by the roof. This feature gives the structure the appearance of having a semicircular hipped roof. On the typical chickee, low-hanging eaves roughly four feet from the ground protect the interior from wind and rain as well as the casual glances of passersby.

As a temporary shelter in a remote, tropical wilderness the chickee is without rival. It affords protection from the sun and rain with maximum exposure to breezes. It can be erected quickly. Two men can build one in a few days. As a permanent residence, however, this kind of building has limitations. It can be cold on a damp winter day. When built well and maintained, one may stand for twenty years, but ten years is considered a long time for a chickee to last, and the roof must be recovered with fans approximately every five years.

The Seminoles modify the basic chickee design according to the type of use the structure is to have. Dimensions of the perimeter, for instance, vary considerably. A small sleeping chickee measures 10' x 16'; a large dining

Interior of a Seminole chickee at Scott Ranch, Okeechobee. Photo by Blanton Owen, Florida Folklife Program. Courtesy of State Archives of Florida.

chickee 15' x 30'; and one built as a recreational hall 20' x 80'. Increasing the size of the structure requires little more than adding extra side and end posts, and extending the rafter system to cover them. Enclosed chickees and those intended for public use usually have eaves of seven feet or more.

On some roofs the overhanging end rises only part of the distance to the ridge creating a half-hipped effect. The most interesting modifications, however, distinguish one type of chickee from another.

Types of Chickees

The sleeping chickee fits the stereotypic image of the general Seminole building. The popular impression of this structure may come from the fact that the Seminoles often use the sleeping chickee as a place for doing crafts work. Inside it a simple platform, set two to three feet above the ground, provides a clean, dry, vermin-free surface for sitting, sleeping, or working. The platform occupies most of the area enclosed by the corner posts, with one side and end of the platform running along the outer edge of the floor plan with enough space on the other side and end to let an individual stand inside the posts. Paul Bowers recalls that as a boy his family had a large sleeping chickee in which there were platforms at each end with a walking space between.

The Seminoles use the plates, beams, and horizontal braces of the roof system in the sleeping chickee for hanging clothes and insect netting at night. These structural members create an excellent storage loft as well. Boards and poles laid across them form shelves. Often during the day, and especially for periods when they plan to be away for several days, the inhabitants of the chickee roll their bedding and place it in this loft.

An open cooking fire is built in the center of the cooking chickee. This type of chickee frequently has a distinctive gable roof. The gable is open; the ridge of the roof extends beyond the corners of the eaves giving an outward slant to the end; and the eaves reach closer to the ground than those on other chickees. According to informants, this design allows smoke to escape easily from the cooking fire and affords good protection for the people inside. Counters, shelves, and cabinets are installed along the sides of the structure, making use of the low eaves; and pots, utensils, lights, and other items hang from the beams and rafters. A secondary work counter, which may be rigged with some type of running water, is frequently located outside nearby.

Other chickees have the basic form with certain identifying furnishings installed. The dining chickee, for example, contains a long table, possibly two if it is a long chickee, with benches on each side. In a large camp of a half dozen structures or more, the dining chickee is relatively near the cooking chickee. The utility chickee contains shelves, cabinets, and perhaps a counter.

CULTURAL ASSOCIATIONS AND TRANSITIONS

During recent trips to the Big Cypress Reservation, it was difficult for fieldworkers, even with the help of tribal members, to find good examples of the camps to document. Most Seminoles no longer live in chickees. They prefer the same advantages that other Americans enjoy in a building: permanence, comfort, and ease of care. A federal housing program, complemented by tribal building contractors and building material suppliers, are gradually filling the need for modern houses.

Current uses of the chickee indicate that they are coming to be regarded as outbuildings. Many of these are utility chickees, others serve as backyard canopies equipped with cement floors. An alternate use of chickees for some Seminoles is the development of a second home complex as a weekend and vacation retreat. Chickee builders working today have incorporated modern materials and conveniences in the structures. The ends of posts and poles in early chickees were notched to cradle the beams and rafters that rested on them. Now they are sawed flat to butt against a crossing structural member. In the old chickees, major joints were pegged, and small ones were tied with strips of hide, vines, or roots. Today the joints are nailed together. Fronds were once secured with a strip from the edge of the frond tied around a rib. Now they are nailed as well. The addition of electricity is perhaps the most striking adaption. Posts and beams carry conduit and wire to switch boxes and outlets, giving contemporary chickees full electrical service comparable to that in any other building.

There was a time within recent memory when young men had to build their own chickee when they took a wife. This tradition is no longer followed. A few boys still learn the fundamentals of construction by helping their fathers and uncles build chickees when the opportunity arises, but they are a minority. Most have other interests, and the general expectation that males will use the art of building chickees as an adult no longer exists.

Chickees continue, however, to have symbolic value. An indication of this fact can be seen in the use of the cooking chickee as the principle image in the seal of the Seminole Tribe of Florida. Chickees are the only buildings used at the sites of the Green Corn Dance, an annual ceremony of tribal affirmations. Many of the structures found on the ceremonial grounds are built with the old notched-pole techniques. Those young men who study tribal medicine with their elders at the Green Corn grounds must re-roof their own chickee each year using the method of tying the fronds with strips of the leaf fiber.

A new demand for chickees has emerged among non-Seminoles. Floridians in cities and subdivisions throughout south Florida want the structures beside their beach lots, pools, and patios. Interestingly, these other Floridians choose four different roof styles: Umbrella (single pole), Hawaiian (hipped), Polynesian (half-hipped), and the traditional Seminole. According to Paul Bowers, a chickee building contractor, the general preference is for the Polynesian. Non-Indian contractors also build chickees for this market, but the Seminoles have a competitive advantage. Because of their experience with the form and the availability of materials on their lands, they can offer high-quality workmanship and the best materials at a low cost.

It seems likely that a generation from now there will be no Seminoles living in clusters of chickees as the people of this tribe have done for over a century. Furthermore, given the rapid rate of decay that these structures are subject to, it is unlikely that any early examples will be preserved except as they are maintained at the Green Corn ceremonial grounds. Nevertheless, this Florida building has been adapted to contemporary life and shows promise of surviving through the enterprise of the people who created the form originally.

Sacred Steel

ROBERT L. STONE

MENTION "STEEL GUITAR" AND MOST PEOPLE WILL THINK OF THE WEEPING sound of the instrument played in country music. Some might think of pedal steel guitars that are routinely found in white country gospel groups and church "praise" bands. Relatively few would know the electric steel guitar has been the dominant musical instrument for more than fifty years in certain African American Pentecostal churches.

The electric steel guitar was introduced into the House of God in the late 1930s and eventually became the dominant musical instrument in its worship services. Over the years, House of God steel guitarists developed distinctive playing styles and repertoire. The unique musical tradition remained little known outside this denomination for more than fifty years, until 1995, when the Florida Folklife Program produced a cassette album titled *Sacred Steel: Traditional Sacred African-American Steel Guitar Music in Florida.* The album was licensed by Arhoolie Records, one of the oldest roots music labels in the country, and distributed internationally. Critics and fans hailed the music as a major discovery, and eight more Arhoolie albums followed. Today this compelling music is commonly known as Sacred Steel. Several groups who play this music are touring internationally, and one has garnered a rock star-magnitude recording contract and two Grammy nominations.

Florida, home to fifty-three House of God churches (far more than any other state), has produced many of the denomination's most influential steel guitarists. But it was in Philadelphia where the steel guitar was probably first used in a religious service. Steel guitar music was first brought to the United States in the early twentieth century by Hawaiian musicians, and the popularity of Hawaiian music continued into the 1940s.

The steel guitar takes its name from the metal bar, or "steel," the player holds in the left hand and presses lightly on the strings to make notes that often have singing, voice-like quality. In contrast, players of standard guitars make notes by using their fingers to press strings onto thin metal frets embedded in the instrument's neck.

The other instruments in House of God musical ensembles are typical of configurations found in many African American churches: drums, bass, a keyboard instrument, and rhythm guitar. Congregants often bring percussion instruments such as tambourines, maracas, washboards, and cymbals to "make a joyful noise" from the pews. The steel guitarist leads the musical ensemble to play driving praise music that moves the congregation to shout and dance ecstatically, provide dramatic emphasis as ministers preach, furnish a musical backdrop during periods of meditation, and play swinging march music for jaunty offertory processions.

The steel guitar was introduced to the Philadelphia House of God by Troman Eason, who learned to play it in the 1930s by taking lessons from a Hawaiian artist he heard over the radio at home. Troman's music making inspired his teenaged brother, Willie, to play the steel guitar in the late 1930s. Rather than play in the sweet Hawaiian manner like Troman, Willie developed a technique that closely approximated the singing he heard in church. Willie Eason found his approach to the electric steel guitar well suited for the celebratory, cathartic worship services of the House of God attended by his family. He could play it rhythmically; it had a strong, penetrating tone; and, because notes made on the instrument were unrestricted by frets, he could imitate the expressive, highly ornamented African American gospel vocal style.

Willie Eason withdrew from high school to travel throughout the eastern United States to play for church services, revivals, and street-corner music ministries. He was a powerful, moving singer with a magnetic personality. He often made his steel guitar echo the words he sang or finish his incomplete sentences. A Macon, Georgia, deejay dubbed him "Little Willie and His Talking Guitar," and the moniker stuck.

Willie Eason first came to Florida in 1940 with the Gospel Feast Party, a troupe of musicians and ministers that traveled from New York to southern Florida to hold revivals and worship services under tents in churches. Soon he struck out on his own to play street-corner music ministries for tips and donations. For many years he spent the fall and winter months in Florida.

Eason knew how to work a crowd and made a good living performing on the streets. One of his most productive spots in the 1940s and 1950s was in front of Buddy B's juke joint on Broadway—today Silver Springs

Willie Eason, ca. late 1940s.

Boulevard—in west Ocala. When Eason plugged in his powerful amplifier and began to perform, the local African American community was drawn to his soulful music. In later years, Eason's memory was impaired by Alzheimer's disease, but his wife, Jeannette, vividly recalled his playing in front of Buddy B's. "So Willie would go down to Buddy B's, and he'd hook up. That loudspeaker, when it went out, people out in the clubs and the bars and even Dr. Hampton, he would open his windows. He was a dentist. He would open his windows to let the patients hear Willie playin."

Eason's renown increased as he made seven 78 rpm records for popular black gospel labels in the 1940s and 1950s. He became somewhat of a living legend among House of God congregations and was a major influence in establishing the steel guitar as the dominant instrument in the church. In 1987, Willie and Jeannette Eason moved to St. Petersburg and opened the Fat Willie From Philly barbeque restaurant at 1371 Sixteenth Street South. The business folded quickly, and they retired.

Willie Eason's first wife was Alyce Nelson of Ocala. Her father, Bishop W. L. Nelson, worked tirelessly to establish dozens of House of God churches along Florida's east coast from Key West to Jacksonville. Most of the House of God churches active in Florida today grew from congregations and edifices established by Bishop Nelson.

Elsewhere in the country, there are more than 8,000 members of the denomination in twenty-six states, most of the churches east of the Mississippi. This denomination, one of the oldest Pentecostal churches in the country, celebrated its centennial in 2003. Pentecostal churches such as the House of God literally interpret the book of Psalms to give God praise through loud, joyful music. The churches place a strong importance on behavioral patterns such as shouting, ecstatic dancing, and speaking in tongues, as manifestations of being infused with the Holy Ghost. Music—especially in combination with dramatic preaching—helps infuse believers with the Spirit.

Willie Eason influenced Alyce Nelson's younger brother, Henry, who went on to become one of the most influential steel guitarists in the House of God. Henry Nelson, who idolized the dapper, charismatic, and freewheeling Eason, took up the steel guitar in 1940 at age eleven. Over the years, Henry Nelson defined what would become the classic form of driving praise music for the church. Nelson died in 2002.

Henry Nelson's son, Fort Pierce native Aubrey Ghent, is recognized as one of the finest six-string lap steel guitarists playing in the House of God today. In addition to his fiery praise music, he is known for his masterfully rendered hymns and powerful baritone voice. His stunning performance at the 1994 National Folk Festival in Chattanooga marked the first appearance of a House of God steel guitarist before a national audience in recent decades.

Ghent influenced a host of younger steel guitarists in Florida including Darryl Blue of Fort Lauderdale; his cousin, Antjuan Edwards of Ocala; his seventeen-year-old son, A. J. Ghent of Fort Pierce; and Elton Noble, also of Fort Pierce. Noble recently reflected on the power of the instrument as he recalled an experience in Lake City. "I played and I let it moan, and a woman jumped up and screamed and fell out [fainted]—just because the guitar was moanin," Noble said. ". . . I want it to touch you. That's what I want. If it touch you, I played. If it didn't touch you, I didn't play."

Another musician who influenced many younger Florida steel guitarists was Glenn Lee of Perrine. While he respected the music of Henry Nelson, he was determined to establish his own, more contemporary musical style. He was one of the first in Florida House of God churches to play the modern pedal steel guitar, an instrument usually heard in country music. Lee died of cancer at the age of thirty-two in 2000. A number of young pedal steel guitarists and his family band, the Lee Boys, carry on his musical legacy.

Members of the Lee family provide the music that drives the spirited worship services at the church built by patriarch Elder Robert E. Lee in west Perrine—one of the most heavily attended of all House of God churches.

In addition to playing for worship services, the Lee Boys enjoy success performing at festivals and concerts throughout the United States, Canada, and Europe.

House of God clergy and congregants take a variety of viewpoints on musicians playing outside the church. The most conservative believe the music should be performed only within the church. The most liberal view the presentation of the music at secular venues as a means of evangelizing. Each musician has to negotiate these issues with fellow band members, family, and local clergy. "Right now, our ministry may not be within the four walls of our church," said Alvin Lee. "But it's spreading the music that came from the four walls abroad, and it's touching a lot of people. And that's what the Lee Boys are all about. To me, that's a part of the ministry."

In March 2000, Crescent City House of God steel guitarist Marcus Hardy and a handful of volunteers produced the first Sacred Steel Convention at Rollins College in Winter Park. The event was open to the public and held in a secular venue, but its energy approached that of an inspired worship service. However, unlike worship services where the ministers are in control, the steel guitarists were in charge; it was their show.

Among those who showcased their talents was twenty-two-year-old New Jersey pedal steel guitarist Robert Randolph. His pyrotechnic performance resulted in an alliance with Jim Markel, a local man who had been looking for a Sacred Steel act to manage. Randolph and his Family Band soon began to perform at secular venues including nightclubs, concert halls, and large "jam band" festivals. By the spring of 2002, he signed a major recording contract with Warner Brothers. In December 2003, his debut CD for the label Unclassified received two Grammy nominations: Best Rock Instrumental and Best Rock Gospel Album. Randolph's commercial success in the secular world is a controversial topic among House of God clergy and congregations, but most wish him well and are proud of his achievements. Much as neighborhood kids shooting hoops aspire to become the next Shaquille O'Neal, dozens of youngsters from the House of God hone their steel guitar licks in hopes of being the next Robert Randolph.

Others choose to keep their music within the church. Fort Lauderdale high school student Eddie Harmon serves as a minister and steel guitarist in the House of God. "I want God to be glorified out of it, not me," said Harmon. "I don't want to get any personal wealth or gain off what I do, because I know it was God that gave me this gift. And so, what better way to show my gratitude than to stay in the House and play the music how God wanted me to play it?"

Even though women are in the House of God clergy and comprise the overwhelming majority of congregants at most worship services, few females have

Elton Noble, Crescent City, 1999. Photo by Robert L. Stone.

ever played steel guitar in church. The only woman doing this in Florida is Lisa Lang, who calls herself "Lady of Steel." Lang, who is the steel guitarist at the Brownsville church in Miami, perceives differences in how the genders approach the instrument: "We're not as aggressive as the males are in our playing. We bring more of a sophistication to it than the males because, you know, they just drive on that aggression, where it's not really in our nature to be aggressive like that." Lang's example has inspired others to break the gender barrier. One of her goals is to assemble a band composed entirely of women to play in church. "It'll happen," she said with conviction.

As Sacred Steel musicians usher their musical tradition into the new millennium, there seems to be something for everyone. Touring groups have audiences from Miami to New York and from Berlin to Paris dancing in the aisles and calling for more. And every Sunday from Pensacola to Florida City, venerated masters and dedicated younger steel guitarists—male and female—make Florida congregations jump for joy as they drive their instruments to sing, moan, and cry.

Musical Practice and Memory on the Edge of Two Worlds

Kalymnian Tsambóuna *and Song Repertoire in the Family of Nikitas Tsimouris*

ANNA LOMAX WOOD

Our bride is the thunder that comes with the storm
Give them as many sweet years
As there are shoots on the mint
—FROM THE "*PARIANÓS*," A KALYMNIAN WEDDING DANCE

NIKITAS TSIMOURIS (1924–2001) WAS ONE OF A FEW DODECANESE BAGPIPERS still practicing at the end of the last century. Experts—who are as rare as the pipers themselves—considered him a master of his instrument, the *tsambóuna*. He was loved and revered in his family and community as a bringer of joy and keeper of tradition and was a living treasure of his adopted home, the state of Florida. Nikitas and his instrument were, however, the standard bearers of a whole universe of song, dance, and poetry shared and often governed by the women of his family, which spilled out of their own intimate circle into the Kalymnian communities of Tarpon Springs and abroad.

It is my purpose to conjure up that world from the behavior and memory of this immigrant family and at the same time to draw attention to the importance of vocal music and its relation to instrumental music in this and by extension other Balkan and Mediterranean village traditions. Additionally, I propose this work as an example of cultural feedback falling within the realm of that rich and diverse field known as public folklore, in which the researcher collaborates with informants to galvanize musical memory, enrich cultural identity, and preserve the more subtle and fleeting—and often neglected—aspects of tradition.

Nikitas Tsimouris. Photo by Anna Lomax Wood.

The tsambóuna is a small bagpipe with two chanters found in the Dodecanese Islands (principally on Karpathos and Kalymnos), Crete, Pontic Turkey, and Thrace, and nearly identical to the sort played in North Africa and the Middle East. It is one of two variants known in Greece, the other being the *gaida*, which has a single chanter and is used in Thrace, mainland Greece, and elsewhere in southeastern Europe. The term "tsambóuna" (pronounced "tsabuna") derives from the ancient Greek word for harmony, an agreement of sounds (*simfonía*). Being a difficult instrument to master and tune, the tsambóuna is not widespread. During the Greek junta of 1967–1974 it was banned as a primitive survival, but it continued to be held in high esteem by cultural insiders. Representing as it does a link with deep tradition, the tsambóuna is still in demand, and there are now some fine young performers in Kalymnos and abroad.

It is often assumed that the tsambóuna is an instrument for solo playing or formal display, but I learned early on in this study that this is by no means so. An audience of sheep and goats would have been the most common beneficiaries of a solo bagpipe performance, but far more often the tsambóuna, like the gaida, served to lead dancing and accompany singing of all kinds and this was their main function. Instrumental music generally was almost entirely a male activity, while women and girls chiefly performed the social and ritual songs it accompanied. Nikitas's sisters and wife often sang while he played. His daughters, grandchildren, and others present clapped and beat the rhythms with their feet while dancing, augmenting the orchestra and spurring on the main performers to greater heights of *kefi* (joyfulness) and inspiration. In short, "it is so beautiful of an instrument to hear . . . that it excites the listener and introduces a sense of enthusiasm and liveliness in a *glendi*" (http://www.olymbos.org/music/).

Nikitas Tsimouris

Nikitas was born in the village of Khora on the island of Kalymnos and immigrated to the United States in 1967. Mountainous, near-barren Kalymnos had been the center of Aegean sponging, known since antiquity. It prospered also through trading and boatbuilding, and was famed for its citrus groves. As Mediterranean sponge fisheries became depleted in the early twentieth century, Kalymnians emigrated in large numbers to Darwin and Melbourne, Australia; the Bahamas; Campbell, Ohio; and Tarpon Springs, Florida—first establishing the sponging industry in Tarpon, and later developing a lucrative niche in industrial bridge-painting nationwide.

Kalymnians were reputed to be wealthy among Aegean islanders, but the years encompassing the two World Wars and the Depression, straddled by the Italian occupation of the Dodecanese from 1912 to 1947, were anything but prosperous. Nikitas was one of eight children. His father, a sponge fisherman and citrus sharecropper, was also a bagpiper, and the family was known for their love of music and dancing. After the third grade, Nikitas went to work in the mandarin orchards and the sponge fisheries to help maintain the family and earn dowries for his sisters, as was the custom. Upon his own late marriage, Nikitas received twenty sheep and goats as a dowry from his wife's family, which he sold in order to provide a dowry for one of his sisters. Even so, two sisters had gone into permanent service with well-to-do families as children and could not marry. Nikitas's father died in 1942, during the worst starvation years of World War II.

Once in the United States, Nikitas worked briefly on the Tarpon sponge boats, as a short-order cook and dishwasher in a Greek restaurant, and then in the stucco plastering trade. In later years he served as custodian of St. Nicholas Greek Orthodox Cathedral. He was a short, rather stocky man, with the large, pale-blue eyes of the dawn sea and a phlegmatic, slightly mischievous air—not above being a tease to exasperate his wife, who, having the care of three daughters, was of a serious turn of mind. For the last ten years of his life the effects of smoking left him unable to play his bagpipes without the aid of a compressor. Nikitas retired several years before his death in 2001. He rarely left home except at Christmas and Easter, allowing his wife and daughters to represent him at church and at parties. When not refurbishing his bagpipes or tending his tiny orchard of perfumed Kalymnian mandarins and the herbs and flowers planted round his modest house, he sat at the kitchen table listening to the Greek radio station and silently rehearsing the lyrics of the old songs.

At the end of his life, Nikitas Tsimouris was heaped with honors. First recorded and brought into the public eye by musicologist Theodore Grame of Tarpon Springs, he came to the attention of folklorists from the Florida Folklife Program, which produced a film about the family and their folkways (*Every Island Has Its Own Song*, 1988). This was followed by a 1989 Florida Folk Heritage Award; participation in the Florida Folk Festival and in the Florida Folklife Apprenticeship Program as a master artist; and numerous magazine and newspaper articles. In 1991 Nikitas became the first Florida recipient of a National Heritage Fellowship from the National Endowment for the Arts. Nikitas is featured in the *Florida Encyclopedia* (1993), and one of his bagpipes is part of the permanent collection of the Museum of Florida History.

The Tsambóuna

The airbag (*touloumi*) of the tsambóuna is made of untanned kidskin (*tragéois*) softened and airproofed with mixtures of honey, milk, olive oil, and sometimes chemicals. It is turned inside out, and the neck, tail, and two leg openings are tied shut with string. Tightly affixed with string to the remaining two leg openings of the bag are a mouthpiece and blowpipe made of olive wood, and a double chanter made of two pieces of bamboo (cane or rush are also used) pierced with a heated metal rod and bound together with string and beeswax. The mouthpiece and tube, which is serrated at one end, are made of olivewood that is carved and burned with geometric designs. Nikitas received his from his grandfather, dating it to the nineteenth century.

The parallel chanters, each having a single reed, are fitted into a single olivewood tube and sealed there with wax. One has five and the other three finger holes, and no thumbholes. To tune them, the piper adjusts the reed lengths with a piece of string and reduces the size of certain holes with bits of beeswax. As noted by Dietrich (1976), air leaks are stopped up with bits of beeswax, and air is kept from escaping out of the mouthpiece by an onion-skin flap affixed on the inside with beeswax.

Nikitas filled his bag with air and squeezed it with his arms, forcing air through the chanters to produce sound. He played standing up, with his arms around the bag, keeping pace by tapping his feet. By varying the air pressure in the bag, he was able to "bend" notes, that is, to ornament the basic melody with flurries of grace notes. He would also occasionally hold the air pressure with his arms while singing a line or two of a song. Although the tsambóunas of Crete and the Cyclades are similar, the manner of playing in the Dodecanese Islands, particularly in Karpathos and Kalymnos, is unique:

> it cannot be classified among either bagpipes with a fixed drone nor those which are solely melodic. In fact, the right pipe completes the hexatonic scale and can, at the same time, find itself in unison with the second degree of the scale, thus covering both melodic and accompaniment functions. The tsambóuna's tuning system possesses qualities which are completely particular, of which the most obvious is the tonal "ambiguity" of the third degree (in relation to the lowest note of the scale). (http://www.olymbos.org/music/)

Melodies played on the instrument consist of one to two phrases—basically a litany—with variety and excitement created by patterns of trills, mordents, pulsing vibrato, and other bitonal effects. These are executed on the second (left-hand) pipe by the index finger, which "can create separate acoustic images and more complex rhythmic structures" (www.olymbos.org/music/). *Lyra* players employ a similar technique, producing trills and tremolos with the left fifth finger. Using a multitiered method of coding each melodic segment, Haris Sarris and colleagues (2008) have studied melodic/rhythmic flow in Dodecanese instrumental music, focusing in one instance on a recorded performance of the "*Pano khoros*" played in Karpathos on the lyra (pear-shaped rustic violin with three strings held upright and bowed across). The authors make the interesting point that if the lyra came into play in the Aegean after the bagpipe as they believe it did, the way it was played was imitative of, and was circumscribed by, the musical range of the tsambóuna.

The limitations of the tsambóuna are similar to those of the gaida: the musician lacks contact with the reeds, so he cannot modulate the continuous flow of sound through them by tonguing, "nor can he play pauses or rests, staccato, or even the same note twice in succession. Furthermore, bagpipes do not have a range of dynamics. Generally speaking, the higher the note, the greater the volume, so the loudest note is E5, while the least sonorous is E4" (Sarris and Tzevelekos 2008). As these authors also point out, the higher registers are the most sonorous.

Nikitas Tsimouris with apprentice Nikitas Kavouklis. Photo by Anna Lomax Wood.

Transmission and Performance Practice

The chanters traditionally were passed from father to son, and are inserted into the skin when a new bagpipe is made. These are learned first, before progressing to the full bagpipe. Nikitas's chanters were made by his father. With this small instrument, which Nikitas began playing at the age of eight, he learned first to play the drone and then gradually to produce ornamented melodies before attempting to master the ensemble of airbag, mouthpiece, and chanters all together. Similarly, when Nikitas's nephew, Nikitas Kavouklis, showed an interest in the instrument, he made him a pair of chanters.

Nikitas learned to play the tsambóuna from his father and other male relatives, who played the instrument to pass the hours while watching their animals. Mrs. Tsimouris's father had been a *megalos voskós* (shepherd owner with a large flock) on Kalymnos and also a bagpiper, and she recalls that family and neighbors often gathered to dance and sing in their courtyard. Nikitas played in the citrus orchards he tended and on the sponge boats he manned seasonally in the Aegean, to entertain the crew and pass the time. When he settled in the tightly knit Greek community of Tarpon Springs, he was followed by his sisters and widowed mother and they all took houses around one shady block between Banana, Lime, and Oakwood Streets in the "fruit salad" district of town. In the evenings they came together with their growing families in one or another's dusty front yard, or in Nikitas's mandarin grove, to summon up the pleasures of their lives on Kalymnos, with laughter, music, and dancing.

Singing Style

Sarris and others have begun to look closely at how gaida/tsambóuna/lyra playing and singing mirror one another in Thrace and Crete. What is the nature of this symphony, and how might it have evolved? In my view, one of the crucial topics to investigate in the folk music of the eastern Mediterranean is precisely the synergy between singing and instrumental music and its possible relationship to pastoralism.[1] Overall, Cantometrics (1976) furnishes the most effective system for profiling singing style and vocal qualities in a comparative framework. With general reference to this method, Kalymnian singing style as manifested by the Tsimouris family is rather loud and medium to high-pitched, nasal, noisy, and forcefully accented. It uses melisma and vowel prolongation; slow to moderate tempo; rather narrow intervals and melodic range; simple melodic forms with considerable variation; and long phrases. Instrumental and vocal preludes and many songs are in free rhythm. I heard only solo and individualized (raggedly blended) monophonic unison singing with occasional passages of heterophony. At least a quarter of the text is repeated throughout most songs.

The Documentation Project

I met Nikitas Tsimouris in the early 1990s with my late husband, William Chairetakis. He was introduced to us by my aunt, Bess Lomax Hawes, whom he had come to know at the National Heritage Awards. He took it as his personal obligation to befriend and look after us, both as compatriots (with the distinct plus that Bill was from Crete, a place and culture high in Greek esteem), and as a mark of respect for my aunt. By then, the first generation of Tsimourises had become stately older parents, uncles and aunts with several grandchildren and more on the way. The old musical pastimes had for the most part been incorporated into weddings, christenings, and other life-cycle parties, now big catered affairs, as well as into community festivals, dances at the St. Nicholas Parish hall, and the Greek nightclubs in the Sponge Docks district of Tarpon. The tsambóuna and the old songs had assumed iconic status and were foregrounded at climactic moments in the order of events.

When Bill died in 1992, Nikitas combined with my father to convince the priest to say the liturgy at the funeral home, which was quite irregular. In a gesture of remarkable solidarity, Nikitas attended with his wife and daughters and played the *mirologia* (laments). A few months later I moved with our young son to Tarpon. Invited into the society of our kind Greek friends, I noticed that village-style dancing thrived, but music and singing had become the province of popular entertainers—dazzling electric bouzouki players and clarinetists, and velvet-throated singers, as was also the case in Greece and southeastern Europe. As in many parts of the world, the unaccompanied singing tradition was being laid aside, both repertoire and style.

Noting a decline in the repertoire, I proposed a documentation project to the City of Tarpon Springs and the National Endowment of the Arts, with the object of capturing on tape the complete range of vocal music and dance still practiced in the Tsimouris family, and of learning more about both instrumental and vocal genres as they functioned in performance practice and in the life and memory of the community. This would be one of the few recorded studies made of singing and tsambóuna together in a naturalistic setting, with fairly sophisticated equipment. It would also be a continuation of the work of cultural feedback begun by the Florida Folklife Program, aiming to consolidate and reflect back to the community, as well as to the Tsimouris family, a rich and relatively unexplored vein of their culture.

Nikitas readily acquiesced to the idea of a recording project, as did his sister Thea Nomikí, who had kept up her singing, but the married women in the family were reluctant at first, having lost the habit of singing regularly. Mrs. Tsimouris's responsibilities would not to allow her to give herself over entirely to frivolities. Nevertheless, she and Nikitas's other sisters, Thea Maria Ellenas and Thea Fotiní (Focaina) Skandaliaras, tentatively agreed to help out. Unlike the children of the Italian immigrants I had worked with several years before, who were shamed by their parents' music because it lacked support or context in the community, the Tsimouris's children and grandchildren were proud to assist, and did so with verve.

We began in early fall 1994. The setting we chose for recording was one in which these activities had often taken place and in which everyone felt most at home: the Tsimouris's kitchen. I used a TEAC portable DAT recorder on loan from the Florida Folklife Program, and Sanheiser stereo cardioid microphones. Achieving a perfectly balanced microphone placement for the bagpipes, vocals, and percussive dancing was beyond my competence, but we concocted a setup that worked fairly well.

Almost at once Nikitas's breath began to fail him. Not one to be frustrated, he devised an auxiliary for his weakened lungs. By trial and error, he had a mechanic friend build him a compressor that would generate a flow of air roughly equivalent to his own breath. To this he attached plastic tubing, and after trying various sizes and lengths for the amount of flow needed, he attached the other end to the air pipe of his bag. Although the compressor was penetratingly loud, if placed at a distance of several feet behind a closed and sealed door, it was drowned out by the sound of the bagpipes and was undetected even by my sensitive microphones. Compressor and tubing, mike stands, recording cables, and improvised baffling; extra people, children, chairs, and stools; and the bulk of the aunts—all had to be accommodated in the Tsimourises' small, agreeable kitchen.

A trickle of cognac, introduced at our first meetings, overcame the reticence of the aunts and gave me the courage to plunge ahead, in spite my limited knowledge of both Greek folk music and digital recording techniques. On September 18, October 7, 15, and 17, and November 2 and 29, 1994, and on March 26, 1998, we recorded five hours of music and commentary, as well as fairy tales told by Thea Focaina Skandaliaras. One session took place on the stage of the Tarpon Springs Cultural Center stage.

A Greek American folklore student from the University of South Florida made a first pass at the song lyrics. I thought that being able to review them at length with the performers would solve the problems of transcription and translation, but Nikitas and his family weren't able to fill in all the gaps and had little patience for the task. The following summer I consulted my mother-in-law, Maria Chairetakis, in Greece, who understood the Kalymnian dialect and knew many of the songs. With her help a near-complete set of lyric transcriptions in Greek was produced. The subsequent theft of the computer containing this work was so discouraging that I put the project aside until 2009.

Repertoire and Song Typologies

The family's repertoire of songs and instrumental pieces consisted mainly of social music, but also included the cycle of wedding songs; cradle rocking verses (a lullaby); and emigration songs, also called mirologia (laments). We recorded twenty-six different songs plus variants—all the songs that the participants could recall at the time with the exception of funeral laments, which are held to be inauspicious to perform out of context, and *kalanda* (carols), of which those the Tsimouris family knew were virtually identical to those sung throughout Greece. Work songs they scarcely recollected but they said that the bagpipe tunes applying to social occasions were used to enliven the men on the sponge boats, the shepherds on the hillsides, and the farmers and laborers in their orchards, and further that the songs used to accompany work were love songs. Though forgotten songs and lyrics later surfaced, the family's core repertoire—at least as it survived and continued to play a part in social life in this country—appears to have been covered. Comparison of this with other, broader collections of Kalymnian songs made in Greece indicates that there may have been gaps and substitutions in the lyrics as sung by the Tsimourises.

The performers described their songs in ways that might be familiar to scholars of Greek music but were new to me, and contrasted with what I had learned about musical typology in southern Italy, where in a given territory a handful of melodies and a characteristic performance style accompanied scores of eight-line lyric poems, many of them unique, others more widely known. Nikitas explained that some Kalymnian songs apply to specific social functions and ritual occasions, but they are classified primarily by rhythmic motif and melodic mode. Melody and rhythm identify songs more than do specific texts; the same verses and refrains turn up in many songs. With Nikitas's help I prepared the following overlapping classification scheme so as to illustrate how Kalymnians variously describe and order their songs.

(1) Social occasion, sequence of activities, and/or *mood*:

- Table songs (*tou trapeziou*)
- Dance songs (*yia khoro*)

(2) Rhythm/dance steps:

- *Issós/Sousta*
- *Kalamatianós*
- *Syrtós*

(3) Tempo (corresponding to rhythm/dance steps):

- Slow
- Moderate
- Fast

(4) Place of origin:

In the Dodecanese cultural and commercial universe:

Kalymnos, Kos, Pari, Kriti, Kefalonia, Kalamata, Halki, Kasos, Leros, Paros

(5) Social function:
- Social songs:
  - *Erotiká* (love songs)
  - *Pismatiká*
  - *Mantinades* (table songs)
  - Serenades
  - *Kantades* (composed popular songs that entered the folk repertoire primarily from Kefalonia and the Ionian region of Greece)
- Ritual songs:
  - *Yia gamos* (wedding songs)
  - *Mirologia* (funeral laments)
  - *Yia apokries* (carnival)
  - *Kalanda* (Christmas season carols)
- Songs associated with work and household tasks:
  - *Nanourismata* (cradle songs)
  - Other songs not remembered
- Patriotic songs:
  - Epic narrative fragments (*akrites*, or border guard songs from the Byzantine period)
  - Songs of emigration, also called *mirologia* (laments)

(6) The way lyrics are deployed:
- *Skopós* (mode, melodic motif) with signature opening verses plus improvised and stock verses added on at will (the more common type).
- Skopós with fixed, designated texts.

A song is identified primarily by its skopós, a term more or less signifying "mode" and designating a melodic motif, pattern, or scale. Traditional Greek instrumentalists rely upon it to describe their pieces, but few sources deal with the concept. A Macmillan music study guide provides an explanation that fits the approach to musical production by the tsambóuna player: "The skopós is built upon a melodic skeleton from which the pitches are connected by ornaments and played in a fixed or free meter." In both multi-instrumental and vocal performances, "a group of musicians called a *paréa* [company, group] play the tune in heterophony, meaning that they interpret the same melody in slightly different ways" (http://spotlightonmusic.macmillanmh.com).

Specific texts, sequences of verses, and storylines are secondary to the skopós. Most songs in the category of social music have a few verses—sometimes only one or two—that are specific to one tune. The remaining verses are "migratory," as Nikitas put it, drawn by the singer(s) from a common pool, as their feelings and memories inspire them. However they begin, the singers often shift to *pismatiká* (see below), when the verses belonging to their original song are exhausted while the singers are still warming up. Thus it is that many songs last as long as the singers wish to sing them. Often, too, when the tsambóuna is being played, one tune will transition into another, and that tune into yet another, producing a continuous stream of music lasting for as long as thirty and forty minutes or more, with singing weaving in and out of the drone of the pipes, quieting down and heating up, in the foreground and receding.

Even as lyrics are handled in this pragmatic and flexible way, they are prized for their poetic content. Nikitas would say that he kept a light heart because the scores of verses he knew "lived in his mind." "The songs of then were really into love," said his daughter, Irene, then about twenty. "They're romantic, like Romeo and Juliet. They touched a woman's feelings."

Love Songs

Pandote ta tragoudhia itan yiá tous érotes—"All [our] songs were about love," Mrs. Tsimouris said. Love songs are a category that embraces nearly all others—dance songs, table songs, pismatiká, kantades, songs for working, wedding songs—if nothing else by means of verses of love and courtship "thrown in" to other songs. *"O Potamos"* (The River), in syrtós rhythm, may also be used as a table song. Its refrain addresses the river: "Oh River with your waves, your whirling waters." Focaina Skandaliaras led the singing, with the group repeating each line.

Opening refrain: *E . . . Potamé, ta kimatá sou*
A ta strifo—, ta strifo ki' i yirismatá sou

Katsisma: *Ela ela me ta ména, ki as' ti mána pou se yenna (2)*

M'íthela, m'íthela tos' sti zoi mou (2)
Akh n'a sou na, na sou na tairi mou (2)

Katsisma: *Ela ela ela pali, khiotiko mou portokali (2)*

Na sou stro—, na sou strono na kimase (2)
Aspro peristeri mou, na sou n'a tairi mou (2)

Katsisma: *Ela ela me ta ména, ki 'as ti mana pou se yenna (2)*

Ta matá—, ta matákia sou ta mavra (2)

Sung as refrain: *Ta matákia sou ta mavra, pou na t'ákhases na ta vra (2)*

To matió, to matió sou to trighiri (2)
To matió, kai o erotas pekhnidhi (2)

Katsisma* [refrain]*: *Ela ela me ta ména, ki as' ti mána pou se yenna (2)*

M'eipa sou, m'eipa sou to skilla [*sic*] *kori (2)*
Sto yialó, sto yialó mi kateveineís [*sic*] *(2)*

Yia ti tha—, yia ti thalassa fortouna
Tha se pa—, tha se parei na pniyeis

K'an me pa—, ki'an me pareis pou tha pao? (2)
Mesa sta, mesa sta vathiá nerá (2)

Kano to, kano to kormí mou varka (2)
A kai ta khe—, kai ta kheria mou koupiá (2)
Ta malliá, ta malliá tis kefalis mou (2)
Alisí—, alisides kai skiniá (2)

Katsisma: *Ela ela ela me ta ména, ki 'as ti mána pou se yenna (2)*

Eh . . . River, your waves
Your whirling—, your whirling and spinning

Come, come with me and leave the mother who bore you

He wanted me, he wanted me so much all my life
Ah, to be—, to be my mate

Come, come, come again, orange from Chios

I will lay—, I will lay you down to sleep
My white dove, to make you my mate

Come, come to my side, and leave the mother who bore you

Your eyes, your pretty black eyes

Your pretty black eyes
Where did you lose them so I can find them?

Your eyes, your dark eyes
Your eyes, and your playthings of love

Come, come to my side, and leave the mother who bore you

I told you, bad girl
Don't go down to the seashore

For the sea, the sea is rough
It will take—, it will take you and drown you

And if you take, and if you take me where will I go?
Down into, down into the deep waters

I will make, I will make my body into a boat
And my hands, and my hands into oars

The hair, the hair of my head
Into chains, into chains and ropes

Come, come to my side and leave the mother who bore you.

"Magdaliní," a family favorite, is a satirical, playful love song.

O Magdaliní Magdaliní
Kateva kato stin avlí
Na se dó, na se gnorizo
Kai na se glikó filiso
Kátisma: *Okh amán, okh amán Magdaliní* **[Repeat all]**

Magdaliní, ton andra sou (3)
Vále to sto zebilli

Kai kremasé to sta psilá (3)
Na min ton fan i psili
***Kátsisma:** Okh amán, okh amán Magdaliní*

Dhen eisoun eisai pou m'oúlegheis [*sic*] *(3)*
San dhen me dhis pothéneis

Kai tora perpatás kai les (3)
Pou m'edhes pou me dhe' kseres

Miskokarfiá mou kokkini (3)
Me saranda fila
***Kátsisma:** Okh amán, okh amán Magdaliní* [**Repeat all**]

Saranda s'agapisane (3)
Mono ego se pira.

Oh Magdaliní, Magdaliní
Come down in the yard
So I can see you, so I can know you
So I can sweetly kiss you
Oh amán [expression of sorrow], oh amán, Magdaliní

Magdaliní, your husband
Put him in your carrying hod

And hang him up high
So the fleas don't eat him
Oh amán, oh amán, Magdaliní

Wasn't it you who was telling me
That without seeing me you die

And now you walk around and say
That you see me and don't know me

My scented red carnation
With forty petals
Oh amán, oh amán, Magdaliní

Forty men loved you
I alone snared you.

Pismatiká

Song lyrics also have a powerful in-the-moment social dimension. Pismatiká (which can be translated as back talk) are teasing couplets usually exchanged by a group of three or four women, followed by a refrain. The verses are improvised as well as pulled from a common reservoir, and may be gossipy or competitive; but the spirit is mainly one of fun, intended to provoke friendly laughter and amusement. I asked why the women so often shifted from other songs into the pismatiká mode. "Because that's what comes up," was the reply—*"Ti allo peksame?"* (What else are we going to play at?). It was evident that the pismatiká are indeed a form of play, and that these island women relished the game as they returned to it again and again.

The pismatiká are a manifestation of the poetic duel, the contest in song, which is one of the most fertile veins in the oral traditions of West Africa, Central Asia, southern Europe, and the Caribbean. Of great resilience and apparently long use (judging by its diffusion among ancient pastoral peoples), the practice may be employed in displays of ethnic supremacy and male proficiency, stamina, and valor. It is used in courtship and as a means of social and political criticism. Its functions may be those of social control or revenge; of harmonization or the provocation of conflict; of winning patronage, respect, or gaining the advantage in a superior love match. Verses can be boastful, flirtatious, teasing, slanderous, admonitory, insulting, or obscene; and no subject or target is sacred. The Central Italian *contraste* were witty exchanges setting forth in song the opposing views and feelings of the participants. Examples of the type range from the toasts of Georgian mountaineers, the lengthy song duels of Sardinian shepherds, the *botta e riposta* of Central Italy, the *controversia* and *décima* of the Spanish-speaking Caribbean, to calypso and many more. Even where there is only one singer, many songs of the circum-Mediterranean region seem to represent one side of a conversation, argument, or act of persuasion or vilification.[2]

In Kalyminian pismatiká, singers take turns leading with the verses they prefer or that come to mind. The couplets and refrains are sung in tonal unison with some rhythmic heterophony. Often the voices in the refrains overlap in such a way as to create rhythmic tension and syncopation so that the pismatiká go into overdrive, becoming a kind of rapping, in spirit and musical effect. Watching the two Nomikís and Focaina lean into the singing circle one by one with their verses, it occurred to me that "playing at" pismatiká could be a pleasurable way of working through tensions and contradictory emotions arising from continuous proximity and interdependence among women confined to a small group of kinsmen and neighbors, as they had been.

"O Voskós kai o Vassiliás" (The Shepherd and the King) is a dialogic song in the issós rhythm that was used in Kalymnos during Carnival, when bagpipers and little groups of revelers went busking from house to house. The performance recorded by the Tsimourises, which morphs into pismatiká, exemplifies the protean character of Kalymnian folk singing. The shepherd lover and his charms is a motif that recurs in a number of songs in the family's repertoire. Alternating solo voices, or solo alternating with group, repeat each verse.

First motif, refrain (repeated twice):
O voskós, amáni, aramáni
O voskós, voskó ki' o vasiliás

Second motif (repeated twice):
O voskós, voskós ki' o vasiliá, stíkhima i vásane [stékhima pron. 'stíkhima']

Stékhima [sic], amáni aramáni
Stékhima, amáni vasane

Stékhima i vásane, kai stekhimatizane

Voskós: *"Pes mou afendi vasiliá, ti pou vazeis stékhima?"*

Vassiliá: *"Vazo ti amáni aramáni,*
Vazo ti vasílissa

Vazo ti vasílissa, me to vasilikí tis"

Vasiliá: *"Pes kai esei, amáni aramáni,*
Pes kai esei, kale voské,

"Pes kai esei, kale voské, ti pou vazeis stékhima?"

Voskós: *"Vaso khília próvata, amáni aramáni*
Vaso khí—, khilia próvata
Vaso khília próvata, me ta aryiró koúdhouna"

Voskós: *"Vazo kai, amání, aramáni*
Vazo kai ena kaló arní

Vazo kai enan kaló arní, me metasko to mallí"

Vasílissa: *"Akh, ki' eimouna, amáni aramáni*
Akh, ki' as ei—, eimoun kómissa
Akh, ki' as eimoun kómissa, n'amou kai tirokómissa"

Additional verses:
Vasílissa: *"Na tirokó—, amání, aramáni mou*
Na tirokó, —ko mou to madrí
N'avgazo kaló tirí kai mizithra dhrosirí"

The shepherd
The shepherd, shepherd and the king

The shepherd, shepherd and the king made a bet

Wager, amani aramani
Wager, amani they laid

They laid a wager and they bet

Shepherd: "Tell me, my lord king, what are you betting for?"

King: "I'm betting, amani aramani
I'm betting the queen"

"I'm betting the queen and her prince"

King: "Now you tell me, amani aramani
You say, good shepherd

Now you tell me, good shepherd, what you're betting on"

Shepherd: "I'm wagering a thousand sheep, amani aramani
I'm wagering a thou—, a thousand sheep

I'm betting a thousand sheep, with their silver bells"

Shepherd: "And I'm throwing in a nice lamb, with hair of silk"

Queen: "Ah, if I were only, amani aramani
Ah, if I were only a goatherd

Ah, if I were only a goatherd, I could be a cheese maker too"

Other verses:
"If I could be a cheese—, amani aramani
If I could make cheese with my flock
I would make good goat cheese and fresh mizithra"

This song transitions naturally into *"Ala Roudja Voskaroudja."* The Tsimourises explained that *ala roudja, roudja, roudja* [or, *routsa*], the typical refrain of the pismatiká, resembles "mana, mana, mana" (Mother, Mother, Mother), a common interjection in Greek folk and *rembetiko* music. Irene Tsimouris and Nomikí and Petroula Sazalis (Nikitas's daughter and granddaughters, of similar age) were present and danced throughout this recorded sequence. The kitchen was packed with family and guests, dancing, stomping, whistling, and singing pismatiká. After the leader, the chorus repeats each couplet and the last two lines of each tercet as well as the refrain.

Panathená ti mana sou,
Kai me ti ne dhikiá mou

Kai me ti ne dhikiá mou,
Kai dhen mas ipadhrévghane
Na sou tora dhikí mou

Katsisma (refrain): *Ela ela me ta ména, na pernás kharitomena*

A, to voskaroúi sto vounoú
Sfirizei kselakonei

A, sfirizei kselakonei
Ki' i eremí tou i sfiriá
Ta mesa mou ta lioni

Katsisma: *Alla roudja roudja roudja, ta mikrá ta voskaroudja*

Kardhiá an eisai apó yiallí
Vastá kai mi raghisseis

Vastá kai mi raghizeis
Kai an eisai apó sidhero
Kalá na yondiseis

Kai an eisai apó sidhero
Kalá na yondiseis

A ghália ghália me keró
K'i ora dhen ikháthei
Ki' ora dhen ikháthei
Kai me ta vótana tis yís
Yia trévonde ta pathi
Katsisma: *Ela ela me ta ména, ki 'as ti mana pou se yenna*

Matia kai fridhia kai malliá
Pou t'akhei to poulí mou

Pou t'akhei to poulí mou
Ma einai kai pismatariko pou lei tha yinei
Ki' kopse ti zoí mou

Katsisma: *Ela ela me ta ména, ki 'as ti mana pou se yenna*

A, ta matia sou einai kafenés
Ta fridhia sou balkoni

Ta fridhia sou balkoni
P'ourkhonde kai glendizoune
I meraklidhes olli

Katsisma: *Ala roúes roúes roués, i mikrés o voskaroúes*

Sto meraklido ta khartiá
Eimai ki'ego grameni

Eimai ki'ego grameni
Eimai sta khili yelastí
kai sti kardhiá kameni

Katsisma: *Ela ela me ta ména, ki 'as ti mana pou se yenna*

Curses on your mother
And on mine too

And on mine too
They should have married us
So you would now be mine

Come, come with me, to live happily

Ah, the shepherd on the mountain
Whistles to gather his flock

Ah, he whistles to gather his flock
And the call of his whistling
Melts my insides

Alla roudja roudja roudja, that little shepherd girl

Heart, if you are made of glass
Hold it so you won't shatter

Hold on so you won't break
But if you're made of iron
You can take it

Slowly, slowly and with time
Time won't be wasted

Time won't be lost
For with the greens of mountain soil
The passions heal

Come, come with me and leave the mother who bore you

The eyes, brows, and hair
My sweetheart has!

That my sweetheart has
But she's stubborn and whatever she says goes
That she scares me half to death

Come, come with me and leave the mother who bore you
She scares me half to death

Ah, your eyes are brown
And your brows are balconies

Your brows are balconies
Where are all the enthusiasts going to party?

Ala roués roués roués, the little shepherd lads

On the roll of the party-goers
My name is written too

My name is written
And my lips are smiling
But my poor heart is burning

Come, come with me and leave the mother who bore you.

Table Songs

At festivities and gatherings, the men and women and friends of the family would sit together after eating to sing table songs in quiet gaiety with wine, spirits, nuts, and fruits before them: *Kathomaste to yiro, pinome krasaki, kai leme kathe tragoudhi* (We sit around the table, drink a little wine, and sing all of our songs). Of old, the Tsimourises would gather every Sunday afternoon to sing, consuming several gallons of retsina between them. The singing of table songs is more than casual merrymaking. It has a quasi-ritual character clearly evident in the *kathisto glendi* in the conservative villages of the island of Karpathos, as well in the toasts and table singing of the Caucasus and the Balkans. For the Tsimourises, as for many Greeks in new lands or for those left behind, table singing served the purpose of integrating cultural memory with present experience, of sharing the experience of personal and historical loss as well as the pleasure of the occasion.

"Varkamou Boyiatismeni" (My Painted Boat) was a favorite of Nomikí A. Tsimouris, who used to sing it to me over the phone, and led it in this recording:

Main motif
Nomikí A.: *E . . . kaimeni mou kardhiá, krata kai mi raghizeis*
Group: *O . . . kaimeni mou kardhiá, krata kai mi raghizeis*

Refrain motif
Leader: *Varka mou boyiá—, varka mou boyiatismeni*
Sta kaponia, sta kaponia kremasmeni
Group: *Varka mou boyiatismeni, sta kaponia kremasmeni* [**Sung as above.**]

Main: *[***Omitted:*** *Kardhiá mou, an eisai apó sidhero]*
Kai . . . an . . . vasaná ta, kalá na t'ayodhiseis

Ela me to ga—, ela me to gazolini,
Pou einai i thala—, pou einai i thalassa galini

E . . . dhen ne boró ta matiá mou psi—, psilá na ta sikoso
[Kai tis kaimenis mou kardhias, parigoriá na dhoso]

Dhen s'arnioume, dhe—, dhe' s'arnioume, dhen s'arnioume
Mono sou pará—, mono sou paraponioúme
Kai . . . kai tis kaimenis mou kardhiás tha—, parigoriá na dhoso

To matió sou, to ma—, to matió to mavradhi
Zotaní me—, zotaní me pa' ston Adi

A . . . dhos mou Thée mou eponomí os ei—, os eidhoses stis petras

A . . . kai Panayiá, Panayiá mou parigora
I kardhiá mou, i kardhiá mas aftí tin ora

A . . . os eidhoseis sto aidhonioú khri—, ssá fterá ki' peta

A . . . Panayiá mou ki' as—, Panayiá ki 'as provalei
Nato dho ki 'as sviyei pali

Akh . . . Thée mou, mi t'a sou kanna (ekane) kai me pedheveis toso

A . . . Panayiá mou dho—, Panayiá mou dhos tous khrónia
San tes lemo—, san tis lemoniá ta klonia

An einai yia pandotiná, pare me na glitoso na glitoso

As . . . sti yí vathó, as sti yí vathó ti yis vrondá,
A . . . sti yis ta pathi mou rotá **[Cuts off before group repetition.]**

Eh . . . My poor heart, bear it, don't break
Oh . . . my poor heart, bear it, don't break

My painted boat, my painted boat
Tied up at the dock

[*Omitted:* Heart, if only you were made of iron
So you could better bear your troubles]

Come bring the gas—, come bring the gasoline
For the sea, the sea is milky blue

Eh . . . I can't raise, I can't raise my eyes
[*Omitted*: I must give my poor heart consolation]

I'm not denying, not, not denying you, not denying you
I'm only complaining to you

Your eyes, eyes, your black eyes
They send me straight to Hell [Hades]
Ah . . . give me patience, my Lord, like you gave to the rocks

Ah . . . and Holy Mother give hope
To my heart, to my heart, right now

Like you gave to the nightingale
Golden wings so it could fly

Ah . . . my Holy Mother, Holy Mother as he comes
See how he goes away again

Ah . . . my God, what have I done that you torment me so?

Ah . . . my Holy Mother, give them, give them years
As many as the lemon trees, the lemon trees have branches

If it's forever, take me and caress me

Let the deep ground, let the deep ground of the earth
Let the earth swallow up my pains.

Table singing is essentially serious and spiritual, a collective, vocalized meditation. The company gathers as though to perform devotions to the emotional-poetic aspect of being. In isolated, conservative villages such as those on Karpathos where pastoralism has been the main source of livelihood, the singing of mantinades was almost exclusively an intensely male ritual (Caraveli-Chaves 1985; Kavouras 1993). The men expressed their views and feelings on a variety of topics, addressing the company in fifteen-syllable rhymed couplets expressing the views and feelings of the singers and appropriate to the occasion. "This form of poetic expression occurs in the context of a sit-down musical celebration . . . amongst a group of men. It often happens spontaneously in various settings while wine and food are served" (Apella Nota).

Even during celebrations, a gathering inward of thought and emotion is mustered for the performance of these songs (see www.olymbos.org/music). Most table songs are in issós (slow and even) rhythm, and some may be danced as well. They are often preceded by introductory phrases sung in free rhythm, or played on the bagpipe if accompanied. These are equivalent to the rubato parlando passages of melody preceding an instrumental piece, known in Arabic as *taksim* or *maqaam*, and in Greek as *taksimi*. The lamentations are called *amanes*, signifying "Alas!" or "Have pity!" from the Turkish, and also form a subcategory of table songs.

Mantinades were similarly sung in the homes and coffee houses of Kalymnos, where, however, pastoralists in patri-groups intersected with a more uxorious horticultural, sponging, mercantile culture. Immigrants have led the way in bringing women increasingly to the fore in family and community life. In gatherings of the vivacious Tsimouris family the female voice prevailed even during table singing. A song about immigration, *"Maroúli"* (Lettuce), is one about which Mrs. Tsimouris commented: *"Aftos einai skopós varismenes"*—this is a very heavy (grave and sad) song.

Leader 1: *E . . . o kaimeni Kálimnos,*
Group: *Kaimeni Kálimnos*
Leader 1: *E . . . kaimeni Kálimnos, —ola roula*
Group: *Mavrisan ta vouná sou (2)*
Group, Leader 2: *O kaimeni Kálimnos, maroúli,*
Leader 2: *Mavrisan ta vouná sou*

Kai éfigan, vlepe tous, Panayiá mou
Efigan ta levendó pedjiá [*sic*]
A ki' efigan levé— ndó pedja, maroúli
Efighen ti khará sou
Efe— to pedja, maroúli
Kai fighen ti khará sou

Thée, kai megalo, —o dhinamé
Thée megalo dhinamé
Thée megalo dhinamé, akh maroúli
Meghalo t'onomá sou!
Megalo dhinamé, akh maroúli
Meghalo t'onomá sou

E . . . filo dhen pefti apó dhendrí
Filo dhen pefti apó dhendrí
O filo dhe peft— apó dhendrí, akh maroúli
Dhikhos to thelimá sou
Filo dhe pefti a— pó dhendrí, maroúli
Dhikhos to thelimá sou

E . . . opios 'gapá me—lakhrinó
Opios agapá melakhrinó
Opios 'gapá me—lakhrinó, maroúli
Prepi na to dhilonni
Opios agapá melakhrino
Prepi na to dhilonni

Kai yiatí ekhei ston'eró— ota
Kai yiatí ekhei ston'eróta, maroúli
Logariasmó na dhosi.
Opa! Clapping

[**Other verses:**
Figane ta omorfiá sou
Pali figane ta khará sou
O kaimeni Kálimnos, maroúli
Mavrisan ta vouná sou.]

Eh . . . unlucky Kalymnos
Poor Kalymnos
Eh . . . unlucky Kalymnos, ola roula
Your beloved mountains are in mourning

And they've gone, look at them, Holy Mother
Your fine young men have gone, maroúli
And your fine young men
Your joys have departed maroúli
The flower of your youth, maroúli
And your joys have fled

God almighty
Oh God, great and strong
God, great and strong, ah, maroúli
Great is Thy name
All mighty, ah, maroúli
Great is Thy name

Eh . . . the leaf doesn't fall from the tree
The leaf doesn't fall from the tree
The leaf doesn't fall, from the tree, ah, maroúli
Against Thy will
The leaf doesn't fall, from the tree, ah, maroúli
Against Thy will

Eh . . . whoever loves a dark-haired man
Whoever loves a dark-haired man
Whoever loves a dark-haired man, maroúli
Better declare it
Whoever loves a dark-haired man, maroúli
Better declare it
Because when you're in love
When you're in love, maroúli
There's a price to pay

[*Other verses:*
Your beautiful ones have gone
And your joys have also fled
Oh poor Kalymnos, maroúli
Your mountains are in mourning.]

DANCE SONGS AND METRIC FORMS

Table singing may be punctuated with dancing, or vice versa. At the Tsimouris home, bagpiping inevitably led into dancing, in the measured issós meter, or with slow songs being sped up to transition into a sousta. All dances are performed by two or more dancers—often a roomful—progressing with linked arms counterclockwise in an arc.

Tsambóuna music is played primarily for dancing, and Nikitas paced along with the dancers as he set the complex seven- and thirteen-beat rhythms. From our first recording session in the Tsimouris's kitchen, it was clear that he was at his best when playing off of the singers and dancers. Nikitas explained that a bagpiper should stand in the middle of the dancers and keep pace with the leader so that the leader would not lose his steps. This places the orchestra at the center of the dance, a typically African arrangement. "At a dance the bagpiper is supposed to control the dance, and listen to the singer and watch the singer. He measures himself with the singer, who dances and sings at the same time."

The Tsimouris family sang as they danced, their stamping feet, clapping, rhythmic whistling, and calls of "opa" making up the rhythm section of their little orchestra. The pismatiká also provide rhythmic texture and drive, and the women often broke out into pismatiká rapping in the excitement of dancing. Occasionally, Nikitas would hold the air pressure with his arms while singing a line or two of a song himself. As mentioned above, singing while playing is also common in the gaida music of Thrace and Bulgaria.

Dances are named and classified by rhythm, and every tune has a rhythmic designation. They are also described by the number of steps in each measure. The issós has five steps, and is written in 2/4 time. Its tempo is slow to very slow. It is danced smoothly ("flat"), without any bounce. The sousta is a speeded-up version of the issós, and is danced with short springing hops and kicks, and can become quite wild. The word "sousta" derives from an Italian word for the springs of a carriage (Dietrich 1976). The issós and the sousta have become the typical dances of the Dodecanese, but each island has its own style.

The "*Kotikos*" or "*I Yialla*" is a dance and song from Kos in issós meter. Nikitas and his sisters said that "i yialla" was an old form of greeting. Since the song is from Kos, which was under heavy Turkish occupation and influence, it is an outside possibility that the phrase derives from the Arabic "*Ya Allah*," which means "Dear God," or "God help me," a form of salutation. Alternating leaders and chorus sing while dancing and clapping.

Katsisma **[refrain]*:*** *E . . . dhos tous, Pana— yiá mou, dhos tous khronia*
San tis lemoniá ta klonia

Leader 1: *E . . . Thée megalo dhiname*
Yialla! Megalo t'onomé, megalo to onomá sou
Leader 2: *E megalo dhinamé*
With group: *Megalo to onomá sou!*

Leader 1: *E . . . dhos tous, Pana— yiá mou, dhos tous,*
T'akhei o nous to logoyismós tous
Group: *Dhos tous, Pana— yiá mou, dhos tous,*
T'akhei o nous to logoyismós tous

[Each couplet is repeated by the leader, then a second leader and/or the group:]

E . . . filo dhen peftei apó dhendrí, yialla!
Khorís to theli—, khorís to thelimá sou

E . . . s'agapo yia— tí eisai oreos
O dhen tou miazi allos neos

Opa!

Ekhoun keró ta matia mou, yialla
Na dhoune ta, na dhoune ta dhiká sou

E . . . ela me to takhidhromo
O pou 'nai ghrighora sto dhromo
E . . . ki'ekhoun paraponо frikhtó, yialla
Na klapsoune pro—, na klapsoune prostá sou

E . . . ela ela, me ta ména
E ki'as ti mana pou se yenna!

Opa!

Kho!

A . . . stin emprostela tou khoroú, yialla
Kai parakí, kai parakí ligaki

[**Omitted**: *Stekete miá miskakarfiá / Me ti mesimeraki*
A . . . Ki' vleppe toutoto mou tous, Panayiá mou
O pou n'einai i pa— rigoriá mou]

A . . . stekete mia ga—, garifalo,
Me to mesime—, me to mesimeraki
Stekete mia ga—, garifalo, yialla
Me to garifalé, me to garifalaki

Op!

A . . . dhos tis, Panayiá, khronakia
San tou dhiosmou, o ta klonaikia

[Dancing and clapping continues.]

Op!

Op!

Op!

Op!

Op!

Opa!
Op! Opa!

Op!

Opa, opa, opa!

Eh . . . give them, Holy Mother, give them as many years
As the lemon tree has branches

Eh . . . almighty God
Yialla! Great is your name, great is your name!
And great is your power
Great is your name!

Eh . . . give them, Holy Mother, give them
Give them reason in their minds (repeat)

Eh . . . A leaf doesn't fall from the tree, yialla!
Without, without Your wish

Eh . . . I love you because you're handsome
Oh other youths don't compare with you

My eyes have time to look at you, yialla!
To see, to see what's theirs

Eh . . . let the mail come soon
Oh may it be quick upon the road

Eh . . . and they [my eyes] have bitter complaints
To weep to you

Eh . . . come, come to be mine [come to me?]
Eh . . . and leave the mother who bore you

Ah . . . at the edge of town [there's a guy], yialla
And just over there, just over there a little

Stands a carnation
With a sunflower [?]

Ah . . . and watch over him, my Holy Mother
Oh, for he's my consolation
There stands a carnation
With the scented blossoms [?]

Ah . . . give them, Holy Mother, as many of those years
As the mint has little shoots

Also notable was an issós performed one evening when the group met at the little theater of the Tarpon Springs Cultural Center. Here their serpentine line dancing had full scope and one can hear the sounds of their feet measuring the 2/4 beat of the issós on the boards. The prolonged, haunting prelude functions to stabilize the airflow from the bag through the pipes, creates suspense and anticipation, and allows the singers to prepare.

They followed this with a sousta performed on tsambóuna, with clapping, dancing, stamping, loud whistling, and singing pismatiká:

Opa

Opa

Leader: *Dhen eimai se dhiáthesi*
Yiá na tragoudhiso
Kharitirei tis pareas mou
Pali tha to kiniso (2)
Group: *Pali tha to kiniso*

Ela ela ela, mikrí mou ela
Ela pou na se feroune
Nekró sti yitoniá mou
Kai na se saranone
Ta khéria ta dhiká mou [**Repeat verse.**]

Khristé mou ki'as i provale
Me to mantili sto lemó
Kai me ti kinaraki

Pismatiká kai pismata
Se ména dhen pernoune
Yiatí eimai eleftheró pedhí
Kai me parakouloune

Dhen eimai se dhiáthesi
To kefi mou einai ligo
Yiatí dhen t'oda símera
To kókkino mou milo

Matia frídhia kai malliá
Pou t'akhi to poulí mou
Einai kai pismatariko
Kai kopse ti zoí mou

Theé megalo dhíname
Pou miazeis kardhiás mou
Kane ta sinefa vrokhí
Na sviseis ta fotiá mou

Coda: *Osi dhen khorevoune*
Einai pou zilevoune.

I'm not in the mood
For dancing
But to bring enjoyment to my companions
I will do it anyway
I will do it anyway

Come, come, come, my girl, come on
Come on, let them bring you
Dead into my neighborhood
So I can wrap you with mourning bandages
With my own hands

My Christ I wish he would appear
A little shepherd lad
With a scarf around his neck
And a staff in his hand

Your wisecracks and retorts
Don't bother me
Because I'm a carefree guy
And they're begging me [to marry their daughters]
I'm not in the mood for dancing
I'm not feeling very inspired
Because today I haven't seen
My little red apple

The eyes, brows, and hair
Of my little bird
They are something to talk about
And they tear me apart

God all mighty
Who knows my heart

Make the clouds rain
To put out my fire

Those who don't dance
Don't dance because they're jealous.

The syrtós uses twelve steps and is in 4/4 time, making a slow three-beat and quick two-beat-quick two-beat pattern. Of ancient origin and enjoyed also by the Ottomans, it is popular throughout Greece and the Diaspora; each island, region, and city has its own variant. The kalamatianós syrtós originated in the southern Peloponnese, where the first battles for independence from the Ottomans were fought, and is one of the oldest Greek dances. It uses the same steps and slow three-beat, two-beat two-beat rhythm as the syrtós, but is in 7/8 time—one of the complex additive rhythms used in Greece and the Balkans. In some areas the syrtós is performed by couples dancing in a circle. The Kalymnians have their own version, but Nikitas preferred the *kritikós syrtós* from Crete. In "*To Argalió*" (The Loom) each line is sung by a leader and repeated by the group.

Kori pou fai—, kori pou faineis st'argalió (2)
Kai faiveis kai ksefaineis, kai to nou mou eisai to pairneis (2)

Spase, Thée-, spase Thée mou t'arghalió (2)
N'avgó na kanno volta, na tin ne dho stin porta (2)

Kori, s'an pas, kori s'an pas stin ekklisia (2)
Proskéna kai yia ména, proskéna kai yia ména (2)

Yia na sothoún, yia na sothoún ta pismatá,
Pou s'oukho kano mena, proskéna kai yia ména (2)

Panáthema, panáthema tin mana sou (2)
Kai ména tin dhikiámou, kai eména tin dhikiámou (2)

Kori pou fai-, kori pou faineis t'arghalió (2)
Kai faiveis kai ksefaineis, kai to nou mou eisai to pairneis (2)

Pismatiká, pismatiká kai pismatá (2)
Se ména dhen pairnoune, se ména dhen pairnoune (2)

Yiatí eimai, yiatí eimai eleftheró paidhí (2)
Kai me perikaloune [**sic**] *kai me perikaloune (2)*

A pane na pis, pane na dheis sti mana sou (2) **[Man to woman or vice versa.]**
Na kanei kai alli yenna, na kanei alli yenna (2)

[Laughter]

Yia na kapsei ki' a-, na kapsi allineis kardhiá (2)
Ose ne kapse ména, na kanei alli yenna (2) **[Or repeat 1st phrase of line.]**

[Discussion]

[Man says to girl:]
Panáthema, panáthemame kai an kholió (2)
Pou s'ekha k'eikha s'ase, pou s'ekha k'eikha s'ase

Mono kholió, mono kholió tous kerous mou
To dhikó mou k'eikha s'ase, pou s'ekha k'eikha s'ase
Pou'ourkhómoun ki' vriskáse

Other verses:
Panathená ti mana sou kai mena, kai mena ti dhikiá mou (2)
Pou dhen mas padhrevasei, na sou tora dhikiá mou (2)

Pismatiká:
Kai me parakaloume
Pane na pis stis manasou
Na kanei kai alli yena
Yan a kapsi ki'allineis kardhiá
Ose kapsene mena

O girl weaving, weaving at the loom
Your constant weaving drives me crazy

Break, break the loom, Lord
So I can go out and see her at her door

Girl, if you go to church
Bow down and pray for [to?] me too

So they'll talk, talk and gossip
About what I've done to you, that you bow to me

Curses, curses on your mother
And on mine, and on mine

Girl, girl, weaving at the loom
You weave and weave and you take over my mind

[Talk, talk and wisecracking
Don't bother me]

[Look at me!] I'm a single man
And they're begging me [they're after me]

Ah, go tell your mother
To give birth to another like you

So she can burn another heart
The way mine burns—let her make another like you

Damn me if I'll grieve—
I had you and then I lost you

I only regret my old times
And the one I had that I lost

Damn your mother and damn mine
For not marrying us so you would be mine now

Wedding Songs and Cradle Songs

The traditional wedding cycle was long and many faceted, extending over days and weeks. We recorded as much of it as the family remembered, beginning with "*Penemata Tis Nifis*" (In Praise of the Bride), a song addressed to the bride before her wedding. Early in the morning before proceeding to the church, female relatives and friends go to the bride's house and gather in her bedroom while she dresses or is being dressed by an experienced woman. At another point in the preparations, praises are also sung to the groom (*gambros*). The women sang unaccompanied, with leaders and group in alternation; Nikitas joined in at the end.

I nifi mas i omorfí ipofaneromeni (2)
Epíre 'n andra emorfo, tin ekhei khadhemeni (2)

I mana ta se yenise evriskonda sta ori
Ki' troye rises tou vounoú kai kame tetia kori (2)

Gambros einai o neo aetos ki' i nifi peristeri (2)
Kai ta aniktá garifala i nei simpetheri (2)

Nifi to velós sou évales, vale kai ti tsimpidha (2)
Ki' omorfiá sou gráftike kai mes tin efimeridha (2)

Gabré mou dhroseré flasté n'apó ton abelona
Na se kharí i nifi mas s' ollo o neona (2)

Nifi, s'an se stoulósane stis ekklisiás sti mesi (2)
Kouniódhou o polli eleós sti yí kato na pesi (2)

Gabré zouboullí khiotiko nifis smirnias vio— lenda(2)
Nifi tis frenimadhes sou tis kánane kouvenda (2)

***Nikitas:** Nifí s'an se stolísane stis ekklisiás sti mesi (2)*
Mikrí megali t'ópane khará tis pou ton ekhei (2)

***Nikitas:** Gabré tin nifi n'agapás kai na mi tin egoghizeis (2)*
San to vasilikó tis yís na tin dhrosologhizeis (2)

***Focaina:** Tha poume alli?* **[Spoken: Shall we sing another verse?]**
Gabré ti nifi n'agapás kai mi ti ne malloneis
Kai na travás to paploma kai na ti koukouloneis (2)

[Laughter]

***Nomikí A.:** Kalá ikséromai.* **[We remembered well.]**

Our beautiful bride is shown everywhere
She got a handsome husband, and he has her spoiled

The mother who bore you was found in the mountains
Eating mountain roots, and she made such a daughter

The groom is the young eagle, the bride is the dove
And the new in-laws are the carnations in bloom

Bride you wore your scarf—put on your veil as well
And they will write about your beauty in the newspaper too

My groom is a fresh grapevine in the vineyard
Let him give joy to our bride all of her life

Bride, if they stood you in the middle of the church
All the hanging oil lamps would fall to the ground

Groom, blooming flower of Chios; bride, violet of Smyrna
Bride, they are extolling your virtues

Bride if they stood you in the middle of the church—
Young and old, we would all wish him happiness

Groom, you better love your bride and not mistreat her
Water her like the basil plant

Groom, you better love your bride and don't scold her
Cover her up in a quilt and cuddle her

The first dance of the wedding is the issós. The very last dance is the parianós, also in issós rhythm. It is a rite of farewell to the bride in which she crosses over to the groom's side. Originating from the island of Paros, it is a very slow dance, similar to the issós but sung only at weddings in the early morning hours. First the bride's family dances, then her husband's goes: the father of the bride begins, then the bride dances, followed by the bride's mother, her mother-in-law, and lastly the other relatives. In the parianós, improvised and stock verses are followed by refrains, here repeated to the near exclusion of other text, leader and group singing each line twice in alternation.

E . . . i ormorfí pou einai nifi mas, melakhrini komati (2)
Ksismata: *O Panayiá dos tous khronia / San tis limoniás ta klonia (2)*

O san ta triandáfila, triandá—fila podhió sto mati (2)
Ksismata: *Dos tous Panayiá mou khronia / San tis limoniás ta klonia (2)*

Vrisko vayia sto gabró louloudhi ton anghelo (2)

Panayiá mou, Panayiá mou, dos ayera tis kardhiás mou (2)

Malamatenia einai klidhí pou aniyi to evanghelio (2)
Ksismata: *Panayiá dos tous khronia / San tis limoniás ta klonia (2)*

I nifi mas einai frondí pou erkhete me ti vora (2)
Ksismata: *Dos tous Panayiá khronaikia / San tous dhiosmous ta kloniakia (2)*

San strapsis stin anatolí tha feksi mesa i khora
Ksismata: *Panayiá mou pou t'avlaki, me to neo zevgharaki (2)*

E . . . i mana sa se yenise evrisketo sta ori (2)
Ksismata: *Panayiá dhos tos khronia / San tis limoniás ta klonia (2)*

Kai etroye ri— ses kai stou vounoú ki 'kame tetia kore (2)
Ksismata: *Panayiá mou, Panayiá mou, dhos aera tis kardhiás mou (2)*

E . . . Apó mesa pou ti Kálimno irthe ena peristeri (2)
Sung like refrain: *To matió sou to mavradhi, zotaní me pane ston Adi*

E ki' fanose i perdhika kai yinna nea tairi (2)
. . . **[Cuts off.]**

[**Other verses, omitted:**

E . . . tin omorfi tis yitonias t'ipofaneromeni

E símera fanoseme perdhika ploumismeni

Kai smikse me ti perdhika ka yinei san tairi

Panayiá, pou khorizei, vlepetei pou kseyorizei]

Eh . . . How beautiful is our bride, our dark-eyed one
Ksismata: O Holy Mother give them years
As many as the lemon tree has branches
Oh like two roses, her eyes are two roses on a stem
Ksismata: O Holy Mother etc.

[*Vrisko vayia sto gabró louloudhi ton anghelo* **(Untranslated)**]

Ksismata: My Holy Mother, Holy Mother, give my heart ease

Golden are the keys to the Gospels
Ksismata: Holy Mother give them years, etc.

Our bride is the thunder that comes with the storm
Ksismata: Give them as many sweet years
As there are shoots on the mint

Like lightning in the east, she lights up the town
Ksismata: My Holy Mother on the porch
With the new young couple

Eh . . . your mother gave birth to you, and [they found you] in the mountains
Ksismata: Holy Mother give them years, etc.

Eh . . . Down into Kalymnos came a dove [young man]
Sung like refrain: The pupils of your eyes
Send me straight to Hell [drive me crazy]

Eh, a partridge appeared and there was a new mating

[*Other verses, omitted:*
Eh . . . the beauty of the neighborhood, and one who shows the most

Eh, today a plumed partridge appeared
And alighted with the [female] partridge and became her mate

Holy Mother, why part them? She's the most beautiful.]

The "kritikós skopós" (Cretan rhythm) segues from the parianós. Sung by the group, with clapping, laughter, and pismatiká, this table song in the form of Cretan-style mantinades is very popular in Kalymnos. It is another song that comes at the end of weddings, when the family sits around the bride and groom and sings to them. Two leaders alternate, sometimes with the group coming at the end of a line or repeating each single line. These are couplets, of which each line is repeated, and sometimes the last phrase of the first line is repeated yet again by the leader. "Every word has a special meaning (*ekhoun noima*)," said Mrs. Tsimouris.

Refrain **[with laughter]:**
Leader 1: *A, na ne stenakso ithela (2)*
Kai fovoume a mi pothano [sic] (2)
Leader 2: *Idha to kosmo khano (3)*

Leader 2: *M'árkhise glossa m'árkhise, tragoúdhise kardhiamou (2)*
Leader 2: *Tragoúdhise kardhiá mou,*
Leader 2: *Yiá na penes—, yiá na penes,* ***with group:*** *—so to kormí mou (2)*
Pou einai dhiplá mou
Leader 1: *Tralalalá lalala*

Leader 1: *Kenouria agapi ka palliá me válane sti mesi (2)*
Leader 3: *Strefo yirizo* **[kai vlepo]** *ti paliá, kenourio dhen m'aresi (2)*

Otan matiá ti kardhiá rotoún, "Kardhiá mou 'nt'akheis lipi?" (2)
"Kardhiá mou 'nt'akheis lipi?"

"Straváste kai dhe' vlepete t'atairi mou pos lipi?" (2)
Matiá kai fridhia kai mallia, kai zakharenio stoma (2)
Leader: *Kai zakharenio stoma*
Group: *E, lala lala lalalá, tralalalá lalala*

Nato i thalassa steriá na ekhei kai parathiria **[Twice, with leaders alternating.]**
Kai ela ela na, na ekhei kai parathiria
Na vlepa to poulaki mou, sta matiá kai sta fridhia (2) **[Girl is talking about man.]**

Nato i thalassa steriá na tin iperpatoúsa (2)
Na tin iperpatoúsa
N'arkhómouna na se dhámona khili kai me kratousa

As eimouna eroplano na peto ston aera (2)
Na peto ston aera
N'arkhómouna se dhámona mia n'ora tin i mera (2)

Vasanismeno mou kormí, tiranimeno soma (2)
Tiranimeno soma
Pote tha se kepasone i petres kai to khoma? (2)

Otan se protognorisa "thio" m'ekheis fonaksi (2)
Kai tora ti kardhoula mou m'ekheis katasparaksi (2)
Tralalala . . . **[Laughter.]**

Ta matiá sou einai kafenés, ta fridhi sou balkoni (2)
P'ourkhounde kai glendizoune i meraklidhes olli (2)

[**Other verses:**
Arkhise glossa mou, árkhises, tragoudhia m'aradhiázeis
Kai tin kalí paréa mas na tin dhiaskedhaseis.]

I wanted to sigh
And I was afraid I would die
I saw I was losing the world [losing my mind]

I brought forth my words [loosened my tongue] and my heart sang
My heart sang
In praise of that being who is beside me
Tralalalá lalala

Between a new love and an old one they put me
I twist and turn to look at my old love
And I don't care about the new one

When my eyes ask my heart,
"Heart, haven't you missed her?"
"Heart, haven't you missed her?"

"Are you blind, don't you see my mate [the girl's heart] is missing?
And eyes, brows, and hair, and mouth sweet like sugar
And mouth sweet like sugar
Eh, lala lala lalalá, tralalalá lalala"

If the wide sea had windows [Twice, with leaders alternating.]
And come on, come on, if it had windows
So I could see my little bird [my man], his eyes and his brows

If I had to journey the wide seas
If I had to journey far
I would come to meet you even if a thousand held on to me

If I were an airplane taking off into the sky
Taking off into the sky
I would come to meet you for an hour every day

My being is troubled, my body is tormented
My body is tormented
When will they throw stones and earth on you?

When I first met you, you called me "Uncle"
And now you have broken my little heart
Tralalala

Your eyes are brown, your brows are balconies
Where the devotees go and party

[*Other verses:*
Start singing, bring forth a song
So this good company of ours can be entertained.]

One of the most beautiful songs in the family's repertoire, remembered only by the older women, was the wedding serenade, *"Mera Merosi"* (Day Has Dawned, a wedding morning serenade), here performed as a table song by the group accompanied on the tsambóuna. Niki Sazalis explained that a mixed group of five to ten singers, unaccompanied or with *violí*, performed this ritual serenade at dawn at the bride's house, which had usually been given to her by her father, in which the bride and groom spent their first night together. It can also be sung when the wedding is over and the guests have left. In that case, the closest relatives and friends sit in a circle around the bride and groom and process through these long poetic lines. Its fifteen-syllable lines are sung in the meter of classical Greek song. The heavily accented irregular rhythm, and the prolongation of lines and verses by means of partial repetition of the text, mark an antique style that is fast becoming a rarity. Group singing was led by Focaina Skandaliaras and Nomikí A. Tsimouris.

Sose
Mera merose tora ki'—, tora ki' avyí kharazi
Tora ke— [—laidhoún], tora ta,
Tora ta pouliá
Tora ta
Tora ta, tora ta

Tora ta pouliá
Tora ta khelidhonia
Tora i pe—
Tora i pe—, tora i perdhikes
Tora i pe—
Tora i pe—, tora i perdhi— kes,
Tora i perdhikes, tora i perdhikoules
Tora ke—
Tora kela—
Tora kelaidhoún

Tora ke—,
Tora kela— aidhoún
Tora kelaidhoún, tora —laidhoún kai lene
Sikhná, afe—
Sikhná, afe—, sikhná, afendi mou
Sikhná, afe—, sikhná, afendi mou
Sikhná, afendi mou
Sikhná, kalé mou afendi
Sikhná ga—
Sikhná galia—
Sikhná galiase
Sikhná ga—
Sikhná galia— ase
Sikhná galiase
Kormí kiparissenio

Ki' aspro le—
Ki' aspro mele—
Ki' aspro melemó
Ki' aspro mele— mó
Ki' aspro mele—mó
[Stithuria] san to khioni

Aspri lí—, aspri lighé—, aspri ligherí

Day is breaking, and now dawn comes
And now they call out
Now the birds
Now the

Now the, now the
Now the birds
Now the swallows
Now the partridges
Now the pa—
Now the pa—, now the partridges
Now the partridges, now the little partridges
Now they cr—
Now they cr—
Now they cry out

Now they cry—
Now they call out
Now they cry, now they call out
Awake, lord
Awake, lord, awake, my lord
Awake, lord, awake, my lord
Awake, my lord
Awake and em—
Awake and embrace
That body like a cypress tree

And white thro—
And white marble throat
And white marble throat
And white marble throat
And breasts like the snow
White form, white form [*Ligheri* untranslated.]

The daughters and granddaughters of the Tsimouris family were raised with nanourismata, cradle-rocking songs, and say they sing to their own babies.[3] "I was in kindergarten," young Irene recalled, "and if my mom or dad didn't come up and tap me and sing [lullabies] to me, I wouldn't go to sleep. My dad used to tell me stories about *o yeros* ['The Old Man,' a child's fable] . . ." In peasant homes the baby slept in a wooden cradle that hung from a rope suspended across the matrimonial bed so that it could be near its parents and could be rocked easily during the night. Sleep is personified as in many southern European lullabies, and is called to take the child away and bring him back "refreshed and tall like a cypress tree." Focaina takes the lead in singing the verses of a nanourisma in alternation with the two Nomikís. Between verses, Nikitas,

Focaina, and others present make joking comments and mimic the baby's cries. Unaccompanied solo, with occasional group singing in alternation.

Kai yémises tous korfous tou me triandáfila kai rodha yia na kanni

[Adult mimicking baby cries]

Ela Ipné mou, kai par to kai pare to sta pervólia
[Cries]
Apó kato pou ti lemoniá, na kovi ta lemonia

Nanni nanni nanní na—anni
To moró mou ya na kanni [sic]

Ipné pou pairneis ta morá, pa— re kai to dhikó mou
Na mou ton ferneis dhroseró, psilós san kiparissi
Nanna nanni, nanni na— nni
To pedhaki mou na kani

***Nikitas* [spoken]:** *Vre yineka, tí ha kaneis? Tha meroseis to pedhí—tí tha kaneis?*

[Laughter.]

Na mou ton fernies dhroseró, psi— lós san kiparissi
***Nikitas* [spoken]:** *Piáse rizase to!*
Na mou ton **[breaks off laughing]**
Various comments

Na mou ton fereis dhroseró psi— lo san kiparissi
Kai na mou to zilevoune s'anatolí kai dhisi
Nanni nanni, to moró mou, na kimiso to mikró mou
[Cries]

***Nikitas* [spoken]:** *Alakse to moró! Katouremeno einai, morí!*

Ela Ipné mou, pare to pa— ne sta pervólia
Apó kato tes lemonés, na pezi ta lemonia
Nanni nanni to moró
E . . . eh!
***Nomikí A.* [spoken]:** *Savá, . . .* **[inaudible]** *nanourisma na kimate*

Nanni nanni to 'Rinió mou
[*Cries*]
Focaina **[spoken in falsetto]**: *Sopa na kimitheis, kanni nanni, kanni nanni!*

Nanni, tou riga tou pedhí, tou vasiliá t'angoni
Na to kouniai i Pana—yiá, me to khrisso sedhoni

Nanni nanni to pedhí mas
Na mi kopsi ti i zoí mas

Nikitas **[spoken]**: *"Klei kai dhen boró na kimithó, dhe kataleveis?"*
Focaina: *"Ti tou kano tora to pedhí? To riksome okso?*
Nikitas: *Grépsato!*
Focaina: *To keró pou t'ekanes dhen to oskseres? Thelei na kimithí. Pas stin alli kamera ki' ekí kimitho!"*

[Laughter, whispering]

Kimate o ilios sta vouná, ki' perdhika sto dhassi
Kimate to pedhaki mou, ton ipno na khortasei

Nani nanni nanni na— ni
To pedhaki mou to ká— ni

[Spoken]:
Nomikí A.: *Endaksi*
Nikitas: *Kai katourise pali.*
Nomikí A.: *Pa na to sfoughizeis!*

Kimate o ilios sta vouná, ki' perdhika sta dhassi
Kimate to Iannaki mou, ton ipno na khortasi
Nanni nanni nanni na, ipno elafrí na kanni
Nanni nanni nanni nannáki

Ela Ipné sti kouniá tou, stavré ste kefalí tou
Ki' Ayí mou Pandelemoná fil— aye ti zoí tou
En an a-a-a-e . . .
Kamu e-e-e . . .

Ayi mou Pandelemoná kai— sei Kirá Psilí mou
Vlepeis to Savaki mou pou— kopse ti zoí mou
Kami e-e-e-e!
[Speaking]: *Etsi tha kimísei tora, kakomira . . .*

And you filled his bodice with roses and pomegranate flowers
So that he would sleep

Come my Sleep, and take him, take him to the orchard
Under the lemon trees, so he can cut lemons

Sleepy, sleep sleep
Let my baby sleep

Sleep, you who takes all the babies, take mine
Bring him back to me fresh, tall as a cypress tree
Sleep, sleep, sleep
Let my little one sleep

Nikitas: Woman, what are you doing? Will you quiet the child?
Bring him back to me fresh, tall as a cypress

Nikitas: Take him and give him the breast!
Bring him back—

Bring him back fresh, tall as a cypress
So they'll envy me him from east to west
Sleep, sleep my baby, let my little one sleep

Nikitas: Change the kid! He peed himself!

Come, my Sleep, take him to the orchard
Under the lemon trees, to play with the lemons
Sleep, sleep, the baby
E . . . eh!

Nomikí A.: Lullaby to sleep . . .

Sleep, sleep my Rini [teasingly to Irene, her teenage daughter]

Focaina: Come now, sleep! Go on off to sleep!

Nanni, child of the lord, grandchild of the king
Let the Holy Mother rock him, in golden sheets

Sleep, sleep, our own child
Don't scare the life out of us

Spoken:
Nikitas: He's crying and I can't sleep, don't you see?
Focaina: What do you want me to do with the child? Throw him outside?
Nikitas: Get rid of him!
Focaina: The time you made him didn't you realize? You want to sleep—go into the other room and sleep!

The sun is sleeping in the mountains, the partridge in the woods
My little baby's sleeping, let him sleep until he's satisfied
Nani nanni nanni na— ni
My little baby's sleeping

Spoken:
Nomikí A.: Alright . . .
Nikitas: Now he's peed again!
Nomikí A.: You wipe him up!

The sun is sleeping in the mountains, the partridge in the woods
My little Johnny's sleeping, let him sleep until he's satisfied
Sleep, sleep, sleep, let him have a carefree sleep
Nanni nanni nanni nannáki

Come, Sleep, into his cradle, make the cross on his forehead
And my Saint Panteleimon [saint of healing], watch over him
En an a-a-a-e . . .
Go to e-e-e

My Saint Panteleimon, and you my Tall Lady[4]
See my little Sava, who gives me such a fright
Go, go to sle-e-e-ep!

Spoken: There, he'll sleep now, poor thing . . .

Immigration

"Dhiosmarí" (emigration lament)—this sorrowful address to Kalymnos laments the loss of the island's young men, its most precious resource, to emigration. Its poetry is laid out on long melodic phrases carried forward by strong, irregular pulses, in which held notes and melismatic passages alternate with triplets. The text also belongs to "Maroúli" (see the translation above), a table song usually accompanied on tsambóuna or violí. Nomikí A. Tsimouris's renditions of this song were much requested at Kalymnian parties. I first heard it when a visiting radio producer requested an immigration song. I thought I had heard all of the family's songs, so this was a reminder of the surprising depths of the folk repertoire in long-continuous, stable traditions such as that of the Dodecanese, where there is always more poetry, always another song.

A mou kaimeni Kálimnos
Dhiosmaraki mou
O, mavrisan ta vouná sou
Siganá, siganá, siganá kai ta peina

Efiga ta levendiá sou
Efigan i khará sou
Siganá, siganá, siganá kai ta peina

Dhen boró ta matia mou
Dhiosmaraki mou
O psilá ta sikosa
Siganá, siganá, siganá kai ta peina

Ah, my poor Kalymnos
My sweet mint
Your mountains have turned black
Softly, softly, softly I tread the earth

Your young men have departed
My sweet mint
Your heart's joys have fled
Softly, softly, softly I tread the earth

My eyes can't bear it
My sweet mint
Oh I grew them tall,
Softly, softly, softly I tread the earth

Of Songs and Sponges

"Why do Kalymnians sing songs from other islands?" I asked Nikitas as he sat at the kitchen table one afternoon. "Long ago, Kalymnians were sponge fishermen (*sfoungaradhes*)," he replied. "They sailed to all the islands and brought their songs back to Kalymnos and we made them our own."

> In those years, in the days of my father, when they came back from the sponge fisheries in September bringing in the sponges, they would bring a song—one each year. All the songs that they sing in these islands around, we sing better in Kalymnos, because the Kalymnians knew how to party *(glendousane)*, and they especially liked to dance. In Kos, for example, they did not. The Kotes sang these songs differently . . . These are simple songs, not made by educated people. But they are better, because all that you have inside of you, you put into song. My grandmother lived to ninety-nine years and she danced the sousta. If you want to live a long time you must sing inside yourself. You must not be sorrowful. You must know all the songs, and keep them in your mind. That is the way I am . . .

[Recited:]

Dhen kleo ego ton pethamenou	I don't weep, for the dead
Oute tha pethano	Not even when I die
Kleo monakha leyo	I only weep when I wonder:
Edho sta skotiná monakhós ti tha kano?	Alone in the dark [of hell], what shall I do?
Etsi to apofasisa	And so I decided
Kai etsi tha to kano	And that's what I will do:
Tha pino kai tha tragoudho	I will drink and I will sing
Eos sou tha pethano.	Until the day I die.

Cultural Transmission:
The Ebb and Flow of Greek Life in Tarpon Springs

With over a hundred kinfolk and relatives by marriage in Tarpon Springs alone, the Tsimourises do not lack for society, and circulate in a continual round of life-cycle celebrations, church lunches, and Kalymnian Society dinners and festivities. When I met them they were living in very modest circumstances and worked hard, but they were serene and exuberant and projected a sense of enormous satisfaction with the progress of their lives. When I asked Mrs. Tsimouris, who was the conscious keeper of the family ethos, about the source of their happiness, she attributed it to their fulfilling their duties as Kalymnian Greeks in the familial, community, and spiritual arenas, and particularly with respect to the conduct of courtship, marriage, and of observances for the dead.

The family saw themselves as doubly fortunate to be directly engaged with the artistic traditions that symbolize and reinforce their Dodecanese heritage and identity, as well as their ties to Kalymnos. These they have repeatedly renewed through extended stays and new bonds of marriage. Their circumstances allowed them to initiate a new coming of age rite, in which the young girls of the family were taken to Kalymnos when they were of an age to begin thinking of courtship and marriage. Whether this produced marriages or not, it had the effect of further binding the young Greek Americans to their Greek identity. It also brought them into generational synchrony with the youth culture of Greece in ways that were highly rewarding and pleasurable. Even the conservative Mrs. Tsimouris fully collaborated in allowing the young people a full and fairly unrestricted nightlife of clubbing and dancing, both in Tarpon and in Kalymnos. A more effervescent group of young people, or more fulfilled adults, would be difficult to find in this country.

Thus the Tsimourises are energetic, engaged, and upstanding people. They produced flourishing, happy children who have tried new paths but have remained securely anchored in the family and community orbit. Inveterate Greek traditionalists, they are at the same time adaptable and flexible, always learning how to make the best of several worlds and how to make their island culture work in interesting ways wherever they are.

Does this sound too good to be true? Of course, like any other, the family has had its dramas and its problems, but while I lived among the Tsimourises as neighbor, quasi-family member, and ethnographer over seven years, they manifested a high level of functioning. It must be said, however, I entered their orbit at a particularly happy conjunction between the degree of assimilation the family had achieved in the United States, and the degree to which Greek village custom had, for them, maintained its moral force and idealized appeal, but had lost most of its fearsome disciplinary power. The Florida community was small, low key, and physically and socially unified, yet it had few of the inconveniences and restrictions of village life in Greece. These conditions and balances will inevitably change, but the people who lived this phase of Kalymnian adaptation will influence at least two more generations.

The Greeks of Tarpon Springs are active in and on behalf of their traditions. Children are immersed in the Greek Orthodox religion, in Greek language taught daily at the church school and often spoken at home, and in Greek regional folk arts, particularly dancing, with several dance groups practicing and performing in the community at any one time. However, the little lyra, violí, or tsambóuna orchestras with singing that used to accompany dancing have been replaced by pan-island and pan-Hellenic electric popular live and recorded music. Tsambóuna music is considered antiquated, but at least as long as Nikitas was alive it continued to serve as a focal point at weddings and other community events. Much more endangered was the beautiful and unusual repertoire of vocal music and accompanying poetry, performed in an antique style. The women who knew the songs were growing old, and the younger ones were only learning them partially at best.

Even so, there is continued interest in traditional music among some young Greek Americans in Tarpon Springs. It would therefore still be possible to encourage the Kalymnians to incorporate the songs and singing styles represented in this collection into their repertoire and performance practice, which could in consequence become more meaningful and interesting. One immense educational and spiritual benefit would be that of learning and absorbing the prosody of the singing and the poetry of the lyrics.

Public Outcome

The National Endowment for the Arts funded the original research project as documentation with a public outcome. Accordingly, the recording phase was followed by a period of public outreach resulting in more exposure for the folk artists and their musical traditions both locally and abroad. Nikitas and his family were featured in newspaper articles and a television program on ethnic traditions. During the much-celebrated Greek Independence week of 1995 the Tsimourises performed at the Tarpon Springs Cultural Center, introduced by Nikitas's daughter Irene. Nikitas Kavouklis, a beginning Florida Folklife Program apprentice under his great-uncle, played tsambóuna. At the 1996 Florida Folk Festival the two demonstrated the outcome of the apprenticeship. The family performed at the Pinellas County Heritage Park Festival in Largo in September 1996, and again in May 1997 at the Florida

Folk Festival in White Springs. One of their recordings was included in *The Florida Music Train*, a curriculum with CD for schools by the Florida Folklife Program. The program notes for these presentations were made available to the family and presenting organizations for their future use. Copies of the original recordings were placed in the archives of the City of Tarpon Springs and of the Florida Folklife Program, and copies of the recordings and photographs were given to the participants.

About the Singers

The main ensemble of singers and bagpiper consisted of Nomikí Tsimouris, Nikitas's wife (vocal and clapping); Nomikí A. Tsimouris, Nikitas's sister (vocal and clapping); and Fotiní (Focaina) Skandaliaras, youngest sister (vocal, songs and stories); and Nikitas Tsimouris (tsambóuna). Dancers, who also provided musical accompaniment with their stamping feet, whistles, and calls of "opa," were Nikitas's daughter Irene, who lived at home, and sometimes his married daughter Niki Sazalis and/or her children, Nomikí and Petroula (Patty) Sazalis, and other visitors.

Nomikí Tsimouris née Makarounas was born in Skalia, Kalymnos, in 1935. She came from a shepherd family and village, and her father had a flock of three hundred sheep. In Tarpon Springs, Nomikí worked for many years at a small warehouse cutting sponges and as a housekeeper in a hotel, rising at 3:00 a.m. to make bread and cookies at a local bakery. She is known for her firm religious principles, her observance of custom, and her propriety and correctness in family and social affairs. She has four children, ten grandchildren, and three great-grandchildren.

Nomikí Antoniou Tsimouris (1928–2010) was born in Khora, Kalymnos. She went to work as a maid for a well-to-do family at age six, and was not sent to school. Unable to raise a dowry, she stayed single and cared for her mother, who died in Tarpon Springs at age eighty-two. Nomikí emigrated to Tarpon Springs in 1970, where she worked for many years cutting sponges. She retired in 1992, supplementing her tiny income by taking care of elderly people, boarding the occasional sponge buyer or visitor, and cooking for parties, where her singing was in demand.

Fotiní (Focaina) Skandaliaris née Tsimouris was born in Khora, Kalymnos, in 1931 and emigrated to Tarpon Springs in 1970. Like many Kalymnian men her husband made a good living as a bridge painter, traveling on jobs all over the country. They had four children. Focaina, who rarely went out except to church, was shy and soft-spoken. She had a special gift for

Left to right: Nomikí Makarounes Tsimouris singing with Nomikí A. Tsimouris and Focaina Tsimouris Skandaliaris. Photo by Anna Lomax Wood.

remembering and telling fairy tales, the lives of saints and holy men, and stories about the old days, *ta khronia*.

Another sister, Maria Ellenas, was an approving and supportive presence at the recording sessions even though, being a widow, she could not be persuaded to fully join in. Her husband had been known for being a great singer and merrymaker. He organized all the family's evening glendis, which the young people remembered with great joy, and his early death blighted these happy gatherings.

Maria lived with her daughter and three grandchildren, all of whom attended college with scholarships. Both grandsons learned to play the tsambóuna with Nikitas, who was a patient and encouraging teacher. "Little" Nikitas Kavouklis was awarded a Florida Folklife Apprenticeship to study the instrument and participated with his great-uncle in the Florida Folk Festival, planning at one time to continue the family tradition. The elder Nikitas estimated that between Kalymnos and Tarpon Springs there were perhaps ten tsambóuna players, but only two or three of any merit, some of the more accomplished being younger men.

Like Nomikí, the youngest sister, Sevastí Tsimouris was sent to work as live-in housekeeper at an early age. Although she, too, never married, she was able to get some schooling and the opportunity to travel, and became the most worldly of the four sisters. Considered the best singer in the family, with the finest voice, Sevastí visited Tarpon once a year and was sought after at parties for her singing.

NOTE ON THE LYRIC TRANSCRIPTIONS AND TRANSLATIONS

The transcriptions and translations were begun with Maria Chairetakis in 2000 and finalized with Mrs. Nomikí Tsimouris in 2009. Niki Sazalis, Irene Rinios, and Katerina Hatzileris explained many idioms and Kalymnian turns of phrase, bridging the language and interpretive gaps between Mrs. Tsimouris and myself. The transcriptions and translations are a work in progress, however, there being a number of words and phrases that remain indecipherable, or that may have been imperfectly translated. The Greek texts have been presented in the Roman alphabet because I could find no one to transcribe them into Greek alphabet while keeping to Kalymnian dialect usage as sung.

ACKNOWLEDGMENTS

The Folk Arts Program of the National Endowment for the Arts provided funding for the recordings through the City of Tarpon Springs. Thanks to Dr. Kathleen Monahan, director of Cultural and Civic Services of the City of Tarpon Springs, for her support of the project, and to Theodore Grame, who first learned of Nikitas. The Florida Folklife Program provided the DAT recorder, and Robert L. Stone of the program kindly tutored me on its use. Kenith Crawford made beautiful black and white photographs at some of the sessions. Katerina Gryparis, Maria Chairetakis, and Mrs. Nomikí Tsimouris worked on the transcriptions and translations with me. Matthew Barton transferred the recordings to CD. I thank Dr. Tina Bucuvalas, Geoffrey Clarfield, Dr. Judith R. Cohen, Ellen Harold, and David Marker for reading and commenting on this paper. I am deeply grateful to Nikitas Tsimouris, Mrs. Nomikí Tsimouris (my *nouná*), and all of the Tsimouris family for their hospitality, patience, and trust. Nikitas will always remain an icon in my heart.

Notes

1. It can often be noted that here traditional singing and/or reed instrument playing is imitative of or harmonious with ungulate vocalization. Can it have played an ancient role in domesticating and herding ungulates in the region? Systematic studies of ungulate behavioral and brain responses to this and other kinds of music and of sing-

ing styles and instrumentation in the oldest pastoral regions of the Middle East and Mediteranean basin are required.

2. Why so strong a predilection for challenge and debate in oral poetry arises in this region is an interesting question. Song dueling may be explained on a case-by-case basis but one might also look for an explanation in the combination of competition for scarce resources in precarious environments and weak statehood that has characterized these regions over most of their history. Such circumstances seem to produce a sort of high individualism and an inclination for intra-group displays of power and skill, particularly among males but also among family groups, and in the past, "estates" (*etats*), or formally established classes of people—the knight and the squire, the peasant and the nobleman, the rustic and the townsman of sixteenth- through eighteenth-century literature, for example. Michael Herzfeld's observations of a Cretan shepherd village (1985) generally support this line of argument. Herzfeld (1985) makes the point that as state government with its controls and subsidies takes on more importance in villagers' lives, competition for cattle and status between agnatic groups subsides, as do the poetic traditions that dramatize these tensions.
3. I did not learn what lullabies they sing or how.
4. Tall Lady: an apparition of the virgin said to have appeared to Greeks fighting at Morova in 1940, among others.

References

Anoyanakis, Fivos. 1991. *Greek Popular Musical Instruments.* Athens: Melissa Publishing.

T' Άχολο Περιστέρι (The Carefree Dove). 2008. Apella Nota Folk Music Productions. Άστική μή Κερδοσκοπική Εταιρεία. www.karpathos.net/ApellaNota.

Baud-Bovy, Samuel. 1935–38. *Chansons populaires greques du Dodecanese. Tomes 1–2.* Athenes.

Caraveli, Anna. 1985. "The Symbolic Village Community Born in Performance." *Journal of American Folklore* 98: 129-57.

Caraveli-Chaves, Anna. 1980. "Bridge Between Worlds: The Greek Women's Lament as Communicative Event." *Journal of American Folklore* 93: 129–57.

Deitrich, Volf. 1976. *Musica popolare del Dodecaneso. Registrazioni sul campo effettuate a Kos, Simi, Nissiros, Rhodes, Karpathos.* Albatross (LP).

Florida Folklife Program / Florida Department of State. 1983. *Every Island Has Its Own Songs* (Film). Directed by Peggy A. Bulger.

Herzfeld, Michael. 1985. *The Poetics of Manhood: Contest and Identity in a Cretan Mountain Village.* Princeton, NJ: Princeton University Press.

http://spotlightonmusic.macmillanmh.com/music/teachers/articles/folk-and-traditional-styles/greek-folk-music.

http://www.olymbos.org/music/.

Kavouras, Pavlos. 1993. "Extempore dialogical song and the symbolism of the ghlendi at Olymbos, Karpathos." *Ethnologia* 2: 155–200.

Lomax, Alan. 1976. *Cantometrics: An Approach to the Anthropology of Music.* University of California Extension Media, Berkeley.

Sarris, Haris, Tassos Kolydas, and Panagiotis Tzevelekos. 2008. "Parataxis: A Framework of Structure Analysis for Instrumental Folk Music." *Proceedings of the Fourth*

Conference on Interdisciplinary Musicology (CIM08). Thessaloniki, Greece, July 2–6, 2008, http://web.auth.gr/cim08/.
Sarris, Haris, and Panagiotis Tzevelekos. 2008. "Singing like the *Gaida* (Bagpipe): Investigating Relations between Singing and Instrumental Playing Techniques in Greek Thrace." *Journal of Interdisciplinary Music Studies* 2 (1 & 2): 33–57.
Sutton, David E. 1998. *Memories Cast in Stone: The Relevance of the Past in Everyday Life.* New York: Berg Publishers.

Eternal Be Their Memory!

STAVROS K. FRANGOS

AMONG THE MANY DOCUMENTED CUSTOMS MODERN GREEKS CONTINUE to practice, as they have since classical times, are those related to observances for the dead.[1] Yet in all the academic accounts written about Greeks in North America, none mention, let alone describe in detail, the cemeteries established or sought out by the early pioneers and how they have been maintained by their descendants.[2] One especially noteworthy gathering of artifacts is found in the Cycadia Cemetery of Tarpon Springs, Florida.

Named after the cycadia palms first planted to mark the cemetery grounds, this community institution was founded in 1886—one year before the city of Tarpon Springs was incorporated. At that time, two early pioneer women, Liola Keeney Beekman and Amilia Meres, began to care for the small gathering of graves. The earliest burial was C. L. Webster, 1872, prior to the formal establishment of the cemetery. It is recalled that Beekman and Meres brought plants and trees to the cemetery in a mule-drawn wagon. In 1887, Beekman donated the land to be dedicated as the cemetery. In November 1904, the women established the Cycadia Cemetery Association.

As the cemetery grew, the management became too much for the local women. Consequently, in 1946 the cemetery was deeded to the city of Tarpon Springs, which continues to manage it today. The Cycadia Cemetery is located just east of U.S. Highway 19 at 1021 East Tarpon Avenue.

In 1905, sponge industry entrepreneur John Cocoris and his brothers brought some 500 Greek spongers from the Saronic Gulf and Dodecanese Islands to the western coast of Florida. Others soon followed. Sadly, the inherent dangers in diving more than ten fathoms (sixty feet) for the best deep-water sponges soon resulted in deaths. As befits those daring sponge divers, their gravestones, mausoleums, and large family plots are unique and artistically distinctive. The overall Greek presence at the Cycadia Cemetery is in direct measure to their demographic standing along the Gulf Coast of Florida. In 1940, there were well over 1,000 men actively engaged in the sponge industry. These men and their families constituted roughly 2,500 Greeks in a town of 3,402. By the late 1970s, an estimated one-third of the residents were Greek or of Greek descent in a town that then numbered some 13,000 individuals.

In the twenty-first century, the total number of Greeks along the western coast of Florida has unexpectedly grown. Retired Greeks and Greek Americans from around the country have flocked to towns all along the western Gulf Coast to the north, south, and east of Tarpon Springs as both permanent and seasonal residents. No reliable statistics are available on the seasonal residents. However, the vast majority own homes or condominiums in the region. One way to document the increase of seasonal residents is the growth of Greek churches in Pasco, Pinellas, Hillsborough, Manatee, Sarasota, and Polk Counties. On October 10, 1909, in Tarpon Springs the St. Nicholas foundation stone was laid, making it the first Greek Orthodox parish in western Florida. Since the 1970s, there are now an additional eight parishes: St. George (New Port Richey); Sts. Raphael, Nicholas, and Irene (Palm Harbor); Holy Trinity (Clearwater); St. Stephanos (St. Petersburg); St. John the Baptist (Tampa); St. Barbara (Sarasota); and St. Sophia (Winter Haven). While a number of these churches today may claim to be of long historical standing, none of them would have reached the current size or stature now enjoyed without the presence of the seasonal parishioners.

In addition to these officially recognized churches, there has been phenomenal growth in small Eastern Orthodox parishes, chapels, shrines, and even monasteries scattered across these very same counties. As in large cities across the country, the appearance of this complex of churches/chapels/shrines/monasteries is similar to their organization in Greek communities throughout the world. Parishioners in these various places of worship encompass a wide social range in terms of immigration, theological beliefs, village or region of origin, economic standing, and other components of Greek identity.

Greek graves and cemeteries in the United States have always differed from those in the villages from which the majority of immigrants arrived from 1880 to 1920. In Greece prior to the period beginning in the 1970s, bodies were exhumed and the bones were washed and placed in ossuaries—then common to all cemeteries. In the rural villages, individual gravesites were family owned with each generation taking their turn in the same designated site. Exhumation is still not an uncommon practice in Greece. As with all Greek customs, funeral rites must be examined and understood on a regional basis, but exhumation is definitely on the decline.

In the late 1970s, a gradual increase in the placement of permanent sarcophagi over the graves began to appear. On the new sarcophagi, the name and birth date are most often inscribed toward the head of the grave. At the head of the tomb there often is a small glass-enclosed box running the width of the sarcophagus. Sliding doors allow family members and visitors to place and display incense burners, icons, candles, and pictures or small mementoes inside. Again, these small items suggest the idea of personal and ongoing contact with the dead. The new sarcophagi may vary in size but not necessarily in type.

What is so striking about the Greek gravesites in North America is that they differ from graves both in the population's village or region of origin. There is often a strongly pronounced individuality. Folklorists as well as historians of popular culture have long recognized connections between cemeteries and other areas of American design. In the Victorian era, when domestic and public buildings were elaborate structures with a strong emphasis on decorative detailing, so were the average gravestones. In the period following World War II, as suburban tract housing with its utilitarian square shape began to encircle urban centers, gravestone designs followed suit with cubes of marble surrounded by cleanly cut lawns. Greek graves at the Cycadia Cemetery, however, did not follow this national trend, and they differ in a number of distinct ways from those that surround them.

As one would expect, many headstones show nearly photographic carvings of sponge boats and deep-water diving helmets. Examples of the sponge boat carvings can be readily seen on headstones for George A. Demopoulos (1949–1983), J. D. Christmas (b. 1920), and especially Nicholas C. Tsourakis (1918–1995). On the tombstones at the Katsaras gravesite, John Katsaras (1902–1979) has a helmet carved below his name and between his dates of birth and death. In addition, immediately under his name is carved "*Kapetanios*" (Captain). In contrast, on Ourania Katsaras's (1910–1994) headstone only the carving of "Mama" appears below her name. There are many other examples.

It is interesting to note that not only sponge boats are represented in Greek tombstone carvings. On Ernest D. Kachikis's (1925–1991) gravestone we see a large merchant marine tanker. Captain Kachikis was a merchant ship captain and a port captain for well over twenty years. He had married into a local family involved with the sponge trade and was an ardent supporter of youth activities at St. Nicholas Greek Orthodox Cathedral.

Georgiou-Vatikiotis gravestone with carved image of sponge boat. Photo by Tina Bucuvalas.

Classical Greek columns, urns, and crosses with intricately carved reliefs document in stone the identification Greeks felt and continue to feel for their ancestors. On a number of the tombstones there are highly accurate carvings of the home island. In one particular case, the Matsis gravesite is not only carved with a map of Rhodes, but it also shows the two different villages from which the couple migrated: Kremasti and Psinthos.

Most of the earliest Greek graves, which are occupied by those who arrived in the 1905 exodus of married men, note from which island the deceased hailed. The Billias gravesite boasts a beautifully carved headstone arrangement noting, "George Born 1870 Naxos Greece Died 1929," as well as "Mary Born 1880 Calymnos Greece Died 1954." The notation of the island of origin is noted on so many different Greek gravestones that it unquestionably quite literally carried to the grave social distinctions strongly felt within the early generation of the community.

No single style or dominant motif runs throughout the Greek graves. In the earlier stones one can see art deco-inspired headstones with majestic sweeps of curving stone, tree trunks wrought from limestone, large and small urns, along with photographic ovals of the deceased—each with a judicious employment of colored marble. The sepulchral monuments for children are unique and heartfelt. In the statuary for the graves of babies we find beautifully carved angels, small lambs, and even the profile of faces. Especially beautiful is the gravesite of Evdokia N. Gonatos (1934–1936). With an oval

Gravestone with photo of Petros Fatolitis in diving suit. Photo by Tina Bucuvalas.

photograph at the top, the scrolled marble headstone bears her name along with the day and year of her birth and death. Carved columns support this top stone with a stunning red and blue marble panel between them. Immediately in front of this colored stone is a foot tall white marble angel with the sarcophagus below.

On the gravestones for teenagers and young adults, sometimes there is only a single name in carved script, such as "Nicky," or a single epitaph, such as "Free Spirit." Musical notes adorn the impressive tombstone dedicated "To Our Sweetest Mother." One recent grave is marked with a wooden cross with not only the deceased's name and dates of birth and death in large scrolling script, but also striking carvings of baskets, wreaths, and sheaves. Individuality, then, is the only common element among the Greek graves.

Aside from the tombstones a number of other means are used to demarcate the gravesite. At times the border of the plot is marked by low rough-cut granite or marble. For other sites, elaborate iron-work fences, marble posts with chains, or even low block walls with the family name carved in stone set at the foot of the grave. On other gravesites, the entire surface of the lot is covered. The surface of these graves varies from a thick cover of white stones, a carefully laid field of cement or baked-clay tiles, or even massive slabs of three-inch to four-inch granite or imported marble. With the usual individual grave plot measuring four feet by nine feet, family sites can be huge expanses of granite or marble. The large family lots often prominently feature statues, benches, large urns, small metal holders for burning incense, enclosed red glass memorial candle stands, trellises, intricate plantings of flowers, and wind chimes. It is striking how many real flowers can be found on the graves no matter what the time of year. And the air nearly always carries the scent of incense and the sound of wind chimes.

Such costly and artful arrangements of space clearly are meant as places where the living can come together with the dead. Gatherings of relatives who come to honor and remember the best of those who have passed on can be seen in any cemetery where Greeks have come to rest.

In terms of the Greek Diaspora, the Cycadia Cemetery would be significant simply for the number and array of sponge divers and boat captains present on its grounds. Yet among them are many other notable individuals, such as Mother Superior Thekla Makris (1910–1992)—said to be the first Greek Orthodox nun in North and South America. Yiorgos Katsaros, one of the earliest and foremost Café Aman style musicians in the United States, is here, as is musician, promoter, and record producer John Gianaros.

Since Greeks in western Florida and across the United States take such direct and continued care of their deceased loved ones, it behooves folklorists, historians, and sociologists to systematically study the ways in which love and respect see enduring expression in the coldness of carved stone.

Notes

1. An earlier version of this article appeared under the title, "The Greek Graves of Tarpon Springs," *National Herald/Ethnikos Kirix* (New York City), 2, no. 84, May 22–23, 1999. My thanks to all those at the Tarpon Springs Area Historical Society is necessary. No reliable contemporary history or cultural study exists on the Greeks of Tarpon Springs. Given this situation *Strangers At Ithaca: The Story of the Spongers of Tarpon Springs* by George T. Frantzis (St. Petersburg, FL: Great Outdoors Assoc., 1962) remains the best general history. Written by a local Greek lawyer who drew upon the memories of the local sponge divers and the Greek community at large the volume suffers from a lack of footnotes and a useful bibliography.
2. A hairline distinction must be immediately made between funeral and folk customs of burial and the nature of tombstones, cemetery design, and gravesite accoutrements. Early references to Greek funerals can be readily found since they appeared exotic to the Protestant American press. One example typical for this early period is "Weird Greek Ritual to be Chanted for the Dead," *Atlanta Constitution*, December 1, 1901. The first English language accounts on Greeks in the United States, such as in Thomas Burgess's *Greeks in America: An Account of Their Coming, Progress, Customs, Living and Aspirations* (Boston: Sherman, French, & Co., 1913), 111–12, do have passing references to funeral rites. In Burgess's case we find a long paragraph filled with generalizations and a translation of a funeral hymn, nothing else. Even the noted historian Helen Zeese Papanikolas speaks directly to funerary customs and folk beliefs, not the

existence or appointment of cemeteries, in "Wrestling with Death: Greek Immigrant Funeral Customs in Utah" (*Utah Historical Quarterly* 52, no. 1 [1984]: 29–49). Nicholas M. Prevas wrote an exhaustive and beautifully illustrated descriptive history, *Gone But Not Forgotten: A Definitive History of the Greek Section at Woodlawn Cemetery* (Baltimore: Greek Orthodox Cathedral of the Annunciation, 2001). An otherwise finely written account, Prevas critically errs when he speculates that the Baltimore church was the first Greek immigrant community to secure extensive cemetery plots. For a review of this volume, see Steve Frangos, "Eternal Be Their Memory," *National Herald / Ethnikos Kirix* (7, no. 343 (May 8–9, 2004). It is well established that the Greek immigrants who arrived in the late 1880s and early 1890s quickly initiated formal fraternal organizations that served, aside from their camaraderie functions, as self-help insurance companies. Long-established work-abroad traditions of Greeks dictated that aid, medical, and funeral/burial services were among the first duties of any such organization. It is still not recognized within Greek American studies that even before local Greek immigrants agreed to establish a church, in the very early period when many fully intended to return to Greece, they nevertheless secured insurance and burial plots. We can note three community histories that independently document that securing burial plots for their members was among the very first formal collective actions taken when legally incorporating their individual communities: "History of the Early Greek Community of Pasadena and the San Gabriel Valley to 1959" by Nikitas J. Tripodes, in *Saint Anthony Greek Orthodox Church 1954–2004* (Pasadena, CA: Saint Anthony Greek Orthodox Church, 2004), 19, "The Cemeteries of St. John" in *Commemorative Album of the Hellenic Orthodox Community 1905–2005* (Pueblo, CO: St. John the Baptist Hellenic Orthodox Community, 2005), 54–55; and *1905–2005 Centennial Anniversary of the Atlanta Annunciation Cathedral* (Atlanta, GA: Atlanta Annunciation Cathedral, 2007), 41.

Richard Seaman's Presence within Florida's Soundscape

GREGORY HANSEN

IN HIS HOME IN JACKSONVILLE'S AVONDALE NEIGHBORHOOD, RICHARD Seaman told me that his homeplace in Kissimmee had burned to the ground long ago. He told me how different the community is from what it was like when he was born on the shore of Lake Tohopekaliga in 1904. He had been back there a few years ago in the 1990s, and he explained that a trailer court was built on the property that once belonged to his father, Lewis Seaman. The land is no longer in the family, he explained, because the property taxes were too high after Disney came in.

I had known Seaman for over a dozen years, but I had never really thought about visiting his old community, until that conversation in 2001. During that spring, I was also doing fieldwork in the Space Coast for the Florida Folklife Program, so I took the opportunity to turn away from the urban sprawl of U.S. 192, found Kissimmee Park Road, and headed west to see the site of his old homestead. New suburban-style homes predominate, but a few of the older vernacular buildings speckle the landscape of this pretty drive. I was surprised to find this pocket of rural countryside in central Florida. Most of the area consists of ranchland and citrus groves. It feels wrong to drive too fast on this old country road, and it felt perfectly appropriate to stop the car a few times to take some photographs of scenes reminiscent of Florida's older landscapes. Nearing the end of the road, the eastern shore of the lake came into view. I saw where the trailer court was located and pulled my car to the side of the road. As I walked toward the lake, I noticed a sign for Tohopekaliga Drive on my right, and I continued to shoot some 35mm slides of the area. I didn't notice another street sign until I had walked back to my car. I looked up and read "Seaman Ave." The dirt road stretched southward before me, and I laughed to myself, thinking, "Mr. Seaman always is waiting with something new to tell me." I photographed the sign, returned to my car, and rolled down Seaman Avenue, taking it to where it ended in a private driveway.

A few days later, I recounted my Kissimmee Park trip to Richard Seaman. He had that twinkle in his eye when I exclaimed that I had found Seaman Avenue, and he affirmed that the road had, in fact, been named after his parents. Just as the sign for Seaman Avenue memorializes the Seaman family's presence on Florida's landscape, Richard Seaman's contributions as a fiddler and storyteller continue to play a vital role in shaping Florida's soundscape. As Murray Schafer writes, a soundscape is an aural environment that helps to create, define, and evoke a sense of place (Schafer 1993:274). Understanding a soundscape requires the art of careful listening. A primary task is separating the background noise out of an environment and learning to listen to the significant sounds that are part of the cultural constructions that are meaningful within an area. These sounds may be part of the natural order. In Kissimmee Park that day, the soundscape included the leaves rustling through the trees, the bees buzzing among flowers, the waves lapping on the lakeshore, and the screech of seagulls just above the water. The elements of the soundscape that then came to my mind were the melodies of Seaman's old-time fiddle tunes running through my head. These tunes, in turn, recalled the lasting impression of his voice. I thought of his stories, and I was struck by how the witty tall tales that he first learned in Osceola County fit the environment. As I walked along Seaman Avenue, the eloquent stories of his own experiences gave me a vibrant sense of how he experienced his homeplace (Lopez 2006:xv–xviii).

The Florida Department of State rightly honored Richard Seaman with a Folk Heritage Award in 2001. The state recognized him for his old-time fiddling and for his gifts as a storyteller. The Governor's Proclamation provided special recognition for his contributions to Florida's next generation of fiddlers. As his Heritage Award affirms, fiddling is an important aspect of Florida's folk culture. Consequently, fiddlers are well represented in the history of this award program. The pioneering bluegrass fiddler Robert "Chubby" Wise and the versatile western swing and bluegrass fiddle player George Custer were early recipients of the award (Hansen 2007:33). Recently, the virtuoso fiddler, James Kelly, has also received this honor along with a number of other fine players. Although Richard Seaman did not have a musical career that reached this kind of high profile, his musical contributions are subtle yet vital contributions to Florida's folklife.

His style is termed "old-time fiddling." The name refers primarily to the traditional dance tunes played for square dances at parties, generally called "hoedowns" but locally referred to as "frolics" or "free-for-alls" in Florida (Bronner 1987:12–17). This music predates contemporary country music and bluegrass, and it has likely been a part of the state's traditional culture since the early English period (Housewright 1991:56 and 66–67). One of the most significant aspects of Seaman's music is that he learned to play the fiddle prior to the widespread influence of radio and recorded music. He learned his initial repertory of dance tunes directly from other musicians who played at house parties in central Florida well over one hundred years ago. In particular, he credits an Osceola County musician named Joe Barber as an important early influence. With this continuity of tradition, Seaman's tunes remain an aural link to the soundscape of nineteenth-century central Florida.

Seaman began attending his community's house parties as a child, but he recalled that he was more interested in learning to play the tunes from Barber and other fiddlers than in dancing to the various sets that were played out on living room floors. As was typical in many parts of the country, Florida dances were held a few times a month when neighbors cleared out what little furniture they had, rolled back the rug, and sprinkled cornmeal or salt on the wood to make a slick surface for dancing (Martin 1994:42). Neighbors would arrive with instruments, cakes and pies, fruit punch, and often moonshine to create a Florida frolic that would last late into the night and often early into the morning. Seaman viewed these dances as one of the only forms of recreation in an area that he saw as starved for entertainment. Along with Sunday afternoon buggy rides, community picnics by the lake, and hunting and fishing parties, the dances were one of the only outlets for taking a break from the work of ranching, tending orange groves, and keeping a house. The fiddler's tunes made important contributions to the community, and the fiddler was valued as a musician, according to Seaman, even if he could play only a few tunes. What mattered the most was the ability to keep accurate time and convey the right sense of rhythm as dancers listened mainly for the bright bounce of the fiddler's syncopated shuffle so they could cut their figures across the room. He noted that sometimes the dances were even held without the play of a fiddle as the swings, do-si-dos, promenades, stars, and allemandes could all be called to the beat of someone merely tapping two broom handles against the floor to set up a rhythm for the hoedown.

One hundred years ago, Kissimmee was a small community. Ranching and tending the citrus groves were major industries, and the region was also known as a pristine area for hunting, fishing, and trapping. The Kissimmee Park neighborhood was formed after Hamilton Disston's late-nineteenth-century land purchase, so the area's recorded history is relatively recent

(Hansen 2007:19). Consequently, the local fiddling tradition mainly features tunes brought in from outside of the area. Many tunes in Richard Seaman's repertory consisted of hoedowns played at the turn of the nineteenth century. The tunes that he first learned in Kissimmee Park constituted an important part of his own core repertory, or the fiddle tunes that he played most frequently in various performances. They were also part of the core repertory of fiddle tunes that once were popular at the dances held in Kissimmee Park. Today, they provide a sample of tunes to which Floridians have danced for well over one hundred years, and they remain important elements of Kissimmee Park's early history. These tunes include

Shear 'Em
Mississippi Sawyer
Flop-Eared Mule
Sally Gooden
I Don't Love Nobody
Whistling Rufus
Stoney Point
Down Yonder
Marching through Georgia
Pop Goes the Weasel
Skip to My Lou
Cindy
Old Hen Cackled
Old Joe Clark
Soldier's Joy
Yellow Gals
Irish Washerwoman
At a Georgia Camp Meeting
Rag-Time Annie
Ida Red
Dance all Night with a Bottle in My Hand (Hansen 1996:85)

According to Seaman, the most popular of these tunes was "Shear 'Em." The hoedown is also known as "Cotton Bagging," and Bob Wills reworked it as a western swing piece titled "Take Me Back to Tulsa/Too Young to Marry." This tune also has lyrics that fiddlers and dancers would sometimes sing:

Makes no difference how you shear 'em,
Makes no difference how or when.
Makes no difference how you shear 'em,
Just shear 'em boys, shear 'em.
(Hansen 2007:140)

Lyrics are usually atypical for many fiddle tunes, but as Erynn Marshall explains, the lyrics and jig couplets are helpful mnemonic devices (Marshall 2006:64 and 80). Remembering the lyrics provides fiddlers with an easy way to learn and remember the melody line when playing by ear. The lyrics to Seaman's tunes are often phrased as couplets and regarded as somewhat frivolous, novelty elements in a song. He recalled the comic lyrics of two other tunes:

"Sally Gooden"
Up on the hill side, seen Sally coming,
Thought to my self, I'd kill myself a running.

Blackberry pie and huckleberry pudding,
Give it all away to see Sally Gooden.

"Old Hen Cackled"
Old hen cackled,
She cackled in the lot.

Second time she cackled,
She cackled in the pot.
(Hansen 2007:139–40)

Like many of the tunes in this core repertory, "Shear 'Em" was documented by folklorists by the 1930s (Linzee 1990). Chubby Wise learned the tune at this time while growing up in the Lake City area, and it remains a part of many Florida fiddlers' repertories today. Other tunes, such as "Mississippi Sawyer," "Flop-Eared Mule," "Stoney Point," and "Whistling Rufus," are commonly played in Florida and across the United States (Beisswenger 2002; Bronner 1987; Cauthen 2001; Guntharp 1980; Kartchner 1990; Marshall 2006; Martin 1994; Milnes 1999; and Wolfe 1997). While not unique to the local community, all of these tunes are characteristic of long-standing local musical preferences. Many of them originated as hoedown tunes for dancing. Some of these tunes, such as "Watermelon on the Vine," "Yellow Gals," "At a Georgia Camp Meeting," and "Pop Goes the Weasel," originally were played at minstrel shows, written by Tin Pan Alley composers, or first performed at play parties. One of the tunes, "Irish Washerwoman," is one of the few jigs in his repertory, but all of these tunes were used for dances early in Kissimmee Park's history. These tunes defined Seaman as an old-time fiddler, and they continue to be played at dances that showcase old-time fiddlers and string bands. One of the most significant aspects of the tunes' history is that they all predate musical genres created in response to mass media. The origin of his old-time fiddle tunes precedes the development of western swing fiddling in the 1930s and the refinement of bluegrass fiddling in the 1940s. Seaman played them in a style that other fiddlers would refer to as "old-time" (Youmans 1992:123–25).

Old-time music also includes other tunes that Seaman added to his repertory. While playing with fiddlers after he moved from Kissimmee to Jacksonville in the early 1920s, Seaman learned other hoedowns commonly played in Florida, including "Liberty," "Fourteen Days in Georgia," "Maple Sugar," "Rubber Dolly," "Up Jumped Trouble," and "Arkansas Traveler." By playing with musicians in Jacksonville, he also learned to perform waltzes, a genre that many musicians would also consider part of old-time fiddling. All of these old-time tunes were typically played either by solo fiddlers or by small string bands, featuring a combination of clawhammer banjo, guitar, mandolin, and string bass. Throughout Florida, variations on this line-up typically are used for live square dances, but string bands were atypical in Seaman's home community. The banjo was rarely played in Kissimmee Park, and he did not hear his first guitar until moving to Jacksonville. Seaman explained that in his community, fiddling was primarily a solo performance tradition. If two fiddlers played for a dance, they generally took turns. One took a break while the other played from a corner of the room, staying out of the way of the raucous dancing, complete with its heavy stomps, wild swings, and flailing kicks. Seaman believed that the old-time style of square dancing was much livelier than contemporary square dancing. He also explained that hosting dances in homes had died out by the 1940s and was replaced largely by dancing in public facilities and new styles of dancing in bars and honky-tonks. In respect to changes he has seen within Florida's social dancing, his life history reflects huge shifts in Florida's history.

These changes are also evident in Seaman's music making. During the 1920s, when he was working as an apprentice machinist for the Seaboard Air Line railroad, he further developed his musicianship within an urban context. Jacksonville was known as a "Fiddlers' Capital" at this time, and the popularity of fiddling is demonstrated in an old program advertising a "Fiddling and Hog Calling Contest." Over thirty fiddlers, including Richard Seaman, had participated in the event on May 15, 1930, and the next day's newspaper reported that over one thousand people were in the audience (Hansen 2007:90–91). Fiddling contests were held throughout the state, but their main draw was in urban areas. In these venues, the fiddler's role shifted away from how fiddlers were regarded within the rural community. Rather than being seen as a participant in the frolic who brought the music in the same way that other neighbors contributed by opening their homes, bringing along baked goods, and offering refreshments, the fiddler became more of a performer who presented his music on a spotlighted stage. The city's different social scene is also reflected in changes in his repertory through the addition of waltzes. Seaman noted that the waltz was rarely played and virtually never danced in Kissimmee Park's house parties. Instead, couple dances were much more popular in the city, where Seaman began playing in new venues. These venues included dancehalls and bars where people attended as couples and ideally stayed together the entire evening.

The city also brought Seaman new commercialized opportunities for performing. He began busking for cash on street corners, in barbershops, and as a hired musician for company picnics and other events. During this time, he frequently played with fellow musicians Jack Pitts, Clyde Kirkland, and Tom Acosta. Acosta later introduced him to Daisy Turknett, a vocalist and pianist whom Seaman married. The Seamans raised a family, and their two children also became well-known musicians in Florida's First Coast. Their home was known for its music, for the Seaman family hosted old-time square dances in their urban neighborhood.

Mass media has significantly affected old-time music. Early recording stars of the 1920s and 30s, such as the Carter Family and Jimmie Rodgers, profoundly influenced local musical traditions (Malone and Stricklin 2003:58). Seaman even met the "Singing Brakeman" when Rodgers bunked in Jacksonville's railroad industry's boardinghouse, where Seaman learned some of his tunes on the guitar. He also began to add tunes to his repertory that were recorded by "hillbilly" fiddlers onto cylinders and eventually 78 rpm records. One of the biggest influences of the new media on Seaman, however, was radio. He and Tom Acosta began playing on a half-hour radio show on WJAX. They called themselves "The Melody Makers," and they crafted a music variety show called *Uncle Josie's Farm.* This show featured old-time music, sentimental parlor tunes, and old hymns, but Seaman and Acosta also ventured into musical comedy in this golden age of radio. With an expression of amused chagrin, Seaman told how their show included comedy sketches, country humor, jokes, and barnyard animal imitations to create the aural ambience of this fictitious farm, owned and operated by the equally mythical "Uncle Josie." The program lasted less than a year, but the show gave him and The Melody Makers a great deal of exposure in north Florida. Seaman continued to play with these musicians after the show's demise, and music making provided a means of subsistence for his family when he was laid off from work during the Great Depression.

Seaman's old-time music is a form of roots music. His style of old-time music has had a major influence on the popular forms of country music that emerged out of a highly mass-mediated soundscape. Florida's fiddling tradition shares some commonalities with the hot Texas contest style, and Seaman learned to play western swing tunes that he added to his repertory. "San Antonio Rose," "Washington and Lee Swing," and "Faded Love" became part of his repertory via listening to Bob Wills and the Texas Playboys in the 1930s, and these tunes also continue to be popular among Florida's fiddlers. The old-time fiddling tradition, however, has had a greater influence on a style of music that Seaman never played: bluegrass music. Bluegrass is rooted in the music of old-time string bands that were recorded in the 1920s and

1930s. Its unique sound is refined by influences from other genres, including blues, gospel, ballads, and Tin-Pan Alley songs. Kentuckian Bill Monroe coalesced the bluegrass sound from this musical mélange in the 1940s, especially after bringing Earl Scruggs with his three-finger style of banjo picking into his band, and Florida's old-time fiddlers have directly contributed to the genre (Rosenberg 1985). Most notable is Chubby Wise, one of Monroe's earliest fiddlers, who is credited with refining the bluesy tone qualities of his fiddling to forge the quintessential bluegrass sound (Noles 2002). Seaman knew Wise, and they both appeared together with another bluegrass/swing fiddler, George Custer, in a workshop presentation at a folklife festival in Jacksonville during their later years (Hansen 2007:33–54).

Old-time fiddle tunes also are the roots for another element of Seaman's own musicianship. His fiddle tunes were important components of the repertory of a family band that he formed and named "The South Land Trail Riders." Consisting of himself on fiddle, Daisy Seaman on piano and vocals, his son Richard Keith on guitar, and his daughter Jeanne on guitar and vocals, the band also included other Jacksonville musicians who sang and played guitar or bass during the late 1940s and 1950s. The band played an eclectic variety of western swing and early country tunes that were recorded by artists like the Carter Family, Ernest Tubb, Bob Wills, Hank Williams, and other radio and recording stars. As the following set list from one of their shows reveals, they also played sentimental parlor songs, novelty songs, and old-time fiddle tunes as part of their performances:

Up Jumped Trouble
Aunt Diana's Quilting Party
When You and I Were Young, Maggie
Sweet Bunch of Daisies
Darling Nelly Gray
Red Wing
Good Ole Summer Time
Silver Bell
I'm Going Where the Roses Never Fade
Alabama Jubilee
Shear 'Em
I Don't Love Nobody
No Name Waltz
At a Georgia Camp Meeting (Hansen 2007:145–46)

Perusing this list shows the interplay between a musician's repertory and audience tastes over a half century ago. Seaman added these tunes to his repertory of hoedowns, waltzes, and western swing because The South Land Trail Riders no longer played mainly for dances. Instead, they were putting on shows for audiences who were sitting down and listening to a country band. Seaman's hoedowns are important, even definitive, components of his old-time style, but they became less prominent in his repertory as his life history progressed. By the end of his life, old-time fiddle tunes only constituted about one-third of the tunes in his active repertory. As folklorists and ethnomusicologists have shown, this variety of musical genres is fairly typical of many traditional fiddlers throughout the country (Cooley 1992:47 and Marshall 2006:178). Rather than thinking of old-time fiddling as representing a pure stream of oral/aural tradition, it is important to recognize the great diversity of a fiddler's repertory.

The South Land Trail Riders was a popular band in northeastern Florida. They played country music shows, picnics, and private parties, and for local fund-raisers. Seaman also continued to play for square dances as a solo fiddler or with another member of his band, until the popularity of the house parties waned and old-time music was largely replaced by newer forms of music by the late 1950s. These commercial genres included the Nashville sound in country music, rock-a-billy, and eventually rock-n-roll. By the mid 1950s, the idea of square dancing in a neighbor's home came to be seen as old-fashioned. The shifts in musical tastes were also coupled with problems with keeping a band together, and Seaman disbanded his group by 1955. At this time, he also quit playing his fiddle and laid the instrument on his mantel for over thirty years. Having a period of time when fiddlers chose not to perform is a common element of other fiddlers' life histories, and the impetus for not playing is motivated by numerous factors (Beisswenger 2002:79–83). Seaman quit playing because there were limited opportunities to perform with other musicians due to changing musical tastes. It is ironic that Seaman stopped playing right before a major folk music revival began in the 1950s.

While this folk music revival had little direct effect on Seaman's music making, it may have influenced him in other ways. He began attending the annual Florida Folk Festival and various bluegrass music shows—as a listener rather than as a performer. The popularity of this folk festival and the many bluegrass shows in Florida are directly related to the revival of folk music in the state, and in attending these events, Seaman became known within Jacksonville's bluegrass music community. Connections that he made finally influenced Seaman to revive his own musical tradition when he met Jack Piccalo, a banjo player and guitarist who encouraged him to resume playing in 1986. Piccalo began backing Seaman's fiddling, and the two began playing together. At first, they played solely in Seaman's living room and at informal jam sessions. Eventually, they formed the Richard Seaman Band. For nearly

Richard Seaman playing with his band at the 1996 Florida Folk Festival. Photo by Gregory Hansen.

the last two decades of his life, Seaman once again performed in public. Some of the new venues included playing for the Duval County Folklife in Education Program, the Florida Folk Festival, bluegrass shows, and an interdisciplinary arts event called "Arts Mania" (Hansen 2007:9–17). Playing at these venues marked a major difference from his earlier performances. Rather than performing as an integral part of a rural community in central Florida or as a semiprofessional musician in the city, Seaman's presentations took on a different tone. His playing became a showcase for a revived tradition. This sense of his music and himself as a living treasure of Florida's rich culture heritage was most poignantly evident when he was honored with the Folk Heritage Award at the age of ninety-six at the Florida Folk Festival. Seaman returned to the festival the next year to make his final public performance in May 2002.

Florida's Folk Heritage Award not only recognized his musical contributions, but also honored him as a talented storyteller. He would frequently include tall tales that he first learned in central Florida in his stage patter during numerous performances in schools and folk festivals. In other events, he was given the stage to present solely his stories. His repertoire consisted of more than thirty tall tales. These narratives are not necessarily unique to the state, but they are representative of various tale types that have been told throughout Florida's history. An excerpt from a telling that he gave at the 1992 Florida Folk Festival provides his versions of AT Type 1889: *Snakebite causes object to swell;* Motif J426.2: *Snake wants to eat frog friend* (also known as the "Convivial Snake"); AT Motif D2156.2: *Miraculous increasing of milk from one cow;* and AT Type 1920: *Contest in Lying* (Thomas 1984:35 and Thompson 1961).

I saw a rattlesnake out there in the potato patch.
I was hoeing potatoes.
And that was the biggest rattlesnake I ever saw in my life.
Well, I didn't have nothing in my hand but a hoe, and that's what I had to kill him with.
So I started hoeing away at that snake,
    and he started fighting back.
And we had our battle royal out there.
    That was a big snake, and he fought awful hard.
I was just framing away at him with this hoe.
    And he was biting at it.
And in the fracas, he bit the hoe handle.
    He didn't bite me,
        thank the Lord,
    But he did bite the hoe handle before I got him killed.
And after I got him killed, I looked over there,
and that hoe handle began swelling,
and it swelled as big as a log.
So I got me a log cart, and I carried it to the sawmill—
    had it sawed up into lumber.
And I brought it home, and I built me a mule shed.
    And I put my mule in it and went to bed.
        It was getting late—
            thought I had done pretty good.
The next morning, when I got up, that there swelling had gone out of that lumber,
and it shrunk down on my mule, plumb to death.

One day, I was fishing down at Kissimmee River—
    That's way down there, down the state.
    It's a beautiful place down there with trees overlapping the river bank.
    And you could sit there and let your feet hang down,
    And fish,
    And just enjoy nature out there.

One day, I was sitting there fishing, and I heard an awful commotion in the bushes there.
    And I went over to see about it.
    And it was a snake that had caught a bullfrog.
    That old water-moccasin had caught a bullfrog,
    and that old bullfrog was croaking and a-hollering,
        trying to get loose.
Well, I knew that snake had to have his dinner,
    but I thought I'd have some fun with him.
So I went over to a willow tree and cut off a branch with a forked end on it,
    and I trimmed it off.
    And I walked over to where that snake was,
    and I pushed that forked stick right down over that snake's neck,
        right in back of his head,
        and held him down.
And I pulled out that frog and let him go.
Well, that frog left there.
He left there in about two directions at the same time.
    He was leaving there.
But while I had him held down there, I reached into my pocket and got a bottle of
white lightning.
Old moonshine.
And I give that snake a good drink of moonshine.
    Poured his mouth plumb full, and then I turned him loose.
And I went on and sat down.
Went to fishing and forgot about it.
And after a while, I felt something tap me on the back, and I turned around,
    And looked.
And there was that darn fool snake with another toad in its mouth.

My sister had a cow that fell in the well down there one day.
The best milk cow they had in Osceola County.
    So we went down there to see about it.
And then we didn't know what we were going to do about the cow in the well.
    Nobody could get it out—
        in those days we didn't have wreckers,
        or anything to pull them out with,
        in an abandoned well,
        out there in the field.

Well, we went down there, and sure enough,
    the cow was in the well.
I told them that wouldn't be no trouble to get the cow out of the well.
So I went into the house, and I got a ladder,
    and I climbed down the well where the cow was.
And I started milking.
Well, I milked that old cow,
    and I kept right on milking her.
And I floated her right out of that well.
There was no trouble to it.

I had a rooster on the farm that was the laziest rooster I ever seen in my life.
He was actually so lazy so when the neighbor's rooster would crow in the morning, he just nodded his head and would say "Amen."[1]

These texts are but a small sample of the many tall tales that comprised his repertory. He told the tall tales because they were inherently interesting and entertaining to modern-day audiences, but it is curious that he rarely had told the stories when he was with The Melody Makers and The South Land Trail Riders over half a century ago. He found that contemporary audiences seemed to appreciate the tall tales more, and Seaman used them to paint a highly stylized portrait of the rural context for his old-time tunes. The stories added variety to his performances and enlivened the flavor of his old-time fiddle tunes, a genre of music perhaps better suited to accompany dancers than to be listened to by a seated audience. On the literal level, the stories provided him with the ability to present salient features of his life experiences in rural Florida, thereby establishing the resonant aspects of the context for his old-time music. On a figurative level, the stories articulated important values that he learned within his home community. The stories' humor and hyperbole typically turn around ideals such as resourcefulness, cleverness, community-mindedness, self-sufficiency, and a subtle sense of modesty that seems to belie the braggadocio implicit in some of the tales.

The tall-tale genre, in turn, is but one of the many genres within a wider repertory of narratives. He told the tall tales and various jokes in numerous public folklore events, but in other settings, Seaman also told vivid accounts of local history, captivating personal experience narratives, and fascinating local legends. His most compelling stories portray a more complicated and nuanced view of Florida. Whereas the tall tales are entertaining to hear, his skill as a raconteur often emerged more powerfully in other stories, that he typically recounted only in private. The tall tales provide one context for his rural upbringing, which he freely presented to public audiences. The more accurate and vivid presentations of this context, however, emerged in the stories that he mainly told in the domestic sphere. From his living room in Jacksonville, Seaman gave an elaborate account of the context for the house parties in Kissimmee Park:

> We lived back out in the woods, and we had no electricity. We had no running water or anything like that. So there wasn't much to do but work.
>
> My Dad took care of a seventy-five acre orange grove for a man by the name of McCool. William McCool, from Beaver Falls, Pennsylvania, he owned that land. And they would come down there in the wintertime and hunt. It was good hunting and fishing around on that lake and them swamps down there.
>
> And that was the only outlet we had—other than taking care of the orange grove and working for Old Man McCool. That's what we had to do, and when I got big enough, I had to get out there and help with them. Plowing and fruiting trees, hoeing trees, taking care of fencing, and mending fence—and anything that happens on the farm. And we had no outlet. When the sun went down, that was it.
>
> We'd generally eat about dark. In the time the supper dishes were washed, why, it was dark. And there was nothing else to do but just sit around. Read a book if you had one. Maybe us kids would play games. Mother would sew a quilt. She was always making something, like making a quilt or mending clothes. Dad would read an old book if he had one.
>
> The only outlet we had was if the neighbors would get together, and your next door neighbor might be three-quarters of a mile or a mile away. They'd get together on a Sunday and go and have a picnic down at the lake. And they'd seine some fish and have a fish fry. We thought that was wonderful.
>
> A lot of Saturdays—evenings—why for something to do, they'd have a square dance somewhere. And there'd be one or two old fiddlers—or someone who tried to fiddle. There was never experts at it. And they would sit down and saw on this fiddle, and they'd dance all night long.
>
> Some of the women still had their old bonnets on and their aprons. But they didn't care. They was having a lot of fun.
>
> And then Sunday, it was just recuperate to go back to work Monday. It was the same routine, over and over. Fishing and hunting was my outlet.

> I had a lot of territory there that I could hunt, trap, fish, and in the wintertime we would catch a few furs, coons and stuff like that, and try to sell the hides to a hardware store by the name of McKinson. That would give me a little spending money. In the summertime, we'd hunt alligators and sit up all night and fight mosquitoes and try to kill us a few alligators. And we thought that was fun. All that is gone now. Everything is gone.
>
> They've got electric lights, and they even got a fire department out there now where we used to live. People have come up there in trailers. And the old place, you wouldn't know it. The old orange groves, the last bad freeze we had, which was several years ago, wiped it out. And that's all dead.
>
> There's nothing out there now like it was. (Hansen 2007:19–20)

This eloquent overview of his homeplace vividly renders Seaman's understanding of the place of fiddling and square dancing in Kissimmee Park. The landscape has changed. The area truly does look very different from Seaman's portrait. There may be fragments of the old forms of recreation, as fishing and hunting remain popular activities, but the old frolics and the spontaneous neighborhood picnics died out long ago.

The old-time fiddle tunes and his stories, however, remain as important features of Florida's aural environment. This soundscape continues to resound with these tunes, and the stories come alive when read aloud. Listeners and performers alike can continue to hear tunes like "Shear 'Em," "Mississippi Sawyer," and "Flop-Eared Mule" and discover musical continuities that stretch from the early twenty-first century back into the nineteenth. The old-time tunes remain part of the state's soundscape, despite the new contexts for hearing the music. Seaman's stories further animate the musical features of the state's soundscape, and the tales and tunes contribute to the audio ambience of Florida.

Richard Seaman's contributions to this soundscape live on in contemporary Florida's folklife. During the annual Florida State Fiddle Contest in 2002, a young Tallahassee fiddler named Maitland Jones played a little-known tune titled the "Annie Seaman Waltz." He had met Richard Seaman a few months previously, and he learned the tune from a tape recording and a musical transcription made by his teacher, Jane Scott. Seaman had written the tune a few years previously, and he named it in honor of his second wife. They married in 1989, when both were well into their eighties, and the story of their December/December courtship commonly is told when fiddlers play this little waltz. Along with his tunes, stories about Richard Seaman himself now accompany the tunes he played and the stories that he told. His own story is now emerging as an important facet of the state's long-enduring but ever-changing soundscape.

At the end of my fieldwork venture into Florida's Space Coast, I returned back to Kissimmee. I had obtained a press pass that allowed me to photograph the Silver Spurs Rodeo in the old arena that was about to be torn down and replaced with a new facility. Leaning against the fence to load a new roll of film into my camera, I paused a moment to listen to the rodeo's band. They had just finished playing "Down Yonder," and I heard the shuffle bowing of a familiar tune. As the cowboy band kicked off "Shear 'Em," I smiled once again, recognizing that Richard Seaman would enjoy knowing that I had the chance to hear his tunes played live in his home community.

Note

1. These texts are traditional folktales that first appeared in print in my 1996 article "The Relevance of 'Authentic Tradition' in Studying an Oldtime Florida Fiddler," *Southern Folklore* 53:87. The story of his sister's milkcow is presented in Kristin Congdon's *Uncle Monday and Other Florida Tales* (Jackson: University Press of Mississippi, 2001), 90. I have transcribed them in a style termed "ethnopoetics." There are various approaches to this style, but the central idea is to change the conventions of writing to render a story more like a representation of a verbal performance rather than a written transcription. I am most influenced by Glassie's rationale for using ethnopoetics as set forth in *The Stars of Ballymenone* (Bloomington: Indiana University Press, 2006), 504–5. His style emphasizes the use of new lines to represent the flow of a narrative and the use of white space to illustrate the logical development of a narrative.

Works Cited

Beisswenger, Drew. 2002. *Fiddling Way Out Yonder: The Life and Music of Melvin Wine.* Jackson: University Press of Mississippi.

Bronner, Simon. 1987. *Old-Time Music Makers of New York State.* Syracuse: Syracuse University Press.

Cauthen, Joyce H. 2001. *With Fiddle and Well-Rosined Bow: A History of Old-Time Fiddling in Alabama.* Tuscaloosa: University of Alabama Press.

Congdon, Kristin G. 2002. *Uncle Monday and Other Florida Tales.* Jackson: University Press of Mississippi.

Cooley, Timothy J. 1992. "When a Tune Becomes a Folk Tune: Fiddling in Southern Illinois." *Missouri Folklore Society Journal* 13 and 14:45–79.

Glassie, Henry. 2006. *The Stars of Ballymenone.* Bloomington: Indiana University Press.

Guntharp, Matthew. 1980. *Learning the Fiddler's Ways.* University Park: Pennsylvania State University Press.

Hansen, Gregory. 1996. "The Relevance of 'Authentic Tradition' in Studying an Oldtime Florida Fiddler." *Southern Folklore* 53:67–89.

———. 2007. *A Florida Fiddler: The Life and Times of Richard Seaman.* Tuscaloosa: University of Alabama Press.

Housewright, Wiley L. 1991. *A History of Music and Dance in Florida, 1565–1865.* Tuscaloosa: University of Alabama Press.

Kartchner, Kenner C. 1990. *Frontier Fiddler: The Life of a Northern Arizona Pioneer.* Edited by Larry V. Shumway. Tucson: University of Arizona Press.

Linzee, Jill. 1990. *A Reference Guide to Florida Folklore from the Federal WPA Deposited in the Florida Folklife Archives.* Edited by Ormond H. Loomis and Deborah S. Fant. White Springs: Florida Department of State/Bureau of Florida Folklife Programs.

Lopez, Barry, ed. 2006. *Home Ground: Language for an American Landscape.* San Antonio: Trinity University Press.

Malone, Bill C., and David Stricklin. 2003. *Southern Music/American Music.* Revised and expanded edition. Lexington: University of Kentucky Press.

Marshall, Erynn. 2006. *Music in the Air Somewhere: The Shifting Borders of West Virginia's Fiddle and Song Traditions.* Morgantown: West Virginia University Press.

Martin, Philip. 1994. *Farmhouse Fiddlers: Music & Dance Traditions in the Rural Midwest.* Mt. Horeb, WI: Midwest Traditions.

Milnes, Gerald. 1999. *Play of a Fiddle: Traditional Music, Dance, and Folklore in West Virginia.* Lexington: University of Kentucky Press.

Noles, Randy. 2002. *The Orange Blossom Boys: The Untold Story of Ervin T. Rouse, Chubby Wise, and the World's Most Famous Fiddle Tune.* Anaheim, CA: Centerstream Publishing.

Rosenberg, Neil V. 1985. *Bluegrass: A History.* Urbana: University of Illinois Press.

Schafer, R. Murray. 1993. *The Soundscape: Our Sonic Environment and the Tuning of the World.* Rochester, VT: Destiny Books.

Thomas, Robert. 1984. "*Non Nimium Credendum Antiquitati:* But Don't Throw the Baby Out with the Bathwater." In *First Citizens and Other Florida Folks: Essays on Florida Folklife.* Edited by Ronald Foreman. 35–43. Publications of the Florida Division of Archives, History and Records Management, No. 1. Tallahassee: Florida Department of State.

Thompson, Stith. 1961. *The Types of the Folk-Tale.* 2nd revised ed. Helsinki: Folklore Fellows Communication no. 184.

Wolfe, Charles K. 1997. *The Devil's Box: Masters of Southern Fiddling.* Nashville: Vanderbilt University Press/Country Music Foundation.

Youmans, Julie. 1992. "Warming the Cold Notes: Style and Boundaries in Old-Time Fiddling." *Missouri Folklore Society Journal* 13 and 14:123–32.

Legacy and Meaning in the Changing Sacred Harp Tradition of the Okefenokee Region

LAURIE K. SOMMERS

ON MAY 4, 1958, SINGING SCHOOL TEACHER SILAS LEE, FROM HOBOKEN, Brantley County, Georgia, took a small group of Sacred Harp singers to the stage of the Florida Folk Festival (FFF).[1] The singers had traveled from their homes in the Okefenokee region of southeast Georgia and northeast Florida to the festival site located in the north-central Florida community of White Springs. They sang three songs from the *B. F. White Sacred Harp, Revised Cooper Edition,* to the polite applause of the audience.[2] This was the first of two late 1950s appearances at the festival by the Hoboken group and the only one recorded for posterity. The 1958 recording is an important sonic benchmark in the history of this significant local variant of Sacred Harp. Silas Lee pitched the singing quite low, so the singers could sing the melodies slowly in a richly ornamented style influenced by their own tradition of Primitive Baptist hymn singing. These two intertwined musical traditions—Primitive Baptist hymnody and Sacred Harp—have been defining genres for this small rural region for well over a century.

Although Sacred Harp became a mainstay of the Florida Folk Festival, the Hoboken FFF appearances were an anomaly. Hoboken singers rarely sang with or for outsiders again for nearly fifty years. Instead, this singing community became more insular and influenced by conservative Primitive Baptist beliefs, especially those of the Crawfordites, the most conservative of local Primitive Baptist subsects who take their name from the nineteenth-century south Georgia elder, Reuben Crawford. By the 1990s, participation had shrunk to a small cadre of Crawfordites, and the nondenominational, community legacy of local Sacred Harp was in jeopardy. In 1994, cousins and current song leaders David and Clarke Lee of Hoboken, Georgia, launched a deliberate effort to open up and change their Sacred Harp tradition in order to save it for future generations. Hoboken and the Lee family subsequently achieved celebrity status among the national Sacred Harp Diaspora;[3] many viewed visits to Hoboken's monthly Sacred Harp sings as "pilgrimages" to the wellspring of "the ultimate traditional Sacred Harp singers."[4] The Hoboken annual All-Day Sing in March[5] "has swelled to become one of the largest Sacred Harp gatherings in the country, drawing several hundred singers a year, an exceptional number for a one-day singing."[6] Members of the national Sacred Harp singing network and scholars (myself included) now inextricably link this Sacred Harp variant with Hoboken, Georgia, and with the Lee family as its exemplar and cultural ambassador. For local folks who have always sung this music, it is simply "Sacred Harp," four-note singing, or singing from the "note book" (as opposed to the words only hymnal, *Primitive Hymns* by Benjamin Lloyd, which many use at local Primitive Baptist churches).

I first met the Lees and attended my first Hoboken Sacred Harp sing in January 1997, just a few years into the remarkable transformation of this singing community. As a folklorist and ethnomusicologist then based in south Georgia, I began to document the singers and sings as part of the South Georgia Folklife Project at Valdosta State University (1996–2006). My tape-recorded interviews from this period, combined with participant observation at many singing events, provide the primary source material for this article. I also involved Hoboken singers in several public programs, including their return to the Florida Folk Festival in May 2000. Nearly fifty members of the Lee family from Georgia and Florida joined with other singers for the Silas Lee Memorial Sing, an event that I instigated as part of a special Okefenokee section of the swampways-themed folklife area. I previously had shared with David Lee a copy of the 1958 festival recording discovered in the Florida State Archives; he deliberately repeated history (and created another sonic benchmark) by opening the sing with the same three songs led by Silas Lee in 1958, three years to the weekend from the death of the elder Lee at age eighty-five. As Johnny Lee, Silas's nephew and David's father, remarked that day, "A lot has changed since 1958, the year we were down here . . . . One thing has not changed: this book (the Cooper revision of *The Sacred Harp*), the heritage, the legacy, the memory, and the meaning. The deep spiritual meaning has not changed."[7]

This chapter chronicles continuity and change in "Hoboken-style" Sacred Harp tradition, using recordings from the 1958 and 2000 Florida Folk Festivals as points of departure: 1958, capturing the in-group community tradition that had evolved in southeast Georgia and northeast Florida, largely

Clarke Lee (*left*) and David I. Lee walk time at the 2001 All-Day Sing, Hoboken, Georgia. Photo by Laurie K. Sommers. Courtesy of South Georgia Folklife Collections, Valdosta State University Archives and Special Collections of Odum Library.

independent of the other traditions of southern Sacred Harp; and 2000, capturing the increasing hybridization of the new public face of "Hoboken style" with traditions from neighboring Alabama, Florida, and elsewhere. I discuss continuity and change through an interpretive history of the tradition, paying particular attention to the factors that shaped Hoboken's distinctive singing style and to the core values that make the singing meaningful to local singers. The focus is Sacred Harp singing, but the Okefenokee regional tradition cannot be understood without examining its symbiotic relationship with Primitive Baptist hymnody. Although Hoboken and the Lees are pivotal, these associations obscure the community nature of the tradition and the deep-rooted patterns of cultural interchange along the border between southeast Georgia and northeast Florida. David I. Lee underscored this point from the stage of the 2000 FFF: "This music has been part of our culture and our life at home around Hoboken for not just the Lee family, but for the entire community and for actually that entire region."[8]

The area that gave birth to Hoboken-style Sacred Harp lies in and around the Okefenokee Swamp of southeast Georgia and northeast Florida. When Silas Lee's group came to the FFF, the local economy still revolved around turpentining and logging, herding free range cattle and hogs, subsistence agriculture (or as David Lee explains it, "farming for groceries"[9]), and the railroad with its great crossroads in Waycross, Georgia, and continuing south through Florida. Most members of the singing community trace their heritage to the British Isles with names like Lee, Carter, Conner, Hickox, Strickland, Dowling, Prescott, and Chesser. Many early settlers had migrated to the region from the Carolinas or further north in Georgia, rather than directly from the British Isles.

The geography of the great swamp shaped the distinctive culture of "Swamper" families who lived at the fringes of the Okefenokee and on islands scattered across its interior. Beginning in 1912, naturalist and folklore collector Francis Harper documented the music, tales, customs, hunting and fishing, material culture, and speech of the Swampers. Harper's documentation provides a fascinating window into the musical culture that surrounded Sacred Harp through the Great Depression. Swampers embraced an oral tradition of unaccompanied ballads, local songs, fiddle and banjo tunes played for frolics, and the yodels or hollers used to signal over long distances, to gather free-range hogs or cattle, or for the sheer joy of hollering. Sacred Harp singing was the only religious music Harper recorded, although his field notes mention Primitive Baptist hymnody (a tradition he likely was not allowed to record due to Primitive Baptist beliefs).[10] He made the first known recording of Sacred Harp in the region, borrowing a battery-powered tape recorder from the Library of Congress in the summer of 1944 and recording some seventy-five minutes of Swamper music and narrative, including four songs from *The Sacred Harp, Revised Cooper Edition* sung by four members of the Chesser family, of Chesser's Island in the Georgia Okefenokee. By the time of these historic recordings, however, the creation of the National Wildlife Refuge had already begun to displace Swamper families, forever altering the unique, place-based culture Harper first encountered in 1912. Some traditions successfully transplanted to surrounding communities in Georgia and Florida. Others simply disappeared. Sacred Harp and Primitive Baptist hymnody are the most enduring of the musical traditions Harper observed, due in large part to the strength of local Primitive Baptist religion and worldview.

The Primitive Baptist faith dominated religious practice through WWII and was a crucial force in the development of Sacred Harp singing along the Florida-Georgia frontier. Even nonmembers attended meetings at the church houses. These spare, wooden buildings served as gathering places in the sparsely populated piney woods. Weekend meetings, and especially the annual or Big Meeting, fulfilled social and spiritual needs for rural families. The oldest surviving churches, or meetinghouses as they often are called, date to the early nineteenth century. High Bluff, Brantley County, Georgia, and Sardis in Charlton County, Georgia, both were constituted in 1819. Pigeon Creek Primitive Baptist Church of Nassau County, Florida, was founded in 1821 and is the oldest of the state's Baptist churches.[11] The term "primitive" refers to members' desire to follow the ways of the original or "primitive" Christian church. Clusters of like-minded Primitive churches banded together in associations, rather than organizing as part of a formal denomination. As Delma Presley observes in *Okefinokee Album*,

> Outsiders often have misunderstood the Primitive Baptists, assuming that such believers are backward, superstitious, or overly emotional . . . Whether the questions concern organized missions, church-supported seminaries, or musical instruments, Primitive Baptists tend to respond that "these things are foreign to the Bible and to the old ways." For their stubbornness and deep-seated conservatism, they have become known as "hardshell" Baptists. They insist on using real wine at communion and on washing the feet of brothers-and sisters-in-the-faith, just as the New Testament commands.[12]

The practitioners of Hoboken-style Sacred Harp historically have been Crawfordite Primitive Baptists whose strict discipline and doctrine follow the interpretations of Reuben Crawford, influential nineteenth-century elder in the Alabaha River Association of Primitive Baptists. The ultraconservative Crawfordites sought to continue most practices "as in the time of Uncle Reuben" and increasingly isolated themselves even from other Primitive Baptist associations.[13] Their slow, metered, ornamented a cappella hymns, many of them lined, represent the most conservative end of the musical spectrum among the region's Primitive Baptists.[14]

From the late nineteenth century, when Primitive Baptists of the Wiregrass South experienced their heyday, through WWII, the Crawfordite Primitive Baptists numbered as many as eighteen churches on either side of the Georgia/Florida line. Each church held its meeting one weekend a month; on the other weekends, members and the community at large visited another church in the Alabaha River Association, of which these churches were a part. In addition to congregational singing during the service, members gathered to sing before the start of the service, a practice that continues today. But hymn singing also occurred frequently outside formal worship, often paired with songs from the *Sacred Harp* book. David I. Lee recalls, for example, how he and his cousin Clarke Lee would "sing for their supper" after the conclusion of the weekend worship at the meetinghouse:

Singing from *Primitive Hymns* by Benjamin Lloyd after a service at Sardis Primitive Baptist Church, Folkston, Georgia, 1997. Photo by Laurie K. Sommers. Courtesy of South Georgia Folklife Collections, Valdosta State University Archives and Special Collections of Odum Library.

> They would prepare a big meal and a lot of people would go by and enjoy being together. Clarke and I, as young men, would be called into the kitchen, . . . and since none of us had radios and none of us had televisions, I guess . . . the ladies that were in there cooking, we were their entertainment. . . . And so while they . . . cooked and bustled about the kitchen, Clarke and I sat there and sang from memory, or we'd gather up the books we needed and sing out of the hymn book or sing out of the shape-note book. The one thing that it guaranteed us was that we were the favorites of the ladies, and so we got the biggest and the hottest biscuit, and we got the biggest piece of cake or the first piece of cake.[15]

Visitors came from further afield and in greater numbers during the yearly annual or Big Meeting, which typically included a Sacred Harp sing on Saturday evening. This network of churches, then, disseminated and maintained the Crawfordite style of hymnody and fostered the close association between Sacred Harp and hymn singing.

Crawfordite hymnody is part of a larger tradition of unaccompanied congregational singing among Primitive Baptists. Crawfordites also share with many other Primitive Baptists the continued use of *Primitive Hymns* by

Benjamin Lloyd (1841), a compilation of poetic texts organized according to topic, which reflect Primitive Baptist belief and discipline. Lloyd completed *Primitive Hymns* at a time when many Baptist churches were abandoning practices of a cappella singing with word-only hymn books in favor of hymnals with printed music used with instrumental accompaniment. Lloyd's was a "new" compilation that preserved the long-established worship practice of lined and unaccompanied hymn singing. As folklorist John Bealle has observed, subsequent generations of Primitive Baptists have associated this little book with their love for the "old sound."[16] The Crawfordites still use the "700" hymn version, as opposed to the 705 tune expansion adopted in 1906, in deference to the old ways, and have subsidized special printings as needed by using the pre-1906 plates.[17] Hymn texts are sung to memorized tunes in the appropriate meter. In her study of Primitive Baptist hymnody, Beverly Patterson describes how the absence of notation fostered rhythmic and melodic freedom and "serves some Primitive Baptists as a stimulus to the kind of heartfelt interpretations they believe were characteristic of the generations before them."[18] Slow tempos allow time to meditate on the spiritual import of the text and to elaborate and embellish the tune. Primitive Baptists frequently use alternate tunes and adjust the tune to fit the words.[19]

Many of these tunes, once part of oral tradition, were later compiled into shape-note songsters like *Sacred Harp*, a book published during the same period as the Lloyd hymnal. This synchronicity, and the fact that the Sacred Harp is also sung without musical accompaniment, explains the enduring popularity of Sacred Harp singing among many Primitive Baptists. For Crawfordites, Sacred Harp was the only approved music outside the hymns of the meetinghouse. Certainly, they were surrounded by secular oral repertoires like those documented by Harper, the music of the public schools, and even popular music of the day. Before joining the church, these genres of music were part of everyday life. But Sacred Harp singing was uniquely situated to meet the social and spiritual needs of the entire community, whether they were Primitive Baptists, other denominations, or not church members at all.

The Sacred Harp, first published in 1844 by B. F. White and E. J. King—residents of western Georgia—is the most popular shape-note songster used in this singing style today. Sacred Harp singing has been part of local community life along the Georgia-Florida frontier for over 150 years. Delorese Conner Lee, born in 1930 and raised in Nassau County, Florida, heard stories of her great-grandparents on both sides of the family singing Sacred Harp. This includes singers from Nassau County on her father's side and the Georgia Okefenokee on her mother's.[20] Pioneering settlers carried with them a variety of shape-note tune books as they migrated to south Georgia and Florida from Sacred Harp hearth areas further north. Hoboken-area singing communities currently use the *B. F. White Sacred Harp, Revised Cooper Edition*, known by singers as the Cooper book. Compiler W. M. Cooper of Dothan, Alabama, first published his revision in 1902. Cooper is widely credited with adding a fourth (alto) line to the bass, treble (or high harmony), and tenor/melody lines of previous *Sacred Harp* editions and revisions.

The Cooper book is popular in much of southern Georgia, Alabama, Texas, Mississippi, north Florida, and the Panhandle. Silas Lee, however, recalled using various books during his long career as a song leader and singing schoolteacher in southeast Georgia and northeast Florida. In addition, many songs were sung orally, "handed down to us by inspired men of old," as stated in the preface to *The Pilgrim's Harp*, also known simply as "the brown book," a self-published compilation of words and tunes to locally sung old favorites by David and Clarke Lee of Hoboken, and Phillip Reeves of Callahan, Florida. *The Pilgrim's Harp* compilers traced these songs and texts to various shape-note songsters and hymnals, among them Georgia-originated four-shape books such as *The Social Harp*, by John G. McCurry (1855); various revisions and older editions to the *Sacred Harp*; classic four-shape books such as William Walker's *Southern Harmony* (1854), the most popular shape-note tune book of the nineteenth century; and various seven-shape compilations used for their words only, since local singers could not read seven-shape notation: the Southern Baptist *Broadman Hymnal* (1940), Stamps-Baxter's *Favorite Songs and Hymns*, Primitive Baptist hymnals such as *The Good Old Songs: The Cream of the Old Music*, compiled by Elder C. H. Cayce, and *The Harp of Ages* (1925). *The Pilgrim Harp* source material illustrates both the variety of hymnals and shape-note books influencing Okefenokee region singing, and the pervasive oral circulation of tunes popular along the Georgia/Florida state line that had been compiled into various published collections. Even though religious beliefs of Crawfordite singers encouraged cultural isolation, other books and tunes entered the tradition.

The singers of south Georgia and north Florida historically shared familial and communal Sacred Harp singing contexts similar to those of other white, Protestant shape-note communities throughout the rural South. The earliest photodocumentation of Sacred Harp singing in the Okefenokee region comes from Francis Harper, who photographed members of the Robert Allen Chesser family in 1922, "singing out of the 4-note book, or Sacred Harp, on the porch of their Chesser's Island home place, deep in the Okefenokee Swamp."[21] Although Harper staged the photograph, it captured the very real home-based setting of much Sacred Harp. Delorese Conner Lee

One of the earliest known photos of Okefenokee region Sacred Harp shows members of the Robert Allen Chesser family singing on the porch, Chesser's Island in the Okefenokee Swamp, Charlton County, Georgia, 1922. Photo by Francis Harper, courtesy of Delma Presley.

recalls, for example, that during her childhood in Nassau County, Florida, her family sang from the Cooper book while sitting together on the porch, around the dining table, and during the evenings of the annual or "Big Meeting" of their Primitive Baptist church. At most of these gatherings, the family also sang from the Lloyd hymnal. Delorese learned by hearing her mother, Carrie Hickox Conner, who grew up in the Okefenokee south of Waycross, Georgia.[22] When Delorese married Johnny Lee of Hoboken, nephew to Silas, it was a marriage of the already intertwined Georgia-Florida singing tradition, as well as a love match. The couple's son, David I. Lee, was raised in Jacksonville and Nassau County until he was fifteen, when the family moved to Hoboken. Like his parents, he grew up with Sacred Harp. "My earliest memories go back to when I was sitting in a chair and my feet were sticking out in front of me. I wasn't big enough for my feet to touch the floor. And holding a book in my lap, singing by myself." David's boyhood memories resound with Sacred Harp: "We'd sing anywhere that we're together, whether it be a funeral, a wedding, a baptism, a group of people around a dining room table, in the kitchen, beside the river."[23] All of these contexts also included hymn singing.

Sacred Harp singing permeated families and communities. One of the strongest traditions originated in Hoboken, Georgia, where in the early

1950s, Brantley County superintendent Herschel Herrin and song leader Silas Lee initiated monthly Sacred Harp sings at the Hoboken School. In Nassau County, Florida, singers periodically gathered in small buildings like a renovated egg house or a simple building constructed just for singing. As David Lee remembers it, "Everybody in our family sang, everybody . . . They learned from their elders and once a year they'd have a singing school at the schoolhouse.[24]

Singing schools are the traditional means for teaching Sacred Harp. In the Okefenokee region, early singing schools occasionally were held in the Primitive Baptist churches (always outside formal worship), but more frequently took place in rural country schools. Delorese Conner Lee recalls that during the mid- to late 1930s, when she was still too young to attend, singing schools were held in Double Branch School in Nassau County, the little one-room schoolhouse where she attended first through eighth grades. She heard stories of her uncle John Newton Conner, who had taught singing schools, but this was before her time.[25] During Delorese's girlhood, the local singing school teacher was Silas Lee, who by his own account taught widely throughout the region beginning in the 1930s:

> The first sing that I tried to lead was in 1932. From then I went on to lead sings and singing schools in north Florida and all over south Georgia . . . That has been almost 50 years ago. Most of the time I was the only one that could lead a sing. . . . When I would go down to Florida for a singing school I would leave on Thursday, and I would pay my way to Hilliard or Callahan. We would have the sing for three days straight. We would start on Friday after lunch, on Saturday at about church time which was 10 a.m., and on Sunday at the same time. And we would sing for as long as we could hold out. The singing school would last for about eight weeks. We would average about 25–30 people and maybe a little more after word got around. Those were the Hoover days [the administration of Herbert Hoover, 1929–1933], so nobody had much. Most of the time, I was offered pay but never got much. Of course, I had syrup and biscuits and maybe some turnip greens and generally enough money for the bus or the train. I always stuck it out because I loved it, and I have continued to follow it.[26]

Itinerant singing school teachers like Silas Lee disseminated Sacred Harp singing styles throughout their geographic sphere of influence. Singing school teachers learned from their predecessors, as one teacher passed the mantle to the next generation. Silas Lee's mentor was his father-in-law,

Martin Dowling. Dowling's mentors can be traced back one more generation, to his maternal uncle Bill Guy and his father Lazarus Dowling, the latter a Confederate veteran who is remembered in Dowling family history as a Sacred Harp song leader, singing school teacher, and deacon of High Bluff Primitive Baptist Church, Brantley County, Georgia. Dowling is the first documented example of a long line of singing school teachers who also led hymns at the meetinghouse, a practice which enhanced the cross-fertilization of the two singing styles.

The singing schools and their teachers promoted far more than the skills of shape-note singing; the schools and associated community sings were important contexts for renewing community ties, expressing religious sentiment, sharing local food traditions, socializing, and courtship. Silas Lee recalled, "It used to be told that out of every sing, there would be a wedding. Sings were a place to gather people."[27] Johnny Lee first saw his future bride, Delorese Conner, at a singing school led by Silas Lee held at a vacant Conner family house in Nassau County, Florida. Martha Mizell Puckett, who grew up in Brantley County, Georgia, attending Martin Dowling's singing schools, remembered that weddings of her generation often took place as part of the grand, all-day sing that closed a singing school. As the groom approached the porch, the singing master led everyone in a "mighty chorus" of "Midnight Cry" from the *Sacred Harp*: "Lo the bridegroom is at hand, Who will kindly treat Him? Surely all the waiting band, Will now go forth to meet Him."[28]

Other community sings occurred throughout the singing school season, when, as Puckett recalled, all the countryside would "come out, and join in, and sing for sheer joy. They would bring their dinner and stay all day long from 10:00 a.m., until 4:00 p.m." A local family fed and housed the singing school teacher for the two days per month of the school, and "it was understood that there would be an evening sing held at that home with the school master leading the singing. Friends and neighbors would come from near and far . . . . All the song books would be brought forth and the singing would begin and would last until late in the evening. Then the lady of the house, assisted by her lovely daughters, would bring out the cakes, pies, cookies, coffee, milk, buttermilk, and fruit juices, and everyone would enjoy the delicious refreshments. According to the season would be the menu, boiled or parched peanuts, or great pans of peaches, Lecont pears, scuppernong grapes, and sugar cane juice—what ever the time and the season afforded."[29]

Accounts of Martin Dowling's singing schools in the early twentieth century provide the earliest descriptions of three important hallmarks of Hoboken-style singing past and present: the practice of walking time, the drone, and an emphasis on the sacred nature of the singing, all of which were emphasized in singing school.[30] A fourth hallmark, distinctive characteristics of vocal performance, was learned informally. It was simply the way everyone sang. None in isolation is unique to this region, but as a group they comprise the essence of Hoboken's local variant of Sacred Harp.

Walking time is taught in Okefenokee region singing schools yet today. Only two Sacred Harp traditions have a custom of walking time: the white singers of southeast Georgia and northeast Florida, and the black Wiregrass Singers of lower Alabama and the Florida Panhandle. We may never know if there was historic contact between these singing communities, but the two styles of walking time are distinctly different. As described by ethnomusicologist Doris Dyen, the African American song leader "walks rhythmically back and forth across the center of the square [a reference to the 'hollow square' seating arrangement of the singers] between the basses and the trebles, making sure always to maintain a basic orientation towards the lead part (tenors) and the onlookers beyond them."[31] Although individual leaders display variations of "walking your time," they often "accentuate the rhythmic structure of the song by including heavy-footed swaying, with intermediary beats shown through a slight bounce after each main step."[32] The walking time tradition of the Okefenokee region in Georgia and Florida is a more straightforward movement around the square, the feet keeping strict time with the meter of the tune. As David Lee comments, "Some people think the leader is dancing, but it's not dancing. We are Primitive Baptists, and we don't dance [laughs], but it's a way of establishing the beat of the song."[33] Dyen suggests that the practice of walking time originated from "the need to move around the square to cue various voice sections (especially in fuguing tunes or anthems, where reduction of voice-parts and staggered entrances during the song are common)."[34]

A second hallmark of Hoboken style, the drone tradition, is more widespread than walking time. In southeast Georgia and northeast Florida, the earliest account of a drone comes from Lottie Lee Carter, who attended Martin Dowling's singing schools in the 1920s. She recalls that Dowling closed singing schools with a drone that was sung to a select group of harmonically suitable songs. Dowling would give the bass, tenor, and treble each their starting note to hold or drone as they marched around in a circle. Facing the marchers, and arranged inside the circle, stood a group of young men who sang the actual notes and words.[35] Variants of the drone tradition are documented among the Old Harp Singers of Tennessee, Sacred Harp singers of central and north Mississippi—where the special drone song "Travelling to the Grave" has closed several recent Mississippi State Conventions—and among Old Regular Baptist hymn singers in Kentucky.[36] The Old Harp tradition appears most similar to Hoboken, with "a quartet singing a lesson of four parts in the middle of the class, [while] the rest of the class would get up, hold the starting chord and march around the room in time to the music while keeping that chord."[37] Accounts of the other two drone traditions do not include "marching" or "walking time." The Hoboken tradition shares with Mississippi the use of the drone to close a sing. The drones today are more often re-stagings of an old tradition rather than vibrant ongoing practices. Beginning in 1996, after their "discovery" of and by the national Sacred Harp Diaspora, members of the Lee family were invited to give special singing schools on Hoboken style where they taught and demonstrated the drone, or they held drones by request at several southern sings. In January 2001, for example, I requested a drone in Hoboken so I could film the event. The last previous Hoboken drone was held in 1984. The Hoboken drone, then, must be viewed as part of a larger, albeit increasingly rare, southern tradition. Perhaps unique to the Okefenokee region, however, is the feel of a drone, a spiritual synergy of movement, chord, and sound that powerfully affects the singers. As Johnny Lee explains it, "Whatever perpetuated the drone, I think it has subliminal qualities that would be difficult if not impossible for most to put into words."[38]

This subliminal, deeply felt spirituality is the third hallmark of Hoboken-style singing, and the most important to the singers themselves. Clarke Lee, one of Hoboken's current song leaders, underscores this essential point in a 1996 letter to Minnesota Sacred Harp singer Steven Levine. Lee explains that Sacred Harp is not about walking time, drones, special performance practices, or even a thorough knowledge of the rudiments and songs in the *Sacred Harp* book:

> To me Sacred Harp is the truest and purest form of religion that I have ever experienced. *The Sacred Harp* song book has songs, hymns, melodies, and all the wonderful glories of its own self, yet to get to the heart of the matter, I believe we must sing spiritually. I say that Sacred Harp is religion in its purest form because it has no boundaries. There are no set rules that one must go by that are restrictive to the spiritualism of this music. There are no restrictions in this art of love.[39]

As John Bealle observes in *Public Worship, Private Faith*, "Many generations [and] countless thousands of people have found this music to be genuine expression of piety and grace," sung with an "atmosphere of reverence and worship."[40] In the Okefenokee region, the spiritual nature of Sacred Harp is particularly intense. In David's words, "Our people can sing their love for each other in ways that they can't talk about. There's another place that we go when we're singing, and I don't know how to get to that place, except to go there by singing . . . . There's things that take place at these sings, there's power exhibited that people can't contrive. There is something here that had to come from Above. We can't make this up."[41] Singers here historically formed a community in the true sense of the word, where one's fellow singers were neighbors, family, and brothers and sisters of the Primitive Baptist faith. Sacred Harp and Primitive Baptist hymnody shared a common core of singers, a common repertoire of tunes, overlapping oral traditions and performance practices, shared singing contexts, and a Primitive Baptist worldview that linked the two styles in all but actual practice: they never sang meetinghouse hymns at singing schools or Sacred Harp sings, and they never sang Sacred Harp at meetinghouse worship services. Sings in this area differed from the mainstream in that they *did not* open and close with prayer, in order to rigorously distinguish Sacred Harp from worship, despite the religious nature of the *Sacred Harp* texts.[42] Crawfordite singers here did not compose new songs, as was common elsewhere, "as that'd be like writing a new chapter to the Bible and asking them to read it at church."[43] As David Lee explains, "The attitude is that these [*Sacred Harp*] books were handed down from Above so they were sacred things. So you were careful with those books. You wouldn't change or alter anything in those books any more than you would the Bible."[44]

Vocal performance practice, so closely intertwined with Primitive Baptist hymnody, is a fourth hallmark of Sacred Harp in the Okefenokee region. The 1958 FFF recording clearly illustrates distinctive aspects of the local sound as it had emerged by the mid-twentieth century.[45] The rendition of "Firm Foundation" (#72 in the Cooper revision) is most illustrative. Although Silas Lee pitches all four parts, only three parts are audible: men and women singing the tenor or melody line, one or two female altos, and men only on the bass. (Alto parts were new to Sacred Harp with the Cooper revision, and large alto sections were not present in Okefenokee region singing until the 1990s. More typically, singing in this area had treble, tenor, and bass, with emphasis on tenor and bass.) This song unfolds at a slow tempo influenced by the meetinghouse (quarter note equals 52 beats per minute on a metronome), beat in 4/4 time as opposed to the 2/2 tempos common in many other Sacred Harp traditions. Silas Lee pitched the song a perfect fourth below the printed notes, so the singers could more easily navigate the slow tempos. Vocal lines are richly ornamented, an unselfconscious "transitioning between the notes" as David Lee describes it, where the embellishments of the meetinghouse spill over to Sacred Harp. "You add those extra notes on purpose, because it'd be mighty spare and dry without it. So you get a whole different tune out of it. . . . I think the page is restrictive . . . you can use that as a guide. The notes in that book is like a skeleton. When you have a complete skeleton you still don't have a person, and when you got just them notes you still don't have a song. You got to flesh it out . . . And I think that's where that ornamentation is. We put that stuff in automatically and do it all the time."[46] As David's generation was growing up, singers sang without the book a majority of the time, reinforcing oral transmission of tunes and the practice of ornamentation.

Ornaments per se are not unique to Hoboken. In his seminal publication, *The Sacred Harp, A Tradition and Its Music,* Buell Cobb elaborates on George Pullen Jackson's earlier comments about ornamentation and the role of oral tradition in Sacred Harp. The most common ornaments are anticipations, passing tones, and "the optional flourishes which garland the central notes of the melody."[47] These types of ornaments characterize southeast Georgia and northeast Florida Sacred Harp, but use of ornamentation here was far more pervasive and integral to vocal practice. Writing in the 1960s and 1970s, Cobb observed that ornamentation was more evident in the singing of black Sacred Harp singers, who were more influenced by the improvisatory traditions of the African Diaspora. At the time, however, Cobb was unaware of the white tradition of the Okefenokee region and the extent to which Primitive Baptist hymnody had shaped its Sacred Harp performance practices, and vice versa.

Would the "sound" of Silas Lee and his little band of singers have seemed distinctive to audiences at the 1958 Florida Folk Festival? The answer depends on the familiarity of the audience with Sacred Harp, but organizers likely invited the Hoboken group to represent Sacred Harp as a genre, not for any particular way of singing.[48] (By contrast, at the time of the 2000 FFF appearance, the Sacred Harp Diaspora had a sophisticated awareness of the varied styles of southern singers and singing families, including "Hoboken style," due to proliferation of sound recordings, communications via the Internet, and personal visits to singings.) The FFF was Florida's exemplar of the burgeoning folk festival movement, intended to raise public awareness of authentic American folksong and to "reconnect Americans with genuine historical roots."[49] Festival organizers would have considered Sacred Harp to be genuine folk music of the sort suitable for their fledgling event. Scholar George Pullen Jackson, who took his specially trained "Old Harp Singers" to folk festivals as early as 1934, had brought a Sacred Harp group to Gainesville, Florida, in 1949 at the urging of University of Florida professor and folksong collector Alton Morris, also an instigator in the 1953 founding of the Florida Folk Festival. In this context, festival participants like the Hoboken singers were part of a larger cultural and intellectual effort to promote authentic folksong as the basis for American national identity. This was an extraordinary moment for a group that had developed outside the larger movement of southern Sacred Harp, seemingly unaware of singing conventions and their associated practices that had been prevalent since the mid-nineteenth century.

White Springs is only one hundred miles from Hoboken, on the other side of the Okefenokee Swamp, but the singers rarely traveled this distance to other Sacred Harp sings, let alone to perform at a folk festival. The two 1950s FFF performances represented both a geographic and a cultural leap. Sacred Harp singers describe theirs as singer's music, not listener's music, so even today, a stage presentation of traditional singing communities is rare outside festival contexts. More significantly, this performance would have been controversial among members of Crawfordite churches. In the Crawfordite worldview, singing on stage would be frowned on as "a show," drawing inappropriate and unwarranted attention to the singers.[50] The Hoboken singers present were church attendees, not actual members, however, and as such not bound by the church's strict codes of conduct.

As remarkable as it was, the 1958–1959 detours to the FFF had no lasting impact on this unique singing tradition. The recording disappeared into boxes of tapes destined ultimately for the State Archives of Florida. The singers returned home, and for the next several decades continued, if not intensified, their self-imposed cultural isolation. Lee family lore recounts how a recording of north Georgia Sacred Harp had such fast tempos that it wasn't even recognizable *as* Sacred Harp. Before joining the church, several singers recall visiting Sacred Harp conventions near Cordele, Georgia, but they preferred their own way of singing and stopped attending.[51] So, for the most part, as David Lee explains, "We never sang with anybody except ourselves. And because of that isolation, we developed a completely different way of singing this music. . . . We were perfectly content with what we had at home, because the entire community was involved in our singing."[52]

By the time of the 1958 FFF, the community Delorese Conner Lee associated with her girlhood—where one's fellow singers were neighbors, family, and brothers and sisters of the Primitive Baptist faith—already had begun to fracture. The long religious and cultural domination of Primitive Baptists was on the wane. As the historian John Crowley notes, after WWII, "the combined effects of desertion of the southern countryside where their main strength lay, the pressures of town and city life, aggressive proselytizing by other denominations, competing worldly entertainments, and their own divisiveness resulted in a sharp and accelerating decline in numbers."[53]

Stephen Marini has suggested that traditional southern singers imbued Sacred Harp with connotations of the vanishing world of agrarian, intergenerational, intimate religious and civic community that existed in many areas prior to 1950. Sacred Harp became a symbol of the old ways with their "web of relationships, culture, and sacrality."[54] Marini argues that Sacred Harp is the only remaining southern institution able to express this web of relationships. By contrast, the Crawfordites of southeast Georgia and northeast Florida refused to abandon the old ways and preserved their Sacred Harp and hymn singing traditions not as a symbol, but as a living legacy of the old ways. They had always sought isolation from the mainstream culture; as the world around them increasingly changed, they strengthened the boundaries that kept them apart. As explained by David Lee (born in 1954), "We didn't have any other kind of music. I was raised in a home without radios and without televisions. Because we were Primitive Baptists, we did not partake in instruments of any kind . . . . The only style of music that we had anything to do with was our style of [hymn] singing, our style of Sacred Harp. I never had anything to do with any other kind of music."[55]

Not long after attending the FFF, Silas Lee, who had sought to keep denominational ties outside singing schools and community sings, gave way to the next generation of leadership. Sacred Harp became associated with and dominated by the religious principles of Crawfordite Primitive Baptists, views that were increasingly unpopular and anachronistic among their non-Crawfordite neighbors. The inclusive, community spirit championed by Silas Lee gradually disappeared, and with it the traditions of fellowship and community-wide participation in Sacred Harp. Sings became confined to small, in-group gatherings of Crawfordites and their families. Factionalism within the church and within families affected the frequency, the joy, and the sense of community that had been a hallmark of local Sacred Harp. Clarke Lee, the latest local song leader, was frustrated and discouraged to the point of abandoning the tradition altogether. David Lee persuaded him to "make one last effort . . . . We just didn't want to see it die."[56]

Around this same time, local singers began to discover the larger Sacred Harp network. David's cousin gave him a recording of the National Sacred Harp Convention in Birmingham, Alabama, and David recalls playing it repeatedly.[57] He also read Buell Cobb's book, *The Sacred Harp*, and wanted to attend one of the sings described but didn't have the contacts to get there.[58] Then in June 1994, Clarke received an invitation to a sing in Tallahassee,

Florida; upon request from a Tallahassee sing organizer, the shipping agent for *Sacred Harp* books had forwarded names of those in the area who had ordered books, including Clarke's. David and Clarke attended, beginning a momentous process of change in their local tradition. David said, "We got our eyes opened to what Sacred Harp could be. And reminded us of what it used to be."[59] A year later they held their first public sing in a local Missionary Baptist Church and began an experiment designed to rebuild a precious and threatened tradition through a deliberate plan of revitalization and change. Over the following year the Lees attended sings throughout Alabama, Georgia, and Florida. These events filled a void by re-creating the fellowship and joy of singing they had experienced growing up: "This is what we were used to, this is what we've been missing."[60]

Unbeknown to the Lees, an underground tape of a home recording of a 1980s Lee family sing was circulating through the national network of Sacred Harp singers (the tape originally was given by a family member to John Garst, one of his professors at the University of Georgia and coeditor of *The Social Harp*). Singers around the country were captivated by the sound. As described by Minnesota singer Keith Willard, "The voices heard were clearly extraordinary and in a style different from any we had previously heard. It seemed to be from another world."[61] Diaspora singers knew the tape came from near Waycross, Georgia, but were hesitant to intrude on what seemed a private, in-group tradition. When the first All-Day Sing in fifty years was held in the Hoboken School in December 1996, it attracted visitors from eight states. Three years later, singers flocked from twenty-eight states. In October 1996 David and Clarke Lee for the first time hosted the Tri-State Sacred Harp Convention, which meets alternately in lower Alabama, the Florida Panhandle, and Hoboken.

Since 1994, when the Lees first "raised the tent flap and peeked out," as Johnny Lee describes it,[62] their world has changed dramatically. The most wrenching change occurred at home. In 1996, the same year they revived the All-Day Sing at Hoboken School, they were thrown out of their church because of their "new style" Sacred Harp. This was an extraordinary and tragic moment in the history of this tradition: tragic in that it severed families, church members, and a singing community; extraordinary in that Sacred Harp was of such significance that a perceived violation of its core tenants caused a schism in the community that had nurtured it for generations. This schism underscores the extent to which Sacred Harp had merged with Crawfordite Primitive Baptist identity and ideology. The "new style" Sacred Harp promoted by David and Clarke Lee adopted the practice, widespread elsewhere, of opening and closing with prayer. These actions violated the basic tenants or Decorum of the Alabaha River Primitive Baptist Association that forbids members from praying with or associating with other religious societies and denominations. New Sacred Harp, for the Crawfordites, had become "worldly entertainment accompanied by Religious practice."[63] Participation of Diaspora singers, for whom Sacred Harp was folk music or Americana, not religious expression, further exacerbated tensions.[64] The schism also revolved around a breach of traditional modes of performance practice, although this was a secondary issue. As explained by song leader Wilson Wainright, Crawfordites felt "new" Sacred Harp deviated too far from inherited practice. It was simply too fast and too loud, thereby drawing unseemly attention, for singers who were still "trying to sing the way Uncle Silas did."[65] As new Sacred Harp exploded on the national scene, private Crawfordite sings continued in homes and in association with Big Meeting, maintaining the longstanding practices. The tradition fractured into old style and new style.

New Sacred Harp rapidly integrated with members of the Sacred Harp Diaspora, who warmly embraced the Lee family as "quintessentially authentic"[66] and linked their unique vocal style to Hoboken. The Lees sent invitations to their sings via fasola.org (the most complete Internet site for information on Sacred Harp). Visiting singers disseminated glowing e-mail testimonials on the listserv describing their first visit to Hoboken. The Lees, in turn, have prompted the moniker "Hoboken slow," as a tempo descriptor in national Sacred Harp discourse and have infused their profound sense of spirituality into previously secular Diaspora singings. Two official CDs of Sacred Harp from the monthly sings in Hoboken Elementary School, "Sacred Harp, Hoboken Georgia 1996" and "Hoboken City Limits," were produced in collaboration with David Lee, and many "pilgrims" to Hoboken made personal recordings. The tradition has been featured in publications, exhibitions, and documentary radio and television. All of this is a remarkable turn of events for a singing community that had been unaware of the rest of the Sacred Harp network just a few short years before.

The Sacred Harp Diaspora was particularly fascinated with Hoboken's vocal style, even prompting comparisons to "a lost tribe" (evoking George Pullen Jackson's famous description of southern shape-note singers as a "lost tonal tribe").[67] As Johnny Lee explains, "We were asked about our style of singing, how did we do it, could we show or teach them, etc. and we were at a total loss to understand. We weren't doing anything but singing."[68] Organizers of Diaspora Sacred Harp conventions across the country and in England invited Lee family members to lead singing schools on "Hoboken style." Inviting traditional singers to lead singing schools is not a new approach for many northern Sacred Harp conventions, but it was new for the Lees, pushing them to become articulate and self-conscious about the hallmarks of their way of singing.

Ironically, the very "Hoboken sound" which so fascinates the national Sacred Harp network is disappearing from the monthly Hoboken sing. To learn about Hoboken style, one needs to attend one of the special out-of-town singing schools. David and Clarke sacrificed the "old style" Sacred Harp and the fold of their church in exchange for the survival of a precious legacy. They deliberately opened their tradition to a national network of singers with whom they share a passion for singing but often little else. They are prepared to lose stylistic features that make Hoboken Sacred Harp unique as part of their strategy to attract more local people to the tradition. Singing schools still take place in Hoboken, and David and Clarke still teach "walking time" along with the note shapes, scales, and rhythms. The local style of singing still is learned informally through oral transmission, but unless they are part of the small group of Crawfordite singers clinging to the past, the next generation of Hoboken-style singers hears less and less of the old unique sound.

Members of the Sacred Harp Diaspora have urged the Lees not to change the performance practices that set them apart. For David Lee, this is not an option:

> This Sacred Harp is a living tradition. And because it's a living tradition it's going to change and evolve . . . Now what happened was there's a few people that want to stop time, and you can't do that. That's what happened to our sing. We tried to go ahead, and there was this struggle. You have to move ahead, because the alternative is to die. I don't feel like we're losing anything. Hoboken is changing its voice. Now we still walk time to some of our songs. Our people down here are accustomed to that. We also have certain tempos and certain ways that we sing particular songs, and we understand how we do that. I think Hoboken still has a voice, but I think that voice is different than it was 20 years ago. I regret that. The sentimentalist in [me] regrets that. But on a more practical level, I want to see this tradition continue. And if I don't try to help it thrive and survive, if we all depend on someone else to do it, it doesn't get done.[69]

The 2000 FFF recording of the Silas Lee Memorial Sing captures the emergent, hybrid Hoboken-style sound six years into the change process. Although this sing had outside participants, including members of the Sweetwater Sacred Harp Singers from Gainesville, Florida, nearly fifty members

Johnny Lee leads at the Silas Lee Memorial Sacred Harp Sing, Florida Folk Festival, White Springs, Florida, May 2000. Photo by Laurie K. Sommers. Courtesy of South Georgia Folklife Collections, Valdosta State University Archives and Special Collections of Odum Library.

of the Lee family attended. The entire event became a memorial lesson for Silas Lee, a Sacred Harp convention practice the Lees had encountered only a few years prior. The most obvious sonic difference between 1958 and 2000 was the sheer number of singers and the audibility of all four vocal parts, including a full alto section similar to what the Lees had first heard in 1994 when they sang at Tallahassee. Songs were pitched higher (and only a half or whole step below the printed notes), in keeping with the faster tempos adopted after increased exposure to singings in Alabama and elsewhere. "Firm Foundation," for example, was sung at 66 beats per minute, as opposed to 52 in 1958. At the faster tempos the ornamentation is less audible and less pervasive. Some song leaders walked time, but the practice is now a more symbolic gesture to heritage. Given the context of this particular event, song leaders were specially selected for their relationship to Silas Lee. Until the recent changes, sings in this region had a single male song leader, unlike the more democratic practice of a different leader for each song common in most southern singing conventions. David and Clarke adopted multiple leaders in order to "involve more of the people in this tradition, and give them more chance to experience the music than it used to."[70] Perhaps most significant of all, singers emphasized the sacred nature of the singing, even in this secular festival context. Clarke Lee compared Sacred Harp to "soul food" for those who were raised on it and encouraged everyone that "if it lifts up your heart to sing to the Lord, that's what we want you to do."

At the singing school held during the 2000 FFF, David Lee gave a brief history lesson about the tradition that has shaped his family, community, and region for well over a century: "I've heard Uncle Silas say how he's been down in Florida teaching singing schools and all over southeast Georgia in several counties teaching singing schools . . . . Prior to him was his father-in-law Martin Dowling, who also taught singing schools all over those parts, and prior to him his daddy . . . . So with this music being a part of our way of life all this time, it is in every part of our local and family culture, it is who we are. When we see each other, we immediately recognize reference to this music."

Along both sides of the Okefenokee Swamp, a cluster of neighbors, family members, and brothers and sisters in the Primitive Baptist faith created and sustained a unique local variant of Sacred Harp. Although never part of a church service, Sacred Harp was intertwined with Primitive Baptist hymnody, featuring similar slow tempos, lower starting pitches, and ornamentation. Much of the singing was done from memory, fostering a fluid orally transmitted tradition, rather than strict adherence to the printed page. Other distinctive features of this tradition include a deeply felt spirituality, walking time in a counterclockwise fashion according to the meter of the tune, and use of the drone. This combination of characteristics gave local singing its uniqueness. This way of singing became an identity marker for communities in this small corner of Georgia and Florida. Within the protective boundaries of their Primitive Baptist faith, local singers created their own "voice," which was instantly recognizable to their fellows. David Lee calls Sacred Harp "a way of communicating. We're always singing to each other and for each other." Sacred Harp communicated love of God, fellowship with one's neighbors, and a rich array of memories and emotions.

This local music community remained remarkably self-contained for generations, developing and maintaining their tradition of Sacred Harp outside the mainstream of southern singing conventions. As David Lee explained at a 1998 singing school held in Seattle: "Until three and one-half years ago . . . we actually had the feeling that we was the last ones on earth that sang Sacred Harp. We had no idea how mistaken we was!"[71] When internal strife caused the community to split in two, it initiated a period of transition and change. The Crawfordites retain the old-style inherited practice as they understand it and perpetuate the strong boundary separating themselves from outsiders. David and Clarke Lee felt that the joy and sweet communion that had once characterized their tradition was gone. Participation dwindled, jeopardizing the legacy for the next generation. As Silas Lee said in one of his final interviews:

> People don't look for it, and they don't have the heart to beg for it, anymore. We have put it under denominations, and it is sad. That's what the threat is now. Splitting it up over denominations. B. F. White didn't organize to be denominational . . . . White organized it to be "Sacred Harp" just like the name says . . . . Keep the good thing a-going.[72]

David and Clarke promised Silas to do just that, preserving the legacy of their forebears by shattering the old in-group boundaries and opening their singing to new practices and a new network of singers.

Folklorist Henry Glassie observes that "the story of change is double, simultaneously a matter of gain and loss."[73] Along the border of southeast Georgia and northeast Florida, Sacred Harp continues in both its old and new forms. It accompanies rites of passage such as weddings, funerals, and river baptisms, much as it always has. Sings still occur during Big Meeting and at community singing schools. The historic connections between hymnody and Sacred Harp have been incorporated into the annual All-Day Sing in March and the tri-annual Tri-State Convention every third October. The evening after the *Sacred Harp* sing, visitors and locals alike are invited to sing from Lloyd's *Primitive Hymns* at Mars Hill Primitive Baptist Church in Hoboken, the new church home for many of those who were thrown out of the Crawfordite churches over "new Sacred Harp."[74]

Hoboken has emerged as the epicenter and public voice of "Hoboken style" with the monthly and All-Day Sings, while other regions of southeast Georgia and northeast Florida continue the tradition more quietly, and more infrequently, out of the public eye. But Hoboken's public voice has changed. The distinctive sound that so fascinates the Sacred Harp Diaspora—especially the richly ornamented vocal lines—is morphing into a different hybrid sound. For the creators of this new voice, Sacred Harp is not about "how we sing," but rather "why we sing." As Clarke Lee wrote in his letter to Steven Levine, "Learning intervals, scales, to walk time, to drone and wiggle notes is not Sacred Harp . . . . When you learn all the book has to offer, you still need to go one step farther."[75] By singing in fellowship with one another, singers find deep spiritual meaning, what Johnny Lee calls the "inner music" that "touches the soul as well as the ear."[76]

For much of southeast Georgia and northeast Florida, Sacred Harp today is a heritage, not a way of life, labeled as such on road signs now posted on the state routes entering Hoboken, and in a newly instituted Social Studies unit for Brantley County eighth graders.[77] A once insular singing community's explosion onto the national scene has been the unlikely impetus for its recognition as a distinctive style, just as that style is in the process of disappearing from the public singing tradition. For the singers of this music, however, the most important things remain: memory, heritage, legacy, and spiritual meaning. This generation of song leaders takes seriously Silas Lee's charge to "keep the good thing a-going." From the stage of the 2000 Silas Lee Memorial Sing, David Lee reminds his family and neighbors "to not let this go. It's bigger than we are. It's a precious thing that was given to our little group of people."

Notes

1. A version of this article with illustrative media such as audio, video, and photos, titled "Hoboken Style: Meaning and Change in Okefenokee Sacred Harp Singing," appears in *Southern Spaces* (http://www.southernspaces.org/). Duplicate sections are reprinted with permission. Portions of this article previously appeared in Laurie K. Sommers, "Continuity and Change in Hoboken (Georgia) Sacred Harp," *Society for American Music Bulletin* 2, no. 3 (Summer/Fall 2000): 1, 34–37, 44. Thanks to David Lee, Delorese Conner Lee, and Johnny Lee, who commented on earlier versions of this paper. Much of the research for this article was conducted under the auspices of grants to the South Georgia Folklife Project, College of the Arts, Valdosta State University: The Okefenokee Traditional Music Survey, funded by the Lila-Wallace Reader's Digest Community Folklife Program, the Let Us Sing exhibit grant from the Georgia Council for the Arts Folklife Program, and grants from the National Endowment for the Arts Folk and Traditional Arts Infrastructure Initiative.
2. Silas Lee, advocate of the nondenominational nature of Sacred Harp, chose three songs which he likely thought would be accessible to the festival audience: "Murillo's Lesson" (#358, a secular song with text dating to the late 1700s), "Coronation" (#63, found in many Protestant hymnals as "All Hail the Power of Jesus Name"), and "Firm Foundation" (#72, also found in Protestant hymnals), during which Lee invited the audience to join in.
3. In using the term "Sacred Harp Diaspora," I adopt Kiri Miller's concept of "the phenomenon of the Sacred Harp conventions that draws many travelers from far-off places rather than the local singing in an isolated area where most participants are related by blood or marriage" (28). The concept is the topic of her book, *Traveling Home, Sacred Harp Singing and American Pluralism* (Urbana and Chicago: University of Illinois Press, 2008). I also use the term "Sacred Harp network," after Dorothy Noyes's reformulation of the term "folk group" under the rubric of social network theory, to distinguish singers whose connection to one another is based solely on Sacred Harp as a hobby or avocation, as opposed to the deep-seated, multifaceted community ties which characterize singers in southeast Georgia and northeast Florida. Noyes suggests replacing the much overused concept of "community" with "dense multiplex network characterized by frequent interaction, a high degree of solidarity, and an equally high degree of social control." Perhaps I am a victim of the nostalgic postmodern longing

for community, but, at least for the historical period through WWII, community does seem more applicable here: a stable cluster of neighbors, family members, and brothers-and-sisters in faith that sustained Sacred Harp and hymnody for a century within one of the more isolated regions in the Deep South (see Dorothy Noyes, "Group," *Journal of American Folklore* 108, no. 430 [Fall 1995]: 449–78).

4. Miller, *Traveling Home, Sacred Harp Singing and American Pluralism*, 102. Miller's book includes a substantive discussion of the Lees' role in the Sacred Harp Diaspora.
5. I use the term "sing" as they do in southeast Georgia and northeast Florida, as opposed to the more common term "singing" used most other places.
6. Miller *Traveling Home, Sacred Harp Singing and American Pluralism*, 102.
7. Johnny Lee, remarks at Silas Lee Memorial Sing, Florida Folk Festival, White Springs, May 28, 2000.
8. David I. Lee, remarks at Silas Lee Memorial Sing, Florida Folk Festival, White Springs, May 28, 2000.
9. David I. Lee and Clarke Lee, interviewed by Laurie K. Sommers, Hoboken, GA, February 15, 1997.
10. Francis Harper and Delma E. Presley, *Okefinokee Album* (Athens: University of Georgia Press, 1981).
11. John G. Crowley, *Primitive Baptists of the Wiregrass South* (Gainesville: University Press of Florida, 1998).
12. Harper and Presley, *Okefinokee Album*, 29.
13. Crowley, *Primitive Baptists of the Wiregrass South*, 109.
14. Crowley, *Primitive Baptists of the Wiregrass South*, 178.
15. David I. Lee, interviewed by Laurie K. Sommers, Hoboken, GA, July 15, 2000.
16. John Bealle, *A Guide to the Film* Sweet is the Day, *a Sacred Harp Family Portrait* (Montgomery: Alabama Folklife Association, 2001), 31.
17. Joyce Cauthen, ed., *Benjamin Lloyd's Hymn Book, A Primitive Baptist Song Tradition* (Montgomery: Alabama Folklife Association, 1999), 92.
18. Beverly Patterson, *The Sound of the Dove, Singing in Appalachian Primitive Baptist Churches* (Urbana and Chicago: University of Illinois Press, 1995), 166–67.
19. Patterson, *The Sound of the Dove*, 103.
20. Delorese Conner Lee, phone interview by Laurie K. Sommers, July 8, 2009.
21. Francis Harper, photograph captions from the Francis Harper Collection, Special Collections, Georgia Southern University, Statesboro.
22. Delorese Conner Lee, phone interview by Laurie K. Sommers, July 8, 2009.
23. David I. Lee, interviewed by Laurie K. Sommers, Hoboken, GA, July 15, 2000.
24. David I. Lee, July 15, 2000.
25. Delorese Conner Lee, phone interview by Laurie K. Sommers, July 8, 2009.
26. *Brantley Enterprise*, "Lee's life entwined with the Sacred Harp," December 11, 1996.
27. *Brantley Enterprise*, December 11, 1996.
28. Martha Mizell Puckett, *Snow White Sands* (Douglas: South Georgia College, 1975, 1978), 95–96.
29. Puckett, *Snow White Sands*, 95.
30. Puckett, *Snow White Sands*, 94, and Lottie Lee Carter, interviewed by Laurie K. Sommers, Hoboken, GA, May 10, 2001.
31. Doris J. Dyen, "The Role of Shape-Note Singing in the Musical Culture of Black Communities in Southeast Alabama" (Ph.D. dissertation, University of Illinois at

Urbana-Champaign, 1977), 292. The phrase "around the square" refers to the traditional seating arrangement of Sacred Harp, with singers grouped by voice part (tenor, bass, alto, treble) in a hollow square formation, with the song leaders located in the center of the hollow.

32. Dyen, "The Role of Shape-Note Singing," 292.
33. David I. Lee, interviewed by Laurie K. Sommers, Hoboken, GA, July 15, 2000.
34. Dyen, "The Role of Shape-Note Singing," 292.
35. Lottie Lee Carter, interviewed by Laurie K. Sommers, Hoboken, GA, May 10, 2001.
36. Larry Olszewski, e-mail to Laurie K. Sommers on the Old Harp drone, February 14, 2002; Karen Willard, e-mail to Laurie K. Sommers on the Mississippi drone, February 13, 2002; Nicholas Pasqual, e-mail to Laurie K. Sommers, February 16, 2002, on Kentucky folk singer Jean Ritchie's remembrance of an Old Regular Baptist drone in the liner notes to her LP *Sweet Rivers*.
37. Larry Olszewski, e-mail to Laurie K. Sommers on the Old Harp drone, February 14, 2002.
38. Johnny Lee, e-mail to Laurie K. Sommers, October 14, 1999.
39. Clarke Lee, letter to Steven Levine, March 10, 1996.
40. John Bealle, *Public Worship, Private Faith, Sacred Harp and American Folksong* (Athens: University of Georgia Press, 1997), 215.
41. David I. Lee, July 15, 2000.
42. John Crowley, "The Sacred Harp Controversy in the Original Alabaha Primitive Baptist Association," *Baptist Studies Bulletin* 3, no. 7 (July 2004).
43. David I. Lee and Clarke Lee, interviewed by Laurie K. Sommers, Hoboken, GA, February 15, 1997.
44. David I. Lee and Clarke Lee, February 15, 1997.
45. Crawfordites still do not allow recordings in the meetinghouse, so I infer historic connections from attendance at contemporary Crawfordite congregational singings.
46. David I. Lee and Clarke Lee, interviewed by Laurie K. Sommers, Hoboken, GA, February 15, 1997.
47. Buell Cobb, *The Sacred Harp, A Tradition and Its Music* (Athens: University of Georgia Press, 1978), 42–43.
48. How then, did a group of these singers end up at the 1958–1959 Florida Folk Festival? We may never know for sure, but the link may be Hoboken School, where Silas Lee and Superintendent Herschel Herrin had recently established a monthly community Sacred Harp sing. The Hoboken School Glee Club and barbershop quartet also performed at FFF, so perhaps the teacher, Miss Griffin, mentioned the local Sacred Harp to FFF organizer Thelma Boulton. According to Tollie Lee, Griffin and Silas Lee became close friends after the second FFF, and Griffin became a regular participant in the Hoboken School Sacred Harp sings. Superintendent Herrin accompanied the groups to FFF, and might have been the point person as well.
49. Bealle, *Public Worship, Private Faith, Sacred Harp and American Folksong*, 113.
50. Delorese Conner Lee, phone interview by Laurie K. Sommers, July 15, 2000.
51. Wilson Wainright, interviewed by Laurie K. Sommers, Nahunta, GA, September 4, 2003.
52. David I. Lee, interviewed by Laurie K. Sommers, Hoboken, GA, July 15, 2000.
53. Crowley, *Primitive Baptists of the Wiregrass South*, 163.
54. Stephen A. Marini, *Sacred Song in America: Religion, Music, and Public Culture* (Urbana and Chicago: University of Illinois Press, 2003), 90.

55. David I. Lee and Clarke Lee, interviewed by Laurie K. Sommers, Hoboken, GA, February 15, 1997.
56. David I. Lee and Clarke Lee, interviewed by Laurie K. Sommers, Hoboken, GA, February 15, 1997.
57. David I. Lee, e-mail correspondence with Laurie K. Sommers, October 12, 1999.
58. David Lee, personal communication, reported in Miller, *Traveling Home, Sacred Harp Singing and American Pluralism*, 101.
59. David I. Lee and Clarke Lee, interviewed by Laurie K. Sommers, Hoboken, GA, February 15, 1997.
60. David I. Lee and Clarke Lee, February 15, 1997.
61. Keith Willard, liner notes to "Sacred Harp Hoboken, Georgia, 1996" (CD), 1999.
62. Johnny Lee, e-mail correspondence with Laurie K. Sommers, October 14, 1999.
63. Minutes of the One Hundred and Fifty-fourth Annual Session of the Alabaha River Primitive Baptist Association held with Oak Grove Church, Brantley County, Georgia, October 12–14, 1996.
64. Crowley makes a similar point in "The Sacred Harp Controversy in the Original Alabaha Primitive Baptist Association," *Baptist Studies Bulletin* 3, no. 7 (July 2004).
65. Wilson Wainright, interviewed by Laurie K. Sommers, Nahunta, Georgia, September 4, 2003.
66. Miller, *Traveling Home, Sacred Harp Singing and American Pluralism*, 102.
67. George Pullen Jackson, *White Spirituals in the Southern Uplands* (Chapel Hill: University of North Carolina Press, 1933), 4.
68. D. Johnny Lee, e-mail correspondence with Laurie K. Sommers, October 14, 1999.
69. David I. Lee and Clarke Lee, interviewed by Laurie K. Sommers, Hoboken, GA, February 15, 1997.
70. David I. Lee and Clarke Lee, February 15, 1997.
71. Wayne Murphree, *Hoboken in Seattle* (video), February 21, 1998, Seattle, Washington. Produced by Wayne Murphree Ent., Inc., 25735 Alabama Hwy. 71, Flat Rock, AL 35966; 256–632–2474.
72. *Brantley Enterprise*, "Lee's life entwined with the Sacred Harp," December 11, 1996.
73. Henry Glassie, *Material Culture* (Bloomington: Indiana University Press, 1999), 15.
74. Mars Hill is a "Bennettite" church, referring to the faction of the Alabaha River Association that split from the Crawfordites during the homestead controversy in the nineteenth century and followed elder Richard Bennett.
75. Clarke Lee, letter to Steven Levine, March 10, 1996.
76. Johnny Lee, October 14, 1999.
77. Both signs and curriculum are initiatives of retired Waycross, Georgia, music educator, Willie Character.

Works Cited

Bealle, John. *Public Worship, Private Faith, Sacred Harp and American Folksong*. Athens: University of Georgia Press, 1997.

Bealle, John. *A Guide to the Film* Sweet is the Day, *a Sacred Harp Family Portrait*. Alabama Folklife Association, 2001.

Brantley Enterprise. "Lee's life entwined with the Sacred Harp," December 11, 1996.

Carter, Lottie Lee, interviewed by Laurie K. Sommers, Hoboken, GA, May 10, 2001.
Cauthen, Joyce, ed. *Benjamin Lloyd's Hymn Book, A Primitive Baptist Song Tradition.* Montgomery: Alabama Folklife Association, 1999.
Cobb, Buell, Jr. *The Sacred Harp, A Tradition and Its Music.* Athens: University of Georgia Press, 1978.
Crowley, John G. *Primitive Baptists of the Wiregrass South.* Gainesville: University Press of Florida, 1998.
Crowley, John G. "The Sacred Harp Controversy in the Original Alabaha Primitive Baptist Association." *Baptist Studies Bulletin* 3, no. 7 (July 2004).
Dyen, Doris J. "The Role of Shape-Note Singing in the Musical Culture of Black Communities in Southeast Alabama." Ph.D. dissertation, University of Illinois at Urbana-Champaign, 1977.
Glassie, Henry. *Material Culture.* Bloomington: Indiana University Press, 1999.
Harper, Francis, and Delma E. Presley. *Okefinokee Album.* Athens: University of Georgia Press, 1981.
Jackson, George Pullen. *White Spirituals in the Southern Uplands.* Chapel Hill: University of North Carolina Press, 1933.
Lee, Clarke. The Sacred in Sacred Harp. Letter to Steven Levine, March 10, 1996.
Lee, D. Johnny. Remarks at Silas Lee Memorial Sing, Florida Folk Festival, White Springs, Florida, May 28, 2000, recorded by Paul Butterfield for the South Georgia Folklife Collection, Valdosta State University Archives.
Lee, D. Johnny. E-mail correspondence with Laurie K. Sommers, October 14, 1999.
Lee, D. Johnny. Interview with Laurie K. Sommers, Hoboken, GA, July 8, 2009.
Lee, David I., and Clarke Lee. Interview with Laurie K. Sommers, Hoboken, GA, February 15, 1997.
Lee, David I. Interview with Laurie K. Sommers, Hoboken, GA, July 15, 2000.
Lee, David I. Singing School at Florida Folk Festival, May 28, 2000, recorded by Paul Butterfield for the South Georgia Folklife Collection, Valdosta State University Archives.
Lee, David I. Interview with Laurie K. Sommers, Hoboken, GA, July 15, 2000.
Lee, David I. E-mail correspondence with Laurie K. Sommers, October 12, 1999.
Lee, Delorese. Interviews with Laurie K. Sommers, Hoboken, GA, July 8 and 15, 2009.
Marini, Stephen A. *Sacred Song in America: Religion, Music, and Public Culture.* Urbana and Chicago: University of Illinois Press, 2003.
Miller, Kiri. "'First Sing the Notes': Oral and Written Traditions in Sacred Harp Transmission." *American Music* 22, no. 4 (2004): 475–501.
Miller, Kiri. *Traveling Home, Sacred Harp Singing and American Pluralism.* Urbana and Chicago: University of Illinois Press, 2008.
Murphree, Wayne. *Hoboken in Seattle* (video). February 21, 1998, Seattle, Washington. Produced by Wayne Murphree Ent., Inc., 25735 Alabama Hwy. 71, Flat Rock, AL 35966; 256–632–2474.
Patterson, Beverly. "Forging Religious Identity: An Exploration of Hymn Singing in Anglo-American Primitive Baptist Churches." In *Benjamin Lloyd's Hymn Book, A Primitive Baptist Song Tradition*, ed. Joyce Cauthen. Montgomery: Alabama Folklife Association, 1999. Pp. 22–28.
Patterson, Beverly. *The Sound of the Dove, Singing in Appalachian Primitive Baptist Churches.* Urbana and Chicago: University of Illinois Press, 1995.

Puckett, Martha Mizell. *Snow White Sands*. Occasional Papers. Douglas: South Georgia College, 1975, 1978.

Noyes, Dorothy. "Group." *Journal of American Folklore*. Special Issue, Common Ground: Keywords for the Study of Expressive Culture, Jeff Todd Titon, ed. 108, no. 430 (Fall 1995): 449–78.

Sommers, Laurie K. "Continuity and Change in the Hoboken, Georgia Sacred Harp Tradition." *The Society for American Music Bulletin* 2, no. 3 (Summer/Fall 2000): 1, 34–37, 44.

Wainright, Wilson. Interview with Laurie K. Sommers, Nahunta, GA, September 4, 2003.

Willard, Keith. "Notes." *Sacred Harp Hoboken, Georgia, 1996*. Compact Disc, Independently produced by Keith Willard, Rodney Willard, and David Lee, 1999.

Nativism and Cracker Revival at the Florida Folk Festival

MARTHA NELSON

THE FLORIDA FOLK FESTIVAL (FFF) BILLS ITSELF AS THE LONGEST RUNNING state-supported folk festival in the United States. For the past fifty-nine years the festival has been the formally sanctioned institution for public display of Florida's collective cultural traditions and multiple ethnic identities. Over time, music performances at the festival have come to be dominated by a group of revivalist musicians who are composers of "Florida Song." Incorporating interlocking themes and stock images, Florida Song renders a nostalgic view of Florida's frontier inhabited by Spanish explorers, Scots-Irish Crackers often working as cowboys, and the remnants of Creek Indians who evaded massacre or forced removal in the nineteenth century by migrating to a continental outpost. At its core Florida Song is defined by valorization of early settlers, paired with lamentation and protest over what has been lost. The purposes it serves extend beyond entertainment or the celebration of cultural heritage.

What is remarkable about Florida Song's domination of state-funded displays of cultural tradition is that its stereotypes of a romanticized wilderness frontier take place in a state that was ranked fourth in the nation for the number of foreign-born residents in 2005. The majority of Floridians are not Scots-Irish, Seminole, or direct immigrants from Spain. The question for folklorists is not "Is the music folk?" but "What is the meaning of the purposeful control of the state folk festival for the dissemination of Florida Song?" Celebrating Florida's phenomenally rich cultural landscape with the annual repetition of songs focused on a small segment of the population during a limited historical period seems to be an odd pursuit for a state folk festival.

Understanding the folklore of Florida Song requires a reckoning with the history and public policies of Florida and the United States, mostly during the twentieth century but extending back to the 1700s. The use of folk song as a tool for agitation and promotion of a political agenda is one of the legacies of the popularization of folk music during its revival in the mid-1900s. Finally, to the extent that public folklore has functioned as advocate and intervention in traditional culture, the folk festival itself influenced the creation of Florida Song.

The Florida Folk Festival's formative years coincided with the earliest stages of the Cold War; but the force of creation for the event came from the National Federation of Music Clubs (NFMC). A philanthropic organization with state chapters, the NFMC was chartered by the U.S. Congress in 1898 and remains the only music organization with membership in the United Nations. It serves as a locus for the promulgation of American music, including advocacy through civic and political action. The group was instrumental in the Florida chapter's lobby of the state legislature in 1935 to proclaim Stephen Foster's "Old Folks At Home" the official state song. By that time the NFMC and the state chapter were already planning construction of a memorial to the antebellum composer along the Suwannee River in north Florida. The NFMC had declared Foster America's first professional songwriter. Its members were actively promoting the Foster Memorial in White Springs as a venue for the performance of American music. When the first building was dedicated in the fall of 1951, the president of the NFMC surveyed the surrounding 250 acres of riverside land and suggested the site would be a perfect location to hold a folk festival.

Folk festivals first developed in America in the 1920s. The nation's experience in World War I and the first rumblings of ambition to become a world power stimulated an interest in roots heritage, accompanied by considerable posturing to strengthen national identity. Policy makers projected an image of America that was multiethnic. The United States adopted its first comprehensive immigration law in 1921, with visas favoring Anglo-Saxon immigrants to complement the existing cultural profile of the nation. Constructing a national identity still required negotiating the different origins of northern and western European immigrants. Staging a celebratory event where distinct heritage would be imbued with pride and value, yet cast in the frame of a national treasure, was deemed an appropriate tool. Folk festivals also had commercial appeal, generating the flow of capital for the purpose of nation building.

In north Florida local and state residents appointed by the governor to the Stephen Foster Memorial Commission hired Sarah Gertrude Knott, founder of the National Folk Festival, to develop a state folk festival. The Florida festival replicated the National's policies of presenting American culture as pluralistic. In the foreword written for the festival program Knott described folk festivals as being "democratically significant in that they promote tolerance and better understanding of our neighbors, whose race or religion may differ from our own." The objectives of the Florida Folk Festival were to "keep flourishing the traditional expressions which reflect life as it has been lived in the United States, and in other countries from which our people have come." Utilizing this wealth of cultural legacies would create "stronger unity of our people," thereby fostering "appreciation of the fundamental cultures of our world neighbors."

At the first festival in May 1953, Czechoslovakian dance and embroidery, Anglo fiddling, French Huguenot storytelling, Minorcan Easter rituals, shape-note singing, children's rhymes, African American folk tales, turpentine camp songs, and the lore of Cow Creek Indians were interspersed with stylized music club and academic renditions of British ballads and southern beliefs. The format was educational with brief histories for each presentation written in the program. On Sunday morning the program of sacred music included Mormon, Jewish, Greek, Danish, African American, and Primitive Baptist singers, as well as one performance on the musical saw. In 1954 the program included preacher tales, traditions of the Scottish Highlanders, and renditions of "Dances of Newer Americans" by music club members.

Also like the national festival, the Florida event aligned itself with academic folklorists. Alton C. Morris and Edwin C. Kirkland of the University of Florida and J. Russell Reaver of Florida State University were festival advisors. Over the next twenty years their expertise would ground event programming in the emerging methods and theories of American folklore studies. Immediately apparent was the focus on text and collecting lore firsthand. Performances by Floridians enacting the traditional customs of other nationalities were common, effectively separating the content of folk song and dance from the context in which it had developed. The emphasis on text reflected the literary interests of the professors, as well as the state of folklore studies generally. Performers also included people who had recently moved to Florida or who maintained residences in other states but relocated to Florida for the winter. The event programs recognized performers sharing folk songs from Arkansas, Montana, Kentucky, and North Carolina. One of these, Bob Pavitt, became a repeat performer at the festival and often shared tunes he had "collected" from miners or other folk singers in Harlan, Kentucky. The festival's planners looked at the state's cultural resources from the vantage point of the early 1950s, and while they reached backward to include ballads, tales, performance styles, and instrumentation with Old World origins, they also recognized that Florida's population and cultural landscape were being transformed. During the 1950s Florida's population increased an astonishing 78 percent.

In 1955 Knott passed the directorship of the festival to Thelma Boltin, a storyteller who had been a performer at the first two events. Boltin's training was in theater and youth club recreation. She encouraged music clubs to perform and added to the schedule school groups performing songs and dances from international folk custom. The NFMC had assembled song sheets and curriculum guides for musical education of all forms, and challenged local clubs to sponsor a community folk festival. Instructions directed programmers to include people of different nationalities and descendants of original settlers. Bibliographies, discographies, and song sheets could be ordered from the NFMC and included both classical interpretations of folk music and field recordings of British ballads by John and Alan Lomax.

During her third year as director, Boltin began referring to some of the performers as "Cousin" and soon thereafter, she became known to everyone as "Cousin Thelma." As she worked to market the festival and commodify folklore itself, Boltin shaped the event's participants into a "folk family." In the foreword to the 1955 program Boltin characterized the festival as reflecting the state's "diversity" with an emphasis on "authenticity"—both being buzzwords in academic folklore as a folk music revival with its own motivations gained momentum across the nation.

In 1956 the Florida Federation of Music Clubs' newsletter recounted a radio broadcast in which President Dwight Eisenhower commended the NFMC for its efforts promoting music as an instrument for international good will. That same year the festival presented for the first time a Florida "Cracker." The term was likely too sensitive to use singularly and was actually listed as "whipcracker." Noted underneath the schedule listing: "From the Spanish and Colonial cattle drivers herding their stock on pasturelands carved out of the wilderness of Florida and cracking long bull whips over them to keep them moving, comes the term 'Florida Cracker.'"

The following year an essay titled "What is a Cracker? Where did the Florida native get his name?" filled nearly half the program's last page. In addition to attributing the nickname to using a whip for cattle driving, the essay read, "Crackers are mainly descended from the Irish, Scotch, and English stock which, from 1740 on, was slowly populating the huge southern wilderness behind the thin strip of coastal civilization." The writer alludes to the true origin of the term "Cracker" when she adds that the area was also being settled "by wealthy planters whose slaves raised cotton, corn, sugar cane, rice, and tobacco. There were the same wide class disparities which characterized the rest of the South, and the poor folk continued to eke out a living from garden plots, firearms, and fishing lines."

The migration of "Crackers" from the English colonies into north Florida is further suggested by "The preponderance of settlers from Georgia as reflected in the lyrics of such fiddle tunes as 'I Want To Go Back To Georgy.'" The writer refers to simple homes, rail fencing, penned plots for growing potatoes, and "scrub cattle." Without explanation for how the cattle came to be in Florida, the writer continues, "The scrub cattle were scrawny from under-nourishment and inbreeding." And further, "But the breed was blessed with the stamina to cover range so sparse that heavier blooded stock would literally walk themselves to death trying to find enough to eat. They could travel through thickets of saw palmetto without lacerating their legs." The scrub cow "knew how to side-step rattlesnakes, keep out of gopher holes, avoid bogging down, wade neck deep after water hyacinths, and perform many other practical feats."

Connecting the history of Florida Crackers with the present, the essayist wrote, "Today it is hard to find a real Florida Cracker, because the native-born Floridians are just the same as folks from other states. When an out-of-stater asked recently where he could find a real Florida Cracker, someone wisely answered, 'You won't be likely to find him leaning on a rail fence at a crossroads. He is a busy, prosperous man, and a prominent citizen.'"

"He is the backbone of our state. He was here before the big 'boom' of the mad 20s and he is the fellow who stayed and stuck it out during the lean years of the 30s. He made the most of what he had and even today would rather 'sell' Florida than sell the merchandise in his own store. He knows that selling Florida means more business for everyone. The 'Florida Cracker' is the fellow who just passed you in the custom-made convertible . . . if you didn't see him, just watch his dust! He's going places!"

What the writer did not say was that for at least four hundred years "Cracker" had been a class-based slur referring to white peasants from the British Isles. Linguists believe the word derives from the Gaelic *"craic,"* a term still used in Ireland to describe conversation infused with such quick wit and verbal agility that it seems to "crack" like the sound of a whip. In a twist of Elizabethan politics of culture, the English used the term to ridicule their Irish neighbors. Not entertained by the Irishman's legendary repartee, English colonizers slurred the Irish "Crackers" as being loud braggarts. The most famous written use of the term comes from Shakespeare's *King John* (1595): "What cracker is this . . . that deafes our ears / With this abundance of superfluous breath?"

The term was carried from the British Isles to the North American colonies by Scots-Irish immigrants, who settled along the eastern seaboard as far south as Georgia. Travelers' accounts from the 1750s to the 1850s contain descriptions of Crackers from Maryland to Georgia. The Scots-Irish settlers were described as a "lawless set of rascals . . . who often change their places of abode." In 1790 a Spanish official in Florida reported the "influx of rootless people called Crackers."

By the time British settlers arrived in Florida, the Spaniards and the French had exhausted several expedition parties in the peninsula. The fortified Spanish settlement of St. Augustine was tenuous but holding, with Portuguese, Jewish, French, Native American, and African inhabitants. Spaniards had imported cattle from the vast plains of Andalusia that proved hardy and adaptable to Florida's climate and topography. In north Florida in the late 1600s, Spanish cattle ranchers were shipping tallow, hides, and dried beef out of the Suwannee and Santa Fe Rivers through the Gulf of Mexico to Cuba. In 1771 during a brief period when Britain held Florida, officials counted 288 whites and 900 black slaves in northeastern Florida. Tropical fevers, poor soil, violent resistance by American Indians, and dense foliage made the area difficult to settle. For the next century as Florida's strategic location on the continent made it a bargaining chip among French, Spanish, and English colonizers, those settlers who survived in Florida were divided between coastal plantations flush with aristocratic wealth and slaves, and the timber cutters and cattle ranchers of the interior who had a wealth of natural resources to exploit.

The "Cracker" essay in the FFF program has two other referents that deserve mention. An Orlando builder recorded impressions during a tour of the Florida backcountry in the early 1900s. He found vast expanses of wilderness and only a few Florida natives, including one family waiting by the roadside, leaning on a fence post, "the genuine, unadulterated 'Crackers'—the clay-eating, gaunt, pale, tallowy, leather-skinned sort."

One of the most critical assessments of Florida Crackers in print, Carl Dann's "Vicissitudes and Catastrophes" continues: "Who, or what, these 'Crackers' are, from whom descended, of what nationality, or what becomes of them, is one of the many unsolved mysteries of the state. Stupid and shiftless, yet shy and vindictive, they are a block on the pathway of civilization, settlement and enterprise wherever they exist . . . The native Florida Crackers are few in number and are rapidly becoming fewer. They have but little influence in the affairs of the counties or in the several communities, but singularly enough, they have preponderance in the state legislature, owing to the manner in which representatives are chosen, and their influence there is not very beneficial to say the least. Time and immigration, however, will change all this condition of things. The best class of these 'Crackers' are the cattle-herders, a tough, rough, and dare-devil, good-natured crowd."

The image of the western cowboy in America has been widely disseminated and carries images of patriotic, brave frontiersmen. Cattle ranchers in Florida have not historically called themselves cowboys and their experience is not well known. The Scots-Irish Crackers took possession of the Andalusian cattle brought to Florida by the Spanish, but their methods for herding and driving cattle originated in the British Isles. Working the open range, Florida cattle ranchers called themselves cow hunters or cow men because they traditionally had to round up cattle from swamps, bogs, and dense hammocks. Cracker cow hunters used cow dogs for herding, and a long braided whip to drive cattle from interior grazing lands to the Gulf of Mexico for shipment to Cuba. The historical record and oral legend contain many tales of cattle rustling in Florida, a carry-over from the British Isles where local lore includes border ballads and tales of cattle thievery. Cattle in Florida were both branded and given distinctive ear crops to identify their ownership on the open range, not to mention the likelihood that their ownership might someday be disputed.

The second referent in the Florida Folk Festival program essay points to the cycle of tales and legends associated with Napoleon Bonaparte "Bone" Mizell, a Cracker cow hunter who worked the open range in the late 1800s and early 1900s. Mizell was the quintessential Cracker cow hunter—witty, uneducated, and an unabashed cow thief who always came out on top of his many scrapes with the law. Like the prototype Irish fast-talker, Mizell's words were always able to skirt over, under, and around any argument or libel against him. Reputed to have been one of the best cow hunters in Florida, Mizell is portrayed in one legend as quitting the range and opening a dry-goods store. For reasons that are not explained, but perhaps intuited, ultimately Mizell was not willing to sell the merchandise to his neighbors. He closed the store and returned to cattle herding.

The folk festival's essay redresses Dann's travelogue insults against the Cracker. Not only will he not be found leaning on a fence post, he will be seen driving a convertible. Prominent and prosperous, he has the expendable income to make that a customized convertible. The crossroads also has a certain symbolic value in the story. Florida's economy and demographic profile were rapidly changing and the Cracker was a fellow traveler on the road to the future, not hesitating and certainly not lounging around some barren fence post. He is neither gaunt nor leather-skinned, but looks just like everyone else.

In 1895 American artist Frederic Remington sketched a portrait of Mizell that was published in the August edition of *Harper's New Monthly Magazine.* Remington's chronicles of the western cowboy were favored by politicians and capitalists whose financial gain depended upon expansion of the western frontier. The artist accommodated them, creating figures that were heroic, full of swagger, and willing to make sacrifices to tame an uncivilized frontier, making it safe and profitable for future generations. Remington could not or did not apply the same mythical proportions to his portrait of Bone Mizell. He wrote that Cracker cowboys "lack dash and are indifferent riders, but they are picturesque in their unkempt, almost unearthly wildness."

Despite the fight and heroics of the Cracker cow hunter from the late 1700s onward, in 1900 Florida was considered by many to be a frontier. The state's population was barely more than 500,000 and population density was 9.8 people per square mile, less than half the national average of 25.7. While Scots-Irish settlers had fought Seminoles, freed and runaway African slaves, panthers, black bear, wolves, alligators, malarial mosquitoes, and diamondback rattlers to claim the territory, the Florida wilderness was recast in the twentieth century for a different kind of settlement. With its subtropical climate, exotic palm trees, and "velvet air," Florida in the late 1800s was marketed as "Paradise." Like the rest of the South after the Civil War, Florida was starved for capital. The state's policy makers courted financiers willing to build railroads along the eastern coast and across the peninsula east to west. Henry Plant and Henry Flagler received embarrassingly generous land concessions from Florida in return for developing transportation and infrastructure. What followed were the construction of luxury hotels and the popularity of winter retreats for the wealthy. With the invention of the automobile, Florida's exotic paradise became accessible to middle-class Americans. For the estimated 400,000 vacationing travelers annually, state entrepreneurs built temporary quarters—mobile homes and travel trailers—and local residents nicknamed the visitors "tin can tourists."

The festival essay's example of Mizell's lack of ambition when he failed to sell the merchandise in his own store is especially rich with meaning in the context of mid-twentieth-century Florida when it seemed everything was for sale. Land speculation was rampant, and the state's pro-business policy makers had been soliciting buyers at least since 1912. Bone Mizell was a hero on the frontier when it was defined by rural working-class sensibilities. By the 1950s the frontier was a real estate developer's paradise. Its value would not be in open ranges, but in high-rise hotels. And Bone Mizell, judged by urban, moneyed financiers, was merely a colorful character from the past.

During World War II the United States established several military bases in Florida, exposing the state's unique landscape to another generation of

Americans. After the war tourism developers bought advertisements in national publications with patriotic sales pitches: "Spend your victory vacation in Florida." The development of air conditioning and the use of DDT for mosquito control radically changed the pattern of winter tourism in the 1940s, as many Americans chose to remain in Florida year-round. Between 1930 and 1950 the population nearly doubled from 1.46 million to 2.78 million. Most newcomers settled from Ocala in the central part of the state, southward to Miami and the Florida Keys. Technology to drain and ditch the Everglades had transformed the southern landscape from an uninhabitable "river of grass" to fertile fields harvested by migrant and immigrant laborers working for giant corporations. In 1949 the governor signed legislation prohibiting open-range cattle ranching. Too many tourists were being injured and killed when their automobiles suddenly collided with a Cracker cow.

By the mid-1950s the nickname "Cracker" also had become affiliated with white bigotry, rooted in the unreconstructed race divisions of the South. Its potency as an epithet was meant to carry the same derisive hatred embodied in the word "nigger." In its mission to educate America's many kinds of people about one another, the Florida Folk Festival worked to redeem the term and restore its meaning to one of pride and heritage. In subsequent years, the festival always included one or more performances emblematic of Cracker heritage. These were sometimes supported with short details in the program, calling the Florida Cracker a pioneer and "the backbone of our nation." Within a few years, at least some Floridians were willing to speak proudly of themselves as Crackers. A story about humorist and storyteller A. E. "Frog" Smith illustrates the point. Asked what he would be if he wasn't a Cracker, Smith replied, "Ashamed."

In 1963 the FFF brought to the stage a native Floridian named Will McLean. Touted as a fourth-generation Floridian, McLean was from Chipley in the northern panhandle. Cousin Thelma called him Cousin Will. Alton Morris noted that McLean had lived all over Florida and wrote songs about the state's folk legends and lore. "He has sung many of his original folk songs on television and radio. None of his songs have been published." That year's performances also included a folk song written by Bob Pavitt after Hurricane Donna ripped through the state in 1960. Cousin Thelma composed a song about Florida sand for the bottlephone. Cousin Jay sang American Folk Songs. The incipient form of Florida Song had arrived at the folk festival.

Around 1965, a report in the FFMC newsletter stated: "We are living in a period of transition and change . . . we all know that 'Music is the universal language' and 'There is pride in belonging.'" On the back cover of the NFMC newsletter, listed with sheet music and curriculum guides for order was a publication titled "Let's Have A Folk Festival."

The folk music revival in America developed shortly after World War I, but did not gain momentum until during and after the Great Depression. Like all folk revivals, it was stimulated by disconcerting shifts in established social and cultural systems. After WWI, the contours of world power and national identity had been redrawn; furthermore, policy changes affecting migration and the economy only increased after World War II. Locked in an ideological battle with the Soviet Union to win the hearts and minds of the world, the United States in 1965 adopted sweeping new immigration reforms raising entry quotas and democratizing opportunities for immigration from countries other than the British Isles and Germany. The idea of a frontier in Paradise proved irresistible. Florida's population increased from 1,897,414 in 1940 to 18.8 million in 2010. The dense clustering of new towns and cities between Ocala and Miami annexed the open range and essentially made Cracker cow hunters the inhabitants of a borderland between Florida's receding past and looming future. After 1965 the majority of the newcomers were from Latin America, Asia, and other states within the United States. In 2010, Florida's population density was 350.6 people per square mile, four times greater than the national average of 87.4.

Singer/songwriter Will McLean was a wandering minstrel. He often slept in the woods and he drank, often. He was considered by some to be Florida's Woody Guthrie. He became known to other folk singers as the Father of Florida Folk, writing the episodic tales of seminal moments and forgotten times in Florida's history. Anytime McLean's "Hold Back the Waters of Lake Okeechobee" is sung, the fans of Florida Song sing along, mournfully, reverently. Their shoulders press against one another and they all sway, and real or imagined, the brittle rattle of cabbage palm leaves disturbed by a lofting wind fills the pause between the lines of the song. "Hold Back the Waters" is the anthem of Florida Song, recalling the West Indies winds that blew with hurricane force in September 1928, flooding Lake Okeechobee and drowning 1,800 to 3,000 people, most of them Caribbean and African American migrant agricultural laborers. Okeechobee has been described as "the liquid heart" of the Everglades. As part of the restructuring of land and water to make the glades useful for agriculture, engineers built an earthen work dam around the lake. McLean's song is a simple telling of the tale, but has ominous overtones implying the futility of man's efforts to conquer nature. The song also credits Seminoles for their "wise words" and their ability to anticipate the storm and take refuge. The same story is told in Zora Neal Hurston's novel, *Their Eyes Were Watching God.* By the time of his death in 1990 McLean had performed at seventeen Florida Folk Festivals.

Folk revivalists created the Will McLean Festival, which holds an annual songwriting contest. Entries "must be some aspect of Florida (history, heritage, land, sky, water, critters, or people) and clearly identifiable as such" and will be judged on "authenticity, originality, quality of the lyrics and melody, and the emotional impact of the song." In 2007 the winning entry was titled, "Florida Cracker Girl." Second place was given to "Spanish Gold" and third place to "While Osceola Cries." Among the twelve remaining entries, one was titled "The Legend of Bone Mizell" and another, "You Can Still See Florida."

Florida Song has three dominant strands and each strand has at least one living iconic singer/songwriter who, like Woody Guthrie, Will McLean, and Bone Mizell, serve as literary symbols, pioneers, and heroes of the Florida Song frontier. Stock images are manipulated and become immediately recognizable as part of the Florida Song movement. These edited views of the past are popularized and authenticated by their annual repetition at the Florida Folk Festival.

The first strand is the *Cracker revival* and Frank Thomas is the iconic figure associated with this strand. Lyrics are overwhelmingly nostalgic and the majority of songs are lamentations of loss, over Cracker cow men, the deceased writers of Florida Song, and the pastoral land that sustained them. The category bears the strongest resemblance to McLean's themes and with the tale-telling style of traditional Scots-Irish ballads. Most Florida Song compositions and tunes employ a solo vocalist with guitar accompaniment. A Florida native, Thomas has performed at every FFF since 1980 and his tunes, like McLean's, are best described as acoustic country. Thomas's "Florida Cowman" speaks directly to the emotionality behind Florida Song:

His beard may be stubbled, like a cut-over sugarcane field.
His clothes may be dirty, but the look in his eyes lets you know he won't yield.
He's from a breed that has died, but he has survived and the world that he once knew is gone.
He's an old Cracker Cowman, existing a long way from home.

Chorus:
Now dirt bikes scream over land that used to be scrub cow trails
And interstate highways have taken the place of old Mr. Flagler's rails
And condos rise from the land and space shuttles fly
And the old Cracker Cowman don't know how it all passed him by.

The second strand is primarily concerned with *environmental movement protest* and Dale Crider is the iconic figure for this feature of Florida Song. This strand resembles folk revival protest song when lyrics are written by singer-songwriters at the state folk festival, but Crider is a retired wildlife biologist whose music is not rooted in symbolic nostalgia, but science education and eco-activism. His performances are interspersed with mini-lectures on the rapacious exploitation of Florida's natural resources and the inevitable consequences of overconsumption. Crider has the composure and intelligence of a scientist and his messages are both compelling and entertaining. His songs sometimes employ romanticized images, for example, "Mangrove Buccaneer" uses seventeenth-century Caribbean pirates to recreate a sense of early exploration of Florida's mangrove swamps. Originally from Tennessee, Crider's songwriting during the past thirty years has often been playful and humorous, with songs like "Mosquito Lullaby" and "Gospel Snakes." Crider's message is about conservation and it is measured and sorely needed in Florida where consumption and profit have destroyed vital aspects of a landscape and ecosystem unique in the United States. Including work by other Florida Song composers, this strand connects with the Cracker revival strand by sometimes casting the Cracker as an endangered or vanishing species. The lyrics of a song written by Steve Blackwell illustrate this song type, using the late-eighteenth-century decimation of plume birds by hunters. A native of Indiana he had lived in Florida thirty-five years when he died in 2006:

Feathers for the ladies' hats
Is what they're for I'm told.
And at $35 for an ounce of them
You know they're worth their weight in gold.

Chorus:
Plumes
Bright explosions of wings—
Once I shoot those crazy birds
I can buy all kinds of things.

They'll just sit right there.
Can you imagine that?
Trying to protect their young
Just feathers in a hat.

The third strand is *nativistic* and Bobby Hicks is the iconic figure for this line of songs. Direct, angry, and confrontational, the songs in this group rail against tourists and developers, despise greed, and vigorously assert the primacy of pioneers on the Florida frontier. Hicks's best-known song carries a bit of brag: "I'm Florida, Need I Say More?"

> I guess I'm a little bit of everything.
> Seen so many flags unfurled.
> Someone still remembers, they come and see us all over the world.
> I'm the Spanish moss hanging from the live oak tree.
> I'm what's left of the panther and the old manatee.
> I'm an eagle in flight, I'm the ocean's roar.
> I'm Florida, need I say more?

Hicks is rightfully proud of a Scottish heritage that has endured five generations in Florida. In a *St. Petersburg Times* interview, Hicks said he "found his calling at White Springs, hearing many people sing about rivers and the land. 'But they weren't really lashing out, naming names. I saw a need for that.'" This strand of Florida Song is raw, blatant, and draws closer to the surface the emotion behind the lyrics. In 1998 Hicks vented his frustration from an amplified microphone while onstage at the FFF, and then briefly absented himself from the festival.

"First of all, those of you that matter, you know how much I love you and you know how much I love this place. And my problem isn't with this place . . . I think it's important that people come here before their name's on the program. And, I promised I'd be nice . . . but if this thing ever becomes the Florida Folk Festival where Florida's not the damn exception here, then I'll come back . . . (*sings 'I'm Florida'*) Isn't it a little different when you listen to someone sing a song about something they grew up in? I'm not taking away from our new songwriters, but you know, there are some of us that didn't have to read a book to figure out what the hell we're talking about. Both sides of my family have been on this Florida soil since 1791. There was never anything wrong enough with my home to leave. So when you're here, you're visiting from somewhere else, you moved here from somewhere else, this is sacred ground. This is my home. This is our home. It's welcome to be your home, but treat it accordingly. (*Song continues*) I'm a Frenchman, I'm British, I'm an Indian and I'm all kinds of things. In fact, I'm proud of our multi-faceted culture. But you all better realize that every time somebody different lands at the airport, that doesn't make it part of the picture. You gotta be here a while before you earn a part in Florida folk culture. And that's why I'm gonna leave you all. I am Florida. You are Florida. And I challenge you to stand up to the challenge to make Florida the rule at the Florida Folk Festival and no longer the exception as you've tried to make it for the last seven or eight years. Good night White Springs!"

Hicks's onstage fury is part of his onstage persona and he is unapologetic. When he turned up the flame of his anger and speech in 1998, he managed to boil down the essence of a long-standing territorial dispute over cultural heritage and belonging at the state folk festival.

The FFF became contested terrain in the late 1970s. Cousin Thelma's health was in decline. Peggy Bulger was hired as a folklorist working out of the park in 1976, and the Florida Folklife Program was formed shortly thereafter. The Folklife Program folklorists exercised diplomacy and sensitivity as they considered the profound reworking of Florida's cultural landscape. Positioning themselves as cultural mediators, folklorists kept Florida Crackers in the program. Boltin had more responsibilities at the Foster Memorial than producing the festival. By necessity she developed a group of stock performers who returned every year. The bureau's academically trained folklorists had greater manpower and professional resources. They conducted fieldwork to access old and new pockets of ethnic settlement throughout the state. Mindful of Florida's elders, they created apprenticeships in cow whip making and offered workshops in whip cracking. Cracker "dignitaries" who had invested significant portions of their lifetime sharing and explaining "crackericity" at the festival were honored with Folk Heritage Awards. Folklorists' research significantly extended the depth and breadth of Cracker representation at the festival as tale-tellers, spur makers, farriers, whip makers, saddle makers, and others whose occupational skills were about Florida cattle ranching were brought to the stage.

Folklorists also are professionally and ideologically committed to furthering cultural democracy. Since the 1960s academically trained folklorists have moved away from definitions of authenticity and text, to ethnographic methods and analyses of folklore as public discourse about the spaces where the individual and society meet. Folklife Program folklorists also worked to fulfill the festival's founding mission—to introduce Floridians to one another in a setting where differences were intentionally being addressed. Event programs contained thoughtful and well-researched background. Stage performances of Cuban dance were no longer disembodied textual representations by music clubs who had studied the sheet music, but by Cubans dancing. Bahamian junkanoo dancers, Mexican piñata makers, Ukrainians, Greeks, Nicaraguans, Haitians, Chinese, Vietnamese, Cambodians, Serbians, and Turks spoke for themselves. The festival program also contained essays distinguishing between unbroken tradition and revival, between composing songs for solo performance and learning traditional songs for performance at social dances.

Florida Song performers responded to the changes in provocative ways. One group began having itself listed in the program as "Mr. Ethnic's Wednesday Night Fiddling Support Group," and another performed as "No Commercial Appeal." When folklorists attempted to restructure the number and content of revivalist performers at the festival, fire and brimstone rained down upon the land. Old associations of power between "natives" and state officials were rekindled. Folklorists were shut out of the series of town hall meetings held by state officials with irate festival performers around the state. Folklorists emerged from the fracas with the realization that "there were unwritten rules" about performer selection at the festival.

Revivalists established their own nonprofit organization to act as marketing agent and political action committee on their behalf. The Friends of Florida Folk (FOFF) posts this statement on its Web site: "Way back when, a 'folk Family' evolved . . . a small group of pickers and singers met regularly at the Florida Folk Festival in White Springs. Close family ties were formed with these people around many a campfire. Will McLean was one of us. We sang the old songs, and someone would always bring along a guitar, the coffee pot, and a kazoo. And everyone would join in and sing. Many from our group were performers at the festival. But in 1982 there came about a change in policy and most of the old stand-by performers were not invited to perform any longer. No one understood why this happened, and anger grew. We decided to form a protest group, hoping to get our friends back on the stage. This was the birth of Friends of Florida Folk. We incorporated as a non-profit organization and we approached the 'powers that be' and made a lot of noise, trying to get things changed back to the way they had been. After a long fight, we won, and our friends were again invited to be a part of the festival."

FOFF's self-written history is revealing. As Cousin Thelma's cousins, the festival's stock performers did decide to define themselves as a "family." For the most part Florida Song performers perform Florida Songs—their own, or those of another Florida Song composer. The definition of "old songs" has been rewritten from Old World to "Since Will McLean circa 1963." Among the revivalists at the FFF, many mastered and help to maintain the repertoire of Old World traditional music, including ballads from the British Isles, Cajun, old-time, Irish, shape-note, bluegrass, and gospel; however, Florida Song musicians generally include very few traditional songs in their performances. Porch pickers, dance bands, coffeehouse regulars, and professional musicians are all represented among the revivalist musicians at the Florida Folk Festival. Considered as a continuum of Scots-Irish and British Isles traditional music, Florida Song has replaced the fiddle with the guitar; it has supplanted group or social dance performance with solo performance in front of an audience, and its lyrics and tune structure are more akin to contemporary folk fusion, blending styles and adding individual expression in what Ellen Steckert called "new aesthetic."

The group's decision to "form a protest group" shows direct influence, not with traditional music or Cracker heritage, but with the folk revival of the mid-twentieth century. The use of tradition to mobilize a populace was a prominent feature of the folk revival generated by left-wing activists between 1930 and 1965. Woody Guthrie, Pete Seeger, and Alan Lomax were instigators and beneficiaries of that foray into the politics of culture. Their political aims were not realized, but they effectively created a popular notion that folk singers write and perform "meaningful" songs, and all profited monetarily from commercialization of traditional music. Folklorists have taken note of the revival's commercialization of what previously had been local and heritage-based expressions of culture. FOFF's primary service to its membership is political advocacy to protect its members' domination of performances at FFF. It also publishes a calendar listing of those performers' appearances in a variety of public venues; and it acts as sales and marketing agents for the members' recordings.

The Florida Folk Festival presented confusing definitions of "authenticity" with classically trained music educators enacting Mexican hat dances and "Froggie Went A Courtin." As the study of American folklore matured and changed its emphasis from text to context and then to discourse, the festival's changing definitions of tradition were disturbing to performers who fit into a "folk" festival for many years and then were declared not to be as folk as they used to be. While essays in festival programs between 1977 and 1995 often addressed the definitions of folk and revival, ultimately the revivalists rejected new models and definitions. The anti-intellectualism of many in the folk revival has been considered from different viewpoints. From the perspective of the FOFF revivalists at FFF, folklorists were sent a pointed message from a stage performance of a newly composed tune, "Pseudo-Intellectual."

The Cracker cattle rancher has adapted to the twenty-first century, maintaining traditions of cow dogs and whips and managing herds inside cow pens. They are listening to bluegrass, gospel, and country and western music. If the presentation of Cracker culture at the festival was central to the turf war between FOFF and folklife programmers of the event, then participation by Crackers would be missing. The public discourse of Florida Song cannot be completely answered by a disregard for Florida's "first" settlers on the festival stage. Rather, folklorists' presentation of the state's dynamic and multiple ethnicities comes closer to the "real" Florida, and Florida Song's depictions of a tunnelized history bear more resemblance to exceptionalism.

As politics of culture, the Cracker's inferior status was exposed when Remington did not lionize the Cracker as a frontier hero on the same scale of the western cowboy. Urban and wealthy newcomers established a new command post for political and economic power in the south of Florida. While cattle ranchers such as Zibe King and Jacob Summerlin earned sufficient income to be called "cattle barons" and "cattle kings" their wealth was paltry as compared to that of Henry Flagler and many who followed him. The rapid influx of new immigrants in the twentieth century created a pervasive sense of disenfranchisement for the Crackers, especially when the tidal wave of new immigrants began arriving after 1965.

It is that profound sense of alienation and displacement that characterizes the impulse behind revivalist movements. Taking the view that alienation leads to folk romanticism, and that a sense of deterioration of tradition results in grassroots preservationism, Florida Song exhibits both qualities. The derogatory image of the European Cracker became mutable when carried to a new continent and a young nation with foreshortened historical memory. Associating the nickname with an occupational tradition was a logical progression in the context of romantic nationalism and its reverence for the pioneers who settled the frontier. That reassignment of meaning is reified through composition and performance of Florida Song.

The second element of the Cracker's revival resulted from the eroding sense of both place and belonging as ranch lands were reallocated for urban development and the population became more diverse. The impulse to preserve the Cracker's sense of power and place in Florida history became one of two primary functions of Florida Song. The second was to establish authority as authentic folk musicians at the state folk festival. Having a privileged position at the festival symbolically reinstates the lost privileges of the past. As folklorists drew lines of separation between unbroken tradition and revivalism, Florida Song created new symbols of group heritage and identity, "masquerading as the old."

Florida Song has strong qualities of an invented tradition in its fundamental impulse to select and idealize one fragment of Florida's past. Rooted in contemporary uses of traditional music and lore, it functions to expound upon social and political issues. Without being cut from the whole cloth, it chooses those elements most expedient to achieve its goals. The whole of Cracker tradition is charting another course, adapting to its place in twenty-first-century Florida.

Strictly speaking, when Florida Song's adherents command a larger share of the state's heritage festival for themselves, the movement enters another frame, that of nativistic protest. Florida Song's lyrics provide salient markers for how things used to be, and their use of pathos tries to move the listener into a sympathetic response, perhaps even to make reparation. Limiting migration, restoring wildlife and habitat, drawing back the lines of encroachment are public policy issues for citizen debate. Not allowing new immigrants the right to perform at the festival, which is to say, withholding the privilege of belonging, is nativism. It perpetuates the primacy of Crackers and it restricts or forbids newcomers, who are foreigners. If Florida Song proponents control who has access to stages at the FFF, the FFF becomes a platform for building a political constituency. Newcomers to the state may join the Florida Song coterie and thereby ameliorate their own culpability in the problems of development, exploitation of natural resources, and disregard of pioneer primacy. To do so requires them to abandon their own history and heritage and adopt the identity and "tradition" of Florida Song.

CONCLUSION

For roughly one hundred years, from the early 1800s to the early 1900s, political power in Florida was concentrated in the families and wealth of the northern part of the state. Beginning in 1912 and accelerating as urban development increased in the south, the seat of power shifted and the Cracker's interests were no longer a priority. The Cracker, like the Seminole, is placed on a pedestal, a relic symbolically revered and otherwise inconsequential. When Florida Song and FOFF engage in political protest to maintain their sense of primacy at the state folk festival, the illusion of political authority is renewed. But it is only illusion. While Florida reinstates the Florida Songsters in modern celebrity roles representing statehood at the festival, they simultaneously pursue policies and create constituencies that may stand in opposition to real-life Cracker interests.

"The Rest Is Up to You and Me"

Sunday Morning Band and Ritual Identity in the Florida Panhandle

JERRILYN McGREGORY

THIS ESSAY SEEKS TO ILLUSTRATE SOME OF THE MATERIAL, VERBAL, AND ritual planes of reality that pervade African American life into death. Past scholars predicted that ritual performances would experience some erasure in modern life.[1] Yet, African Americans have ritualized social relationships into a repetitious cycle through the maintenance of organizations such as Sunday Morning Band (SMB). The SMB functions as a secret society, allowing for an interrogation into a rich array of culturally specific African American traditions that enable participants to experience a symbolic spiritual journey.

The first SMB was organized in Columbia County, Florida, on August 8, 1868. At one time, as many as five hundred bands existed throughout the state. They are essentially burial leagues, a kind of mutual aid society.[2] African American burial societies historically existed to administer to the distressed and to help bury the dead. Proper interment, mourning, and honoring the recently deceased are prominent elements in a belief system that privileges ancestral forces. Initially, the SMB conferred on its members such amenities as the construction of a pine box. Given the immediacy of its formation after the period of enslavement, the SMB speaks to the disruption of respectful funeral customs by slave owners, who tended to delay or haphazardly and disrespectfully discard the remains of African Americans' loved ones.[3]

Though often spoken of in the past tense, burial leagues still function to ensure the survival of a core community in times of crises.[4] As an extension of a communitarian outlook, mutual aid members also provide services such as dispensing health care to the sick or infirm, chopping wood, and—when dependent on an agrarian economy—planting or harvesting crops. Additionally, women often outlive husbands, so widows receive special considerations. In this manner, burial leagues meet the needs of any member who is incapacitated or suffering other losses. There is an annual state conference of the SMBs during the last week in May, and host lodge members customarily open their homes to delegates unable to find affordable accommodations.

The Wiregrass region, which encompasses parts of the Florida Panhandle, southeast Alabama, and south Georgia, supports a number of similar organizations with a cornucopia of names such as the Loyal Americans, the International Benevolent Society, Independent Bands I & II, and the 9th of Moses. Close to the Alabama state line, Cottondale is a virtual hotbed of such organizations.

TRADITIONS OF THE TURN OUT

The SMB probably derives its name from an African American spiritual song with the same name. However, contemporary members say the name alludes to the temporal sequence regarding the day of the week and the portion of the day when the annual Turn Out, or anniversary program, customarily occurs: Sundays at 11 a.m. As a colloquial expression, "turn out" means to arrive at a place for a special festive purpose.[5]

On the day of a Turn Out, members march two abreast from their lodge to a nearby church. Along the way, they sing traditional spirituals before uplifting their signature song, "What Band is this / Sunday Morning Band." They make a distinct, rhythmic trampling noise with their feet while periodically crossing underneath an upheld pair of decorated staffs. Members wear specialized colors—women dress entirely in white (sometimes with capes), and men wear white shirts or black suits (sometimes with sashes). The purpose of the Turn Out is not to evangelize but to honor new initiates along with the recently departed and, ultimately, to recruit.

As secret societies, these associations retain elements of African origin. Famed sociologist, historian, and literary figure W. E. B. Du Bois wrote: "Secret societies have always played an important part in West Africa. They include a large variety of associations, of which, the majority are mutual benefit clubs. Membership confers social distinction and one method of bestowing charity."[6] Beyond ensuring proper interment, the foremost function of these lodges is to promote morale and religion. They are mainly Christian organizations. To become a member, accordingly, one must be asked, must be

SMB#363. Photo by Jerrilyn McGregory.

Christian, and must be at least twelve—though children are integrated into a juvenile division at a younger age. So, in addition to being charged with the responsibility of administering to sick members and aggrieved widows, the SMB represents a secular-sacred performance community, which promotes rituals that enhance the survival chances of its constituency.

Like most secret societies, these bands consider themselves clandestine organizations but, as commonly expressed, "with nothing to hide." Initiation is a requirement for membership. Usually, the day before the Turn Out new members are "made," which probably still involves some elements of hazing. Each lodge has a password, but members of other lodges may discern it through an avenue of questioning. In addition, the lodges have secret knocks, handshakes, signs, and a certain walk. If the confidentiality is broken, according to tradition, the culprit's tongue will be cut out. The latter denotes the seriousness of the undertaking, for joining is a lifelong commitment. Sharoreiser White provides an eyewitness account: "Upon seeing them, everyone listens to the familiar theme, listens to the timed shuffle of feet, the systematic clapping of hands, and watches the 'jazzy' dipping of the uniformed train of band members."[7] They constitute a band not only in the sense of being a musical group, but as a unified company pledged to share its resources.

The structure of the Turn Out offers interesting layers of ritualization, decorum, ceremony, liturgy, and celebration.[8] Folks turn out to demonstrate

Band #363 assembles to march into their lodge. Photo by Jerrilyn McGregory.

support, witness the rituals, and enjoy the fellowship. Each band maintains a lodge building. Lodge #363 was constructed from lumber taken from a now defunct African American public school and is constantly refurbished. Joseph Johnson serves as the superintendent of the Sunday School and church steward for Henshaw Chapel African Methodist Episcopal Church. Annually, on the second Sunday in September, Band #363 "marches in," forming a procession from their lodge to the anniversary program site at Henshaw. It is Johnson's voice that bellows out the signature song, based on a Negro spiritual, "Sunday Morning Band," upon entering the churchyard.

Folklorist Roger Abrahams indicates that the festive events of enslaved Africans were "animated by the style, spirit, and social and aesthetic organization of sub-Saharan Africa."[9] For example, processions fulfill a particularized canon of taste throughout West Africa and the African Diaspora.[10] They represent a continuous, documented part of the social life in Freetown, Sierra Leone, Carnival in the Caribbean, and Mardi Gras in the United States. Although tame in comparison, during the SMB's procession the ritualized trampling of feet denotes that their movements intend to evoke more than a mere "marching in." Performance theorist Margaret Drewal stipulates that in Nigeria such rituals are conceived of "as journeys—sometimes actual and sometimes virtual." Unlike parades, processions are ritual acts performed in fulfillment of a spiritual identity.

According to the historian Sterling Stuckey, "The Circle is linked to the most important of all African ceremonies, the burial ceremony."[11] Yet, the SMB ritual privileges the line at their Turn Outs. On one hand, the ritual act suggests hybridity, but could it also be inversion? In traditional African societies the circle furnishes the principle metaphor for the life process, but knowledge of the line was not foreign. In African cosmology the horizontal axis of the cross "signifies the sea or river that divides the world of the living and dead, the heavens above and the earth below, this world and the next."[12] The association with SMB funerary custom is too perfect to ignore. For as Stuckey proposes, "By operating under the cover of Christianity, vital aspects of Africanity, which some considered eccentric in movement, sound, and symbolism, could more easily be practiced openly."[13] SMB movements syncretize well with Masonry and American marching units and so do some of their regalia. In the privacy of their lodge buildings and at actual funerary occasions, I would conjecture more circularity.

Color symbolism too requires examination. White constitutes the prominent ritual color of all the Bands. Universally, cultures associate white as being sacred and pure. In many traditional African societies, adherents wear the color white to appease spirits and to symbolize the journey connecting humans with the spirit world. Its ubiquitous presence in numerous African American sacred contexts syncretizes well with Christian beliefs, especially as white relates to rebirth. In Yoruba culture, the cloth of ritual novices is white—which is in keeping with the Turn Out's practices.[14]

As symbolic objects, the staffs act as one of the primary material components and are imbued with meaning. Crossing sticks was a way that enslaved Africans showed commitment to one another. As part of initiation rites, staffs were crossed to honor and bless the new life that was about to begin. The staffs symbolize the strength and vitality of trees. The rules of decorum dictate that only Band members are qualified to march underneath them. Many members, like the Johnsons, are active Masons. African Americans gave their own expression to the Masonic movement, dating back to the Revolutionary War era. Masons refer to such staffs as rods. Due to the sanctity afforded many of their symbolic objects, the associative meaning is unclear, but the *Encyclopedia of Freemasonry* suggests rods to be "an emblem of power."[15]

The signature song, "Sunday Morning Band," conforms to the antiphonal, syncopated, polyrhythmic style of spiritual songs. The Bands issue the following schematized variant of the original spiritual song's lyrics in a call-response pattern that is sung a capella:

Oh, what Band is this?
Sunday Morning.

Oh, what Band is this?
Sunday Morning.
Oh, what Band is this?
Sunday Morning,
Sunday Morning Band.

There's one,
There's two,
There's three, little angels.

There's four,
There's five,
There's six, little angels

There's seven,
There's eight,
There's nine, little angels
Ten little angels in the Band.

Oh, I'm tramping, tramping
Heaven must be my home.

Oh, I'm tramping, tramping
Heaven must be my home.

Overall, the ceremony demonstrates the degree to which African Americans utilize a musical system that does not isolate song, dance, and drama from one another.[16] The singing, trampling of feet, and secretive ritual movements reinstate long-standing traditions. Ethnomusicologist John Miller Chernoff identifies the definitive feature of the African musical sensibility as a "functional integration" of music and culture. Similarly, SMB Turn Outs bring all these interdependent elements together.

After the program, the Turn Out develops into more of a celebration. Queues form to sample homemade lemonade, ladled out of the traditional steel drum. A festive spirit spontaneously moves the group, and some men become tipsy (not from the lemonade) as others eat.[17] The event changes into a homecoming or family reunion, attracting those who have migrated to return annually. Various groupings assemble around their vehicles, not to tailgate, but to hoodgate. The hoods of cars are heavily laden with food dishes transported, as customary, in cardboard boxes. With the graveyard in such close proximity, one cannot escape a sense of the ancestors also being fed.

As one local resident escorted me around, a constant exchange ensued: "Do you have any possum?" Response: "No, but I know where you can get some goat." This refrain possibly alludes to esoteric knowledge and includes the hint of a password. When an outsider asks about the goat, the typical response is: "It's something you eat." In this neck of the woods, goat is a popular item in the daily diet. Yet, on these occasions, it insinuates so much more.

The process of initiation is referred to as "riding the goat," or as one participant said, "If you want to join, you got to ride the goat." The goat is a root metaphor (i.e., a pervasive cultural metaphor);[18] and as one respondent indicated, "they kn[o]w this is trouble." Much of the original meaning has dissolved into a number of categories derived from it. As part of the hazing process, "somebody would get out and sound like a goat and they would have a big bell or something and they would ring it and people would say, 'Get back, hold that goat . . . they just bamming on the side and stuff.'" Initiates may be blindfolded or an odd assortment of tools may be placed in view during a period in which initiates are being questioned. One informant stated, "They used to put the belt on you years back and you'd be sore for days." This behavior corresponds to the ordeal as a standard feature of initiation rites, "culturally induced suffering that dramatizes what might otherwise be a mundane physiological change."[19] For SMB #363, the metaphor of the goat is now bowdlerized into a skit, a folk drama, for recruitment purposes.

PILLARS OF TRADITION

In the booming metropolis of Cottondale (pop. 900), it is estimated that 90 percent of African American residents belong to a lodge. Two large SMBs coexist: #363 is deemed the citified Band and its rural neighbor is #339. No individual epitomizes the commitment to the tradition more than SMB #363's long-term president, Joseph Johnson.[20] During his tenure as president, which began in 1986, his lodge experienced notable growth. As he likes to express it, he "was born into the Band," by virtue of the fact that his mother was a presiding officer. Born August 24, 1947, in Jackson County, Florida, Johnson continues to be a major local tradition bearer. Although a longtime resident of Tallahassee, Cottondale remains his true home and he retains a homeplace there. During the Turn Out season from September to October,

Rural SMB#339. Photo by Jerrilyn McGregory.

he serves as the song leader by assisting at least eight other Bands. As expressed by one of the community elders who knew his parents and grandparents, "If there is something going on in the Cottondale community, Joe is there to help get it moving in the right direction because he never forgot where he came from."[21] Since he recently retired from his job as a radiologist at Tallahassee Memorial Hospital, he has more time to oversee the continuity of this little-known tradition.

As the presiding officer of the state convention, Johnson officiates in numerous capacities. He described the "good of the Band" through the members' duties: "Five dimes, belong to a church, accept Jesus Christ as Lord and Savior. It's a holy Band." In this manner, Johnson reiterates its affordability and the rewards of membership. He is a consummate tradition bearer, granting administrative leadership and musical prowess to his sacred and secular Wiregrass communities. As expressed by one of his admirers, he accomplishes everything he does in "the Fruit of the Spirit." His religious conviction sustains not only himself but also his community of origin.

Possessing superb vocal skills, Johnson is one of the greatest traditional gospel quartet singers in the region. In 1964, at the age of seventeen, he organized his quartet, the Jubilives, and remains its only original member. Johnson's brother, James, articulates: "I fondly recall the times that Joe would sing in his sleep in preparation for an upcoming program."[22] In 2008, Johnson received the Florida Folk Heritage Award for his commitment to the SMB and gospel traditions. Accolades from his fellow Band members, Cottondale civic leaders, and fans poured in to support his nomination.

Johnson illustrates the customary organizational leadership pattern among African Americans. Efficient leaders often function like benevolent monarchs who seldom abdicate. The annual election or vote of confidence usually has the same outcome. Only death disrupts this structural flow. The perpetuation of a performance community requires the dedication of only a single soul, male or female. In some ways, the Sunday Morning Band and the Jubilives rely heavily on Johnson's stamina to preserve them. And due to his leadership, singing abilities, and strength of character, yearly SMB Turn Outs are deeply anticipated events.

Like Joe Johnson, Inez White, longtime chairman of rural lodge #339, exemplifies community standards. White heads the largest SMB organization in the state. She lives on historic grounds in the vicinity of Bethlehem AME Church, the oldest African American church in Florida. Bethlehem AME was founded by Henry W. Call in 1863, prior to emancipation. On that Thursday night there was a general handshaking, "while the white overseer looked on unaware of anything more than a prayer meeting." During reconstruction, Henry Call and Jacob Livingston became presiding elders in Jackson County, playing a major role in many newly established AME churches and becoming a testament to the denomination's aspirations in the region.

Born August 6, 1937, White lives the Whitesville community on the homeplace where she was born, in clear view of the churchyard. Her band holds its anniversary celebration on the third Sunday in October. African American women usually access greater power with age, and the hierarchical structure is often a ruse that subverts the Western model. According to the sociologist Bennetta Jules-Rosettes, such patterns indicate a distinction between "rites of power and roles of power." In practice, men may dominate in ceremonial leadership positions, as sanctioned by church affiliates, but women preside over their sacred performance communities, undertaking many key responsibilities for their entire lifetime.

In the 1970s, White first served as the head of her lodge's juvenile auxiliary, which includes children as soon as they are able to walk. I would conjecture that it is of utmost importance to members to indoctrinate their young to ensure the tradition's survival. Many joined at an early age in keeping with family tradition, including all five of White's sons. The first woman chair, White has served thirty years in this capacity—the longest ritual leader. She also has been treasurer for the state convention for thirty years. She insisted on the maintenance of the auxiliary to prepare youth to assume leadership positions. For example, she appointed Brandon Killins as vice president when he was about ten years old, and at the age of twenty-one he served as the interim chair when White experienced a stroke.

Although rules of decorum, ceremony, and the liturgy are similar, the celebrations of the two Bands have some observable differences—so these two large Bands in close proximity show both continuity and change. A video taken in 1993 by my student reveals that once inside the Henshaw Chapel fellowship hall, Band #363 performed rhythmic tramping of their feet, letting them explode downward on the hardwood floor. The tables were already set up for the ritual repast, perhaps hindering another formation. Participants formed a square along the baseline. I have observed that after its Turn Out, the citified Band lines up outside for a brief ritualistic exchange of patterned, kinetic hand movements above the waist. They execute a series of the customary enigmatic hand gestures while wearing the patented white gloves: holding hands above the head; two hands grasping from side to side; a rolling pin arm motion. Before promenading into the church's fellowship hall, they maintain a linear formation.

In comparison, another video recording captured the Bethlehem Band conducting its recessional after its Turn Out program. Upon entering its nearby lodge (a vacated brick school building), it produced an explosive furor, encircling the room and loudly tramping upon the hardwood floor. Their movements fall within the sacred mode of dancing, as members never cross their feet. Unlike the renowned counterclockwise movement of the African American ring shout, however, dancers moved in a clockwise direction. Traditionally, such an inversion signifies memory. Their enactment otherwise reconstitutes the ring shout—one of the oldest documented African retentions among African Americans in the United States. Musicologist Samuel Floyd describes the characteristic movements as "the shuffling around in a ring, the upper-body dancing of African provenance, the ever-present singing accompanied by the hand clapping and thudding, repetitious drumming (of feet in this case), and the extended length of the activity."[23] Much should be made of the Bethlehem Band consistently shifting from its opening linear processional to a circular orientation at the close of its ritual event.

CONCLUSION

I have illustrated not the existence of cult beliefs and practices, but the constitutive planes of reality—material, verbal, and ritual—that pervade African American life into death. As the moderator of an independent band stated, "Company is good to the grave. Now, when you pass you need somebody at the graveside also. You need somebody there to prepare flowers, to let you down, to move you in and out of church and what not." According to Drewal, ritual journeys represent a part of the greater journey of the human spirit.[24] Via their Turn Outs, ritual participants reflexively experience a leg of this journey.

Derrida speaks about the work of mourning: "the pathology and the normality of mourning."[25] Groups like the SMB make this expression of sorrow more palatable. Burial societies work to help the departed rest in peace and extend the concept "that life must have a proper ending" into a principle.[26] Funerary customs for people of African descent speak to connectedness with a broader community—the ancestors, who represent the matrix of memory.[27] One is as concerned for their comfort as the living. As the saying goes, "The rest is up to you and me."

Notes

1. John L. Fisher, "Psychology and Anthropology," in *Biennial Review of Anthropology*, ed. B. S. Siegel (Stanford: Stanford University Press, 1965), 234; *Essays on the Ritual of Social Relations*, ed. Max Gluckman (Manchester, UK: Manchester University Press, 1962), 36–37; and Ronald L. Grimes, *Beginnings in Ritual Studies* (Washington, DC: University Press of America, 1982). On the other hand, Robert Bocock extends the boundaries to include repetitive events into his calculation of what constitutes ritual in an industrial society. See Robert Bocock, *Ritual in Industrial Society: A Sociological Analysis of Ritualism in Modern England* (London: George Allen and Unwin, 1974).
2. Roberta Wright and Wilbur Hughes, *Lay Down Body: Living History in African American Cemeteries* (Detroit: Visible Ink Press, 1996), 267–68.
3. Ibid., xiii. Also, see Albert Raboteau, *Slave Religion* (New York: Oxford University Press, 1978), 230, and Bessie Jones, *For the Ancestors* (Urbana: University of Illinois Press, 1983), 46–48.
4. See "Burial Society" chapter in *Lay My Burden Down*.
5. Both the terms, Band and Turn Out, are used in the context of Carnival fetes in the Caribbean. In *Carnival, Canboulay and Calypso: Traditions in the Making* (Cambridge: Cambridge University Press, 1999), John Cowley utilizes them as anglicized vernacular expressions. Moreover, a quotation (139), which he cites, harkens back to the 1890s in Trinidad.
6. W. E. B. Du Bois, *The World and Africa* (New York: International Publishers, 1965), 160.
7. Sharoresier White, student paper, "The Sunday Morning Band," submitted December 8, 1994.
8. See Ronald Grimes, *Celebration*, 274, for attendant discussion of each of these elements.
9. Roger Abrahams, *Singing the Master* (New York: Penguin, 1992).
10. See John Nunley, *Moving With the Face of the Devil* (Urbana: University of Illinois Press, 1987), and Margaret Drewal, *Yoruba Ritual* (Bloomington: University of Indiana

Press, 1992). Roger Abrahams attributes the practice exclusively to an imitation of the English elite, missing a rare opportunity to provide and acknowledge the acculturation process. African Americans often cloak African retentions within Christianity.

11. See Sterling Stuckey, *Slave Culture* (New York: Oxford University Press, 1987), 11. He also provides the reference regarding its metaphoric link to the life process (15). No doubt, after emancipation to foster a public display event privileging a circle ceremony would draw unnecessary attention and support the larger society's charges of retrogression into barbarism. The ring shout, a circular dance, continued in practice but was decidedly performed clandestinely.
12. Ibid., 65.
13. Ibid., 35.
14. For discussions of the significance of white in West African traditions, see Drewal and Elisha Renne, *Cloth That Does Not Die* (Seattle: University of Washington Press, 1995).
15. Albert Gallatin Mackey and H. L. Haywood, *Encyclopedia of Freemasonry* (Chicago: Masonic History, 1946), 863.
16. This is a widely dispensed notion, but for reference, see George Lipsitz, *Time Passage* (Minneapolis: University of Minnesota Press, 1990), 239.
17. Ronald Grimes, "The Lifeblood of Public Ritual," in *Celebration: Studies in Festivity and Ritual*, ed. Victor Turner (Washington, DC: Smithsonian Institution, 1982), 277.
18. See Victor Turner, *Dramas Fields and Metaphors*, for a definition of root metaphor.
19. Barbara Myerhoff, "Rites of Passage," in *Celebration*, ed. Victor Turner, 121.
20. Florida Folk Heritage Award winner, 2008.
21. Support letter, Florida Folk Heritage Award, Mildred Hollins, dated September 27, 2007.
22. Support letter, Florida Folk Heritage Award, James Johnson, dated September 18, 2007.
23. Floyd Samuel Jr., *The Power of Black Music: Interpreting Its History from Africa to the United States* (New York: Oxford University Press, 1995), 37.
24. Drewal, *Yoruba Ritual*, 46.
25. Jacques Derrida, *Specters of Marx* (New York: Routledge, 1994), 178, footnote #3.
26. Melville Herskovits, *The Myth of the Negro Past*, reprint (Boston: Beacon, 1990), 197. Herskovits extensively researched sites throughout the African Diaspora as well as West Africa and recognized delayed funerals as an African survival among African Americans. As he expressed it, "to the extent that European religious beliefs have been taken over, the extinction of the cult does not mean that its spirit has disappeared or that its sanctions have not persisted" (199). The importance of a lavish funeral to create harmony between the ancestral world and their descendants has been well documented by others, such as Stuckey, *Slave Culture*, 5.
27. See Karla Holloway, *Moorings & Metaphors* (New Brunswick, NJ: Rutgers University Press, 1992).

Maritime Folklife

FLORIDA FOLKLIFE PROGRAM, FLORIDA DEPARTMENT OF STATE. INTRODUCTION BY NANCY MICHAEL, ORAL TRADITIONS BY NANCY NUSZ, BOATS BY DAVID TAYLOR, FISHING GEAR BY ORMOND H. LOOMIS, MUSIC BY PETER ROLLER, FOODWAYS BY MERRI BELLAND

INTRODUCTION

FLORIDA'S TEEMING COASTAL WATERS AND INLAND LAKES AND RIVERS HAVE spawned two long-standing, vigorous, fishing traditions: one recreational and the other commercial. Both are important to the state, but despite its significance, the traditions of maritime occupations are often overlooked.

Images of recreational fishermen are familiar to most—a child walking to the river carrying a cane pole and a can of worms, an angler attaching a bright fly to the line of his rod and reel, a scuba diver exploring a colorful coral reef. Opportunities for sport and relaxation have attracted countless recreational fishermen who have contributed to the state's economy through purchases of goods and licenses.

Commercial maritime activities are less familiar. Commercial fishermen, extracting their living directly from inland as well as coastal waters, are the first link in a chain. They sell their catch to processors and wholesalers, to restaurants and retail outlets, and ultimately to the consumer. Included with them in the complex of maritime occupational folklife are people in allied trades such as boatbuilding, net-making, and gear-making, oyster shucking, and crab picking.

The significance of maritime occupational folklife lies in the historical role of maritime enterprise and the distinctive character of the local culture that produced and sustains enterprise. Throughout Florida's history, shipping and boatbuilding have figured as major industries, and seafood has been essential to the diet. Today, Florida continues to have a strategic importance

Cletis Anderson empties oysters onto the culling board. Photo by David Taylor/Florida Folklife Program. Courtesy of State Archives of Florida.

in navigation and shipping, and it is a leader in seafood production, ranking fifth among the states in the value of the catch in 1985.

From Pensacola to Jacksonville to Key West, small communities abound in which fishing and related work are central to the way of life. In these communities, established fishermen's families, boatbuilders, net-makers, and others are well known as sources of traditional knowledge and skill. Many of them follow in the footsteps of other family and community members. They share with neighbors, friends, and family the folk traditions that they have inherited informally—communicating them in anecdotes, names, and other forms of verbal art, teaching the techniques and processes of crafts by example, and passing local histories and beliefs from parent to child.

Verbal arts are still a vigorous expression of maritime culture. Boatbuilders, gear-makers, and other craftspeople are still active. Music and foodways may be local symbols of individuality but are less reflective of distinctive maritime community life than they once were. Some of the traditions, such as the local names for landmarks and objects, are not recognized for their distinctive character by residents; other elements of the folklife, such as the unique speed of Apalachicola oyster cracking tools and technique, are a source of pride.

It is easy to forget that Florida's traditional maritime culture is as fragile a resource as the natural environment with which it is associated. Natural disasters and the loss of natural resources can mean a corresponding loss of folk traditions. When a red tide killed sponges around Tarpon Springs, for example, it also stilled the use of sponging themes in local Greek songs. Mass culture and mass media affect maritime traditions as well. The din of machinery is drowning out group singing in fish houses, and fewer local boatbuilders and gear-makers compete with mass-produced items. Florida's maritime folklife needs increased attention in efforts to maintain what is distinctive about the state.

ORAL TRADITIONS

Fishermen in Apalachicola, Big Pine Key, Clewiston, Crescent City, Cortez, Fernandina, Steinhatchee, and other maritime communities throughout Florida maintain numerous oral traditions. Workers in a packing house use terms with meanings that may only be familiar to area residents; neighbors quote well-known sayings as they forecast the weather; and men on boats weave entertaining stories to pass the long hours during slack times or while performing boring tasks.

The varied oral or verbal lore that Floridians who live around and work on the water share are some of the most vibrant examples of their folk expression. At times, people perpetuate the same terms, sayings, legends, and stories used or told by their fathers or mothers—about a location, phenomenon, boat, or character. More often, the actual words or texts vary from earlier applications or tellings, but are recast in traditional forms. In fact, such variation is characteristic of items of folk culture. In every instance, however, these traditional verbal arts, or folk literature, reflect local values and contain specialized information that is particular to maritime folklife.

Fishermen are similar to workers in some other occupations in their reliance on traditional verbal arts. Folklorist Robert McCarl, for instance, studied firefighters in the District of Columbia. He concluded that the knowledge necessary for the occupation was shared among the men in general conversation, in special terminology, and in stories. Like firefighters, fishermen use verbal arts not only to entertain, but to teach and remind one another of community values and aesthetics.

Naming Practices

People in maritime communities depend on specific terms that apply to gear, places, fish species, people, events, and techniques. Names like "kicker" for outboard motor and phrases such as "on the hill," meaning the land, may be shared by commercial fishermen across the state. On the other hand, some objects are referred to by localized names by people in different regions of Florida. For example, Billy Burbank Jr., a net-maker from Fernandina, refers to a certain type of net that employs a large hood over a tongue that drags the bottom as the "mongoose" while he reports that fishermen from parts of the Gulf of Mexico coast call the same type of net a "cobra."

Fishermen have detailed knowledge of the geographic regions they work in, and they assign names to places that are important to them. The names designate locations, landmarks, and boundaries for fishermen in the same way that neighborhood names function for the city dweller. Usually such names are recognized only by those who work in the area; rarely are these names familiar to the outsider.

Albert Mora, who began commercial fishing in Cortez at age nine, commented on the importance of local names, saying: "Newer ones [fishermen] use different names, and I don't know what they're talking about. You tell me the names I know, and I'll tell you where you are."

Fishermen use physical characteristics to name locations on shore, underwater, or on the water. For example, fishermen in Cortez refer to "Cream and Honey" to describe a particular place in the Sarasota Bay that is muddy and has excessively bothersome mosquitoes. In Apalachicola, residents talk about "the Miles" to designate the westward portion of Apalachicola Bay going toward Indian Pass and the mile markers that are found along the way. Oystermen who work on Apalachicola Bay refer to the oyster bars, the underwater ridges where the oysters grow, by names such as Cat Point, Paradise Bar, and Platform Bar. When new bars come into existence, naturally or because of organized planting and cultivation, oystermen soon give them names that emerge from conversation.

Signs and Beliefs

Commercial fishermen face a multitude of occupational hazards. Sudden changes in weather, engine trouble, long working hours during the day and night, and an unpredictable catch are among the stresses faced routinely by fishermen. Such conditions endanger their lives or destroy their livelihood by ruining their investment in expensive gear.

Cultural observers have noted that people in highly stressful occupations are especially likely to develop and use traditional beliefs. Folklore about weather and fishing serve a psychological function by partly relieving the fisherman's anxiety. Signs and beliefs, like magic, help the user predict tomorrow or suggest courses of action and therefore give him or her some feeling of control over the unknown.

Often beliefs are expressed in witty phrases, rhymes, or other easily remembered forms. Folk sayings that apply to weather predictions, a category of beliefs that is nearly universal among fishermen, illustrate the rhyming. Perhaps one of the best-known traditional weather sayings is

Red sky in morn, sailors take warn
Red sky at night, sailors' delight.

Weather lore also applies to the productivity of some fish. Ken Folsom, an Apalachicola Bay oysterman, uses wind direction to judge how large the oysters will grow. He says the north wind fills the bay with fresh water, which gives the oysters what they need to grow. A south wind, on the other hand, retards growth because it fills the bay with salt water.

Folsom uses a rhymed weather belief to predict how good his catch will be:

If the wind blows east,
You get the least;
West is best.

Fishermen may use other natural signs to help determine when fishing will be good. Albert Mora says that he "goes by the moon to catch fish. A full or new moon is better." If the full moon results in a small catch, there is always hope that the upcoming new moon will bring the big catch.

Sayings about avoiding bad luck and securing good luck are also prevalent among fishermen. The beliefs they express reflect feelings of anxiety about the unknown in a high-risk occupation. Some fishermen feel that any practice to ward off bad luck, especially observing beliefs that have been tested through time, is worth the effort. Familiar beliefs about bad luck include

Leaving the dock on Friday is bad luck.
It's bad luck to have a woman on board a boat.
Whistling on the water can whistle up a storm.
Don't turn a hatch cover upside down.
Don't bring a black suitcase on board.
Don't say "alligator" on a boat.

The extent to which people actually adhere to the beliefs they can cite is difficult to know. Not everyone accepts all the bad luck beliefs. Nevertheless, many of the fishermen who laugh and call the beliefs superstitions also tell stories about the bad luck that befell someone who ignored the belief. Netmaker Billy Burbank tells a humorous story about a friend's woes:

> There are some captains who would say "You don't say alligator on my boat." To give you an example, one day I was on a guy's boat, and I got to talking about the Florida Gators. They just went berserk you know; they ran me off the boat. "Don't you ever come back on here if you're going to say alligator on this boat again." And they were just superstitious for the rest of the day.
>
> Well, that afternoon, they came out to my house, and we had dinner out there. And we went back to look at and check on their boat and everything, and they had tied it up with their spring lines too short. The tide dropped and the boat was just hanging sideways on the dock.
>
> And they said, "See what I told you?"
>
> I said, "That's all bull, you tied that boat up wrong, that's all that was."

Storytelling

Storytelling is a vital part of the oral repertory of maritime communities. Stories are told for entertainment, but they teach as well. Historic information that would otherwise be lost or forgotten is preserved in narratives about everyday life and events. Whether a storyteller is proving that beliefs work, illustrating some other point, recounting an event in local history, or trying to entertain an audience, it takes skill to hold a listener's interest. Common topics for folk narratives include storms that wrecked a community, colorful local characters, descriptions of supernatural happenings, personal experience with dangerous situations, the illegal drug trade plaguing Florida's coastal communities, and stories of buried treasure.

In recent years, hurricanes have been hard on communities along the northern Gulf Coast of Florida. Local people will readily point out highwater marks on area buildings or recount the name and date of the hurricane that did the most damage to their town. Glen Philmon, a stone crab fisherman from Steinhatchee, tells of a hurricane during the 1986 season. Philmon recalls that high water was predicted for the area, and residents were asked to evacuate their coastal community, but most residents decided not to leave because the wind was a "Northeaster" (blowing from the northeast). According to him, people in Steinhatchee believe northeasters blow the water away from their town creating lower water, not higher as was predicted.

The residents assumed that, although they might have bad weather, the area would not flood. Acting on the traditional knowledge of their fishing community, which was based upon years of observation, they chose not to evacuate the area, and the water did not rise.

Stories often outlive the people who survived the disasters and serve as the community's memory and folk oral history. For instance, the actions of Key West sponger Charlie Coker became part of the local record when he performed heroically under stress during a storm. In 1939, Stetson Kennedy documented the following version of the story for the Federal Writers' Project, in dialect from the Conchs.

> Coker was captain of the *Heron*, one of the old-time sailin spongers in the days when spongin was a big thing in Key West. 'E was the best in the trade.
>
> There are lots of stories told about 'im. I know one to be a fact. 'E was caught in a 'eavy storm up at Bay Hundy that the *Heron* couldn't live into. Coker luffed into the wind and lowered the sails to keep em from bein torn to shreds. The wind was drivin the *Heron* straight to'rd the reef, so 'e bellowed to the crew to 'eave over the anchor.
>
> The anchor weighed 500 pounds, and the whole crew of three men was up there on the bow a-straining their guts tryin to get it over the side before she went on the reef. They was all good men, and was puttin out everything they had, but they couldn't manage to get the anchor over. The wind and current was drivin the *Heron* a-hellin for the reef, and old Charlie was a-cussin the men for all 'e was woith!
>
> Finally 'e seen she was goin on the rocks for true if the anchor wasn't got over in a 'urrry. So 'e jumped up on the bow and nearbout knocked the other three men overboard. Then 'e stooped over, picked up the anchor, and 'eaved it over the side, proper, without so much as a grunt!

Many legends, like the one about Coker, are perpetuated about local characters who possess extraordinary strength, special ability, or unusual stupidity. Longtime residents of a community are likely to know such tales about individuals from their area. Glen Philmon recalls that his parents told him stories about Shade O'Stein, who lived in Steinhatchee years ago. Before boats with outboard motors were widely used, area fishermen used "pull skiffs," which were rowed with oars. The fishermen would row out to the Gulf, fish all day, and then row back to dock. According to Philmon, Shade O'Stein was a big healthy guy. Someone you might call "above average" in strength. O'Stein was so strong that at the end of the day the tired fishermen would throw him their lines, he'd hook them to his boat and pull all the boats back in behind him.

Fishermen sometimes have experiences or visions on the water that have no logical explanation and seem to be in the supernatural realm. Because others, particularly outsiders, are skeptical about such events, fishermen seldom talk about them publicly. Jimmy Carden, a net-maker from Panama City, cautiously described an experience he had:

> I saw an occurrence, and I never said very much about it. . . . It was in the bay, and it never really got close enough for me to really see it, but it was right down off town, off straight out from the city marina.
>
> And I watched it come in from the Gulf. And it come in and went across a bar where it's shallow. There's no way a ship that big could cross it. And it appeared to be a big schooner-type, a big sailing ship of some type. And to me, there was no explaining it away. It was a ship [that] come in there and went across that bar.
>
> But I don't know what it was. And I was curious about it, but I never said much about it because you talk about stuff like that and people will say, "Oh, you're crazy." So, you just don't talk about it.
>
> But, this vessel come in from the Old Pass, just like it would have done a hundred years ago. And it come in and it crossed Courtney Point, and Courtney Point is too shallow. And when it crossed it went behind the day marker, and still went right on up the bay towards St. Andrews. And then it just wasn't there.

Daily activities in Florida's maritime communities are steeped in traditions that reach to times long forgotten and to places the world over. Traditional verbal arts in the maritime setting teach occupational jargon, aid in coping with the unknown, reinforce systems of belief, promote community values, and provide entertainment. Maintained by heirs to the lifestyle and occupations the waters have to offer, maritime folk literature contains some of the most priceless pearls of Florida's rich cultural heritage.

BOATS

Most Floridians live relatively close to water and the influence of watercraft, especially small boats, is strong. It is unusual to travel through even the most inland community without seeing many small fishing boats, sailboats, and other pleasure craft resting on trailers beside homes. In coastal communities, harbors often are jammed with commercial and recreational craft and dock space is at a premium.

The vast majority of all boats found in Florida are the products of mass production, a twentieth-century phenomenon. Based on standard designs drawn by naval architects and built of fiberglass, aluminum, and other synthetic materials, they are created by professional boatbuilders working in industrial settings who have acquired their skills on the job.

Not long ago boats in Florida, and throughout the world, were made by men who lived near water and built boats of local woods. People learned how to build boats informally, by observing and imitating relatives and neighbors in their communities. They were not full-time professional builders. They built boats for themselves and others on a part-time basis, and usually followed other occupations. Social and economic changes, combined with mass production and synthetic materials, have eliminated many local boatbuilding traditions in Florida. Nevertheless, traditional boatbuilding still goes on in several locales.

Although little research has been devoted to traditional boats and boatbuilding in North America, maritime scholars agree that large numbers of regionally distinctive craft were common in the recent past. Howard I. Chapelle, the most prolific documenter of North American boat types, writes in his book *American Small Sailing Craft,* "In the days of sail, particularly in the last half of the nineteenth century, about two hundred distinct types and subtypes of small boats were in use in North America. Each had been developed to work in its home waters and weather conditions and to meet the physical requirements of its employment" (1951:3). Most of these boat types were working craft of one sort or another: fishing vessels, cargo carriers, pilot boats, passenger vessels, or tugs.

A number of work boat types could also be found in Florida waters during the early years of the twentieth century: the Key West smackee, cat-rigged sharpie oyster boat, sloop-rigged fishing sharpie, Cedar Key seine skiff, gill-net rowing skiff, menhaden purse-seine boat, Greek sponging boat, skipjack, and others. Some of these boats reflect the influence of traditional knowledge brought to Florida by regional or ethnic groups. The Greek sponging boats of Tarpon Springs, for example, possess characteristic features of Mediterranean design and construction practices. Others were probably developed in Florida, such as the glades skiff, used in the shallow, Everglades "river of grass."

In many small fishing communities on the Atlantic and Gulf Coasts, as well as along the St. Johns River and other in-land waterways, boatbuilding knowledge is still relatively widespread. Men in these areas use knowledge about boat design and construction that is part of the folk tradition they have inherited, to build boats for themselves and others. The vessels that they create are mostly work boats—fishing craft in particular—which are built to suit local conditions.

Boats built according to tradition are shaped to suit local waters, weather conditions, and use requirements. Rarely do builders depart significantly from past practices. This conservatism is partly due to builders' unfamiliarity with alternative designs, building materials, and construction methods. It is also due to builders' reluctance to change design or construction practices which have produced boats that have worked successfully in the local environments for years. Changes, when they do occur, are usually small in scope and are introduced gradually.

Construction practices have been significantly affected by the availability of marine plywood, waterproof glues, and other modern materials. Builders rely less upon locally grown lumber today than in the past. The basic shapes of local boats, however, have remained very stable.

Similarly, builders' attitudes about the boats they produce have undergone little change. Today, as in the past, most builders of small work boats try to construct craft at a reasonable cost that perform well over a certain period of time. The adoption of new, and in many cases better, materials is a way of continuing to produce craft well suited to local needs and conditions.

The local names for boat types are interesting, if sometimes confusing. Boat types, like the Everglades skiff, or the Okeechobee skipjack, are often named after the places where they are used. Names sometimes recognize influential builders. For example, a certain model of oyster skiff, built by the late Joseph Lolley of Eastpoint, is known as the Lolley boat. Similarly, a type of Okeechobee skipjack is known as the Gillis boat in recognition of its builder, Leo Gillis. Distinctive hull shapes sometimes foster names as well. The tunnel boat, used primarily for gill netting mullet along the Gulf Coast, is so named because a tunnel is cut in the bottom of the boat from the midship motor well to the stern. Like the shapes of the boats, names of boat types may vary from place to place. The basic boat type that is known as a tunnel in one area is referred to as a mullet skiff in a second area, and a bird dog boat in a third.

Builders and Their Boats

Many of Florida's commercial fishermen build boats in a traditional manner: men like Theadus Corbin, who builds bird dog boats in Steinhatchee; Sonny Polous, who builds mullet skiffs and oyster skiffs in Apalachicola;

Gloria Polous shucks oysters at D. W. Wilson Seafood in Apalachicola. Photo by David Taylor/ Florida Folklife Program. Courtesy of State Archives of Florida.

and Charles Herrin, who builds shrimp trawlers near Jacksonville. Using the folklore of their communities they construct boats for themselves or others. Some, like Bobby Shiver of Eastpoint, have specialized and spend most of their time building boats for others.

Charles Herrin is a forty-seven-year-old commercial shrimper who began shrimping when he was eleven years old. He fishes out of the small community of Mayport, located at the mouth of the St. Johns River. Herrin fishes in the Atlantic, mainly between Fernandina Beach and St. Augustine, in waters from two-tenths of a mile to five miles offshore. When he fishes he is usually accompanied by his two brothers, Donald and Thomas, with whom he has fished for many years.

Although commercial fishing is his primary occupation, Charles Herrin is also a boatbuilder. He has built boats for his own use, in order to save money and to produce vessels well suited to his needs. Over the years, he has owned six shrimp boats, three of which he built himself with help from his brothers. The first boat that he built was made of steel and named *Herrin Boys,* after the three brothers. The second was built of wood and named *Miss Virgie,* after his mother. The third boat, also built of wood, was named *Miss Joann,* after his wife.

A part-time builder, Herrin learned techniques such as the proper way to shape and install a stem with a "Greek notch" from experienced builders. A large portion of his knowledge came from observing the shapes of local boats and testing boats of various designs over the course of his fishing career. He rightly claims that, with a few minor exceptions, no one taught him how to build boats. Yet, to a large extent, the shrimp boats he builds embody the knowledge of the boatbuilders of northeastern Florida who preceded him. This legacy of ideas helps Herrin determine such things as how boats should be put together, what shapes are "right," what gear to use, what colors are appropriate, and how interior space should be arranged.

In 1984 and early 1985, Herrin worked on the design of a new fifty-two-foot shrimp boat. Working at his kitchen table and periodically taping the drawing on the wall to stand back to check his work, he sketched a scale drawing on a long piece of white butcher paper. It included the side or profile view and the shapes of the timbers at key hull cross-sections or stations. According to Herrin, he worked from "a picture in [his] mind." The design featured a "chine" hull, selected because he had observed that it was more stable than others he had tested, and better suited to his fishing requirements.

After many corrections, Herrin was finally satisfied that his design was right, and he and his brothers began to gather construction materials. Live oak was obtained for the bow stem, pine for the keel and ribs, cypress for the planking, and plywood for the deck and pilot house. The vessel was constructed outdoors on a site adjacent to the inlet where the boat would be tied up.

The complicated process of construction proceeded in an orderly way. The first step was the building of the shaft log. Next, the shaft log was set up on the keel, and the shaft hole was drilled. The pieces of the bow stem were cut out, bolted together, erected in an upright position, and braced. The stern assembly was shaped, erected on the keel, and braced. Next, four moulds for hull cross-sections were fashioned, erected on the keel at regular intervals, and braced. At this stage the basic shape of the hull had been determined. The bottom and side ribs were installed, then the stiffeners and deck beams. Next, the deck was laid. Planking began at the top, or sheer, of the hull. After planking, the hull was caulked, sanded, and painted.

In October 1985, with Herrin's family and friends looking on, the hull was launched and towed to the dock. By the end of January 1986, he and his brothers had completed the deck house and installed the deck gear, much of which they had made as well, and *Miss Joann* was ready to go fishing.

Bobby Shiver of Eastpoint makes his living as a boatbuilder. He was born in 1939 in the small Apalachicola Bay village of Thirteen Mile. Like many men in the area, Shiver's father was a fisherman who also farmed. At an early age, Bobby and his six brothers began fishing with their father and gradually acquired fishing skills. Unlike his brothers, he never enjoyed fishing and began to search for other ways to earn a living. He tried auto mechanics, then turned to carpentry where he found satisfaction in the creative element of woodworking.

Shiver was interested in building boats and local fishermen began to come to him with requests for boats. To expand his knowledge and refine his skill, he went to experienced Eastpoint boatbuilders Charles Raffield and Joseph Lolley for guidance. Both men agreed to let him ask questions and watch them work. In 1963, based on what he learned from Raffield, Shiver built a twenty-eight-foot flat-bottom oyster skiff of cypress. Later, he was persuaded to build a nineteen-foot V-bottom oyster skiff of the type made popular by Lolley. He has lost count of the number of boats he has built since then.

The oyster skiffs that Shiver and others in the community build are usually of the Lolley design, in lengths from twenty to twenty-eight feet. They are beamy, outboard-powered boats with sharply upturned bows and wide rails. Oystermen stand on the rails when "tonging." The small boats are sometimes fitted with cabins at the stern. Larger boats have bow cabins, are sometimes equipped with inboard engines, and are frequently rigged to serve as both oyster boats and bay shrimpers.

Today, Shiver is the region's principal builder of oyster skiffs, although he also earns money as a housing contractor. He builds the skiffs to a modified Lolley design that is customized to suit the preferences of his customers. In addition to these craft, Bobby has built a fifty-two-foot planked shrimp boat, bird dog boats up to thirty-two feet, ten- to sixteen-foot "bateaux" used for flounder and bream fishing, and six- to six-and-a-half-foot "pirogues" that fishermen use to paddle out to boats riding on moorings.

It takes Shiver two weeks to construct an oyster skiff. The materials used include marine and exterior plywood for sides, bottoms, decks, and rails; cypress for the keel; juniper or cypress for the timbers; and pine for the transom. He begins by establishing the basic shape of the hull with the aid of a "master timber," or mould, around which the plywood side panels are bent. He moves the master timber around until a hull shape is realized that is pleasing to his eye. Fashioning the cypress keel and bow stem, joining together lengths of plywood to form the sides of the boat, building a transom out of pine boards and plywood splines, installing chine stringers and sister keelsons, and erecting the timbers are the key steps in the construction. The boat parts are held together with stainless steel boat nails and waterproof glues.

Charles Herrin and Bobby Shiver are both examples of contemporary traditional boatbuilders. Using knowledge that has been handed down to them informally, they build boats that are well suited to local conditions and use requirements. The products of their work represent, in physical form, the heritage of ideas, modified over time, which have been passed down in their communities.

FISHING GEAR

Enter a hardware or marine supply store in a maritime community and consider the items for sale. The array can be fascinating. Along with the standard inventory found in hardware stores throughout the country, there are artifacts that reflect the folklife of the region. In Florida, for example, such stores may contain deck boots, castnets, crab traps, culling irons, floats and weights, net twine, oyster knives, seine nets, and other distinctive gear. The type, abundance, and source of these objects will vary in different parts of the state, and they will tell a careful observer about the region in which the store is located.

Considering the geography of our state, most Floridians are likely to know a crab trap from a dip net. Nevertheless, few people other than those who live and work in maritime communities can discern the relative merits of one trawl net versus another, or have the skill to make an oar. Such knowledge and skills are traditional in communities where fishing gear is part of the immediate world.

Fathers introduce their sons to fishing at an early age by taking them on their boats and having them help repair gear. Later, teenagers find they can make money during the summer by running a line or setting their own net, serving as a crew member on a boat, repairing nets, or working at some of the other fishing-related jobs around their community. People in a maritime area learn about rigging and mending nets or shucking oysters as readily as they learn to make and repair boats or to follow the patterns of the weather.

Understanding the preference for traditional gear requires a knowledge of maritime life. When a shrimper describes the advantages of his net for increasing his catch or an oyster shucker describes the speed a cracking machine gives her, the significance of their folk gear becomes clear. For an individual who has lived and worked around the water, the choice between one style of gear and another—for example, between using a wooden-handled rather than a plastic-handled knife to shuck oysters—involves a sophisticated decision, a decision informed by knowledge that has been refined by repeated use and passed from one generation to another.

Outsiders who want to learn about the equipment that characterizes Florida's maritime communities must realize that each object is part of a fishing complex. For example, the gear used for catching shrimp is different from that used to catch crabs, oysters, or finfish. The investment in gear—as well as the investment in experience—leads fishermen to specialize in one kind of fishing or another. Some fishermen are involved with more than one kind of fishing to keep working when a preferred catch is out of season. For instance, a stone crabber may also fish for bay shrimp, but such diversification is costly.

Shrimp: Nets

Shrimpers generally divide themselves according to those who fish off-shore and those who fish in bays and other shallow waters. Off-shore shrimpers travel from Texas to the Carolinas to fish, pulling large nets behind their boats, usually in pairs, from outriggers. They use various sizes and types of nets depending upon the size of boat they operate, the season and species of shrimp they want to catch, and personal preferences in design. Their nets are treated roughly and several different nets must be available for use, making it difficult for off-shore shrimpers to fashion and repair their own gear. Consequently, deepwater shrimpers often turn to professional net-makers such as the Burbanks of Fernandina and Costa Buzier of Apalachicola for their gear. On the other hand, bay shrimpers and other shallow water shrimpers use relatively small nets pulled from a single boom. Fishing in familiar, more protected waters, these shrimpers can learn the locations of snags and avoid them, thereby minimizing damage to their nets. To keep their overhead costs low, they frequently work on their own nets.

Shrimpers work with trawl nets, essentially long, tapering, mesh bags. At the wide, front end of the net are two flaps called "wings" that extend outward, one on each side of the net, and two wood panels or "doors" on the wings that attach to the cables from the shrimp boat. As the boat pulls the net through the water, the pressure of the water on the doors holds the net open, and the net scoops up anything in its path. At the trailing end of the nets, a section called the "tail bag," made of a heavy mesh netting, collects the catch as it funnels in.

Crabs and Lobsters: Traps

Crabbers and lobsterers use traps: wire traps for the blue crabs that are taken along the entire Florida coast, or heavier wooden traps for the stone crabs found along the Gulf Coast and for the spiny lobsters in the Lower Gulf Coast and Keys regions. Wooden traps are less likely to injure the catch.

Crabbers and lobsterers frequently make their own traps because the cost of buying equipment must be subtracted from the sale of the catch. They sometimes rig their boats with extra decking to carry large numbers of traps. It is not uncommon to find their boats rigged with small winches fixed to the side or stern as well, to lower and raise the traps.

The common blue crab trap measures roughly two by two by one and one-half feet. It is made of woven wire fence material: medium gauge, galvanized wire mesh is sometimes used, but the current preference is for lighter gauge wire with a plastic coating because it weighs less and resists corrosion better than galvanized. This wire box is divided horizontally into two chambers. The bottom chamber has two or sometimes four openings, or "mouths," one each on opposing sides, and a small cylindrical cage in the center to hold bait. The upper chamber, which has a hinged door on it, is separated from the lower by a partition with a funnel-like slit in it. Crabs enter the bottom through the mouth to get the bait, and eventually crawl through the slit into the upper chamber in an attempt to escape. When the trap is retrieved, the crabber removes the crabs through the door.

Wooden traps are made of slats, rip-sawed from large stock. They are nailed or stapled to interior framing pieces to form a cage. A stone crab trap is square, or nearly so, whereas a lobster trap is rectangular. The base of both traps is made of poured cement, which provides weight to keep the trap at the bottom of the water. The mouth on these traps is a hole made of a ring of slats or a section of plastic pipe located in the center of the top of the trap. A door next to the mouth allows the fisherman to empty the catch.

Oysters: Tongs and Culling Irons

The pieces of gear that characterize oystering are the tongs, culling board, and culling iron. Gloves, buckets, bushel bags, and other items are necessary but they are also associated with other maritime activities and are not unique to oystering.

Oyster tongs are the most distinctive of the oysterman's tools. They consist of two long handles with a pair of jaws at the bottom. The handles are made of yellow pine poles that are pinned, like scissors, about two feet above the lower end. Fixed at right angles to the handles, the jaws of welded steel bars look like two halves of a cylindrical cage, with meshing teeth along one seam. The length of the handles varies from twelve feet to eighteen feet depending on the depth of the water in which the oysterman works. The width of the jaws varies from fourteen inches to thirty inches, but they are measured by the number of teeth. In Apalachicola, for example, a standard set of tongs is fourteen feet long with sixteen-tooth jaws (thirty-three inches long).

Thomas Herrin constructs shrimp boat *Miss Joann* at Mayport. Photo by David Taylor/Florida Folklife Program. Courtesy of State Archives of Florida.

An oysterman plucks oysters from the bottom with the tongs. As he searches the bars, raising and lowering the tongs with his hands, a skilled worker balances on the deck or gunnel on one foot and guides the tongs from side to side with the other foot. A skilled oysterman, say people in Apalachicola, can feel with the handles whether or not the oysters at the end of the tongs are of marketable quality.

Raising the tong over the side of the boat, the oysterman turns and deposits the catch on a culling board, where the oysters are separated and sorted. The culling board is little more than a sheet of plywood with two-inch by four-inch planks nailed to the long sides. The planks form a lip on the plywood that channels water and dirt away from the inside of the boat. Often an assistant works at the culling board. An oysterman working alone may tong until he piles a mound of shells and then stop to sort them.

Culling involves knocking clumps of oysters apart with a culling iron to separate the mollusks into singles or pairs. The culling iron is simply a flat, metal bar about one-half inch by one and one-half inch and two feet long. Usually one end of it is padded with a length of hose or some other material for a handle. These days, it is common to see a three-and-one-eighth-inch notch cut in the upper edge of the plank near the seat where cullers sort the oysters. They measure the oysters by the notch to make sure that the oysters they keep are of legal size; smaller oysters are thrown back into the water to mature.

Finfish: Lines, Traps, and Nets

Professional fishermen, those who make a significant portion of their living from selling what they catch, seldom use rod and reel. They rely on luck as much as a serious recreational fisherman does, but they cannot depend on inefficient gear that catches one fish at a time. Instead they use various longlines, traps, and nets.

Longlines, trotlines, and catlines are terms for the commercial rig that employs hooks and line. To increase the yield, fishermen string a series of short lines with a hook on each, from a single, main line. Local fishermen say it is one of the least expensive types of gear for starting into fishing. This equipment can be used in saltwater to catch deepwater fish, but it is most popular in fresh water for catfish.

Several fishermen working along the St. Johns River use trotlines. Their approach with the catline, as they call it, is discussed by folklorist Mary Anne MacDonald (1985:5–6).

> To make a catline, a fisherman takes a main line of nylon and ties 1' to 2' "staging" lines with hooks along the main line every 2' to 4'. A standard length for a catline is 500 hooks, and fishermen may have as many as four lines out at one time. . . . When a fisherman puts the line out, he will use a float, such as an empty bleach bottle, to mark the beginning of the line so that he can easily find it. Fishermen also use an anchor at the beginning to keep the catline in place.
>
> There are two ways to fish with a catline. To run a "stationary" catline, a fisherman goes out in his boat in the morning and pulls up each hook, removes the catfish, if there is one, and moves on to the next hook. In the evening he runs the catline again, this time putting on bait. When running a catline by the "jump" method, a fisherman runs his line in the morning and takes the fish off his hooks, but he pulls the line into the boat with him and takes it back to shore. Once on shore he arranges the catline into an ingenious contraption called a "catline box." [A wooden frame, about 1' square and 2" high, with 25 grooves on each side. Several such boxes are used in tiers.] . . . A hook goes into each groove, and the staging lines and main line are coiled in the middle. The catline is baited in the early evening. Then the fisherman takes his catline box out on the river, puts out the float and anchor, and runs his boat forward at a moderate pace. The . . . catline plays out of the box . . . and the fisherman removes a tier every 100 hooks.

Fish traps are used primarily for catfish. The older wooden types are required by law along small rivers such as the Suwannee, but in some large bodies such as the St. Johns River and Lake Okeechobee, wire traps are allowed. Trapping fish involves dropping the baited traps at specific points along a river, much as a crabber would leave traps. A day or so later the traps must be retrieved before the catch dies.

Wooden catfish traps are four to five feet long. On some, the slats are nailed to a series of hoops, fifteen inches in diameter, to form a cylinder; on others, a series of foot-square framing pieces give the trap a box shape. One end of the traps is closed. At the other end, two inverted funnels, or "throats," of triangular slats create a one-way passage that leads fish to a bag of bait in the interior chamber. A door along a side of the trap allows for removal of fish.

Like crab and lobster trappers, many fishermen make their own traps to save on the cost of their gear. The two types of wooden traps found in Florida, round and square, illustrate the presence of two major cultural traditions. Cylindrical traps are usually regarded as having southern origins whereas the box-shaped traps are associated with northern fishing practice. Today, mass-produced traps can be purchased from a marine supply company in Tennessee, but local makers are active in parts of Florida where the traps are used.

Fishermen use hanging nets such as gill nets, trammel nets, haul seines, and pound nets, to catch many types of finfish in inland waters: pompano, redfish, trout, and most of all, mullet. These varieties are available in varying numbers depending upon the time of year. A fisherman's "luck" often depends on his knowledge of what fish are running, where they are running, and what net to use to catch them. Although other types of fish bring a better price than mullet, mullet is the staple catch, the catch that sustains a commercial fisherman when other types are unavailable.

The gill net is the most popular type of hanging net. It is essentially a single sheet of webbing, or mesh, with ropes, or lines, tied along each long edge. The top line is buoyed with floats, the bottom weighted with lead. Gill nets are commonly about five hundred to six hundred yards long. In use, the mesh hangs suspended between the top and bottom line. When a fish of the right size swims into the net, it is caught by the gills. The head of the fish must be small enough to pass through the mesh but its body must be too large to follow.

Another well-known net is the trammel net. It consists of three panels of mesh hung between a top and bottom line. The two panels on the outside have relatively large mesh and the inner panel has small mesh. A fish swimming into the trammel net pushes the inner mesh through a hole of an outer panel creating a pocket that entangles the fish when it tries to escape.

The nets are used in a process called "striking." Anthropologist Linda Lampl describes the process well in the following passage from her observations of the Pine Island area along the southwest coast (1986:36).

> Striking includes several separate but related activities. The fisherman must throw the buoy or lead "let go," make a compass, wait for the fish to hit the net, pick up the net, clear the net. . . . The let go is a weight attached to the cork line. The opposing action of the let go and the moving boat pulls the net off the back of the boat into the water. . . . As the net goes out, the fisherman steers the boat around to "make a compass," which is to move the boat so that the net runs out in an ever decreasing circle. Once the net is out, the fisherman waits until the fish stop striking the bunt, then begins the task of picking up the net and clearing the fish, if there are fish in the net, tossing the fish into the iced fish box, and restacking net.

Although fishing with castnets is not a major source of income, castnets fill a significant niche in the array of gear. People in maritime communities often use these nets to supply fish for the home menu. The castnet is primarily a tool for subsistence fishing. Young people learning to use the castnet are introduced to the complexity of maritime activities as well. They observe the movement of fish in relatively safe, in-shore waters and learn to anticipate the behavior of their prey. They learn to read the tides and the weather. They learn to care for the net—how to use it without unnecessary damage and how to maintain it for extended use.

The basic design of the castnet has remained unchanged since it was introduced by the Spanish during Florida's settlement period. Today there are few net-makers who know how to make the old-style netting that was used for centuries in castnets and other types of nets. The old style required tying each knot by hand. Within the last forty years, most net-makers have converted to the use of machine-made netting that they buy from marine supply companies.

The castnet consists of a circular piece of net that is rimmed with a rope called a "leadline," which is threaded through small lead weights. The line is connected at the center to another rope, or "handline," for retrieving the net after it has been thrown. When thrown properly, the net spreads to a full circle and traps fish within its perimeter as it settles to the bottom. Then as it is pulled in, it forms a bag that holds the fish until the fisherman can remove the catch. The nets can be thrown from a boat, pier, dock, bridge, or shoreline. Those who have access to shallow inshore waters, such as those found along Florida's Gulf Coast, often wade into the water to cast the net.

Throwing a castnet requires skill. The aim is to spread the net fully so that it will fall over the broadest possible area. Usually the fisherman coils the retrieving line in one hand and drapes the bulk of the net behind it over the forearm, clenches a short piece of the leadline in his teeth, takes a section of the leadline in the free hand, and throws the net, spreading it with a rotation of the arms and upper body.

There are two varieties of castnets: the English, or "brail net," type and the Spanish, or "bag net," type. They differ in the way they are rigged to work when retrieved. A brail net has a ring, or "horn," tied into the center. The handline passes through the horn and attaches to numerous smaller "brail lines" which are tied at regular intervals along the leadline. When the handline is pulled in, the brail lines draw the outer edge of the net to the center, forming a purse around the fish. A bag net has a series of short lines, also called brails, from the leadline to a distance inside the perimeter of the netting. The handline is tied to the center of this type of net. When pulled in, the net forms a pocket along the edge, which holds the fish.

Maritime specialists generally recommend the brail net for casual users, those who fish for sport from a boat or a structure such as a bridge. According to the author of a booklet on making castnets, brail nets are "much more effective in shallow water because it touches bottom, but it is also effective in deep water without touching bottom. In deep water, as soon as the net settles over the fish, it must be hauled in quickly. The English net therefore has a distinct advantage over the Spanish net because it can be used in both shallow and deep water" (Floyd 1965:1).

Folk tradition, however, provides an alternative perspective. Those who fish in shallow inshore waters say they prefer the Spanish net. They find it easy, when wading, to reach in the open bottom of this net, remove fish from the bag that is formed along its edge, and put their catch in a mesh bag that they carry. Opening the brail net involves either a trip back to the shore or the risk of dropping fish from the open bag and tangling the brail lines. With castnets and other fishing gear, local folks learn from tradition, as well as from outside authorities, what works best for their region.

MUSIC

Florida has many maritime communities, where people make their livelihood by going to sea, and music has a place in all of these communities. In some, music is only a reminder of activities from bygone days, such as ship wrecking or sponging. In others, it serves a vital function today. A look at this expression of maritime folklife can inform us about the people who work and live in maritime communities.

Maritime music fills two different functions in these communities: music can aid people working in maritime occupations, and it can serve as entertainment. A song's rhythm has often been used to coordinate work activities. Songs are sometimes used to simply relieve the monotony of work. Maritime music of an entertainment nature does not usually accompany work, but reflects the activities and cultural groups that are prominent in maritime communities.

Many examples of maritime work songs exist in Florida's history. African American stevedores sang as they unloaded boats at the docks of Jacksonville and Tampa. Some of the earliest African American songs to be documented were sung by slaves as they rowed boats among the sea islands of the southern Atlantic coast. The song "Jump Isabel" was sung by slaves as they rowed off Fernandina in the 1850s.

Jump, Isabel, slide water,
Ho, my aunty, ho!
Jump, Isabel, slide water,
Ho, my aunty, ho!

We jump in de boat, an' away we go
Ho, my aunty, ho!
Jump, Isabel, slide water
Ho, my aunty, ho!

Work Songs

The sea chantey is another example of work-related music in Florida's past. Chanteys were sung on large sailing ships to make communal activities such as hoisting the heavy anchor or raising the sails easier. Often the leader sang a verse and the chorus of workers sang their answer as they worked. Typical of such sea chanteys is "Ranzo's Son," a song collected by Alton Morris in Pensacola and included in his *Folksongs of Florida.*

Leader: Oh, if I was old Ranzo's son
Crew: Ranzo, boys, Ranzo
Leader: I'd build a ship ten thousand ton
Crew: Ranzo, boys, Ranzo

Leader: Oh if I was old Ranzo's son
Crew: Ranzo, boys, Ranzo
Leader: I'd give my sailors plenty of rum
Crew: Ranzo, boys, Ranzo

The menhaden (pogy) fishermen who worked in the Atlantic, out of Mayport and Fernandina, and in the Gulf, out of Apalachicola and Port St. Joe, used chanteys to help pull in nets. Between the late 1800s and the 1940s, menhaden were harvested by groups of men in "purse boats" who pulled in one large net using synchronized motions. When the nets seemed too heavy, a chantey was started and the net was slowly pulled in, a little more with each chorus. Many of the menhaden fishermen were black, and the verses they sang were similar to the work songs performed by African Americans setting railroad ties or chopping cotton.

African American women who worked at fish houses on the Atlantic and Gulf coasts sang church songs while they (de)headed shrimp or shucked oysters. Some of them performed their work to the rhythm of the song, but the main reason they sang was probably to help take their minds off the repetitive work. Anglo-American women in the oyster-shucking houses of Apalachicola and Eastpoint also sang religious songs, Sacred Harp hymns, and ballads while performing their work.

Most work music died out because of mechanization and modern technology. When motor-driven ships with mechanical winches replaced sailing ships in the early 1900s, sea chanteys were no longer needed. Similarly, menhaden chanteys lost their purpose when power rigs were introduced to pull in the nets. Noisy, modern, oyster-shucking machines and other mechanical seafood processors make it difficult to hear songs in the processing houses, and singing in Florida fish houses has declined in the last two decades.

Topical Songs

Music that serves primarily as entertainment has not been as adversely affected by modern technology as work songs, although radio, television, and records now compete heavily with the performers of music. People in maritime communities enjoy and retain songs that refer to seagoing activities or name their local area. Some of these songs are old folk songs that have been localized to contain references to a particular community. Others are topical songs that describe a particular town. Water-front cities such as Key West and Apalachicola have inspired a number of topical songs—for example, "Beautiful Isle of Key West," "Apalachicola Mood," and in recent years a growing number of odes to Florida's bodies of water have been written by environmentally concerned songwriters.

Apalachicola Bay, for example, has inspired topical songs in the country and bluegrass styles favored in that area. Xuripha Miller, whose family owns a fish house in Eastpoint, remembers a song that she and some other local "pickers" wrote, called the "Fisherman's Boogie." They composed it during the late 1940s, when blues songs with "boogie" in the title were popular in country music. Xuripha and other workers sang in the fish house at night as they waited for trucks to arrive and load the day's fish.

Pulled on my boots, buttoned up my coat;
Grabbed my lunch bucket, headed for the boat.
Doing the fisherman's boogie, in the fisherman's way;
Doing the fisherman's boogie, by night and day.

Topical songs may also contain references to the tools or activities of the maritime trades. An Eastpoint oysterman named Mack Novak recently released a 45 rpm recording of "Oyster Man's Blues," an original country song performed with full Nashville-style production. The song mentions many aspects of oystering: going to the "bars" to "tong up the oysters," and "grouper troopers" from the Department of Natural Resources who use a "measuring stick" to see if the oysters are of legal size. Referring to the twelve-to-sixteen-foot wooden-handled tongs used by oystermen, the song's chorus says:

His hickory sticks, they're slapping out a tune
And it's called, those oysterman's blues.

According to a local legend, this song was played so often on a jukebox in a fishermen's bar that a customer paid the bar owner a high price for the record so that he could break it!

Greek Music in Tarpon Springs

The songs that are handed down in maritime communities can tell us about its sea-going activities and their importance to the community. The music that is popular for dancing or as a background for socializing will often reflect the cultural groups that have shaped the maritime community and may serve as a focal point for their identity.

Most of the traditional music in Tarpon Springs today was brought by people who came from the Dodecanese Islands, in southeast Greece, to work in the sponge industry. Sponging flourished in Tarpon from 1905 until a deadly red tide in 1947 killed the sponge crop. Songs associated with the sponging days are still fondly remembered in Tarpon Springs's Greek community. During the peak of the sponge industry, the coffee shops near the sponge docks were filled with Greek sailors waiting for their next sponging trip or returning from six months at sea. One song popular with these men, *"Tirlandada,"* was brought from the island of Kalymnos. The leader sang verses praising the blondes and brunettes waiting for him on shore or describing "the sponges selling like gold," and the chorus clapped their hands, answering each line with "da, da, tirlandada."

Tarpon Springs musicians were recorded by Skevos Zembellas in the late 1940s, and a number of the songs were on maritime themes. Zembellas rewrote the words to some of the songs to include references to Tarpon Springs and to sponging. In a Greek love song called *"Kalymnaki"* (The Kalymnian Youth), Zembellas added the words:

> A sailboat from Tarpon sets off for sponge fishing
> And a young sailor on board, sighs and looks back at the shore.

Ethnic recordings made by other collectors seldom sold well, but more than five hundred copies of "Kalymnaki" were sold in Tarpon Springs alone. Today, songs such as "Kalymnaki" and "Tirlandada" are a source of pride for the Greek community when they are sung at weddings or other special events, reminding people of the sponging days.

Bahamian Music in Key West

Key West is in many ways a model of the way music can inform us about the history and cultural identity of a maritime community. Early songs described the occupations that drew people to the Florida Keys. The "Wreckers Song" is a ballad about the ship wreckers and salvagers who waited for large sailing ships to run aground on the reefs off the keys. It was recorded in John Audubon's journal from the singing of the crew of a sailing ship. Key West author Love Dean cites it as follows:

> Come all ye good people one and all
> Come listen to my song;
> A few remarks I have to make,
> It won't be very long.
> Tis of our vessel stout and good,

As ever yet was built of wood;
Among the reef where the breakers roar,
The wreckers on the Florida shore.

Key Tavernier's our rendezvous,
At anchor where we lie;
And see the vessels in the Gulf,
Carelessly passing by.
When night comes on we dance and sing,
Whilst the current some boat is floating in;
When daylight comes, a ship's on shore,
Among the rocks where the breakers roar.

The song "Sponger Money," remembered by many people in Key West, describes the riches of the sponge trade, which became a major Key West industry in the late 1800s. The song was recorded by a WPA expedition in 1940 from Theodore Rolle, an Afro-Bahamian fisherman. Rolle was an entertainer at house parties in Key West's black community. The lyrics in "Sponger Money" refer to the fact that the wages in sponging were higher than in Key West's other major industry at the time, cigar making.

Sponger money never done, sponger money,
Cigar makers on the bum, sponger money,
But I'll treat them just the same, sponger money,
Keep them boys from feelin' shame, sponger money.

Look in my trunk and see what's there, sponger money,
One hundred dollars was my share, sponger money,
I'm gonna take away your woes, sponger money,
I'm gonna buy you fine clothes, sponger money.

Rolle sang two other maritime songs for the WPA researchers. One was "Hoist Up the John B. Sails," a Bahamian folk song about an unfortunate trip aboard a sailing ship. The chorus, "I feel so break up, I wanna go home" is familiar to many. The second was "Bellamena," about a ship that made port at Key West. It has the sexual overtones found in many Bahamian calypso songs.

Bellamena, Bellamena,
Bellamena in the harbor;

Gonna put Bellamena on the dock,
Gonna paint her bottom black, black.

Oh the Maisie, oh the Maisie,
That boat she sets me crazy;
Gonna put Maisie on the dock,
Gonna paint her bottom black, black.

Bahamians who came to Key West to work as wreckers, spongers, and fishermen brought with them their Christmas and New Year's street parade, Junkanoo. Out of this tradition a band, the Key West Junkanoos, was formed. The members began as teenagers beating pots and pans, saws, and other household objects to simulate the syncopated marching rhythms of the Junkanoo parade. They sang Bahamian songs their parents enjoyed, including "Sponger Money," "Bellamena," and "Hoist Up the John B. Sails."

The Junkanoos expanded their repertoire by collecting records from the Bahamas and eventually replaced their homemade instruments with piano, bass, conga drums, and maracas. Besides entertaining at parades, parties, and nightclubs, the Junkanoos have played for the arrival and departure of large cruise ships in Key West. The many references to both maritime activities and Key West in their songs as well as the Bahamian flavor of their music, make the Junkanoos a fine expression of Key West's maritime history through music.

The Cortez "Grand Old Opry"

The small fishing village of Cortez, near Bradenton on Florida's Gulf Coast, is not a place where one would expect to find a Grand Old Opry. Nonetheless, Cortez has a musical family whose talents are so widely acclaimed that the house they occupied for many years is known locally as the "Cortez Grand Old Opry." The Culbreath family's musical legacy started with James Culbreath, a prize-winning contest fiddler who moved his family to Cortez from northern Florida in 1921 and became a Gulf fisherman. James taught three of his sons to play fiddle, and others took up guitar and harmonica. The Culbreath Family Band played at local square dances and performed on a live radio program called the "County Cracker Jubilee." Most important, they played music evenings and Sundays in their home where community members were always welcome to stop by and listen.

Only "Goose" Culbreath, the youngest of James Culbreath's children, carries on the family's tradition of fine fiddling. A mullet fisherman by profession, Goose had a large following as a square dance fiddler at one time and still plays the traditional dance tunes that he learned from his father such as "Boil Them Cabbage Down" and "Arkansas Traveler." He also plays driving bluegrass tunes, such as "Black Mountain Rag" and "Orange Blossom Special," that he learned from listening to the Grand Old Opry broadcasts.

Goose is not the end of the Culbreath family music tradition. His son Lloyd backs him on guitar and is a country singer. Goose's nephew, Richard, plays fingerstyle guitar that is inspired by his father, Hal Culbreath, and influenced by Merle Travis and Chet Atkins. Lloyd's and Richard's children have also taken up instruments. Every New Year's Day the Culbreath family holds a "picking party" to which the whole town of Cortez is invited. Old and young, captains, crew, and fishermen, all attend to hear and participate in the music. The highlight of the party comes when Goose takes up his fiddle and performs his trick version of "Listen to the Mocking Bird."

The significance that the Culbreath family's music holds for the people of Cortez reveals how music played for entertainment can become a part of the identity of a maritime community. The Culbreaths share their music with their neighbors openly, a measure of the cohesiveness often found in maritime communities. Although they do not sing sea chanteys or perform nautical ballads, the Culbreath family's music is linked to the identity of a distinctive fishing village and represents the maritime music of today.

FOODWAYS

Modern Florida is the source of a tempting blend of culinary styles that are part of the folklife of the diverse peoples who have made the state their home. American Indian, Spanish, French, English, African, Minorcan, Greek, Cuban, and more—the settlers influenced the cuisine of the state as well as its demographic and economic growth. It is not surprising that a number of fish and seafood dishes have become associated with our state. With Florida's hundreds of miles of coastline as well as inland waters, people in coastal and inland communities have made fish and shellfish the basic ingredients in many of their recipes.

For a taste of Florida's regional and ethnic specialties, it is usually necessary to visit the communities that are the source of traditional recipes. Although non-seafood products and some imported foods may be used in regional maritime dishes, most cooks prefer to use the local catch as primary ingredients.

Minorcans of St. Augustine

Minorcans came to Florida through the efforts of Dr. Andrew Turnbull, an English colonist who brought workers from the Mediterranean region to establish a plantation in New Smyrna in 1777. The Minorcans enjoyed spicy foods, and they brought seeds with them to grow their favorite seasonings in their new home. From the time of their earliest settlement, Minorcan cooks used the best available ingredients. "Back then," as a modern Minorcan said, "everybody knew the ocean and the sea." When Turnbull's efforts faltered, the Minorcans relocated to St. Augustine. More than two centuries later, traditional Minorcan foods, with the spicy seasonings, are still in evidence and are identified as part of the cuisine of the historic city.

A prominent ingredient in Minorcan cooking is the datil pepper, a small hot pepper. It is used in making datil pepper sauce and datil pepper jelly. Because of its strength, the sauce is referred to locally as "bottled hell." The most important use of datil peppers is in "cook-down seasoning," a key ingredient for Minorcan clam chowder and Minorcan pilau. The three following recipes are characteristic of the traditional Minorcan seafood recipes from St. Augustine.

Geraldine Maguire's recipe for "cook-down seasoning" provides the flavor base for the chowder and pilau recipes. Geraldine rarely refers to a recipe. She says, "You know when the consistency and proportions are right when you've cooked it all your life."

Cook-Down Seasoning

½ lb. bacon
1 or 2 whole datil peppers
1 chopped green pepper
4 chopped onions
¼ tsp. thyme
2 16-oz. cans of tomatoes
salt and pepper to taste

Cut bacon into small pieces and brown in iron skillet. After bacon is browned, remove and save. Sauté the chopped green pepper and onion in the remaining bacon drippings until pieces turn slightly transparent. One or two whole datil peppers are added according to taste and may be removed after cooking. Add remaining ingredients and "cook-down" over low heat, stirring frequently, until it reaches the right consistency. If it is to be used in pilau, the seasoning should be the consistency of tomato paste—it must be so thick that you can push it to one side of the skillet and it will stay there.

Minorcan Clam Chowder

½ lb. bacon
1 chopped green pepper
4 chopped medium onions
2 16-oz. cans of tomatoes
1 or 2 whole datil peppers
½ tsp. thyme
1 qt. chopped clams
1 c. clam juice
4 diced large potatoes

Prepare "cook-down seasoning" to half the thickness of tomato paste. Drain clams and save juice (add water to make one cup). Add chopped clams and diced potatoes to mixture. Cover and simmer until potatoes are fork tender. Add clam juice, stir, and then serve.

Shrimp Pilau

½ lb. bacon
2 c. white long grain rice
2 chopped green peppers
4 chopped medium onions
2 16-oz. cans of tomatoes
2 lbs. cleaned shrimp
3½ c. water
¼ tsp. thyme
salt and pepper to taste
1 or 2 whole datil peppers

Prepare "cook-down seasoning" to consistency of tomato paste. Add water and bring mixture to a boil. Add rice and shrimp, reduce heat, and cook slowly for 1 hour, or until rice is done, and serve.

Pilau, pronounced locally as púr-lo, can be prepared using any of a variety of meats including poultry, beef, crab, oysters, shrimp, or fish. When meat is not available, speckled butter beans or other leftover vegetables can be added for a meatless main dish.

Crackers of Cedar Key

Cedar Key, sometimes called "the island city," has been a fishing community for more than one hundred years. It was named for the large stands of cedar trees that once covered the island. Linked by rail to Fernandina in 1861, the town was an active shipping port, although rail service was interrupted during the Civil War. Fish, especially oysters, were exported on a large scale, and sponges from Tarpon Springs were brought to Cedar Key for shipment. Toward the end of the century, however, the oyster beds began to be depleted. By 1909, the oyster canning plant was converted into a factory for making palmetto fiber brushes.

Today many inhabitants of Cedar Key earn an income by oystering, fishing, clamming, and crabbing. They maintain a tradition of living from the sea, a heritage passed down from English, Welsh, Irish, and Scottish people who settled in the area. Most locals believe that the environment of the islands improves the flavor of their seafood. For example, the balance of salt water and fresh water from the Suwannee River to the north and the Waccasassa River to the south reportedly gives the oysters a wonderfully salty taste.

Most folks learn about seafood at an early age around Cedar Key. One woman spoke of her experiences in her uncle's oyster house when she was thirteen. Her first job was pulling mullet gizzards from the gut-bucket. She soon advanced to fish gutting and later ran the oyster house. In the industry, she said, "Learning is not a process of trial and error. When someone is showing you what to do—it's learning on the job. Things start fitting into place. You learn by watching."

One of the favorite traditional activities in the region is roasting oysters, usually organized as a family affair on the beach. A fire is started early for the occasion. Around it, supports hold a rack of corrugated tin. When the fire has burned down to form a bed of coals, the oysters are dumped on the tin. Family and friends gather to eat as soon as the oysters pop open. Today, charcoal and commercial grills often replace the driftwood fires and old tin roasting racks, but the tradition of roasting oysters is still enjoyed.

Dishes using mullet are widely known on Cedar Key. Smoked and fried mullet are both local favorites. Many people have homemade smokers constructed of old refrigerators or fifty-five-gallon drums that are modified according to personal preference. Smoking fish is a lengthy process, usually taking between six and eight hours. The secrets of good fish smoking are in the wood—green oak or bay woods are commonly used—and the seasoning applied to the fish. In Cedar Key, the preferred fish for smoking is mullet because it is easy to catch and the mullet's large, heavy scales, thick skin, and plentiful supply of oil keep the flesh moist. Smoked mullet can be a meal in itself but it can also be made into a dip, as the following recipe from Susie Day of Cedar Key shows.

Smoked Mullet Dip

½ c. mayonnaise
½ c. buttermilk
2 c. sour cream
1 tsp. Good Seasons Italian (dry mix)
2 c. boned smoked mullet

Mix the mayonnaise, buttermilk, and seasoning mix and let stand. Chop mullet and mix with other ingredients. Fold in sour cream.

Mullet is the only fish with a gizzard so people call it a "fowl" fish. Folks in Cedar Key fry mullet gizzards to eat for snacks or use in a hearty stew. The recipe for this unusual dish was provided by Susie Day.

Mullet Gizzard Stew

2 to 3 qt. mullet gizzards
4 T. bacon drippings
2 c. chopped onions
2 to 4 garlic cloves chopped
½ c. white wine
2 cans cream of mushroom soup
2 c. sour cream

Clean and trim mullet gizzards and let soak in water until ready to fry. Drain water from gizzards. Pour (wet) gizzards with onions and garlic into hot (not smoking) bacon drippings in a six-quart cast-iron dutch oven. Cover tightly, reduce heat, and let simmer (one to one and a half hours), stirring occasionally, until gizzards are tender. Mix together remaining ingredients and stir in with gizzards. Turn burner up to medium and heat until mixture bubbles, then remove from heat. Mixture should be the consistency of gravy. Serve over rice or noodles.

Inland Fishermen

Freshwater fishermen have been active in Florida for more than a century. Commercial fishermen first began harvesting the catfish, mullet, and shad along the St. Johns River in the 1880s. The inland waters of the state also supply eel and game fish, such as bream, bass, and perch, that people who live and work around fresh water enjoy in their diets.

Folks living along the St. Johns River or near Lake Okeechobee, for example, are particularly fond of the several types of catfish that live in the river. The "King of Catfish" is the channel cat, a slender catfish that is exceptionally good eating. Red cat, named because of its reddish tinge, is said not to have such a fine taste. The underbelly of the butter cat is very yellow, as the name would suggest. The butt head has a very wide head. Blue cats are another type of channel cat. Whatever the variety, perhaps the most mouth-watering fillets are from the young fingerlings, six to eight inches long.

Neighborhood and church catfish fries are a common event. They provide an opportunity for socializing as well as good eating. Clewiston, at the lower end of Lake Okeechobee, has become famous for its annual fish fry at which people gather for catfish fresh from the lake and hot from the pan. The following recipe describes one of the foods prepared on such occasions.

Fried Fingerling Catfish

Use about 2 pounds of skinned, pan-dressed fingerlings. Combine one egg with a small amount of milk. Dip the fingerlings into the egg mixture and then into corn meal. Fry fingerlings in hot oil until golden brown and, as they are removed, place them to drain on absorbent paper. Serve with hush puppies and grits.

Another dish made with catfish shows considerable variation among fishermen's families. African Americans often use catfish heads in a stew. Like the recipes for pickled pig feet, cracklin' bread, and chitterlings, recipes for catfish stew produce a tasty meal from ingredients that to many are inedible. Anglo-Americans are less likely to include the fish head. Cindy Noles of Crescent City prefers fillets from the large channel cats in her recipe. "It's a meal in itself," she commented, "and it's even better the next day."

Catfish Stew

1 large can tomatoes
6–8 large potatoes, thinly sliced

6–10 strips of bacon
6–10 catfish fillets
salt, pepper

Fry the bacon in a deep pot on top of the stove. Then, layer the ingredients over the cooked bacon with grease in the following order: potatoes, onions, two or three fillets. Salt and pepper each layer to taste. Repeat layers. Do not add water. Cover pot and cook over *low* heat until fork tender, about two hours for a small pot, up to three or four hours for a large pot. About thirty minutes before the stew is done, pour in tomatoes and let simmer.

Greeks of Tarpon Springs

The sponge business was founded in Tarpon Springs in the 1880s. Hundreds of Greeks settled there to work in the business. By the early part of the twentieth century, the town was known as the sponge capital of the world and was sometimes called "the Athens of the South." More than two hundred boats operated out of the port.

Spongers were often at sea on ships that stayed away from home four or five months. The men ate fresh fish often, but to break the monotony of their diet they brought along *kavourma,* a preserved meat that was made into meat dishes and stews. The crew was responsible for preparing enough kavourma before a voyage to last the whole trip, and making kavourma became both a social occasion for the crew and a necessary step in preparing for the long months at sea.

Kavourma is still made in Tarpon Springs although the preserved meat is no longer a necessity in the fishing industry. Today, only four sponge operations remain from the great days of the sponge industry. Competition from manufacturers of synthetic sponges and the cost of harvesting natural sponges discourage many. The making of kavourma is now a social occasion and a means for remembering the old days and a vanished lifestyle. The following description of making kavourma was collected from Nick Tsourakis and George Kindinis.

Kavourma

When the spongers were preparing for a trip they would generally preserve between 350 and 400 pounds of meat, preferably beef, or goat or lamb. The meat was cut into two-inch squares and seasoned with salt and pepper. It was stored in boxes overnight which gave the seasoning time to set. The next day the meat was cooked, a process which took all day. The kavourma was cooked in huge tubs over a pit about 4 feet wide and 2 feet deep which contained the fire. The meat was boiled in a small amount of water and drained. The fat from the meat was ground, so it would melt easily, and rendered in 25 or 30 gallon tubs. After the fat was melted the meat was added. Processing the meat in the fat meant 2 to 2½ hours of constant stirring with a wooden paddle shapped like an oar. After cooking, the meat was stored in 5 gallon cans and covered with fat. The processed meat would keep for a year. A six man crew would dig out 3 to 4 pounds of meat for stew, adding variety to their diet of fresh fish.

Greek cooks use seasonal vegetables and local ingredients, including those from the sea. Each housewife takes pride in preparing a variety of Greek dishes. The recipes contain special cooking "secrets" that she hands down to her daughter, as her mother did. Baked fish *(psitó psári)*, fish patties *(psári keftédes)*, shrimp and rice pilaf *(garídes piláfi)*, fish roe cakes *(tárama keftédes)*, stuffed squid *(kalamária gemísta)*, squid with rice *(kalamária me ríze)*, and octopus in red wine *(khtapódhi krasáto)* are examples of Greek seafood dishes prepared in Tarpon Springs today.

Key West

The settlers in the Florida Keys—Spanish, Bahamian, Cuban, and English—ate seafood and tropical foods such as avocado, plaintain, guava, coconut, and key limes. Huge green sea turtles weighing up to three hundred pounds were a major food source until conservation rules prohibited their use. Anglo-Saxon descendants of Bahamians came to be named after the conchs because the shellfish were a staple in the diet.

Because there was no refrigeration, canned condensed milk was in demand. With it, the natives created the famous key lime pie, probably Key West's most celebrated food. Variations of the key lime pie recipe are available in many cookbooks. Local opinions vary as to whether the pie crust should be a flaky pastry or made of Graham crackers, and there is even controversy about the toppings: some folks consider the meringue topping, using leftover egg whites, the most traditional, while others insist that the original topping was made of sweetened whipped cream.

One widely used condiment enjoyed in most Key West households is a tangy mixture called "old sour." A fermented sauce of key lime juice, bird peppers, and other ingredients, it is used on fish and other seafood. Hot bird peppers, about half an inch long, are found on bushes growing in most yards.

Old Sour

6–8 key limes
1 T. salt
2–4 bird peppers

Squeeze enough key limes to make one or more cups of juice. The pulp should be strained. For each cup of key lime juice add one tablespoon of salt. Bird peppers are added to taste but 2–4 of the small hot peppers are usually enough. The mixture ferments two to four weeks at room temperature in a tightly stoppered bottle and keeps for about a year.

Crawfish was regarded as an inferior food until it gained status as a delicacy under the name Florida lobster. A favorite Cuban dish was crawfish enchilado. Families carried the ingredients for making a huge cauldron of spicy enchilado to Stock Island where children waded until the picnic was prepared. Served with Cuban bread, crawfish enchilado was delicious poured over rice.

Crawfish Enchilado

½ c. white wine
oregano
salt and hot pepper
6–8 crawfish tails
½ c. olive oil
1 chopped green pepper
1 clove garlic
16-oz. can tomato sauce
small can tomato paste

Sauté onions, green peppers, and garlic in hot oil until onion is transparent. Add tomato sauce and tomato paste, salt, hot pepper and oregano to taste. Cut raw crawfish tails into small pieces and add to mixture. Reduce heat and simmer for about one hour until mixture is thick. Crawfish enchilado is usually served over rice.

From one end of the state to the other, Florida's foodways are as varied and exciting as are its citizens. Maritime communities and the regional cooking which makes them distinctive reflect the traditions of the diverse peoples who have settled in the state. This culinary diversity is a tribute to those who brought their traditions with them from other places.

References

Bernard, H. Russell. "Greek Sponge Boats in Florida." *Anthropological Quarterly* 38 (1965): 41–54.

Chapelle, Howard I. *American Small Sailing Craft: Their Design, Development and Construction.* New York: W. W. Norton, 1951.

Boatbuilding: A Complete Handbook of Wooden Boat Construction. New York: W. W. Norton, 1941.

The National Watercraft Collection. 2nd ed. Washington, DC: Smithsonian Institution; Camden, ME: International Marine Publishing Co., 1976.

Dahlem, Ted. *How To Smoke Seafood.* St. Petersburg, FL: Great Outdoors Publishing Co., 1980.

Dean, Love. "The Wreckers: Fact, Fiction, and Legend." *Florida Keys Magazine* 4 (1981): 32–39.

Federal Writers' Project. *Florida: A Guide to the Southernmost State.* New York: Oxford University Press, 1939.

Florida Folklife Program. Florida Department of State. *Fishing All My Days.* White Springs, FL: Florida Folklife Program, 1986. Video documentary.

Floyd, Hilton M. *Castnets Constructed of Machine-Made Netting.* Washington, DC: U.S. Dept. of the Interior, Fish and Wildlife Service, Bureau of Commercial Fisheries, 1965.

Folsom, Ken. Interview by Nancy Nusz. November 6, 1986. Fieldnotes. State Archives of Florida, Tallahassee, FL.

Frangos, Steve. "Songs of an Indiana Island: The Grecophon Record Company of Gary, Indiana." *Resound* 4 (1985): 2–4.

Frye, John. *The Men All Singing: The Story of Menhaden Fishing.* Norfolk, VA: Dunning, 1978.

Green, Ben. *Finest Kind: A Celebration of a Florida Fishing Village.* Macon, GA: Mercer University Press, 1985.

Greenhill, Basil. *Archaeology of the Boat: A New Introductory Study.* Middletown, CT: Wesleyan University Press, 1976.

Herrin, Charles. Interview by David A. Taylor, July 31, 1986. Tape recording. State Archives of Florida, Tallahassee, FL.

Kennedy, Stetson. *Palmetto Country.* New York: Duell, Sloan & Pearce, 1942.

Lampl, Linda L. *Feeding the People From Generation to Generation, an Ethnography of the Pine Island Fishermen.* Tallahassee, FL: T. A. Herbert & Associates, 1986.

Lebovitz, Richard. "Apalachicola's Skiffs Keep Its Oyster Business Thriving." *National Fisherman* 63 (1983): 45–50.

Lipke, Paul. *Plank on Frame: The Who, What and Where of 150 Boatbuilders.* Camden, ME: International Marine Publishing Co., 1981.

McCarl, Robert S. *The District of Columbia Fire Fighters: A Case Study in Occupational Folklife.* Smithsonian Folklife Series, No. 4. Washington, DC: Smithsonian Institution, 1985.

MacDonald, Mary Anne. "Commercial Fishing on the St. Johns River." In *33rd Annual Florida Folk Festival Official Program Guide.* White Springs: Florida Folklife Program, Florida Department of State, 1985. Pp. 4–10.

Mora, Albert. Interview by Nancy Nusz, March 4, 1987. Fieldnotes. State Archives of Florida, Tallahassee, FL.

Morris, Alton. *Folksongs of Florida.* Gainesville: University of Florida Press, 1950.

Mullen, Patrick B. *I Heard the Old Fishermen Say: Folklore of the Texas Gulf Coast.* Austin: University of Texas Press, 1978.

Novack, Mack. "Oyster Man Blues." 45 rpm disc recording. St. George Sound Records, CSS-152. n.d.

Perez, Ruth, and Brenda Vidal. *Margaritaville Cookbook.* Key West, FL: Vipco, 1984.

Philmon, Glen. Interview by Nancy Nusz, August 18, 1985. Fieldnotes. State Archives of Florida, Tallahassee, FL.

Polvay, Marina, and Marilyn Fellman. *Florida Heritage Cookbook.* Miami: Florida Consultation and Management, 1976.

Shiver, Bobby. Interview by David A. Taylor, November 3, 1986. Tape recording. State Archives of Florida, Tallahassee, FL.

Watson, Verona. *Cedar Key Cookin'.* Gainesville, FL: Rev. J. R. Gallups, 1972.

Selected Florida Folklife Bibliography

American Folktales from the Collections of the Library of Congress. Edited by Carl Lindahl. 185 *"La mata de higo / The Fig Tree,"* told by Ziomara Andux. Recorded by Stetson Kennedy and Robert Cook, Ybor City, Florida, August 23, 1939. 186 *"Senorita Martinez Cucaracha y Senor Ratoncito Perez /* Miss Martinez Cockroach and Mr. Perez Mouse," told by Evelia Andux. Recorded by Stetson Kennedy and Robert Cook, Ybor City, Florida, August 24, 1939. 187 *"Antonio, cortador de lena /* Antonio the Woodcutter," told by Martin Noriega. Recorded by Stetson Kennedy and Robert Cook, Ybor City, Florida, August 23, 1939. Translated by Martha Ellen Davis, 2003. New York: M. E. Sharpe, 2005.

App, Lawrence J. "The Professionalization and Commodification of Steel Drum Music in Florida: Musical Continuity and Change in the Caribbean Diaspora." M.A. thesis, Florida State University, 1997.

Bernard, Harvey Russell. "Greek Sponge Boats in Florida." *Anthropological Quarterly* 38 (1965): 41–54. Reprinted in *Man and the Sea: Human Factors in Marine Environment.* Edited by Raoul Anderson and G. Stiles. New York: Simon and Schuster, 1971.

Blackard, David. *Patchwork & Palmettos: Seminole/Miccosukee Folk Art Since 1820.* Fort Lauderdale: Fort Lauderdale Historical Society, 1990.

Bloodworth, Bertha E., and Alton Morris. *Places in the Sun: The History and Romance of Florida Place-Names.* Gainesville: University Presses of Florida, 1978.

Boggs, Ralph Steele. *Bibliography of Latin American Folklore: Tales, Festivals, Customs, Arts, Magic, Music.* B. Detroit: Ethridge-Books, 1971.

———. "Spanish Folklore from Tampa, Florida." *Southern Folklore Quarterly* 1 (September 1937): 1–12; 1 (December 1937): 9–13; 2 (June 1938): 87–106.

———. *Index of Spanish Folktales.* (Folklore Fellows. FF communications.) Suomalainen Tiedeakatemia, Academia Scientiarum Fennica (1930).

———, and Mary Gould Davis. *Three Golden Oranges and Other Spanish Folk Tales.* New York: David McKay Co., 1967.

Borland, Katherine. "Final Report, Nicaraguan Traditions." Unpublished manuscript, Historical Museum of Southern Florida, 1991.

Boswell, Thomas D., and James R. Curtis. *The Cuban-American Experience: Culture, Images, and Perspectives.* Totowa, NJ: Rowman & Allanheld, 1984.

Briggs, Betty. *Cracker in the Glades: A Family Portrait of Robert Storter, Fisherman, and His Family.* Naples, FL: Betty Briggs, 1980.

Bucuvalas, Tina. "Cuban Folk Arts in the Miami Area." In *A Guide to the 34th Annual Florida Folk Festival, May 23–25, 1986*. White Springs: Florida Folklife Program, Florida Department of State, 1986. Pp. 4–7.

———. "Epiphany in Tarpon Springs." *Florida Heritage Magazine* 7, no. 4 (Fall 1999): 8–13.

———. "Greeks." In *The New Encyclopedia of Southern Culture*. Vol. 6, *Ethnicity*. Edited by Celeste Ray. Revised edition. Chapel Hill: University of North Carolina Press, 2007.

———. "Greeks" and "Little Havana." In *Encyclopedia of American Folklife*. Edited by Simon J. Bronner. New York: M. E. Sharpe, 2006. Vol. 2. Pp. 519–23 and 703–6.

———. "Little Havana: The Cubanization of Miami's Cultural Heritage." *CRM: Cultural Resource Management* 20, no. 11 (1997): 54–56.

———. "Sponge Divers Bring Greek Culture" and "Sponges." *FHC Forum* 30, no. 2 (Summer 2006): 37–41.

Bucuvalas, Tina, Peggy A. Bulger, and Stetson Kennedy. *South Florida Folklife*. Folklife in the South Series, edited by William Lynwood Montell. Jackson: University Press of Mississippi, 1994.

Bulger, Peggy A. "Stetson Kennedy: Applied Folklore and Cultural Advocacy." Ph.D. dissertation, University of Pennsylvania, 1992.

———. "Stetson Kennedy: Folklore and the Struggle for Human Rights." *The Folklore Historian* 8 (1991): 56–66.

Buxbaum, Edward Clarence. *The Greek-American Group of Tarpon Springs, Florida: A Study of Ethnic Identification and Acculturation*. New York: Arno Press, 1980.

Cantrell, Brent. "The Folklore of Little Haiti." In *Arts of the African Diaspora: African American and Haitian Miami*. Edited by Tina Bucuvalas and Brent Cantrell. Miami: Historical Museum of Southern Florida, 1990. Pp. 3–13.

———. "Key Largo to Marathon: A Report on the Folklife of the Upper Keys." In *South Florida History Magazine* 3 (Summer 1990): 19–22.

Capron, Louis. "The Medicine Bundle of the Florida Seminole and the Green Corn Dance." In *A Seminole Sourcebook*. Edited by William C. Sturtevant. New York: Garland, 1987. Pp. 159–69.

Congdon, Kristin G. "Mario Sanchez." In *The New Encyclopedia of Southern Culture*. Folk Art volume. Edited by Carol Crown. Revised edition. Chapel Hill: University of North Carolina Press, forthcoming.

———. "Nicario Jimenez." In *The New Encyclopedia of Southern Culture*. Folk Art volume. Edited by Carol Crown. Revised edition. Chapel Hill: University of North Carolina Press, forthcoming.

———. *Uncle Monday and Other Florida Tales*. Jackson: University Press of Mississippi, 2001.

———, and Tina Bucuvalas. *Just Above the Water: Florida Folk Art*. Jackson: University Press of Mississippi, 2006.

———, and Natalie Underberg. "Religious Inspiration in Ruby C. Williams' Creative Practices: Presentation and Teaching Approaches in Folkvine.org." *Journal of Cultural Research in Art Education* 3 (2005): 29–40.

Curtis, James R. "Miami's Little Havana: Yardshrines, Cult Religion, and Landscape." In *Rituals and Ceremonies in Popular Culture*. Edited by Ray B. Browne. Bowling Green, OH: Bowling Green University Popular Press, 1980.

———. "*Santería*: Persistence and Change in Afro-Cuban Cult Religion." In *Objects of Special Devotion: Fetishism in Popular Culture*. Edited by Ray B. Browne. Bowling Green, OH: Bowling Green University Popular Press, 1981.

DeCosmo, Janet L. "Listen to the Joy of Junkanoo!" *FHC Forum* (Winter 2004): 24–27.

Densmore, Frances. "The Seminole Indian Today." *Southern Folklore Quarterly* 18 (December 1954): 212–21.

———. *Seminole Music*. Smithsonian Institution, Bureau of American Ethnology, Bulletin 161. Washington, DC: 1956.

Doering, Eileen Elita. "A Charm of the Gulf of Mexico Sponge Fishers." *Journal of American Folklore* 52 (1939): 123.

Doering, J. Frederick. "Folk Customs and Beliefs of Greek Sponge-Fishers of Florida." *Southern Folklore Quarterly* 7 (June 1943): 105–7.

Downs, Dorothy. *Art of the Florida Indian: Nineteenth- and Twentieth-Century Seminole and Miccosukee Indian Art*. Hollywood, FL: Seminole Art & Culture Center, 1989.

———. *Miccosukee Arts & Crafts*. Miami: Miccosukee Tribe of Indians of Florida, 1982.

Duany, Jorge. "Popular Music in Puerto Rico: Toward an Anthropology of Salsa." In *Latin American Music Review*. 5, no. 2 (Fall/Winter 1984): 186–216.

Edic, Robert F. *Fisherfolk of Charlotte Harbor, Florida*. Gainesville: Institute of Archaeology and Paleoenvironmental Studies, University of Florida, 1996.

Encyclopedia of Southern Culture. Edited by Charles Reagan Wilson and William Ferris. Chapel Hill: University of North Carolina Press, 1989.

First Citizens and Other Florida Folks. Edited by Ronald Foreman. Tallahassee: Bureau of Florida Folklife Programs, 1984.

Florida: A Guide to the Southernmost State. American Guide Series. Compiled and written by the Federal Writers' Project of the Work Projects Administration for the State of Florida. 1939. Reissued, with a new introduction by John I. McCollum, as *The WPA Guide to Florida: The Federal Writers' Project Guide to 1930s Florida*. New York: Pantheon Books, 1984.

Florida Folklife from the WPA Collections. American Folklife Center/Library of Congress. http://memory.loc.gov/ammem/flwpahtml/flwpahome.html.

Florida Folklife Program, Florida Department of State. "Maritime Folklife. 'Introduction' by Nancy Michaels, 'Oral Traditions' by Nancy Nusz, 'Boats' by David Taylor, 'Fishing Gear' by Ormond H. Loomis, 'Music' by Peter Roller, 'Foodways' by Merri Belland." In *A Guide to the 35th Annual Florida Folk Festival, May 22–24, 1987*. White Springs, 1987. Pp. vi–18.

Florida Folktales. Edited by J. Russell Reaver. Gainesville: University of Florida Press, 1987.

Foster, Charles C. *Conchtown USA: Bahamian Fisherfolk in Riviera Beach, Florida*. Boca Raton: Florida Atlantic University Press, 1991.

Frantzis, George Th. *Strangers at Ithaca: The Story of the Spongers of Tarpon Springs*. St. Petersburg, FL: Great Outdoors Publishing Company, 1962.

Garbarino, Merwyn S. *The Seminole*. Indians in North America series, edited by Frank W. Porter III. New York: Chelsea House Publishers, 1989.

Georges, Robert A. *Greek-American Folk Beliefs and Narratives: Survivals and Living Tradition*. New York: Arno Press, 1980.

———. "The Greeks of Tarpon Springs: An American Folk Group." *Southern Folklore Quarterly* 29 (June 1965): 129–41.

———. "Greek Folk Remedy in America." *Southern Folklore Quarterly* 26 (1962): 122–26.

———. "*Matiasma*: Living Folk Belief." *Midwest Folklore* 12 (1962): 69–74.

———, and Michael Owen Jones. *Folkloristics: An Introduction*. Bloomington: Indiana University Press, 1995.

Greenbaum, Susan D. "Marketing Ybor City: Race, Ethnicity, and Historic Preservation in the Sunbelt." *City & Society*, June 1990, Vol. 4, No. 1, 58–76.

Greenlee, Robert F. "Folktales of the Florida Seminole." *Journal of American Folklore* 58, no. 228 (April–June 1945): 138–44.

———. "Medicine and Curing Practices of the Modern Florida Seminoles." *American Anthropologist* 48, no. 3 (June–September 1944): 317–28.

Hansen, Gregory. *A Florida Fiddler: The Life and Times of Richard Seaman.* Tuscaloosa: University of Alabama Press, 2007.

———. "The Relevance of 'Authentic Tradition' in Studying an Oldtime Florida Fiddler." *Southern Folklore* 53 (1996): 67–89.

Hauptmann, O. H. "Spanish Folklore from Tampa, Florida." *Southern Folklore Quarterly* 2 (1938): 1–30.

———. "Spanish Folklore from Tampa, Florida." No. 4, "Superstitions." *Southern Folklore Quarterly* 2 (1938): 11–30.

———. "Spanish Folklore from Tampa, Florida." No. 7, "Witchcraft." *Southern Folklore Quarterly* 3 (1939): 197–200.

Henderson, Ann, and Stetson Kennedy. "The WPA Guide to Florida: A Conversation Between Ann Henderson and Stetson Kennedy." *Florida Forum* 9 (Fall 1986): 10–13.

Hendricks, George D. "Florida Folk Beliefs." *Western Folklore* 17 (1958): 210–11.

Housewright, Wiley L. *A History of Music and Dance in Florida, 1565–1865.* Tuscaloosa: University of Alabama Press, 1991.

Hurston, Zora Neale. *The Complete Stories.* Introduction by Henry Louis Gates Jr. and Sieglinde Lemke. New York: HarperCollins, 1995.

———. "Dance Songs and Tales from the Bahamas." *Journal of American Folklore* 43 (July–September 1930): 294–312.

———. *Dust Tracks on a Road.* 1942. Reprint, with restored text, foreword by Maya Angelou, and afterword by Henry Louis Gates Jr. New York: HarperPerennial, 1996.

———. *Folklore, Memoirs, and Other Writings.* New York: Library of America, 1995.

———. *Go Gator and Muddy the Water: Writings by Zora Neale Hurston from the Federal Writers' Project.* Edited and with a biographical essay by Pamela Bordelon. New York: W. W. Norton & Company, 1999.

———. *Mules and Men.* Reprint, with a foreword by Arnold Rampersad and afterword by Henry Louis Gates Jr. New York: HarperPerennial, 1990.

———. *Seraph on the Suwanee: A Novel.* 1948. Reprint, with a foreword by Hazel V. Carby, and afterword by Henry Louis Gates Jr. New York: HarperPerennial, 1991.

———. *Their Eyes Were Watching God: A Novel.* 1937. Reprint, with a foreword by Mary Helen Washington. New York: HarperPerennial, 1990.

Huss, Veronica, and Evelyn Werner. "The Conchs of Riviera, Florida." *Southern Folklore Quarterly* 4 (September 1940): 141–51.

Jackson, Joyce M. "African American and West Indian Folklife in South Florida." *South Florida History Magazine* 3 (Summer 1990): 11–18.

———. "African American Folk Culture in Miami." In *Arts of the African Diaspora: African American and Haitian Miami.* Miami: Historical Museum of Southern Florida, 1990. Pp. 14–24.

Jansonius, Remko. "Island Fantasies." *South Florida History Magazine* 1 (Winter 1991): 12–15, 28.

Jumper, Betty Mae. *Legends of the Seminoles*. Foreword by James E. Billie, introduction by Peter B. Gallagher. Sarasota, FL: Pineapple Press, 1994.

Kennedy, Stetson. "Cantantes Callejeros y La Cucaracha." *Southern Folklore Quarterly* 6 (September 1942): 140–50.

———. "Enrique and Amanda." Folklore Project, WPA Federal Writers' Project, 1939. In *American Life Histories: Manuscripts from the Federal Writers' Project, 1936–1940*. Washington, DC: Library of Congress, National Digital Library Program, 1998. http://memory.loc.gov/ammem/wpaintro/wpahome.html, accessed June 30, 2000.

———. *Grits & Grunts: Folkloric Key West*. Sarasota, FL: Pineapple Press, 2008.

———. "Mrs. Amelia Devoe." Folklore Project, WPA Federal Writers' Project, 1939. In *American Life Histories: Manuscripts from the Federal Writers' Project, 1936–1940*. Washington, DC: Library of Congress, National Digital Library Program, 1998. <http://memory.loc.gov/ammem/wpaintro/wpahome.html>, accessed June 30, 2000.

———. "Mister Homer." Folklore Project, WPA Federal Writers' Project, 1939. In *American Life Histories: Manuscripts from the Federal Writers' Project, 1936–1940*. Washington, DC: Library of Congress, National Digital Library Program, 1998. http://memory.loc.gov/ammem/wpaintro/wpahome.html, accessed June 30, 2000.

———. "Nanigo in Florida." *Southern Folklore Quarterly* 4 (September 1940): 153–56.

———. *Palmetto County*. New York: Duell, Sloan and Pearce, 1942. Reprint, with a new afterword by the author. Tallahassee: Florida A&M University Press, 1989.

———. "La Paloma in Florida." *Southern Folklore Quarterly* 7 (September 1943): 163–64.

———. "Pedro and Estrella." Folklore Project, WPA Federal Writers' Project, 1939. In *American Life Histories: Manuscripts from the Federal Writers' Project, 1936–1940* (Washington, DC: Library of Congress, National Digital Library Program, 1998), http://memory.loc.gov/ammem/wpaintro/wpahome.html, accessed June 30, 2000.

———. "Way Down Upon . . . Gathering Tales of Folklife in Suwannee Country." *FHC Forum* 17 (Spring/Summer 1993): 22–27.

———. "The W.P.A. Florida Writers Project: A Personal View." *FEH Forum* 12 (Spring 1989): 1–4.

Kersey, Harry A., Jr. *The Florida Seminoles and the New Deal, 1933–1942*. Boca Raton: Florida Atlantic University Press, 1989.

———. "Seminoles." In *Encyclopedia of Southern Culture*, edited by Charles Reagan Wilson and William Ferris, 440–41. Chapel Hill: University of North Carolina Press, 1989.

Kral, Jon. *Cracker: Florida's Enduring Cowboys*. Ft. Pierce, FL: Long Wind Publishing, 1998.

Linzee, Jill. *A Reference Guide to Florida Folklore from the Federal WPA Deposited in the Florida Folklife Archives*. Edited by Ormond H. Loomis and Deborah S. Fant. White Springs: Florida Folklife Program, Florida Department of State, 1990.

Loomis, Ormond H. "The Seminole Family Camp." In *A Guide to the 33rd Annual Florida Folk Festival, May 24–26, 1985*. White Springs, FL: Florida Folklife Program, Florida Department of State, 1985. Pp. 17–20.

Louis, Liliane Nérette. *When Night Falls, Kric! Krac!: Haitian Folktales*. Englewood, CO: Libraries Unlimited, 1998.

McGregory, Jerrilyn. *Wiregrass Country*. Jackson: University Press of Mississippi, 1997.

———. *Downhome Gospel: African American Spiritual Activism in Wiregrass Country*. Jackson: University Press of Mississippi, 2010.

McWhiney, Grady. *Cracker Culture: Celtic Ways in the Old South*. University: University of Alabama Press, 1988.

Mohl, Raymond A. "Black Immigrants: Bahamians in Early Twentieth Century Miami." *Florida Historical Quarterly* 65 (January 1987): 271–97.

Mormino, Gary R., and George E. Possetta. *The Immigrant World of Ybor City: Italians and Their Latin Neighbors in Tampa, 1885–1985*. Urbana: University of Illinois Press, 1987.

Morris, Alton C. *Folksongs of Florida*. 1950; rpt. Gainesville: University of Florida Press, 1990.

———. *Florida Place Names*. Sarasota, FL: Pineapple Press, 1995.

———. "Mrs. Griffin of Newberry." *Southern Folklore Quarterly* 8 (1944): 133–98.

Murphree, Alice H. "Folk Medicine in Florida: Remedies Using Plants." *Florida Anthropologist* 18 (1965): 175–85.

Owen, Blanton. "Traditional Florida Ranching." In *32nd Annual Florida Folk Festival, May 25–27, 1984*. White Springs: Florida Folklife Program, Florida Department of State, 1984. Pp. 2–16.

Proby, Kathryn Hall. *Mario Sanchez: Painter of Key West Memories*. Key West, FL: Southernmost Press, 1981.

Ramirez, Manuel D. "Italian Folklore from Tampa, Florida." *Southern Folklore Quarterly* 5 (June 1941): 101–6.

Reaver, J. Russell. "'Embalmed Alive': A Developing Urban Ghost Tale." *New York Folklore Quarterly* 8 (1952): 217–20.

———. "Folk History from North Florida." *Southern Folklore Quarterly* 32 (1968): 7–16.

———. "Henry, the Pole-Vaulting Fish." *Journal of American Folklore* 61 (1948): 313–14.

———. "Legends of the King's Highway: Anecdotes from St. Augustine." *Southern Folklore Quarterly* 20 (1956): 225–39.

———. "P'noblums." *Journal of American Folklore* 62 (1949): 63.

Rosenberg, Jan. "Robert James Rudd: Cypress Furniture Maker." In *South Florida History Magazine* 2 (Spring 1989): 10–15.

Ste. Claire, Dana. *Cracker: The Cracker Culture in Florida History*. Daytona Beach: Museum of Arts & Sciences, 1998.

———. "The Cracker in Florida Folklore." Florida History Notebook. *Arts & Sciences Magazine*, Winter 1993.

Shubow, David. "Sponge Fishing on Florida's East Coast." *Tequesta* 29 (1969): 3–16.

Simmons, Glen, and Laura Ogden. *Gladesmen: Gator Hunters, Moonshiners, and Skiffers*. Gainesville: University Press of Florida, 1998.

Smith, G. Hubert. "Three Miami Tales." *Journal of American Folklore* 52 (1939): 194–208.

Sommers, Laurie K. "Caribbean Music in Miami." In *A Guide to the 34th Annual Florida Folk Festival, May 23–25, 1986*. White Springs: Florida Folklife Program, Florida Department of State, 1986. Pp. 13–16.

———. "Caribbean Music in South Florida." *South Florida History Magazine* 3 (Summer 1990): 5–10.

———. "Final Report, Nicaraguan Traditions." Unpublished manuscript, Historical Museum of Southern Florida Folklife Archives, 1991.

Stone, Robert L. "Florida Ranching Traditions." *Florida History & The Arts* (Fall 2007). http://www.flheritage.com/services/magazine/index.cfm?action=article&season=07fall&article=113.

———. "Sacred Steel." *FHC Forum* (Winter 2004): 28–31.

———. *Sacred Steel: Inside an African American Steel Guitar Tradition.* Music in American Life Series. Champaign: University of Illinois Press, 2010.

Underberg, Natalie, and Kristin G. Congdon. "Folkvine.org: Ethnographic Storytelling in Folk Art Web Design." *Visual Anthropology Review* 23, no. 2 (2007): 151–61.

Warren-Findley, Janelle. "Journal of a Field Representative: Charles Seeger and Margaret Valiant." *Ethnomusicology* 24, no. 2 (May 1980): 169–210.

Zimny, Michael. "Dog-trots, Saddlebags & Shotguns: Vernacular Houses in Florida." *Florida Heritage Magazine* 4, no. 2 (Spring 1996): 20–23.

Appendix I

EARLY FOLKLIFE RESEARCH IN FLORIDA

THIS BOOK OFFERS RECENT ESSAYS BY ETHNOGRAPHERS WORKING IN Florida since the 1960s. Yet their work was often foregrounded by the extensive documentation of earlier scholars. Florida provided a rich field of research for many nationally respected ethnographers from the 1930s to the mid-twentieth century. It would be disrespectful not to take this opportunity to consider at least briefly their significant contributions to the study of Florida folklife. Many of the early researchers worked for the Works Progress Administration or WPA (later called the Work Projects Administration), which employed 8.5 million people on public projects in order to provide work during the Great Depression. In addition to the most prominent researchers profiled here, many others published essays on Florida folklife in a variety of journals.

Frances Densmore (1867–1957) was an important researcher and scholar of Native American music. The Bureau of American Ethnology and the Smithsonian Institution sponsored her research from 1907 through 1957, which included recordings and field studies of many native peoples and resulted in 140 publications. Although based on data collected from 1931 to 1933, Densmore's *Seminole Music* (1956) remains the only serious exploration of the topic.

Margaret Valiant (1901–1982) studied and performed as a classical pianist and vocalist for fifteen years in Europe before returning to the United States. Musicologist Charles Seeger invited her to apply for a job with the Special Skills Division of the Resettlement Administration, which had been created to alleviate poverty and to empower economically marginal groups. One of their projects was to create "homesteads." The Special Skills Division then tried to create a sense of community within the new settlements through music and drama. Valiant made field recordings of music and talent shows she recorded at the Cherry Lake homestead in Madison County in 1936, including an early recording of fiddler Chubby Wise. She made further recordings of traditional music in Florida and other states in the later 1930s.

One of the foremost scholars of Appalachian folklore, Elizabeth Barnicle (1891–1978), taught Folklore and English at the University of Minnesota, Connecticut College, Antioch College, New York University, and the University of Tennessee. During the 1930s and 1940s, her Greenwich Village home was a center of the folk music revival. She and her husband, union organizer Tilman Cadle, collected traditional songs in Tennessee and Kentucky from 1937 to 1942 and created a collection considered one of the best in the field of folklore. In 1935, Barnicle organized the research expedition with Alan Lomax and Zora Neale Hurston to Florida, Georgia, and the Bahamas for the Florida Federal Writers' Project.

Zora Neale Hurston (1891–1960) was an African American anthropologist, folklorist, and novelist. In her books Hurston often depicted her hometown, Eatonville, as a place where blacks could enjoy their lives without the interference of white prejudice. She attended Howard University, Columbia University, and Barnard College. At Barnard she studied with anthropologist Franz Boas, who encouraged her to document southern African American culture. From 1927 to 1932, Hurston conducted field research in Florida, Alabama, Louisiana, and the Bahamas. However, her first fieldwork was undertaken in Eatonville and surrounding areas, where she maintained strong family connections. Her best-known folklore collection, *Mules and Men* (1935), includes music, games, oral lore, and religious practices largely based on her field research. She later collected folklore in Jamaica, Haiti, Bermuda, and Honduras. *Tell My Horse* (1938) was a collection of folklore from Jamaica and Haiti. As a participant in New York's Harlem Renaissance from the mid-1920s to 1930s, Hurston achieved fame for novels based on her childhood and fieldwork in Florida: *Jonah's Gourd Vine* (1934), *Their Eyes Were Watching God* (1937), *Moses, Man of the Mountain* (1939), and *Seraph on the Sewanee* (1948). During the 1930s, Hurston worked for the WPA's Federal Theatre Project in New York (1935–1936) and the Federal Writers' Project (FWP) in Florida (1938). For the latter, she again collected African American folklore in central Florida, working with Alan Lomax and Stetson Kennedy. Hurston's fame declined in later life, but in the 1970s her writings were rediscovered by a new generation and today receive international acclaim.

Ralph Steele Boggs (1901–1994) was a folklorist of international reputation who specialized in Hispanic and American folktales, riddles, and proverbs. Due to his initial interest in linguistics, he studied with folklorist Archer

Taylor, and received a Ph.D. in folklore and Spanish from the University of Chicago in 1930. He soon published the *Index of Spanish Folktales*, the first of many major works dealing with the folklore of Spain and Latin America. Boggs was also recognized for his collection of Spanish folklore from Ybor City, compiled during the 1930s. For twenty years Boggs taught Spanish at the University of North Carolina, where he founded the Curriculum in Folklore in 1939—one of the first folklore graduate programs in the country. His friendship with Stith Thompson brought him into contact with Indiana University, where he helped to develop the first Folklore Institute. Boggs later did substantial work in the Dominican Republic, and married Dominican folklorist Edna Garrido. In 1950 he joined the faculty at the University of Miami, and continued research in Florida and Latin America both before and after his retirement in 1967. He was a charter member of the Florida Folklore Society, and in 1987 received the Florida Folk Heritage Award.

Alan Lomax (1915–2002) was part of a family of important folklife scholars—the son of pioneering folklorist John A. Lomax, brother of Bess Lomax Hawes, and father of Anna Lomax Wood. In the 1930s and early 1940s, Alan and his father assisted in the development of the Library of Congress Archive of American Folk Song. They also recorded thousands of songs and oral histories throughout the South, Northeast, Lake States, Midwest, Bahamas, and Haiti. Among Lomax's earliest collaborators and longtime friends were Zora Neale Hurston and Stetson Kennedy. In 1935, he and Hurston undertook fieldwork in Florida that included Eatonville, the Everglades, and other areas. Lomax later conducted significant research in Europe and North Africa. He enriched national folklore archives, created interest in indigenous folk music, and compiled one of the first world music anthologies for Columbia Records in the 1950s. After 1960 he undertook comparative research on world music and dance with a variety of collaborators. This work culminated in the early 1990s with the Global Jukebox, a multimedia interactive database that attempted to discover relationships between expressive style, human geography, and social organization.

Alton C. Morris (1913–1979) was a fourth-generation Floridian from the Lake Okeechobee region. He began research into Florida folklife as a fieldworker for the Folklife section of the WPA's Federal Writers' Project in the 1930s—where he worked alongside Zora Neale Hurston and Stetson Kennedy. He used the results of that fieldwork as the basis for *Folksongs of Florida* (1950; reprinted 1990), the only such collection of Florida folk songs. Morris taught folklore classes in the English department at the University of Florida, where he was a longtime professor. He also served as the editor of *Southern Folklore Quarterly* from 1936 to 1966. In the early 1950s Morris convinced the Florida Women's Music Club to hold a Florida Folk Festival, and he played an influential role in the festival's first years. He also wrote *Places in the Sun: The History and Romance of Florida Place Names* (1978) and was posthumously awarded the Florida Folk Heritage Award in 1988.

Florida Folktales, collected, edited, and with commentary by J. Russell Reaver (1915–2002) is a fine collection of folktales and legends. Reaver provided excellent annotations for the tales, including information on informants as well as tale types and motifs identified by folklore scholars. Reaver was born to a family of Pennsylvania Dutch and Quakers, which instilled in him a sustained love for folk culture. During his lengthy tenure as a literature professor at Florida State University, he pursued this interest by documenting and writing about Florida's narrative folklife. He also contributed to the development of public folklore in Florida through his assistance in establishing the Florida Folklore Society and Florida Folk Festival. In 2002 he received the Florida Folk Heritage Award for his work as a researcher, writer, and advocate for Florida folklife.

Born in Jacksonville, Stetson Kennedy (b. 1916) began documenting Cracker and African American sayings while in his teens. Kennedy spent several years in Key West exploring Conch culture in the mid-1930s. In 1937, he became an interviewer for the Florida Writers' Project, producing the "Key West Tour" section of *Florida: A Guide to the Southernmost State*, and the "Inventory of Key West Conch and Cuban Folklore." He directed the Federal Writers' Project's Folklore, Life History and Social/Ethnic Studies Units from 1938 to 1942, during which time he worked with Alan Lomax, Zora Neale Hurston, and many other ethnographers to preserve thousands of Florida folksongs, tales, and legends now available at the Library of Congress and Florida State Archives. His first book, *Palmetto Country* (1942), was based on unpublished materials from FWP files and examined aspects of traditional life among Florida's Crackers, African Americans, and Cuban Americans. During the 1940s, Kennedy published several short essays on Florida folklife. More recently he coauthored *South Florida Folklife* (1995) with Tina Bucuvalas and Peggy Bulger and published *Grits and Grunts* (2008) about Key West folklife. During his long career, Kennedy has dedicated himself to social causes, especially racial politics. Kennedy donated his collections of WPA folklife materials to the Florida Folklife Program and the University of South Florida in order to preserve Florida's heritage for future generations. He is a recipient of the Florida Folk Heritage Award (1988) and was inducted into the Florida Artists Hall of Fame (2005).

Most know Robert A. Georges for his innovative theoretical works on narrative and folkloristics or for the fine teaching skills that enriched the generations of young folklorists at UCLA. Georges's work stresses folklore as a behavioral phenomenon expressive of physical, cognitive, and psychological states and processes. However, during the 1960s he conducted field research on a variety of topics in Greek communities in Tarpon Springs and other locations in the South. His language skills and knowledge of the culture assisted his research into narrative, beliefs, and customs. Georges's research resulted in such publications as "The Greeks of Tarpon Springs: An American Folk Group" (1965) and *Greek-American Folk Beliefs and Narratives* (1980) and is incorporated into more general works such as *Folkloristics: An Introduction* (1995).

Appendix II

PUBLIC FOLKLIFE PROGRAMS IN FLORIDA

IN FLORIDA, AS IN MANY OTHER STATES, THE ADVENT OF PUBLIC FOLKLIFE programs in the 1970s and 1980s accelerated the pace of folklife scholarship. This appendix documents public programs that have been established throughout the state.

Florida Folklife Program

The Florida Folklife Program (FFP), a component of the Florida Department of State's Division of Historical Resources, is one of the oldest public folklife programs in the nation. The program began when the Stephen Foster Memorial in White Springs, which was run by the Federation of Music Clubs, received a grant from the National Endowment for the Arts. Peggy Bulger was hired in fall 1975 to conduct a one-year survey of Florida folklife to improve the Florida Folk Festival. Bulger was not only retained, but by 1978 seven positions opened. Bulger and others, including Brenda McCallum and Dwight DeVane, completed substantial fieldwork. Merri Belland McKenzie was hired to run an Artist Residency Program during that period.

In 1979 the legislature transferred the Florida Folk Arts component of the Stephen Foster Memorial to the Department of State. It authorized appointment of a folklife director to oversee the Bureau of Florida Folklife Programs, which was charged with documenting and presenting the state's folklife and tradition bearers. The Folklife Program eventually expanded to six professional staff members, who conducted research and implemented presentations at the Stephen Foster State Folk Culture Center in White Springs—Ormond H. Loomis and Doris Dyen were among the first hired. In 1995 it was moved to Tallahassee, where it became the Florida Folklife Program, a unit within the Bureau of Historic Preservation. Today it continues to coordinate a wide range of activities and projects designed to increase the awareness of Floridians and visitors about Florida's traditional culture—for example, the Folklife Apprenticeships, Florida Folk Heritage Awards, exhibitions, radio shows, publications, research, and special events or projects.

Over the years, many folklorists who have led public programs throughout the country worked for the Florida Folklife Program either as permanent staff or contractors, including, in addition to those above, Tina Bucuvalas, Debbie Fant, Gregory Hansen, Teresa Hollingsworth, Jon Kay, Jill Linzy, Doug Manger, Bill Mansfield, Nancy Nusz, Blanton Owen, Betsy Peterson, Jan Rosenberg, Riki Salzman, Laurie K. Sommers, Robert L. Stone, David Taylor, and Blaine Q. Wade.

Historical Museum of Southern Florida

The Historical Museum of Southern Florida in Miami has been a consistent source of documentation and presentation of south Florida folklife for over twenty years, resulting in a plethora of exhibitions, short publications, recordings, and local events. In 1986, The Florida Folklife Program teamed up with the Historical Museum of Southern Florida (HMSF) to obtain a grant from the National Endowment for the Arts that placed folklorist Tina Bucuvalas at HMSF. During her tenure from 1986 to 1991, Bucuvalas established the Folklife Program; administered and/or conducted folklife surveys of the Keys, as well as Latin American, Caribbean, African, and Jewish communities; curated *Tropical Traditions: South Florida Folklife*; and co-curated *Sign of the Times: Haitian Sign Art in Miami* with Brent Cantrell. She also brought outside scholars to conduct research, including Brent Cantrell, Laurie K. Sommers, Joyce M. Jackson, Robert L. Stone, Jan Rosenberg, and Remko Jansonius. Cantrell coordinated the Folklife Program from 1991 to 1995. He administered the Nicaraguan project, hiring Laurie K. Sommers and Katherine Borland to conduct fieldwork, and conducted fieldwork in African folklife in Miami. Stephen Stuempfle headed the Folklife Program and was chief curator from 1995 to 2008. He curated several research-based exhibitions, including *Calypso: A World Music, Caribbean Percussion Traditions in Miami*, and *Florida Folklife: Traditional Arts in Contemporary Communities*. Stuempfle also initiated surveys of South American and Indo-Trinidadian music, hiring Martha Ellen Davis, Joanne Hyppolite, Nina Wood, and other ethnographers to conduct research. In early 2008, Haitian American novelist and folklorist Joanne Hyppolite became chief curator and Folklife Program coordinator and Mike Knoll was hired as a folklorist/community researcher. In 2010 HMSF changed its name to HistoryMiami.

Central Florida Centers

In the mid-1970s, ethnomusicologists Kathleen Monahan and Theodore Grame settled in Tarpon Springs. Monahan initially surveyed Greek folk arts for the City of Tarpon Springs and established a city program of apprenticeships in such Greek traditional arts as bouzouki music. Grame was the first to record and publish about National Heritage Fellow Nikitas Tsimouris and his highly ornamented and complex Kalymnian *tsambóuna* music. Grame also authored small booklets on local Greek foodways and general culture. In 2009, Tarpon Springs hired Tina Bucuvalas as the curator of Arts & Historical Resources in order to develop programs and events that would encourage the continuation of local folklife and augment its role in cultural tourism.

A group of anthropologists and folklorists in the Tampa area joined together in the mid-1980s to document the traditional culture of Ybor City and present it at the Ybor City Folk Festival. Scholars included anthropologists Pat Waterman, Susan Greenbaum, folklorist Loretta Rhoads Van Winkle, and a number of local historians. Although the collaboration and event survived only a few years, they left an excellent body of scholarship on the surviving cultural expressions of the Cubans, Italians, Spanish, and others who had settled in the area.

In the late 1990s, Kristin Congdon of the University of Central Florida in Orlando worked with the FFP to establish a folklife program. Although the resulting Cultural Heritage Alliance hired Natalie Underberg and operated a public program for only a few years, under Congdon's leadership a team of cultural specialists and digital media experts broke new ground by creating *Folkvine*, an innovative, interactive Web site exploring Florida folk arts and artists. This was followed by *Chinavine*, which includes a Web site, television and radio shows, and exhibitions that educated English-speaking audiences about Chinese folk art and traditional culture. Congdon has led other innovative projects that present traditional culture with the help of new media. For the *Cultural ByWays* project, Robert L. Stone documented folk culture along a bus route through downtown Orlando. It resulted in a series of short documentaries exploring traditional culture along the bus route, which was keyed to a GPS system on the buses so that passengers viewed them as they passed the sites.

American Folklife Center / Library of Congress / Florida Folklife from the WPA Collections

Although not based in Florida, in 2002 the American Folklife Center at the Library of Congress launched a comprehensive Web site that interpreted and provided access to many of the ethnographic materials collected by the WPA in Florida. *Florida Folklife from the WPA Collections* at http://memory.loc.gov/ammem/flwpahtml/flwpahome.html is a multi-format collection of materials from African American, Arabic, Bahamian, British American, Cuban, Greek, Italian, Minorcan, Seminole, and Slavic communities. Scholars such as Robert Cook, Herbert Halpert, Zora Neale Hurston, Stetson Kennedy, and Alton Morris created the collection while working for the Florida Federal Writers' Project, Florida Music Project, and the Joint Committee on Folk Arts of the Work Projects Administration. The on-line materials include traditional music, tales, interviews with tradition bearers, recording logs, transcriptions, correspondence between WPA workers and Library of Congress staff, an essay on Florida folklife by Zora Neale Hurston, and an essay by Stetson Kennedy about the experience and legacy of the WPA in Florida. There is also an extensive bibliography, and a guide to Florida's ethnic and language groups.

State Archives of Florida / Florida Memory Project / Florida Folklife Collection

In 2005, the Florida State Archives completed a project to enhance access to and provide educational tools based upon the Florida Folklife Collection. The materials consisted of the field notes, images, and sound recordings created by folklorists with the Florida Folklife Program from inception through 1995. Many materials were added to the Florida Memory Web site (FloridaMemory.com). In addition to the Florida Folklife Program research files, the collection also includes the recordings and images from the WPA and from the annual Florida Folk Festival, the nation's longest-running continuous folk festival. The fine team of specialists in education and preservation at the archives has also released several compact discs of music from the Florida Folklife Program files.

Contributors

Katherine Borland is associate professor of comparative studies at Ohio State University, where she teaches folklore, international studies, and general humanities classes. She has written several articles on Latin American and Latino folklore as well as two books: *Creating Community: Hispanic Migration to Rural Delaware* (2001) and *Unmasking Class, Gender, and Sexuality in Nicaraguan Festival* (2006). She is currently working on a critical ethnography of international volunteering.

Tina Bucuvalas is curator of Arts and Historical Resources for the City of Tarpon Springs and president of the Florida Folklore Society. She worked for the Florida Folklife Program from 1996 to 2009, serving as director and state folklorist (2000–2009). Previously she coordinated the Folklife Program (1986–1990) and was curator of the Object Collection (1990–1991) at the Historical Museum of Southern Florida (HMSF). She served as exhibition review editor for *Journal of American Folklore* (2006–2010) and on the Florida Folklife Council. In 2006–2007, she researched public folklife programs in Greece as a Fulbright Scholar. She coauthored *Just Above the Water: Florida Folk* Arts (2006) with Kristin Congdon, *South Florida Folklife* (1994) with Peggy Bulger and Stetson Kennedy, and published numerous articles on Florida folklife. Among the exhibits she curated are The Greek Community of Tarpon Springs (Tarpon Springs Heritage Museum, 2010–present), Florida Cattle Ranching: Five Centuries of Tradition (co-curator, 2008–2011), and Tropical Traditions: Folklife in Southeast Florida (HMSF, 1991). She has a Ph.D. in folklore from Indiana University and M.A. in folklore and mythology from UCLA.

Brent Cantrell is the executive director of Jubilee Community Arts in Knoxville, Tennessee. Native to rural Warren County on Tennessee's Highland Rim, Cantrell worked in the Peace Corps in Togo before earning a Ph.D. in folklore from Indiana University. He has done folklore fieldwork in Togo; in Haitian, African, and other ethnic communities in Miami while working for the Historical Museum of Southern Florida; and in Tennessee. His unusual perspective on culture reflects both academic training and intense social experiences near and far from home.

Martha Ellen Davis, anthropologist and ethnomusicologist (Ph.D., University of Illinois), has conducted fieldwork in the Dominican Republic, Puerto Rico, Spain (Madrid, León, and la Gomera/Canary Islands), Brazil, Peru, Mexico, Trinidad, New York City, Miami, and north Florida. Her many publications and audiovisual productions include *La otra ciencia: el vodú dominicano como religión y medicina populares* (*The other science: Dominican* vodú *as folk religion and medicine*), 1987, which received the National Nonfiction Award of the Dominican Republic. She currently serves as advisor and researcher in oral history for the National Archive of the Dominican Republic and is affiliate faculty in anthropology and music at the University of Florida. The article in this volume was generated by a Historical Museum of Southern Florida project that documented the Peruvian, Colombian, and Venezuelan communities in Miami-Dade County.

Anthropologist **Stavros K. Frangos** is an independent scholar who has worked on museum exhibitions, archival collections and oral history projects over the last thirty years. Frangos's writings include *The Greeks in Michigan* (2004); "The Greek Slave" in *Founded on Freedom and Virtue* (2002); Stavros Frangos and Alexandros K. Kyrou, "Diaspora Studies: Hellenic Diaspora" in *Greece in Modern Times* (2000); articles in the *Journal of Modern Hellenism*, *Journal of the Hellenic Diaspora*, and others; and over 500 newspaper and magazine articles on the Greek experience in North America. In 2010, Frangos received the American Hellenic and Progressive Association's Academic Achievement Award.

Joyce M. Jackson is director of the African and African American Studies Program and associate professor in the Department of Geography and Anthropology at Louisiana State University, Baton Rouge. Both a folklorist and ethnomusicologist, she does performance-centered research on rituals in Africa and the African Diaspora. She is currently completing a book on the New Orleans Mardi Gras Indians and she is the author of *Life in the Village: A Cultural Memory of the Fazendeville Community*.

Gregory Hansen is an associate professor of folklore and English at Arkansas State University, where he also teaches in the Heritage Studies doctoral program. Hansen specializes in the folklife of America's southern states and teaches courses on folklore and public heritage programming. He is the author of *A Florida Fiddler: The Life and Times of Richard Seaman* and various scholarly articles, instructional resources, and program guides. Hansen has completed public folklore projects for a range of organizations, including the Smithsonian Institution, Danish Immigrant Museum, Kentucky Center for the Arts, and the Florida Folklife Program.

Ormond H. Loomis grew up in the Tampa Bay area. During the 1970s, he earned a doctorate in folklore at Indiana University and worked as an independent researcher/consultant. From 1982 through 1995, he served as state folklorist and chief of the Bureau of Florida Folklife. In 1996, he segued to Florida State University where he taught nonfiction writing, composition pedagogy, and folklore. He officially retired in 2009. These days he lives in Nova Scotia most of the year—where he attends weekly *cèilidhs*, documents local material culture, volunteers with the St. George's Bay Folklore Society, and maintains a modest vineyard—and returns to Florida for sun in the winter.

Jerrilyn McGregory is an associate professor of folklore in the Department of English at Florida State University. She is the author of *Wiregrass Country* (1997) and *Downhome Gospel: Spiritual Activism in Wiregrass Country* (2010). Wiregrass Country is a little known region of the South, which includes Georgia, Alabama, and Florida. *Downhome Gospel* highlights sacred music performed outside of Sunday morning worship from Sacred Harp to contemporary gospel. This examination shows how sacred music fortifies spiritual as well as social needs. She is currently conducting ethnographic research and writing a book on Boxing Day in the African Diaspora, focusing on North Florida, The Bahamas, Belize, Bermuda, St. Croix, and St. Kitts.

Martha Nelson received an M.A. from the University of North Carolina Folklore Program. While employed as the folklorist for the Creative Arts Guild in Dalton, Georgia, she documented Mexican American immigrants and organized the exhibition Among Ourselves: Traditional Art and Culture in Northwest Georgia. Nelson subsequently worked for several years at the Stephen Foster State Folk Culture Center in White Springs, Florida.

Folklorist/ethnomusicologist **Laurie K. Sommers** (Ph.D., Indiana University) has worked for the Indiana Division of State Parks, Bureau of Florida Folklife, Smithsonian Office of Folklife Programs, Michigan State University Museum, and Southern Arts Federation. Her research on Sacred Harp singing began in 1997 while directing the South Georgia Folklife Project at Valdosta State University. The South Georgia Folklife Collection website, at the Valdosta State University Archives and Special Collections, won the 2007 McCallum Award from the American Folklore Society. Sommers is the author of publications for academic and general audiences, among them *Fiesta, Fe, y Cultura: Celebration of Faith, Culture and Community in Detroit's Colonia Mexicana* (Michigan State University Museum, 1995), *Beaver Island House Party* (Michigan State University Press, 1996), and *The Florida Music Train*, a multicultural educational resource on traditional music in Florida (Florida Folklife Program/Department of State, 2003), which won the 2003 Dorothy Howard Award for folk arts in education from the American Folklore Society. She currently lives in Michigan, where she is a free-lance consultant.

Robert L. Stone is an independent folklorist, photographer, and media producer based in Gainesville, Florida. He worked with the Florida Folklife Program as folklife specialist then outreach coordinator from 1990 to 2009, and as state folklorist from 2009 to 2010. His projects have included two eight-part radio series and co-curation of the exhibition Florida Cattle Ranching: Five Centuries of Tradition for the Florida Folklife Program; producing nine CDs for the Sacred Steel Guitar series and directing the *Sacred Steel* documentary video for the Arhoolie Foundation; writing *Sacred Steel: Inside an African American Steel Guitar Tradition* (2010); and creating *Sunshine State Cowboys*, a photo exhibit displayed at the Center for the Study of Southern Culture. His current work includes continued documentation of the sacred steel tradition and Florida cattle ranching culture, and new documentation for HistoryMiami's jai-alai project.

Stephen Stuempfle is executive director of the Society for Ethnomusicology, based at Indiana University in Bloomington, and is an adjunct associate professor in IU's Department of Folklore and Ethnomusicology. He received a Ph.D. in folklore from the University of Pennsylvania and has conducted field research in Trinidad, Texas, and Florida. He is the author of *The Steelband Movement: The Forging of a National Art in Trinidad and Tobago* (University of Pennsylvania Press, 1995) and is coeditor of *Music, Memory, Resistance: Calypso and the Caribbean Literary Imagination* (Ian Randle Publishers, 2007). He has also written about Caribbean music for several journals and encyclopedias. Before joining SEM, Stuempfle served as folklife curator (1995–2000) and chief curator (2000–2007) at the Historical Museum of Southern Florida in Miami, where he directed a range of projects on the history and cultural traditions of Florida and the Caribbean.

Anna Lomax Wood is an applied and theoretical research anthropologist and project manager. A Grammy Award winner, she is also a writer, editor, translator, and lecturer with a research focus on the music and folk poetry of Italy and Greece, micro-cultural variation and its importance to international disaster management and recovery. A speaker of Spanish, French, Italian, and Greek, Lomax Wood contributes to the field of Mediterranean folklore as a working scholar. As executive director of the Association for Cultural Equity she balances her Mediterranean research interests with facilitation of all aspects of the Alan Lomax Archive, especially the community repatriation of specific collections. She also directs the multi-decade Performance Style and Culture Project. Daughter of the late Alan Lomax and granddaughter of the late John A. Lomax, she is the third generation of Lomaxes who have dedicated their careers to cultural preservation and equity. She holds a Ph.D. from Columbia University in cultural anthropology. Having spent much her childhood and adult life in Europe, Lomax Wood now resides and works in New York City.

Index

Abrahams, Roger, 228
Acosta, Tom, 167
African Americans, xii, xiv, xviii, xix, 10–15, 90–95, 189, 192, 209, 225–36, 259, 269
Africans, xviii, xx, 212, 226, 228–30
American Folklife Center, 290
Anderson, Benedict, 32
Antonio, Giomar, 76, 81
Apalachicola, 239, 240–41, 251, 259–60
architecture. See *chickee*
Asians, xvii, xix, xx, 216

Bahamians, xvi, xviii, 3, 15, 20–22, 98, 220, 261–63
Baker, W. C., 14
Balarezo, Luis "Cotito," 69–70, 76
Bardos de América, 69, 77, 80
Barnicle, Elizabeth, 283
Barrel, Virginia, 15
Bealle, John, 184, 190
Belland, Merri, xii
Beneby, Bruce, 20–22
Bennet-Coverly, Louise, 18
Big Cypress Seminole Reservation, 86, 88
Big Pine Key, 239
Billie, James, 85
Blackwell, Steve, 218
Blaes, Richard, 7
boat building, 5, 237–38, 245–50
boats, xii, 244–50; back country skiff, 5; bird dog boat, 246; dory, 63; Everglades skiff, 246; Greek sponge boats, 245; Okeechobee skipjack, 246; oyster skiff, 246, 249–50; shrimp trawlers, 247–48, 253; tunnel or mullet skiff, 246
Boggs, Ralph Steele, 283–84
Boltin, Thelma, 210, 215, 220, 221
Borland, Katherine, xii, 288, 291
Bowers, Paul, 88
Brawner, R. R., 6
Brighton Seminole Reservation, 86
British people, xviii, xix, 3, 212–13
Broward County, 67, 71, 74–75
Brown, Elgie, 9
Bucuvalas, Tina, xiii, 288, 289
Bulger, Peggy, xi, 220, 287
Burbank, Billy, Jr., 240, 242
Buzier, Costa, 251

Cadle, Tilman, 283
Cantrell, Brent, xii, 288
Carden, Jimmy, 244
Carnival, 20, 36–39, 42, 45–47, 228
Carter, Doretha, 15
Casanova, Víctor Manuel "Chocolatín," 69–70, 76
cattle ranching, xix, 210–14, 222–23
Cedar Key, xvi, 245, 267–70
cemeteries, 154–60
Chávez, Ernesto "Lefty," 77–78, 80
Chernoff, John Miller, 230
chickee, 84–89
Chirino, Willy, 30–31

cigars, xv–xvi, xviii–xix
Clewiston, 239, 269
clothing, 63–64
Coconut Grove, 15
Coker, Charlie, 243
Columbia County, 225
Conchs, xix, 3, 6, 8–9, 285
Congdon, Kristin, 289
Cook, Robert, 290
Corbin, Theadus, 246
Cortez, xvi, 239, 240, 263–64
Cottondale, 225–36
cow hunters. *See* cowmen
cow whips, xix, 220, 222
cowmen, xix, 207, 214, 216
Crackers, xiii, xiv, 207, 210–18, 220, 222–24, 267–70
Crescent City, 239, 269
Crider, Dale, 218
Cubans, xi, xiii, xv, xvi, xviii, xx, 3, 23–34, 272, 285, 289
Culbreath, "Goose," 263–64

dance, 17, 20, 28–29, 33, 52–56, 58, 76–78, 97–98, 102, 105, 123–31, 133, 162–66, 230
Davis, Martha Ellen, xiii, 288
Daye, Alice, 13
del Villar, Martha, 69, 71, 73, 80–82
Densmore, Francis, 282
domestic arts, 14–15
Dowling, Martin, 187–88, 199
Drewel, Margaret, 228
Du Bois, W. E. B., 226
Dueñas, Isaac, 29
Dyen, Doris, 189, 287

Eason, Willie, 91–93
East Europeans, xvii
Eastpoint, 246, 247, 248–50, 259–60
Eatonville, xv, 284
Everglades, xix, 284

Fant, Debbie, 288
Fernandina, 239, 247, 259
Ferrer, Pedro, 78, 80
festival arts, 27–33, 52–59, 64. *See also* Carnival; Junkanoo; patronal festivals
Finns, xvii
fishing, xviii, 3–5, 237; gear, 237, 250–57; mullet, 246, 267–68. *See also* maritime folklife
Flagler, Henry, 222
Flores, Esther, 30
Florida Federation of Music Clubs, 210, 215, 287
Florida Folk Festival, xiii, 84–85, 148–49, 169–71, 178, 192–93, 197–99, 207–36, 285, 287, 290
Florida Folk Heritage Awards, 99, 162, 170, 220, 232–33, 285, 288
Florida Folklife Apprenticeship Program, 101, 148, 150, 288
Florida Folklife Program, xi, xii, 99, 148–49, 220, 285, 287–88, 289, 290
folk medicine, 15
Folsom, Ken, 241
foodways, xii, 8–9, 19–20, 59–62, 230–31, 264–72
Fort Mose, xv
Frangos, Stavros K., xiii, 292
Friends of Florida Folk, 221–22, 224
Ft. Pierce, 93
Fuller, Lucille, 19
furniture, 63

Gálvez, Arturo, 72, 82
Garcia, José and Eugene, 6–8
Georges, Robert A., 285–86
Georgia, xii, xiv, 11, 178–206, 211, 226, 283
Gervais, Alan, 41, 48
Ghent, Aubrey, 93
Gillis, Leo, 246
Glassie, Henry, 176, 200
goldsmithing, 63
Grame, Theodore, 99, 289
Greeks, xiii, xvii, 96–153, 154–60, 220, 260–61, 270–72, 285, 289; Kalymnians xiii, 96–153, 289; Karpathos, 97, 118
Greenbaum, Susan, 289
Gulf of Mexico, xvi, xviii, 213
Guthrie, Woody, 216–17, 222
Gutierrez, Chony, 55, 57, 64–65

Haitians, xvi, 220
Halpert, Herbert, 290
Hansen, Gregory, xiii, 288
Harper, Francis, 181, 184–86
Hawes, Bess Lomax, 102, 284
Herrin, Charles, 247, 248, 250, 253
Herzfeld, Michael, 152
Hicks, Bobby, 219–20
Hispanics. *See* Latin Americans
Historical Museum of Southern Florida, xi, xii, xx, 3, 288
HistoryMiami. *See* Historical Museum of Southern Florida
Hoboken, Georgia, 178–80, 182, 186–87, 189–90, 192, 193, 195–97, 200
Hollingsworth, Teresa, 288
House of God, 90–95
Huambachano, Nedda, 73, 75–76, 80–81
hurricanes. *See* storms
Hurston, Zora Neale, xv, 216, 283–84, 290
Hyppolite, Joanne, 288, 289

Italians, xvii–xviii, 289

Jackson, Joyce M., xii, 288
Jacksonville, xvii, 92, 165–69, 186, 238, 247
Jamaicans, 17–19
Jansonius, Remko, 288
Jews, xvi, xviii, 209, 212
Johnson, Joseph, 228, 231–32
Junkanoo, 21–22, 220, 263

Kavouklis, Nikitas, 101, 148
Kay, Jon, 288
Kennedy, Stetson, 283–85, 290
Kernahan, Michael, xiii, 35–49
Key West, xii, xv, xviii, xix, 24, 92, 238, 243, 259, 261–63, 285
Keys, xii, xvi, xviii, xix, 3–9, 215
King, George, 5
King, Zibe, 222
Kissimmee, 161–66, 171, 174–76
Knoll, Mike, 289
Knott, Sarah Gertrude, 208–10

Lake Okeechobee, 216, 269
Lampkin, Jesse, 20
Lang, Lisa, 95
Latin Americans, xv, xvi, xviii, xix, xx, 23–34, 50–83, 216, 283–84. *See also* Cubans; Nicaraguans; Peruvians
Lee, Alvin, 93–94
Lee, Clarke, 179–80, 182–83, 185, 190, 194–95, 197–200
Lee, David I., 179–80, 182–83, 185–87, 189–96, 197–201
Lee, Delorese Conner, 184–87, 193
Lee, Glenn, 93
Lee, Johnny, 179, 186, 188, 190, 195–98, 200
Lee, Silas, 178–80, 187–88, 191–92, 194, 197–200
Lee Boys, 93
Liberace, 40
Linzee, Jill, 288
Lolley, Joseph, 246, 249–50
Lomax, Alan, 222, 283–84
Loomis, Ormond H., xii, 287

Mama Dolores, 30
Manger, Doug, 288
Mansfield, Bill, 288
Mardi Gras, 228
maritime folklife, xii, xvi, xix, 3–8, 237–74; crabbing, 6–8, 237, 251–52, 255; gear, 252–53, 260, 267; lobstering, 251–52, 255; nets, 6, 237–38, 240, 250–51, 255–57; oystering, 237–38, 240, 250, 252–53; rope work, 5–6; sail making, 5; shrimping, 247, 251; sponging, xvi, xvii, xviii, 3, 98, 105, 146, 154–55, 156, 158, 159, 239, 243, 260–62, 267, 270–71; traps, 6–7, 251–52, 255; weather lore, 240–43. *See also* boats; boat building; foodways
Masaryktown, xxvii
Masons, 229
masquerading, 20–21, 46
Mayport, 247–48, 250, 259
McCarl, Robert, 239
McGregory, Jerrilyn, xiii
McLean, Will, 215–17, 221
Miami, xvi, xviii, 10–22, 35–49, 67–83, 215–16
Miami-Dade County, xviii, xix, 10–22, 35–49, 67–83

Miccosukee, xiv, xix
Michael, Nancy, xii
Middle Easterners, xvii
Miller, Xuripha, 260
Minorcans, xvii–xviii, 265–67
Miskitos. *See* Nicaraguans
Mizell, Napoleon Bonaparte "Bone," 213–14, 217
Molineaux, Othello, 36
Monahan, Kathleen, 289
Montalvan, Alonso, 56
Mora, Albert, 241
Morris, Alton C., 193, 209, 284–85, 290
music, xii, xiii; African American, 12–14, 90–95; bluegrass, 167–69, 222; blues, 13–14; calypso, 17–18, 45–47; fiddle, xiii, 161–77, 209, 263–64, 283; Florida Song, 207–24, 225–36; gospel, 12–13; Greek musicians, 159; Kalymnian *tsambóuna* and song, 96–153, 289; Keys, 9; *lyra*, 100; marimba, 56; maritime communities, 257–64; Nicaraguan Creole, 58; old-time, 161–77, 263–64; Peruvian, 67–83; reggae, 17–18; Sacred Harp, xii, 178–206; Sacred Steel, xiii, 90–95; soca, 17; Sunday Morning Band, 229–30; *tamboo bamboo*, 37; *tassa* drumming, 37; West Indian, 16–18, 35–49. *See also* pans; steelbands; *tsambóuna*
mutual aid organizations, 23–25, 225–36

Nassau County, 182, 184, 186–88
National Endowment for the Arts, 287–88
National Federation of Music Clubs, 208, 210
National Heritage Fellowships, 99, 102, 289
Native Americans, xiv, 207, 209, 212. *See also* Miccosukee; Nicaraguans: Miskito; Seminole
nativism, xiii, 219–20, 224
needlework, 63–64
Negrini, Luis Enrique "Quique," 69, 73, 75–76, 80–81
Nelson, Henry, 93
Nelson, Martha, xiii
New Smyrna, xvii
Nicaraguans, xii, 50–66, 220; Creoles, 50–51, 58, 61–65; Mestizos, 50–61, 63–65; Miskitos, 50–51, 58–59, 61–62, 65
Noble, Elton, 93, 95
Noles, Cindy, 269–70
Novack, Mack, 260
Nusz, Nancy, xii, 288

Ocala, 92–93, 215
Okefenokee Region, xii, 178–206
oral tradition, 18–19, 59, 104, 170–75, 238–44, 285
Orlando, xx
O'Stein, Shade, 243–44
Owen, Blanton, 87, 288

Pacific Islanders, xvii
Palm Beach County, xvi, xvii, 74
Palomino, Ramón and Dennis, 29
Panama City, 244
Panhandle, xiv, xviii, 185, 189, 215, 225–36
pans, 17, 35–49. *See also* music
patronal festivals: Cuban, 23–34; Nicaraguan, 52–58
Pensacola, xviii, xx, 238
Peruvians, xiii, 67–83
Peterson, Betsy, 288
Phillip, Michael, 35
Philmon, Glen, 242–43
Polous, Sonny, 246
Port St. Joe, 259
Pratt, Carol, 18
Puckett, Martha Mizell, 188

quilting, 14–15
Quinn, Nancy, 9

Randolph, Robert, 94
Ranger-Brown, Lucille, 18
Reaver, J. Russell, 209, 285
religion, 11–14, 23–27, 33, 52–58, 74, 90–95, 155, 159, 178–206, 225–36; African Methodist Episcopal, 12, 228, 233; altars, 57–58; Baptist, 11–12, 178–206, 209; Catholicism, xv, 12, 23–34, 50–66, 74; Church of Christ, 12; Moravians, 50–52, 58, 62; orthodoxy, Greek, 102–3,

148, 155, 159; Pentecostal, 12. *See also* music: Sacred Harp; music: Sacred Steel; patronal festivals
Remington, Frederic, 214
Reyes, Juan, 69, 73
ritual, xiii, 225, 227–31, 234–35
Roberts, Llewellyn, 20
Roberts, William, 5–6
Rolle, Billy, 20–21
Roller, Peter, xii
Rosenberg, Jan, 288

Salzman, Riki, 288
San Antonio de las Vueltas, Cuba, 23, 25–28
Scots-Irish, 207, 210, 212–14, 217, 222
Scull sisters, xi
sculpture, 7–8
Seaman, Richard, xiii, 161–77
secret societies, 225–36
Seeger, Pete, 222
Seminole, xii, xiv, xix, 84–89, 207, 214, 282
Shiver, Bobby, 247, 248–50
Silva, José, 54
Smith, A. E. "Frog," 215
soap making, 15
Sommers, Laurie K., xii, 288
Spanish people, xiv, xv, xix, 72, 207, 212, 284, 289
sponging. *See* maritime folklife
St. Augustine, xv, xvii–xviii, xx, 247, 265–67
St. Johns River, 245, 247, 269
St. Petersburg, xvii
State Archives of Florida, 290
steel drums. See *pans*
steelbands, 35–42
Steinhatchee, 239, 242, 243
Stephen Foster State Folk Culture Center, xiii, 208, 287
Stone, Robert L., xiii, 288, 289
storms, 243; hurricanes, 215–16, 242
Stuempfle, Stephen, xiii, 68
Sulca, Miguel, 78–80
Summerlin, Jake, 222
Sunday Morning Band, xiii, 225–36
supernatural, 244
Sutherland, Shirley, 19

Tampa, xv, xvi, xvii, xx, 24
Tarpon Springs, xiii, xvi, xvii, 96–153, 154–60, 260–61, 267, 270–72, 285, 289
Tavernier, 5, 9
Taylor, David, xii, 238, 288
Thomas, Frank, 217
Tobagans, 19
Trinidadians, 16–17, 20, 35–59
Tripoli Steel Orchestra, 39–42, 45
tsambóuna, xiii, 96–153
Tsimouris, Nikitas, xiii, 96–153, 289
Tsimouris family, 96–53
Turnbull, Andrew, xvii, 265
21st Century Steel Orchestra, 35–36, 42, 44–48

Underberg, Natalie, 289
University of Central Florida, 289

Valiant, Margaret, 282–83
Van Winkle, Loretta Rhoads, 289
Vega, Manolín, 29
Virgen de la Asunción, 56–57
Virgen de la Candelaria, 25, 27, 33

Waide, Blaine Q., 288
Waterman, Pat, 289
Wellborn, Ida, 7
West Indians, xii, xvi, 10, 15–22, 35–59. *See also* Bahamians; Jamaicans; Tobagans; Trinidadians
White, Inez, 233–34
Wise, Robert "Chubby," 162, 168, 283
Wood, Anna Lomax, xiii
Wood, Nina, 288
WPA (Works Progress Administration), 20, 258–59, 279, 281–83, 286–87
Wright, Charles, 13

Ybor City, xv, xvi, xviii, 289